General Lee's
College

George Washington by Charles Willson Peale.

Robert E. Lee as photographed by Mathew Brady.

General Lee's College

THE RISE AND GROWTH OF WASHINGTON AND LEE UNIVERSITY

by Ollinger Crenshaw

Random House · New York

First Printing
2, 3, 4, 5, 6, 7, 8, 9

Copyright © 1969 by Washington and Lee University
All rights reserved under International
and Pan American Copyright Conventions.
Published in the United States by Random House, Inc., New York, and
simultaneously in Canada by Random House of Canada Limited, Toronto.
Library of Congress Catalog Card Number: 69-16417

Manufactured in the United States of America
by The Haddon Craftsmen, Inc., Scranton, Pennsylvania
Designed by Andrew Roberts

THIS STORY OF THEIR ALMA MATER
IS FOR THE
Alumni and Students
OF WASHINGTON AND LEE UNIVERSITY
AND IS DEDICATED TO THE MEMORY OF
John W. Davis

Preface
and Acknowledgments

My purpose in the preparation of this history has been to trace the evolution of Washington and Lee University from obscure beginnings on the Virginia frontier through mutations into academy and college in the eighteenth, nineteenth, and twentieth centuries. All this has been done to explain how Washington and Lee came to be what it is: *sui generis* in American higher education—an institution for men comprised of two undergraduate divisions, the College and the School of Commerce and Administration, and a graduate division, the School of Law. I have attempted to relate this story in a proper state, regional, and national setting, as well as to the history of American colleges and universities. Withal, I have sought to produce a readable, reasonably complete, and critical account of an important Southern college.

As far as I am aware, no comprehensive history of Washington and Lee has been published. Ephemeral and episodic articles appeared in the first half of the last century, and Henry Ruffner's valuable *Early History of Washington College* . . . , No. 1 of the Washington and Lee University *Historical Papers* (Baltimore, 1890), was supplemented and continued to 1848 by his son William Henry Ruffner in the same *Historical Papers*, Nos. 4 (1893), 5 (1895), and 6 (1904). Others, notably Dr. Douglas S. Freeman in Vol. 4 of his magisterial *R. E. Lee*, have dealt with Washington and Lee's history. Gaping lacunae, however, have remained, and my objective has been to bring the Washington and Lee story together in convenient form, not only for those alumni and friends of the institution who may have especial interest in it, but also for general readers with concern for American history and the development of American higher education.

This book has been made possible by the support of the board of trustees of Washington and Lee University, whose sympathetic interest I much appreciate. At the same time, I am also grateful for the complete freedom in research, interpretation, and presentation of the University's history which they have accorded me. My obligations and gratitude are great also to several Washington and Lee officials consulted over the years: the late President Francis Pendleton Gaines, President Fred C. Cole (1959-1967), Dean William W. Pusey, III, (Acting President, 1967-1968), and President Robert E. R. Huntley, in office since February, 1968. I could not have asked for greater cooperation and understanding than they have given me. The Treasurer of Washington and Lee, Mr. James W. Whitehead, has speeded the process of publication, and Mr. Romulus T. Weatherman, Director of Publications at Washington and Lee, has aided me in many ways in the last phases of the book's preparation.

Librarians throughout the nation, beginning with Mr. Henry E. Coleman, Jr., and his staff of the McCormick Library on the Washington and Lee campus, and ranging from Boston to New Orleans and Austin, have gone beyond the call of duty in finding pertinent materials for my use.

Descendants of the early residents of old Rockbridge have generously furnished materials or information from family papers and traditions. Mr. and Mrs. Matthew W. Paxton, the late Dr. Reid White, Jr., the late Mr. and Mrs. Stuart Moore, Miss Louise P. Moore, all of Lexington, Virginia, and Mrs. James P. Alexander of Fairfield, Virginia, have given me valuable assistance. Miss Ellinor Porcher Gadsden of Lexington, and her late sister, Miss Anzolette Page Gadsden, generously made the *Pendleton Family Papers*, then in their possession, available to me. Dr. Festus P. Summers of West Virginia University, biographer of William Lyne Wilson, furnished me with valuable suggestions and materials, and the late Mr. Herbert A. Kellar, long-time Director of the McCormick Historical Association Library, then in Chicago, made research delightful and worthwhile.

My colleagues at Washington and Lee, Professors W. G. Bean and Allen W. Moger, experts in the field of Virginia and Southern history, have given me steady encouragement and critical advice, and Professor

Charles W. Turner, a moving spirit of the Rockbridge Historical Society, has called attention to materials in that organization's library.

In the later phases of the manuscript's long journey to completion, I was fortunate enough to enlist the services of Mr. M. M. Kreeger of the Tulane University of Louisiana, New Orleans. He brought into manageable proportions a lengthy, heavily documented manuscript, and in the process much improved the style of the book. Mr. Kreeger and I proved to be *en rapport* in our outlook, and I am deeply indebted to him. At Random House, I was lucky enough to have the expert advice and suggestions of Mr. Albert Erskine, and it was a pleasure indeed to work with Miss Cordelia Jason in shaping up the manuscript.

Every author must rely upon the expertise of a professional typist, and it was my good fortune to have Mrs. Robert Stewart of Lexington, Virginia, prepare the final versions of the manuscript. I came to rely upon Mrs. Stewart's judgment too, and am grateful for her contribution.

My wife Marjorie has given me unflagging encouragement and assistance at every stage in the long period of the book's preparation, for which she has my deep and affectionate gratitude. She has been my best critic.

Finally, it must be clear that while enumerating and thanking for their help those named above, I am solely responsible for statements of fact and interpretation in the ensuing pages. In a last word, perhaps I may be pardoned a reference to Henry Ruffner's preface to the first history of old Washington College, dated "Montovis" (near Kanawha Salines, Virginia), October, 1857. Dr. Ruffner remarked that he hoped the reader would find in his history something "more interesting than the commonplace incidents of a seminary of learning." If not, the historian advised, "he can leave the remainder unread and console himself with the reflection that if he has lost an hour in its perusal, the poor author has lost many a weary hour in its composition." It is surely true that I, while sharing President Ruffner's hopes for the reader, have also devoted a considerable period of time to this book's "composition"; during this time, however, I have learned much American history from the sources.

OLLINGER CRENSHAW

Lexington, Virginia
June, 1968

Contents

[*xi*]

List of Illustrations

George Washington—*Charles Willson Peale portrait*

Frontispiece

Robert E. Lee—*Mathew B. Brady photograph*
(U.S. Signal Corps photo in the National Archives)

Frontispiece

Ruins of Liberty Hall Academy

Following page 176

The Colonnade at Washington and Lee

Rectors and Presidents Since 1782

The funeral procession of General R. E. Lee
—*Michael Miley photograph*

President R. E. Lee and the Washington College Faculty

Deans of the School of Law

[xv]

BOOK ONE

Old Washington College

Chapter
I

The Origins

Washington and Lee has evolved through a process that may be likened to the growth of an oak from an acorn or to the progression of stages in metamorphosis. Whichever simile may be preferred, the University developed from a much simpler and humbler form. The seed—or the egg—was a small, peripatetic Latin school organized in the mid-eighteenth century, largely to start boys toward study for the Presbyterian ministry. From that institution emerged successively an academy, a college, and the University.

The history of Washington and Lee properly begins, however, with the great migration of the Scotch-Irish to America; for the predecessor institutions of the University arose in response to the special educational requirements of those people.

The term Scotch-Irish designates the Lowland Scots who colonized the province of Ulster in Northern Ireland in the seventeenth century. The appellation is extended to their descendants, great numbers of whom came to America during the five or six decades before the Revolutionary War. The majority landed at Philadelphia. As the eastern parts of Pennsylvania were already heavily settled by English and Germans, and coastal areas of adjacent colonies also were well populated, most of the newcomers moved westward toward the frontier.

[3]

The advance was deflected by the Alleghenies southward into the "Great Valley," of which the Valley of Virginia forms a part. Through this corridor the Scotch-Irish moved into the back country of Virginia and the Carolinas, where land could be acquired at nominal cost. In the 1730's many settled in Augusta County, Virginia, parts of which later became Rockbridge and Botetourt counties. One historian writing on this migration has described Rockbridge as "the most distinctively Scotch-Irish county in America, as it is one of the most strongly Presbyterian." He has called Washington and Lee the "Scotch-Irish University of America."

Like the early settlers of New England, the Scotch-Irish were characterized by piety, industry, and a respect for education. They believed especially in a learned clergy and their ministers became known "for vivid pulpit oratory and for an erudition which set them apart from their fellows of other faiths." Those who remained in Pennsylvania and those who settled in Virginia were active in setting up schools to prepare boys for collegiate education, particularly at Princeton, and for theological study thereafter. One of these schools came to be called Augusta Academy and was eventually to be transformed into Washington and Lee University.

It would never have occurred to the colonial schoolmasters that they were making history and therefore should leave the kind of documents from which history is supposed to be written. The continuity from Latin school to university cannot therefore be demonstrated by official record. But it is evidenced in letters and other writings of the early nineteenth century by men who learned the story from older residents and who were familiar with local traditions. Such traditions are often well preserved through oral transmission.

Augusta Academy was established by Robert Alexander, a native of Ulster, who migrated to America in 1737 with his brothers, William and Archibald. William died soon after arrival. Archibald became the grandfather of a noted Princeton theologian of the same name. The Alexanders lived for a year or two at Nottingham, Pennsylvania, then moved to the environs of Norristown, and about 1746 pushed on to Virginia where they acquired tracts of land in Augusta County. Little else is known of Robert Alexander's background. Old writings identify him as a graduate of Dublin University and one reference suggests that he attended Edinburgh University, but inquiries made in 1946 indicated that he was never enrolled at either institution.

Historians of Washington and Lee have accepted the validity of accounts that place the founding of the academy in 1749. One document shows, indeed, that the estate of one James McNutt paid Robert

Alexander an unspecified sum "for schooling James and Robert Mc-Nutt, one year, 1748." There is no evidence that the schooling took place in the academy, which would then have had an earlier beginning than the accepted date of 1749.

The school was situated near the present town of Greenville, about fifteen miles southwest of Staunton. Strong local tradition placed it near "Larkin's spring," not far from the border of Augusta and Rockbridge counties, just north of Spottswood. The location is described differently in various accounts—probably because it was changed from time to time. It was not uncommon in those days for a school to be moved about. With low enrollment and little equipment, the rural seat of learning could be relocated now and then as the needs and availability of students required.

In several references Alexander's academy is described as the first Latin, or classical, school in a sizable area whose boundaries were described as "west of the Blue Ridge," or even more indefinitely as "that part of the valley." In any case, it was a pioneering venture to serve pioneering people.

Historians have called the school the Augusta Academy, but it is not known when that name was first applied, or what Alexander himself called it. This title seems to have been in use in the 1770's and perhaps was derived from the practice of referring to "the academy in Augusta."

A more significant question is what and how the pupils were taught. Presumably Alexander's Latin school was like others of its time, concentrating on the classics and requiring much memorization of text, conjugation, and inflection. Tradition has it that Alexander wrote out from memory various exercises, which manuscript volumes were used by his pupils.

In the absence of official records that might have told us something about Alexander's pupils, some inferences may be drawn from later accounts dealing with the school in the decades soon after its founding. The pupils seem to have been in their middle or late teens, and their purpose was to acquire the foundation in the classics necessary to enter college. Princeton was their principal objective. In one list of eight pupils, three have been identified as later becoming Presbyterian ministers—Samuel Doak, James Houston, and John Montgomery. Doak, who was born in the year that the school was started, worked on his father's farm until the age of sixteen, "then made a profession of religion, and shortly after commenced a course of classical study in a grammar school, in the neighborhood of his father's house, kept by a Mr. Alexander." After graduating from Princeton in 1775 he served as a tutor at Hampden-Sydney College, and eventually founded two colleges in the frontier state of Tennessee—Washington (now defunct) and Tusculum.

Alexander conducted the school until the early 1760's; one account gives the date of his departure as 1762. It is known that in 1760 he resigned from the Augusta County vestry because of failing health. He must have given up teaching soon afterward.

Alexander's immediate successor appears to have been one James Campbell, who was "afterwards licensed to preach." Although not a "graduate," he was considered a good Latin scholar and knew "something of Greek."

For several years the school was under the jurisdiction of the Reverend John Brown, pastor of New Providence and Timber Ridge. The evidence indicates that Mr. Brown exercised general supervision, leaving the pedagogy mostly to others. In the 1780's he sponsored another Latin school, distinct from the institution that directly succeeded Alexander's academy.

The names of several teachers have come down to us from the early years. One list includes a John Buchanan, who apparently assisted Robert Alexander. J. Edmundson, Ebenezer Smith, and Robert Archibald taught during Brown's tenure. Smith was a graduate of the academy, having attended with Doak, Houston, and Montgomery. Edmundson and Archibald were both graduates of Princeton and both became licensed preachers. The latter is reported to have been deposed from the ministry for preaching erroneous doctrine. Edmundson also became a physician and Archibald studied medicine, though it is unclear whether he reached the point of practice.

Thus far we have viewed the formative years of Augusta Academy dimly, through a mist of tradition and sketchy information. Now we turn to the advent of William Graham and the emergence of the academy into the clear light of history.

Chapter
II

William Graham and
the Academy of Liberty Hall

WILLIAM GRAHAM headed the academy for twenty-two years. During that time it attained at least a quasi-permanent footing; it was moved to Lexington, its ultimate home (but not to the present campus); and began to confer degrees, although not yet assuming the title of "college."

It must not be inferred that the advances of the Graham era created an institution even remotely resembling, in character or stability, the Washington and Lee University of the twentieth century. The historical material suggests a bewildering absence of the orderly administration, the broad curriculum, the heterogeneous student body of predictable size and origin, and other aspects of the college that are basic and taken for granted today. Many decades would pass before it would be possible to plan the budget a year in advance and to select a freshman class from a "pool" of qualified applicants, much less to prepare for any development in the future.

Nevertheless, the basis for historical continuity was definitely laid during the period of William Graham's association.

GRAHAM WAS BORN IN PENNSYLVANIA in 1746 of Scotch-Irish parents. The family lived for a while in Lancaster County and afterwards in Paxton Township near Harrisburg on the frontier. On one occasion they narrowly escaped an Indian attack. William worked on his father's farm and although he had little time for schooling, he is reported to have studied zealously and to have mastered all that the common schools had to offer.

One biographer states that William, influenced by a neighboring family, in his middle teens grew "excessively fond of frolicking, as it was called, and of dancing." He concealed his vice from his parents and afterwards repented to become "one of the most determined enemies of that practice, that ever lived." In fact he considered it "one of the most effectual means that ever was contrived for the destruction of souls."

His conversion from frivolity progressed far enough to induce him, at the age of twenty-one, to decide on a career in the ministry. Although it was relatively late in life to begin the necessary education, he undertook to prepare himself for Princeton. Such was his determination that he completed his preparation and college course in five years, despite the need to devote part of his time to teaching in order to meet his expenses. He stood near the top of his class and attracted the attention of tutors and classmates for his "genius, industry, and piety." Among his classmates was Henry Lee, who was to become "Lighthorse Harry" of the Revolutionary War and the father of Robert E. Lee. Many years later the Graham family in Rockbridge County had in its possession a book with Lee's name struck out and William's name inscribed in Lee's handwriting. According to family records the book had been presented to William in gratitude for helping Lee in successfully preparing for an examination.

After graduating from Princeton in 1773 Graham studied theology with a neighbor, the Reverend John Roan, a Presbyterian "divine of considerable distinction" who had been a missionary in Virginia in 1744.

At about the same time Graham married Mary Kerr of Carlisle, Pennsylvania, who has been described as "a woman of fair countenance and modest appearance," but "of weak mind, and greatly wanting in discretion." One biographer has reflected that if Graham had married differently "he would have been far more amiable, more useful, and more comfortable." Details or examples of Mary's influence upon her husband are lacking, however, and Graham appears to have borne his marital burdens, if such they were, in silence.

WHILE GRAHAM WAS PURSUING HIS EDUCATION the Presbytery of Hanover in Virginia was concerning itself with the promotion of a school in the valley. In October of 1770 a motion was put forward suggesting a public school in Augusta County, and in the following year the presbytery urged its members to give thought to the proposal. By October of 1773 the body resolved "to fix the publick Seminary for the liberal education of youth" in Staunton.

To find a qualified teacher, the presbytery sought the aid of the Reverend Samuel Stanhope Smith, tutor at Princeton and afterwards president of that college, who had been a missionary in western Virginia. Smith recommended his former student William Graham, and urged Graham to accept the position.

And so in October of 1774 the presbytery agreed "to establish and patronise a publick School" in Augusta County, to be "managed by Mr. William Graham . . . under the Inspection of the Revd. Mr. John Brown." Graham's appointment was tentative. He was to be in charge "at present," but the presbytery reserved the right to determine at a future session "the person by whom it [the school] shall be conducted, and the place where it shall be fixed." Plans to locate the institution at Staunton were set aside because there was "no person to take the management of it" at that place and prospects were considered "very uncertain that there ever will."

The presbytery recommended the school to its several congregations, exhorting them to make gifts compatible with their financial circumstances in order to provide a house, a library, and "other apparatus of learning." Seven ministers were assigned to raise subscription for the seminary in specified areas of Augusta County and environs.

Although the presbytery resolved "to establish" a school, it is evident that, in fact, the body assumed responsibility for continuing an educational enterprise already in being under the supervision of the Reverend John Brown. The minutes of the presbytery do not make this clear. Possibly the members did not consider a peripatetic classical school, existing precariously from year to year, as a tangible institution. Even after they were lending their active patronage to education, they seemed to make a distinction between the Latin school and the seminary. The minutes of February 1, 1775, contain a brief reference to "the school in Agusta,"* and those of April 15 mention the "academy to be established in Agusta." The future infinitive appears especially significant because the presbytery was meeting at the time in the vicinity of the existing school "under the Direction of Mr. Brown,"

* The spelling "Agusta" was commonly used in the minutes at that time.

and its members even visited classes. They "attended a Specimen of the proficiency of the Students, in the Latin and Greek Language," and heard orations "with which they were well pleased."

The presbytery thus appeared to consider the setting up of a permanent academy or seminary at a fixed location as something genuinely creative and entirely new. The members looked upon this as the foundation and not the transformation of an institution. Such a concept is implicit in later historical references ascribing the origin of Washington College or Washington and Lee University to the efforts of the Presbytery of Hanover in the 1770's.

But as early as 1796 the continuity between Robert Alexander and William Graham was tacitly recognized by the trustees of Liberty Hall, in a petition to President Washington. They reported that the institution "as early as the year seventy-six . . . (before conducted in these parts under the form of a Grammar School) received the nominal Title of an Academy. . . ." It is hardly reasonable to believe that the trustees would not have bothered to include that parenthetical allusion unless it referred to a longer span than the two years between the appointment of William Graham as manager of a classical school in 1774 and the titular designation of academy in 1776.

The school of 1774 was conducted in a log building on Mount Pleasant "in a beautiful forest of venerable oaks" about a mile southwest of the town of Fairfield on the Timber Ridge range of hills. In reminiscent writing it has been informally and hyperbolically called the "Log College."

It would be difficult to classify the institution's level of instruction in terms current today. An account of a visit to Mount Pleasant says the students appeared to be from ten to twenty years of age—a span not normally found in any present-day American school. The author of the recollection was Dr. Samuel L. Campbell, a graduate, a trustee, and briefly rector of the academy. His visit was made in boyhood and his description was written many years later. Nevertheless, as he was well acquainted with the school in its formative years we must assume that his observation was reasonably accurate.

Dr. Campbell recalled hearing some of the students in a Greek recitation that sounded beautiful to him even though he did not understand it at the time. The boys and young men presented themselves in groups to Graham, while those not reciting sat apart and studied their assignments. Graham heard the recitations without himself using a textbook, smiling at good performance, and generally leaving it to the students to correct one another's errors.

An indication of the students' curriculum and reading matter is found in a record preserved in the Trustees' Papers of the University. It relates a trip Graham took to Philadelphia to purchase books and apparatus. The book titles included many theological discourses and commentaries and volumes of sermons as well as the traditional classical works. In addition, Renaissance literature was represented by Erasmus' works, *Don Quixote*, Cellini's autobiography, and a ten-volume edition of Shakespeare. Such then "modern" authors as Alexander Pope, Joseph Addison, and Laurence Sterne also were present, along with sets of *The Spectator* and *The Tatler*.

The list of apparatus shows that natural science had a definite place in the educational scheme. The list included an orrery, or device to represent the motions and phases of the planets; a circumferentor, an instrument used in surveying; a protractor, a sector, a prism, double-convex lenses, and a Hadley's quadrant. The scientific equipment at the school included also an electric machine with apparatus and barometer, an air pump, a solar microscope, and a telescope with double reflector.

Early in 1776 the Augusta Academy seemed to be well established at Mount Pleasant. John Brown wrote to the father of a prospective student: "It is a very good school and well attended. And I frankly tell you that my house and heart are open for the reception of your son and I will treat him as my own." In May of that year the presbytery, after conducting examinations, observed the improvement of the pupils in classical studies and in "pronouncing" orations, and warmly approved the students' proficiency and the "Diligence and Abilities of the Teachers." But, despite these signs of stability, moving day was again at hand.

IN OCTOBER OF 1775 WILLIAM GRAHAM, after examination by the presbytery, had been licensed to preach the gospel. On May 4, 1776, he accepted a call as pastor of the united congregations of Timber Ridge and Hall's Meeting House. Meanwhile Captain Alexander Stuart, ancestor of "Jeb" Stuart, and Samuel Houston, father of the Texas hero, each offered to donate forty acres of land at Timber Ridge as a new location for the school. Neighbors offered "to build an Hewed Log House, 28 x 24 feet, one Story and a half high besides their subscriptions, and assuring us of the probability that fire Wood and Timber for the Buildings, will be furnished gratis, for at least Twenty years." The presbytery accordingly agreed to shift the academy southward nearer the scene of Graham's pastoral charge. Graham was appointed rector, this time without strings, and John Montgomery was named as assistant. Twenty men, including Graham (ex officio) and four other Presbyterian clergymen, were selected as a board of trustees, "those intermediate guardians" of the academy.

The change in site was accompanied by a change in name, signifying the Revolutionary sympathies of the "guardians." In the trustees' minutes of May 13, 1776, appears the earliest preserved reference to the school as "the Liberty Hall Academy."

The trustees applied themselves diligently to the construction of buildings, the raising of funds, and other matters concerned with the organization of a new institution. And in the fall of 1776 an advertisement appeared in the Williamsburg *Virginia Gazette*, signed by William Graham, announcing that "An Academy to be distinguished by the name of Liberty Hall, is now established, for the liberal education of youth, on *Timber Ridge*, in *Augusta* county, where all the most important branches of literature, necessary to prepare young gentlemen for the study of law, physick, and theology, may be taught to good advantage, upon the most approved plan." The notice included an assurance that "those peculiarities which form the complexion of any party shall have no place in the scheme."

Liberty Hall had only a brief sojourn at Timber Ridge, plagued by the problems of wartime and an inflationary economy. The effects of the price spiral may be indicated by the rise in the charge for board from £6 10s. to £15 within a year. Through a committee the academy petitioned the general assembly of Virginia, although it is not clear whether the request was for a charter, for financial assistance, or both. Attempts to raise funds by subscription were unsatisfactory, although Graham himself had some success in solicitation on a journey through the East as far as New England. The high hopes of the trustees, the generosity of Stuart and Houston, the interest of the neighbors, and the ability of the rector went for naught.

William Graham, badly affected by the currency depreciation and unable to derive sufficient support from his farm at Timber Ridge, decided to move to a place on North (now Maury) River near Lexington. About 1779 the trustees granted permission for the transfer, provided he would visit the academy every week and sometimes stay for two or three days. Graham's house at Timber Ridge was converted to the use of students.

The trustees intended to maintain the school at Timber Ridge, and continued planning for new buildings. But in 1780 the academy ceased to function there. It was too greatly weakened by the gradual withdrawal of William Graham and the departure of many students to join the armies of the Revolution. Several of the pupils, however, followed

Graham to North River and received private instruction from him. They boarded with him or in the neighborhood. The library and scientific apparatus of Liberty Hall were installed in his dwelling. One of Graham's biographers has remarked: "In this sequestered spot some very valuable men received their education." There the spark of the academy was kept alive until it could spring again into flame.

Liberty Hall students were called out to bolster patriot armies in the Carolinas against Cornwallis' campaigns, and drafted in large numbers for the militia in the area of Augusta and Rockbridge counties. The hardened farmer-soldiers had a low opinion of the student volunteers and conscripts. But Liberty Hall boys in the army of Nathanael Greene acquitted themselves well at the Battle of Guilford Courthouse on March 15, 1781, which forced Cornwallis to withdraw to Wilmington, North Carolina.

William Graham had volunteered his services shortly after the outbreak of war and had been elected captain of a company which, however, never took the field. His closest proximity to combat came in the summer of 1781. Returning to Lexington from clerical business in Staunton, he fell in with some members of the Virginia legislature fleeing before the advance of a British force under Colonel Tarleton. Graham organized the group to spread a warning and urge all militia officers to call up their men and converge on Rockfish Gap, where a stand could be made against the enemy. On his arrival home he sent a messenger to the militia officers of the neighborhood informing them of the danger. Next morning a number of men gathered at Graham's house and proceeded with him to Rockfish Gap, which was already well defended. Tarleton retreated without a fight. Graham and some of the other Americans advanced toward Charlottesville and met Lafayette's army near that town. Informed that the campaign would be a lengthy one, Graham returned home to study war no more.

WITH THE ASSURANCE of peace and independence the trustees of Liberty Hall set about to revive the school in a new location and with a new sanction. They petitioned the Virginia legislature and were granted a charter in December of 1782, the first awarded by the new state to an institution of learning. Unfortunately the records do not indicate the reasons that impelled the trustees to turn toward government and, at least in form, to renounce church control. The charter contained no word of creed or doctrine and no mention of the presbytery. But it did name a self-perpetuating board of twenty trustees, all strict Presbyterians and four of them clergymen—in fact, they were the same men who had been appointed in 1776 by the presbytery, or persons closely related to them.

The trustees considered reestablishing the academy within the comparatively new town of Lexington, but decided instead to locate it outside the town on a hundred acres of land given by William Graham, Joseph Walker, and William Alexander. They began anew their old and continuing struggle to raise funds, to get buildings erected, to recruit and retain tutors who were paid meager salaries for arduous duties.

They also authorized the granting of degrees. The suggestion of college-level standards had been conveyed in the announcement of the establishment of Liberty Hall in 1776, which had stated that full preprofessional studies were available. No degrees were then offered. In August of 1784, however, the trustees designated the second Wednesday of September, 1785, as commencement day—the first in the history of the institution. On that day the Bachelor of Arts degree was conferred upon twelve young men: Samuel Blackburn, Samuel Carrick, Moses Hoge, Samuel Houston, William McClung, Andrew McClure, John McCue, James Priestley, Adam Rankin, Archibald Roane, Terah Templin, and William Willson.

The academy had one more brief affiliation with the Presbyterian Church before the formal ties were finally severed. In 1791 the Synod of Virginia began discussion of the possibility of establishing two theological seminaries, one in Rockbridge County with the Reverend William Graham as president, and the other in Washington County, Pennsylvania. The suggestion was made that the seminary in Rockbridge be formed by a "coalition" with Liberty Hall. The trustees of the academy, facing a financial crisis as usual and being staunch Presbyterians, welcomed the patronage of the synod. Under the agreement, vacancies in the institution's board of trustees would be filled only with members of the Hanover and Lexington presbyteries. Negotiations were completed in 1793.

The relationship of synod and academy temporarily stimulated contributions of funds, or at least the solicitation of contributions, and possibly added some students. As the religious fervor of the early 1790's declined, however, the theological branch of the academy began to lapse, and within a few years was silently dropped. The last reference to Liberty Hall in synod records was in October of 1796.

William Graham, after turning down an offer of the presidency of Hampden-Sydney College, continued as rector of the academy until 1796. Then he resigned and migrated westward. (He also served as pastor of the Lexington Presbyterian Church from its formation until his departure from the town.) Correspondence between Graham and several friends indicates that various motives prompted his move. After twenty-two strenuous years with the academy, during which time he was but poorly compensated for his work, he approached the age of fifty with gloomy financial prospects. Land speculation was rife in western Virginia at the time and in that he found some hope of prosperity. Letters to Graham from old friends hint at other reasons for his leaving. "Scandalous reports" and "the Scourge of tongues" were mentioned.

Graham also held positive political opinions, some of which must have made enemies for him. He expressed severe criticism of Thomas Paine as an "audacious Blasphemer." Vilifying Tom Paine for his supposed atheism was, to be sure, a popular sport among pious folk in the post-Revolutionary period, and Graham could not have incurred much censure on that score. But some of his other views were not as well accepted. He distrusted the framers of the Constitution, and beheld in the document "every species of tyranny and despotism." He sought unsuccessfully to be elected a delegate to the Virginia convention, so that he could vote against ratification, and contemplated publishing a pamphlet to expose the Constitution as "arbitrary," "very expensive," and "inadequate to the end proposed." In 1794 he opposed a synod resolution which by implication condemned the "Whiskey Rebellion" by Pennsylvania distillers against an excise tax on their product. He issued a pamphlet in support of the projected state of Franklin, in which he was said to have purchased land. The tract involved him in a bitter dispute with the Reverend Hezekiah Balch of the Abingdon Presbytery and Graham believed Balch had instigated the people in the area of the proposed state to burn him in effigy. A few of Graham's opponents even doubted his Christianity.

Graham died in Richmond on June 8, 1799, amidst a protracted lawsuit growing out of his attempt to acquire a tract of land on the Ohio River. The academy trustees, apparently unimpressed by the scurrilous gossip concerning his later years in Lexington, took steps to show their esteem for him. At their direction the Reverend George A. Baxter, rector of the academy and a former student of Graham's, delivered an address on the life and services of his late predecessor. In 1804 the board undertook to obtain an "elegant tombstone" for him and appointed a committee to arrange removal of his remains to Lexington. It was not until 1911, however, that the reinterment was accomplished. As Graham's family was destitute, the trustees decreed that his son William should be educated without charge.

During an especially trying period William Graham preserved the continuity of the institution that is now Washington and Lee University. The effects of his services have been summarized by his one-time pupil Dr. Archibald Alexander:

The extent of the influence exerted by this one man over the literature and religion of Virginia, cannot be calculated. As the stream which fertilizes a large district is small in its origin, but goes on continually increasing until it becomes a mighty river, so the influence of the Rev. William Graham did not cease when he died, but has gone on increasing by means of his disciples, who have been scattered far and wide over the West and South.

Chapter
III

Academy Students—
Gentlemen and Otherwise

THE ASSUMPTION that every student is a gentleman and will act as such, basis of the venerable honor system of Washington and Lee University, had not been made during the academy period. Trustees and faculty believed stern discipline was necessary to cope with the post-Revolutionary "degeneracy" which was said to have replaced an earlier piety and zeal for learning among youth.

A CODE OF RULES provided for careful control of behavior. A student monitor was designated each week to record and report all violations. In addition, every student was expected to report any violation he knew of, and the trustees decreed that no one should in any way "distress" the informant. The rector was authorized to enter student rooms if he deemed it necessary, "either by bursting the door or otherwise." Local members of the board of trustees were often assembled to hear cases of misconduct. On some occasions, at least, the accused were interrogated under oath.

We may well wonder how much of this strictness was justified. The records do contain many instances of misbehavior, and student discipline seems to have been quite a problem among other educational institutions at that time. For example, the historian Thomas J. Wertenbaker has written about difficulties at Princeton, which college academy officials generally regarded as a paragon. In 1807 the academy trustees appointed a committee to cooperate with William and Mary and other schools in Virginia in asking the legislature for power to compel attendance of witnesses and to administer oaths in hearings on breaches of rules.

Professor Wertenbaker has suggested that the poor psychology employed by teachers in human transactions caused many of the troubles at Princeton. And the list of rules in force at the academy indicates a rigidity that today would certainly be judged extreme.

Some of the regulations, to be sure, were reasonable enough even by present-day standards. Cursing, swearing, lying, intoxication, and creating disturbances during study hours were forbidden. On the other hand, there were restrictions and requirements that the students must have regarded as challenges to infringement. A student could not call his fellows by nicknames, or "presume to play at ball in Lexington at any time." (!) He was not permitted to "play cards, dice, or any unlawful game"; to visit a tavern "at unseasonable hours"; to "engage at any dancing School" or in "any debauching revel whatever (commonly known by the names of frolicks Dances Balls Entertainments)." When the rector or tutor entered a room every student was required to "rise up with a decent bow." Students were enjoined to "treat all persons with decency and respect especially their known superiors and the Families where they lodge."

As might be expected, card playing and profanity were especially widespread—so much so that on one occasion the trustees commended five lads for being innocent of such offenses, so that "their Names should stand on record to their Honour." In 1784 a board committee reported that Liberty Hall boys were "generally guilty of playing cards," and admonished them to refrain from the "highly pernicious" practice. One student, convicted of both card playing and swearing, was expelled and unanimously censured, but was given the privilege of readmittance "on his Making Publick Concessions to the Rector and not otherwise."

In 1787 the trustees met to investigate reports of misbehavior that included card playing, meeting at night "for the purposes of Drinking and Frolick," swearing, and two offenses not specifically covered in the rules—conspiring to burn down the academy and stealing a beehive from a local citizen. The threat of arson was dismissed as a jest, but a number of students (many of them "nearly related" to the trustees) confessed to complicity in the purloining of the beehive. The record does not show what punitive action was taken by the trustees or the bees.

Soon afterward the board heard a complaint by John McKee, Jr., a student, against William Graham. McKee claimed that Graham had expelled him without sufficient cause, had called him a perjurer, and had declared he was "nearer the gallows than he expected." The board held that Graham had overreached himself and that McKee could be reinstated if he would publicly apologize to Graham for "indecently" contradicting him during the hearing.

In 1794 Archibald Mills was expelled for a list of offenses that included annoying, kicking, and verbally abusing other students, threatening to intimidate some with a pistol, telling people he was "the Devil according to his Magnitude," and impersonating the devil.

The following year David Flournoy was expelled after being found partially guilty on a series of charges comprising mistreatment of three persons, "abusing" someone's hat, misconduct at table, and beating Edward Graham, steward and tutor in the academy.

The trustees were twice called upon to discipline John J. Crittenden, who was to become a member of two presidential cabinets, representative and senator from Kentucky, and author of an unsuccessful compromise proposal which sought to avert secession and civil war. The would-be conciliator of 1860 was a belligerent lad in 1804, when he and several other students were summoned to declare under oath whether they knew anything of an attempt by certain students to "fight or abett in a Duel." The witnesses declined to testify and were suspended.

Crittenden was evidently reinstated, for a month later he was on the carpet again. One day, in a pique, he had thrown a biscuit at the steward because the biscuits had been passed to other students before him. The following day he became irked when the steward rebuked him for eating during the blessing, and he advanced upon the unhappy official with two knives. Warned that he would be answerable to the officers of the academy, Crittenden declared that, rather than suffer a rebuke from a steward, he would submit to expulsion from the academy and from heaven too. The trustees obliged him insofar as their jurisdiction extended.

Following a humble and flowery apology, Crittenden was readmitted to the next session on probation; but he moved on to the College of William and Mary. By 1842 he had gained such prominence that the newly organized Society of Alumni of Washington College invited him to deliver the Anniversary Address. The statesman declined the invitation through pressure of business, but recollected the kindness of the people of Lexington to him during his student days there.

Other cases heard in 1804—apparently a vintage year for devilment —involved charges of duelling, intoxication, fighting, attending a ball, disorder at table, "profane swearing," participating in street affrays, and holding a "Mock Imitation of Divine Worship."

In the same year several academy youths were involved in a fracas with Robert Gold, a townsman, whose house was near a public pump where students congregated to bathe. Gold objected to "the indecency of young men to be stripped naked in the public street in a clear moonlight night between the hours of 8 & 9 . . . and because the law of the town forbade bathing there." Among the boys in the melee was Robert Butler, later treasurer of Virginia. William Crump, one of those suspended earlier for refusing to testify regarding the duel— afterwards member of Congress and minister to Chile—was "charged with running naked through the streets of Lexington." Crump admitted that he had romped unclothed through the staid village at 7:30 A.M. While Butler and several others were suspended for the remainder of the session, "naked Crump" was let off with a reprimand after confessing his crime and promising future good behavior.

William Cabell and Samuel Swan were suspended in 1806 after a series of incidents culminating in a brawl with a townsman, during which they had fired upon their opponent and chased him about Lexington.

Among cases heard by the board in the following year was an appeal by Nathaniel Henry, son of the immortal Patrick, from a suspension imposed by the rector and faculty. Henry had caused a disorder in the dining hall, referring to the soup as slop, throwing bread under the table, and threatening to beat the steward and any teachers who might interfere. He also had spoken of going to a tavern. Young Henry was apparently as much a rebel as his father, though with hardly a comparable cause or eloquence. He had been suspended from New London Academy in Campbell County, expelled from Hampden-Sydney College, and denied admission to Drury Lacy's school. In his ingenuous plea to the academy trustees he conceded his immaturity and imperfection; after all, he had only called the soup "slop"; he had merely been joking about going to a tavern; the piece of bread he had thrown under the table was just a small one, and had had some "flees" in it; his remarks about whipping the steward and teachers were confidential and conditional.

In 1809 the board designated Washington's birthday and July 4 as holidays for students, who would "not be subject to the penalties for dancing on those days" provided their conduct was otherwise good. These generous concessions were balanced by a declaration that if a student were absent from his room while a dance or "other expensive entertainment" was in progress, it would be assumed that he had attended and he would be held liable to penalties.

The academy became embroiled in an extended difficulty with several students in 1810. Early in the session six youths had been suspended after they had created a disturbance in rooms of the school, denied entry to the rector when he sought to quell the commotion, and cast stones at him. Although academy rules forbade suspended students to come within two miles of Lexington, several of those involved returned to town and proceeded to air their grievances "in terms of high crimination." They tried to appeal their case to the trustees and frequented the academy where "they formed a party." One of them, Jesse Irvine, accosted the rector, Dr. Baxter, and threatened him with physical violence. That night Irvine cropped the manes and tails of Baxter's horses, stabbed one of his cows, and injured another. The rector appealed to civil authority, by whom Irvine was bound to keep the peace. Richard Norris, father of one of the boys, threatened to sue for reinstatement of his son but nothing further appears in the records of the affair.

Academy files, like the daily newspapers, tell us more about the breaches of law than about its observance. Except for the five boys who were not caught playing cards or swearing in 1784, we have no statistics on the students who went soberly and conscientiously about their business. We may assume that these constituted a large majority at all times, or nearly all. "Morality is greatly encouraged and vice severely censured," wrote student Allen Taylor in 1794. In the uproarious year of 1804 a Lexington citizen expressed the opinion that "for some considerable time the laws have been pretty generally exercised with moderation and prudence, but it is very difficult to govern such a number of young men of various dispositions, and many of whom have not been accustomed to any restraint."

Scattered letters and lecture notes give us some glimpses of the more serious aspects of student life. Young men did go to the academy for an education; and as well as the heavily emphasized classics and theology, they could learn much of the current knowledge of the world in which they lived. Allen Taylor observed in 1794: "As for what is studyed Here may be said in a few words. . . . the Latin and Greek languages the most useful sciences or indeed any Science a Person Pleases." A decade later William Radford expressed a wish to study politics during the next session, and mentioned several books on the subject, among them Montesquieu's *The Spirit of the Laws* and Vattel's *Law of Nations*.

A student's lecture notes reveal something of the subject matter treated in William Graham's course in "mental philosophy." In lecture 4, for example, such questions were recorded as "What is perception? What is to be considered in every perception? Agent, object, and energy." In lecture 6 it was asked, "Is emotion and passion the same thing? What is the difference between passions selfish and benevolent? May passions be of a mixed nature? What is impulse? Are things out of our power generally objects of desire?" In lecture 7 a distinction was called for between passion and "appatite," and in number 14 the will, moral agency, and free will were defined.

An invaluable educational adjunct of American colleges in the nineteenth century was the literary and debating society. It not only trained future politicians and writers in the techniques of their professions, but supplemented the classical curriculum and other subjects that might now be called social sciences. The societies probably gave the students the opportunity to go more deeply into great issues of the day than lectures or even tutorial studies.

Such societies, or at least their prototypes, existed at Liberty Hall in the 1790's. A letter written in 1792 by student Robert Willson said that on the following day students were to bring their "pieces" into a "society." Years later Robert Stuart, a friend and roommate of George A. Baxter at the academy, recalled that Baxter "had been instrumental in establishing" a debating society there. According to Willson, the rector served as president of the society, and lectured on the topic to be treated at the next meeting. Students took notes as he spoke, and also took notes on other students' "pieces" in order to offer comment afterwards. Upon conclusion of this "society," another was constituted comprising young men under the care of the presbytery, into which students brought their writings.

One of the students under the care of the presbytery of Lexington deserves particular mention. He was John Chavis, a Negro, who afterward became widely known and respected as a teacher and Presbyterian minister in Virginia and North Carolina. He is said to have been privately educated by Dr. John Witherspoon of Princeton before he attended Liberty Hall. Little is known about his residence at the academy, but his name appears on a list of students in the winter session of 1795. A few writers have mentioned Chavis' association with Lexington, where he lived as late as 1804. It should be kept in mind that the generation of Virginians that included Thomas Jefferson, Patrick Henry, George Mason, and George Washington deprecated slavery, wished for its ultimate extinction, and regarded it as at best a necessary evil. There seems to have been far less racial consciousness then than there was later, after the abolitionist crusade was launched, and it is likely that Chavis received the same instruction and privileges as his fellow students.

Young men of the academy overtly demonstrated an interest in public affairs. A letter by student Thomas L. Preston tells of the manner in which students and townsmen responded to the news of Thomas Jefferson's election as President by the House of Representatives in 1801:

> On the 23rd day Feby there was a very eligant dinner given here by the Students to the citizens, at which, a large number of the most respectable attended. It was done to commemorate Genl Washington's birth day,* and at the same time express our approbation at the increased spirit of republicanism. Fortunately, certain information of Jefferson's election came to hand that evening; . . . the Academy was illuminated, as well as . . . private houses in Lexington. The Students marched to town in great order, with torches in their hands, and were met by all the republican citizens, at which greeting there was an *immortal shout* raised, expressive of our joy on the occasion. The whole party then marched up and down the streets huzzaing for Jefferson and Liberty.

When the youths departed from groups of citizens they gave three cheers. March 4, the day of Jefferson's inauguration, was similarly celebrated in academy and town. Preston added: ". . . nor do I expect it will terminate there with the students, as there is now a talk of addressing Mr. Jefferson."

Samuel McDowell Reid, a student in 1810, also described gay times on Washington's Birthday. At noon one John Paxton delivered "an excellent oration" at the court house; and in the evening the students "had a most splendid ball furnished by Mr. Dilworth in the steward's house" at the academy. It was a successful occasion, he declared, at which the fair sex looked lovelier than ever. Next year the same student described the celebration of the Fourth of July in the town: "Gustavus Jones a student delivered a verry excellent oration. At 2 o'clock we sat down to a very good dinner & drank as usual 17 toasts in the evening." The beverage and size of containers were not identified; therefore the effect of seventeen toasts cannot be surmised.

Academy students had hopes, problems, and complaints similar to those of college youth of any generation. A somewhat extreme opinion, perhaps, was expressed in the memoirs of William C. Preston of South Carolina, afterward a United States senator, to whom Henry Clay made his famous remark that he "had rather be right than be

---

* The dinner was held on the twenty-third probably because in 1801 the twenty-second fell on a Sunday.

president." The academy was, Preston recalled, "superintended by lazy and ignorant Presbyterian preachers, and filled with dirty boys of low manners and morals." In six months at the place, he continued, he "unlearned as much as was possible for a boy of sprightly parts to unlearn."

In 1842, some 33 or 34 years after Preston's period of unlearning, the trustees conferred upon this distinguished alumnus the degree of Doctor of Laws.

Chapter
IV

Washington's Patronage—
and Some Consequences Thereof

THROUGHOUT CHANGES in name, location, and governance, the academy consistently retained one attribute characteristic of educational institutions. It remained in precarious financial circumstances.

Trustees and clergymen were continually engaged in soliciting funds for the school, and in exhorting those who had promised contributions to make their pledges good. In some instances, such as the donations of land at Timber Ridge and near Lexington, the academy had good fortune. But the records abound with references to difficulties in obtaining support and in filling the needs of a functioning institution. There was never enough money to pay for necessary construction and supplies or to compensate tutors and stewards.

In 1778 the struggling academy petitioned the general assembly of Virginia. It is not clear whether the object was financial assistance, a charter, or both. Financial considerations were important in the decision to accept the synod's proposal for adding a theological branch in 1795. Despite the intervention of the synod and the sporadic contributions rounded up through solicitation, the trustees in 1794 again deemed it necessary to petition the Virginia legislature, and this time they definitely asked for monetary assistance. They urged that in view of eighteen years of experience and the "present flourishing state of the

Academy," the institution should be made more "extensively and permanently useful." Specified objectives were enlargement of buildings and establishment of an endowment. The endowment would be used to augment the teaching staff. The trustees did not ask for a direct grant from the legislature, but suggested that the lawmakers turn over to them the rights of the commonwealth in certain lands liable to escheat in Rockingham and other counties.

The trustees also sought approval for operation of a lottery. They discountenanced the use of lotteries for private gain or "to accomplish trifling objects," but thought that "for virtuous purposes they ought to be & have been approved by the best and wisest men." Surely no purpose could be more laudable than that of "endowing . . . Seminaries for the liberal education of Youth in a young and growing empire." The trustees' suggestion was really quite in order, as at that time lotteries for religious, educational, or other constructive ends were regarded as fully legitimate. Indeed, such a method of finance was employed by Harvard, Dartmouth, William and Mary, and Hampden-Sydney.

On none of the requests from Liberty Hall did the legislature see fit to take action; so again, in the fall of 1795, supplications for public aid were transmitted to Richmond. Liberty's Hall's past praiseworthy service and its "flattering prospects" were recounted once more, and this time the petition declared that if public funds were not forthcoming the school could exist no longer, but this plea also went unheeded.

WHILE SUCH FUTILE AND FRUSTRATING EFFORTS were being made to give the academy a firm financial footing, an event was taking shape that would prove of profound significance to the history of the institution. The gift George Washington made in 1796 has probably been exceeded in importance to the school's development only by the appointment of General Lee to its presidency in 1865. The academy's future became interwoven with the name of the Father of His Country, a name that was to be universally revered after the political bitterness of the Federalist period had receded. To be sure, the Washington donation did not bring affluence or even provide an immediate solution to the most pressing difficulties; but it created a unique identification, and was the first great step in the second major transformation of this institution—from a provincial academy to one of the country's distinctive smaller universities.

The gift consisted of one hundred shares of stock in the James River Company, an enterprise chartered by the Virginia legislature in 1785.

The purpose of the company was to attain a partial fulfillment of a suggestion made by Washington himself, when still just a private citizen, that the state undertake surveys of the James and Potomac river routes with a view to the construction of canals which, together with portages, would link the Ohio and Kentucky country to the Atlantic.

The legislature conferred the hundred shares of stock upon Washington as a means of winning public confidence in the James River project. Governor Benjamin Harrison urged him to accept the award as a token of Virginia's gratitude for his services. Washington, already one of the country's wealthiest men and sternly opposed to "the principle of gratuities," was embarrassed by the action; yet he feared that an outright rejection would tend to undermine confidence in the canal scheme. He therefore concluded to accept the stock with the understanding that it would be applied to some public purpose. The legislature agreed that the "tolls and profits accruing therefrom" would be devoted to "such objects of a public nature" as Washington should direct. The stock remained in his nominal custody until near the end of his Presidency when there was the prospect that the shares would soon become productive.

Washington believed education was the most worthy object of his philanthropy, and requested the legislature to designate an area from which an institution would be chosen to receive the benefit. The lawmakers, however, unable or unwilling to decide among rival claims of different sections of the commonwealth, returned the matter back to Washington and asked him to appropriate the shares "to a seminary at such a place in the upper country as he may deem most convenient to a majority of the inhabitants thereof." That recommendation was made probably because the lower country had William and Mary and other academies and colleges, but no endowment had been made for an institution west of the Blue Ridge.

At this point Washington's attention was called to Liberty Hall by Congressman Andrew Moore of Rockbridge County, trustee of the academy and alumnus of its antecedent school, and his colleague Francis Preston of Washington County, whose family had been connected with the school since its earliest years. Moore urged William Graham and his associates to apply for the endowment. In January of 1796 the trustees, who had been busy petitioning the presbytery, the synod, the general assembly, and the public, drew up another document—to the President of the United States. They dealt with the origins of Liberty Hall as a grammar school, with its receipt of "the nominal Title of an Academy" in 1776, the arguments for selection of the James River valley, and the difficulties encountered by the school during the Revolution. From 1783, they told Washington, buildings had been constructed in the Woods Creek area of the "forks of the James," about a mile from the North River and from the town of Lexington, "a place for 'calm and undisturbed retirements.' "

The *Washington Papers* in the Library of Congress indicate that at least seven possible locations were under consideration—the towns of Fincastle, Lynchburg, Charlottesville, Staunton, and Lexington; the New London Academy in Campbell County and Hampden-Sydney College.

Governor Henry Lee expressed the opinion that either Staunton or Lexington should be chosen. Leading the partisans of Staunton was Archibald Stuart, alumnus and trustee of Liberty Hall, whose father Alexander Stuart had given land to the school in 1776. Thomas Jefferson predicted that New London would be chosen.

Late in 1796 Washington made his decision in favor of Liberty Hall. Representative Moore has been quoted as saying the President had assured him that the choice was influenced most by the fact that "zealous and persevering exertions had been made, for the promotion of learning" which were unique in the upper country. "These exertions he found had begun before the war, and been continued through it, and were still continued; and so far as he could discover, those who had so perseveringly exercised a fostering care over literature were more likely than any others to make a proper use of the James River fund at his disposal."

The grateful trustees hastened to change the name of the institution to Washington Academy, writing to their benefactor:

> Convinced, as we are, that public prosperity and security are intimately connected with the diffusion of knowledge, we look around with the highest satisfaction on its rapid advances in these United States; unfeignedly rejoicing that the citizen who has long been distinguished as the asserter of the liberties of his country, adds to this illustrious character the no less illustrious one, a Patron of the Arts and Literature.

From the congenial shades of Mount Vernon the retired President wrote to the trustees:

> To promote literature in this rising empire, and to encourage the arts, have ever been amongst the warmest wishes of my heart. And if the donation, which the generosity of the Legislature of the Commonwealth of Virginia has enabled me to bestow on Liberty Hall, now by your politeness called Washington Academy, is likely to prove a means to accomplish these ends, it will contribute to the gratification of my desires.

Thus it came to pass that the Anglican gentleman of the tidewater, whose Cavalier great-grandfather had left England for America because of a reversal in family fortunes caused by the triumph of the Puritans, gave his patronage to the upcountry academy of the Presbyterian Scotch-Irish.

IT WAS TO BE SOME YEARS before any income would be realized from the Washington endowment, the value of which is reckoned at about $50,000. Meanwhile, as an indirect result of the gift, the academy faced a totally unexpected threat that might have changed its essential character for all time to come.

In December of 1796, some three months after Washington's announcement of his decision, the Virginia legislature adopted "An act for erecting Liberty Hall Academy into a College." Unlike earlier changes at the school, this move would have in fact created an entirely new institution, styled the "College of Washington." This college would have had four "schools": languages; natural philosophy and astronomy; mathematics; and logic, moral philosophy, and belles lettres. Each school was to have a professor, one of whom would be appointed president. The professors would constitute a corporation entitled "the President and Professors of the College of Washington in Virginia." The corporation was to be authorized to control "all the property of the college"; to appoint tutors, the treasurer, and lesser officials; to adopt rules for government of the school; and to prescribe educational policy and curriculum.

A nineteen-man board of visitors was established, with the power to appoint the president and professors, to fix their salaries, to remove them for cause, and to appoint replacements. The original visitors were named in the act. Thereafter they were to fill vacancies by election. Thus the institution had the status of a state college under the control of a self-perpetuating board.

The bill completely disregarded the academy's board of trustees, its current president and faculty, and the charter of 1782. Neither the board nor the charter was specifically abolished or superseded. Each was merely ignored, as if it did not exist.

Why and how such a peculiar measure was adopted in this manner is by no means clear. The haste of the action—the academy trustees seem to have had no forewarning—suggests that most of the legislators simply concurred in a plausible proposal as it was presented to them, without considering or even being aware of its implications. The bill on its face must have appeared to serve a constructive educational purpose and to provide an enduring memorial to a great Virginian.

Moreover, the transfer of James River shares to the academy was viewed as a conveyance of public funds to a private school. The lawmakers probably thought this an appropriate reason for the conversion of Liberty Hall into an enlarged and more useful state institution.

The board of visitors named in the bill included no clergymen and only a minority of Presbyterians. The act would thus have taken governance of the academy away from the Scotch-Irish community that had created and fostered it. Historians of the institution have speculated whether the removal of Presbyterian control was a deliberate motive behind the legislation. The influence of Thomas Jefferson has been suggested because of similarities between the structure and curriculum of the proposed College of Washington and those later prescribed for the University of Virginia. It is possible, however, that the form of organization was adapted directly from European universities where faculties were given larger administrative authority than in typical American colleges.

Quickly the trustees of Liberty Hall moved to have the act repealed. They drew up a strong protest based on the contention that the legislation was "a singular instance of infringement on the Rights of an incorporated Body which had not by any Act of theirs violated their Tenure or gave cause for the abolition of their Charter." They held that the law was not only unjust in its essence but menacing in its tendency: "The same principle if admitted in one case may be extended to every such Corporation throughout the State. Their Charters may be violated and their estates in whatever way acquired may be wantonly sported with just as caprice or folly may dictate."

The trustees declared that if the act should go into effect, the work of education at Liberty Hall must necessarily be interrupted for a long period and "greatly impeded for the future"; that the dissolution of the corporation would result in the reversion of property to the original donors; and that in future "the liberal will be discouraged from contributing to similar Institutions." The protest dealt with difficulties in handling debts of a dissolved corporation, with the embarrassment of alienating property given the board in trust, and with the local belief that the legislature's action was contrary to the wishes of "those good Citizens who for the promotion of Virtue and Literature gave largely of their estates to the Academy."

A committee was appointed to inform other Virginia corporations of the assault upon Liberty Hall's charter and to compose a remonstrance to the legislature. A statement of the academy's case also was dispatched to the trustees of Hampden-Sydney College. President Archibald Alexander of Hampden-Sydney, an alumnus of Liberty Hall, and two trustees replied with an expression of warm agreement as to the injustice of the act and its threat to corporate bodies. They believed, however, that the legislation had been passed inadvertently and hoped for its prompt repeal.

Zechariah Johnston, trustee of the academy and member of the house of delegates from Rockbridge, took up the cause of Liberty Hall in the legislature; and early in 1798 the act was repealed. The status quo under the charter of 1782 was explicitly restored, with the unexceptional change in the name of the institution to Washington Academy.

The principle enunciated by the Liberty Hall trustees became the core of the argument of Dartmouth College in a similar defense of its charter, voiced before the United States Supreme Court by the eloquent Dartmouth alumnus, Daniel Webster. Partisan political and sectarian controversies had brought about an attempt to convert the chartered, privately administered college into a university under public control. In 1819 Chief Justice John Marshall, speaking for the court, ruled in favor of the colonial charter and the college. Thus two old American institutions of higher learning, one through legislative and one through juridical channels, won victories of profound significance not only to education but to the integrity of business corporations and all other kinds of legally chartered organizations.

ANOTHER CONSEQUENCE that followed from Washington's endowment was the decision of the Virginia division of the Society of the Cincinnati to turn over its funds, under certain conditions, to the academy. Protracted negotiations over more than forty years, including a petition to Congress and culminating in court action, were necessary before the funds were finally made available to the school. When received in 1848 they amounted to about $25,000.

The Society of the Cincinnati was founded in 1783 at the inspiration of General Henry Knox, and Washington was its first president general. Its original membership was limited to officers who had served on the American side in the Revolutionary War. Membership thereafter was to be hereditary, descending in the eldest male line, or in failure thereof to members of collateral branches who should be judged most worthy. A division was organized in each of the thirteen states and one was created for French officers who had participated in the war. Every member contributed the equivalent of a month's military pay at his rank to establish an invested fund, the income from which would be used to assist needy members or dependents of members.

The hereditary feature of the society, smacking of an order of nobility, drew widespread opposition in the newborn republic. Among the critics were such men as Benjamin Franklin, Samuel Adams, John Adams, and of course Thomas Jefferson. In response to the attacks Washington, as president general, urged that the hereditary provision be dropped. At its first general meeting, in 1784, the national society voted to follow Washington's recommendation. Not all the states ratified the decision, and the societies in six of those that did not have been in existence continuously to the present day. The Virginia society, however, no doubt influenced by the attitudes of the state's two most prominent men, adhered to the decision to admit no more hereditary members. Thus it had no means of replenishing its original membership.

(Several decades later, when Americans could accept the presence of hereditary organizations without fear of a reversion to monarchical practices, the Cincinnati opened membership to certain descendants of Revolutionary officers. The Virginia division was revived in 1889.)

But for a time, at the beginning of the nineteenth century, the Virginia Society of the Cincinnati thus faced the prospect of ultimate extinction. Knowing this, its members discussed means of disposing of the funds which were more than adequate to meet current pension needs and which would some day be utterly inapplicable to their designated purpose. Foremost in their thoughts was the support of an educational institution.

In this situation the trustees of Washington Academy petitioned the Cincinnati for appropriation of the funds to their school. Hampden-Sydney also put in a bid. In 1802 the society voted narrowly in favor of the academy—18 to 16. Washington's patronage of the institution at Lexington seems to have had a strong influence on the result.

This decision was far from final; it was qualified by the requirement for confirmation at a subsequent meeting in 1803. Some members also objected to use of the funds for any purpose other than that stated in the constitution of the society. A conclusive majority of the membership could not be obtained by the next meeting. Meanwhile the newly established Ann Smith Female Academy at Lexington made an appeal for the money which, however, was not seriously considered.

In 1807 the society resolved that the funds should be turned over to Washington Academy when the number of the society's members should become so reduced that a general meeting could not take place for three consecutive years. A further condition was that "there shall be established and continued in the said seminary a military school, in which shall be taught [at least] the Science of Fortification and Gunnery."

Before the attrition of the membership prevented the holding of annual meetings—the last of which was in 1824—the society transferred its funds to the treasurer of the commonwealth of Virginia, Jerman Baker, for administration and for eventual bestowal upon Washington College, as the academy had by then been named. Baker misappropriated moneys from the Cincinnati fund and committed suicide. The Washington College trustees sued his securities, but appeal and other delays prevented a final decree in their favor until 1845. Even then it was necessary to obtain another court order to bring execution of the judgment in 1848.

During these years the trustees also faced the problem of meeting the requirement for teaching military subjects in order to qualify for the Cincinnati gift. On accepting the offer of the funds in 1807, they voted to hire a "Cincinnati Professor" for the appropriate duties as soon as their finances should make it possible. Shortly before the War of 1812, when military fervor was being fanned, they petitioned Congress for consideration in the event that national military schools should be established. In 1825 the trustees resolved that "a military school be & is hereby established"; but the resolution was not implemented. In the late 1830's, when the Virginia Military Institute was founded in Lexington, an agreement was effected whereby a member of the institute faculty was appointed the Cincinnati Professor of Military Science in the College. A decade later a full-time position of Cincinnati Professor of Mathematics and Military Science was created, and was continued until 1865. Since then a course in "fortifications, gunnery, and ballistics" has been offered, in theory at least, under the title of Military Engineering, for "qualified students who may request it." No students have requested that particular course. The establishment of a Reserve Officers Training Corps unit in the University, however, has provided instruction which the original Cincinnati would no doubt consider more than adequate.

In their 1807 resolution accepting the society's gift the trustees stipulated also that as soon as the funds were received, a student should be appointed to make a public address expounding the views, principles, and general character of the organization. The Cincinnati oration was initiated in the 1840's as a commencement honor to the best scholar in the graduating class. In 1891 a gold medal was created to be awarded to the student delivering the oration. In recent times an award has been offered for the best student essay, if there is one of sufficient literary and historical merit, dealing with the "principles upon which the Society of the Cincinnati was founded."

Chapter
V

Old Troubles
in a New Century

THE CLOSING MONTHS OF 1796 constituted a momentous period for the fortunes of the academy. In September George Washington reached his decision regarding the endowment. In October the trustees accepted the resignation of William Graham, who had steered the institution through critical years. In December the legislature made its attempt to usurp control of the academy. Also, apparently, it was around this time that the seminary sponsored by the Synod of Virginia, which had once been expected to bolster the academy, quietly expired.

As we have noted, the material benefit of Washington's gift was deferred, and the magic of his name and patronage could not quickly overcome the difficulties that beset the trustees. These "intermediate guardians" continued to experience chronic or recurrent problems in filling the rectorship, obtaining and keeping faculty members, maintaining a reasonable level of enrollment, and financing operations. The negative influences obtaining in 1796 outweighed the positive.

FOR THREE YEARS after Graham's departure the academy was without a real rector although one of the trustees, Dr. Samuel Legrand Campbell, nominally held the position. The faculty was further weakened by the

[*34*]

resignation of one of the most competent tutors, Conrad Speece, an alumnus of Liberty Hall and afterwards a well-known Presbyterian clergyman. Enrollment plunged to a new nadir and in the fall of 1799 the school had but seven students.

Conditions took an upturn with the appointment of the Reverend George Addison Baxter as rector in October of 1799. Not only did his arrival restore effective leadership, but he brought with him a principal faculty member and ten students from New London Academy, where he had been teaching. Other students are said to have followed. The faculty member was the Reverend Daniel Blain who, like Baxter, was an alumnus of Liberty Hall.

Baxter was born in 1771 in Rockingham County, Virginia. He received his early education from a learned Irish indentured servant believed by the family to have been a revolutionary. Baxter enrolled at Liberty Hall in 1789 and graduated in 1796 after an interruption caused by ill health and a stint of teaching at New London in 1793. Like so many of his fellow students he was involved in disciplinary trouble, on one occasion being charged in court with defaming a local citizen. Also like many Liberty Hall men, he turned to theology; and in 1797 he was licensed to preach by the Lexington Presbytery. In the same year he returned to teach at New London. For six months he traveled through Virginia and Maryland, preaching as a missionary and soliciting funds for the New London Academy.

Baxter's marriage to Anne C. Fleming in 1798 probably promoted his future connection with Washington Academy; for his father-in-law, Colonel William Fleming, had been on the original board of trustees appointed by the Presbytery of Hanover, and commanded much influence in the region of Botetourt and Rockbridge counties.

Descriptions of Baxter's appearance, character, and personality have been left by his daughter Louisa and his intimate acquaintance Dr. John Leyburn of Lexington. "Old Rex" the students dubbed him, despite the academy's official disapproval of nicknames. The appellative may have been inspired either by his imposing physical size or his masterful style as teacher and preacher. He was large in body and head, says Leyburn, "with an expanded, massive brow, in which the very majesty of mind seemed enthroned." He walked with a limp because of a shortening in one of his legs, caused by an accident. "His peculiar footstep," Leyburn continues, "with the striking of his cane, and his manner of clearing his throat, were sounds with which no student of Washington College at least was ever unacquainted: they were too often alarm signals to those who might have been better employed."

Like Demosthenes, he conquered a speech impediment to become a fluent speaker. His sermons were usually brief, almost laconic, and delivered extemporaneously. In teaching he employed the Socratic method to stimulate his students to reach their own conclusions—or absurd contradictions. During his regime the students founded two literary societies whose weekly debates Baxter attended. Sometimes, when the opposing sides had apparently reached a standoff in eloquence and logic, the rector "summed up"; then "the shadows instantly flew away, and the truth, clear as the sun, stood forth, in all its native majesty."

Although his sermons were devoted to evangelical rather than political and social topics, Baxter found other channels through which to state his views on current issues. He published a pamphlet on slavery in 1836, expressing opinions characteristic of eighteenth-century Virginia rather than of the newer generation after 1840. Baxter and the members of his faculty, together with a number of trustees, became much interested in the American Colonization Society which effected the transportation of some twelve thousand Negroes to Sierra Leone and Liberia. The society's proposed solution to the rising slavery problem made a strong appeal to the people of Lexington and environs. Baxter was associated with the local newspaper for a brief time and was a moving spirit of the short-lived *Virginia Religious Magazine,* published at Lexington in 1805–1807. On the whole, however, he wrote relatively little.

EARLY IN BAXTER'S ADMINISTRATION the academy suffered a reverse that was extreme even for that care-ridden institution. The principal building, a limestone structure erected in 1790, burned to the ground in January of 1803. The cause was not determined, and although there was some suspicion of arson committed by students there is no actual evidence of such an act. A lugubriously ornate picture of the disaster has been preserved in a public letter "to the Citizens of Lexington," signed by "A Student," published in the Lexington *Virginia Telegraphe and Rockbridge Courier,* April 12, 1803. The author's purpose, on the eve of his departure from the community, was to thank the townsfolk for their kindness and hospitality on that sad occasion. "On the 9th of January, that doleful night! when the cry of 'fire, fire' echoed and re-echoed through my ears, (ignorant of the consequences awaiting it) I boldly rushed to save our only place of retirement, but was compelled to withdraw by the all-devouring flame—" As nothing could stop the blaze, "that magnificent building, which was supported by the illustrious Washington, was, in a short time, reduced to a pile of ruins." The ruins are still visible, a half mile from the University campus, and are known locally as Liberty Hall.

The work of the academy was temporarily continued in rented buildings in Lexington, and in 1804 the institution was moved to a portion of its present grounds. About two months after the fire Andrew Alexander had proposed to exchange his house near town, and two acres adjoining, for the property of Liberty Hall, provided the academy purchase designated contiguous field lands at $60 per acre. Terms for payment over twenty years were offered. The trustees were confident that the townsmen would cover the required down payment of a hundred pounds. They noted also that John Robinson (a later major benefactor of Washington College) "proposed to aid with two acres of land, or £40 either in corn or other property for use of the Academy to be delivered at his house when required or in cash at the end of 12 months," and that Robinson would contribute a hundred bushels of corn.

The arrangements were agreed to. Plans were drawn up for the erection of two academic buildings and a steward's house on the new campus. The plant was ready by the end of 1804.

The new expenses of construction and land purchase added to the financial woes of the academy; and so the rector set out on fund-raising expeditions, as William Graham had done before him, and as Baxter himself had done for New London.

Baxter made several tours on horseback through Virginia, Maryland, the District of Columbia, and North Carolina. Through letters which this devoted husband wrote to his wife in 1804-1805, we see something of the problems encountered in the quest for support of education, problems with which every college or university administrator today is well acquainted. Then, as now, the need for money was endemic among seats of learning. Many of Baxter's prospects demurred on the grounds that they had contributed to Princeton or other seminaries, or to local projects such as churches and academies. "Academies," he wrote, "are every where on hand and none of them will come to any thing." He described his procedure and typical responses: "I shew my papers; talk about the Academy and ask for money. Sometimes they give liberally, sometimes penuriously; and sometimes not at all. It is strange to hear independent, and rich men talk of their poverty, and some close men say they have run themselves so hard by their former bounties, all for an off put . . ." Among contributors was President Thomas Jefferson, who gave fifty dollars. Baxter mixed preaching with solicitation and on December 8, 1805, preached at the Capitol by invitation.

The rector not only asked others to help the school but set an exceptional personal example of generosity. According to his daughter Louisa he surrendered his own salary for a number of years in order to obtain other teachers and tutors. He lived upon his own resources and the compensation he received from the congregation of New Monmouth, the pastorate of which he had taken upon coming to the academy.

Under a policy continued from the previous century, the tuition fees were divided among the faculty. One-half was assigned to the rector; one-third to Blain, who in 1802 was appointed professor of languages; and the remaining one-sixth to the tutor or tutors. These allotments were augmented by annual payments from other income. In 1804 the James River stock began to be productive and enrollment increased gradually, although it averaged only about forty-five until the War of 1812. The trustees were able to make some increases in salaries. Nevertheless, in 1807 Baxter and Blain sent a protest to the board about the insufficiency of their pay, and in 1818 the trustees recognized the inadequacy of faculty remuneration. William Henry Ruffner has calculated that about the time of the onset of the war Baxter received some $750 per year and the use of a house, Blain $420, "and the poor tutor about $200." As Baxter and Blain also drew pastoral salaries and operated farms, Ruffner concluded that they got along rather well. Yet they could do so only by eking out their academic incomes. "Moonlighting" is by no means a purely modern practice among teachers.

Despite persistent financial adversity and the advent of war, the rector and trustees indicated hopefulness in a petition to the Virginia general assembly on December 5, 1812, for a change in nomenclature from academy to college: "This application is made under an Expectation that the funds of the Institution will soon be competent to enlarge the professorate in such a manner as will comport with the title we wish to assume, and it is supposed that by being invested with the title of College we should be enabled to render more essential services to the interests of literature." We may wonder whether that expression reflected real optimism or merely salesmanship. Its tone is certainly familiar to anyone in a present-day college or university who has had any part in writing "proposals" to government agencies or foundations, or who has engaged in the business of "grantsmanship."

The change was authorized by the legislature early in 1813. It marked no abrupt departure—the academy had been granting degrees since 1785—but an upgrading of the instructional capacity of the institution can be identified with this period.

BEFORE BAXTER'S ARRIVAL the teaching had been conducted by the rector and tutors, with assistance from some of the trustees as occasion demanded. The tutors were mostly graduates of the academy who were studying for the ministry. They were somewhat equivalent to the "graduate assistants" so widely utilized for undergraduate instruction in today's large universities. Baxter, Daniel Blain, and such tutors as were employed, shared the work of the institution. Baxter was responsible for the two upper classes, Blain for the two "inferior" classes, and both helped with the grammar school which was still maintained. In April of 1813 Edward Graham, brother of William Graham, was appointed professor of mathematics and natural sciences. The faculty thus had three persons of professorial rank for fewer than sixty students, including grammar school pupils. Tutors continued to assist in the instruction but reliance upon them presumably decreased considerably.

As to the instruction the students received, contemporary evidence is scanty. Several decades later Colonel John T. L. Preston, who had attended Washington College in the years following the War of 1812 (and sent all his seven sons to his alma mater), attempted to describe conditions of his student days. The College "was then and a good many years later . . . far from what it is now [1866], and by no means what it ought to have been then." Regarding the curriculum: "We got a little Latin and less Greek, Mathematics, of which the measure would be the even root of a negative quantity, Physics on the Homeopathic principle, textbook Belles Lettres, and superficial philosophy." In another reference, in 1878, Preston commented on the narrow Bachelor of Arts curriculum of his day, taken from Princeton, with no electives. The prescribed mathematics included algebra, six books of Euclid, and trigonometry; but the colonel observed: "Our class heard nothing of Conic sections, and particularly nothing of the parabola and projectiles." The textbook in natural philosophy was Cavallo's Philosophy (1803) and in chemistry "Mrs. B's Conversations." No natural history was available during Preston's time at the College.

Yet Preston pointed to the libraries of the College's literary societies which afforded good books to occupy the young men, and he praised the training of the literary societies' weekly debates. There the students gained a "mastery of speech which all the rules of Blair and Campbell never could have conferred." And lest his judgment upon the old-time College be thought unfair, Preston reminded his audience that "one of the ripest scholars in Virginia, Rev. Dr. [William H.] Ruffner, never was a student at any other college." True, it was actually through studies after graduation that he made himself what he was, but he began his learning at Washington College.

Daniel Blain died in 1814. The difficulty in replacing him illustrates the persistence of problems of finances. The Reverend Martin L. Hurlbut, principal of the Beaufort Academy in South Carolina, inquired about the position but withdrew his candidacy in a curt note when he found the proffered salary was half of what he was already making. The Reverend Andrew Heron, a native Scot, was persuaded to undertake the professorship, assisted by a tutor. As he was pastor of two churches in Rockbridge County, the academic pay represented an addition to his income. He soon found the work of three offices too much, however, and resigned the chair at Washington College in 1818.

Early in 1819 the Reverend Henry Ruffner accepted appointment as professor of languages, beginning a long and distinguished association with the College. The senior faculty was thus completed and remained intact for the next decade. "Old Rex," Edward Graham, and Henry Ruffner, with tutors, constituted the corps of professors throughout the 1820's.

The War of 1812 seems to have added little to the woes of the institution until the British capture of the city of Washington in the summer of 1814. Students had been made subject to militia duty, and a heavy draft was imposed following the disgraceful debacle at the national capital. Collegians from other states retreated out of the limits of Virginia. Enrollment, placed by the trustees at about 60 early in 1814, plummeted to 29. Between 60 and 70 students were registered in the session of 1817–1818, but the hard times of 1819 sent the number down again, and fewer than 30 were present in December of 1820. In 1826 the total had risen to about 65 and Edward Graham, Jr., expressed the hope that the College would "be a place of some importance yet." There were still 4 grammar school boys on the roster, though, and 25 "irregular pupils." One source indicates that the average yearly enrollment from 1824–1825 to 1835–1837 did not exceed 26.

As might have been expected, the pecuniary situation of the faculty continued to be something less than satisfactory. Late in 1819 Edward Graham wrote an importunate letter to his young physician son asking that the latter send him aid at once. The Graham family letters in the next decade indicate no improvement in the professor's financial condition.

A POSSIBLE MEANS of ending the College's difficulties presented itself in the form of Thomas Jefferson's project for establishing a "central university," the capstone of a planned statewide system of education.

The people of Lexington and the trustees of Washington College eagerly desired that the university be located in their community. They offered a subscription to the commonwealth amounting to $70,000. John Robinson, the wealthy bachelor who had helped the College to rebuild after the fire of 1803, committed himself to transfer his entire holdings to the state if the university should be situated within four miles of the town.

Apparently the trustees had completely reversed their position since they had successfully resisted the legislature's effort to take over Liberty Hall Academy following George Washington's patronage. Two decades of struggle and frustration, with no relief in sight, could well alter the viewpoint of any body of men, especially when accompanied by changes in personnel. There also were important differences in the circumstances. In 1796 the state government had made a sudden, gratuitous attempt to usurp control of an institution with seemingly bright prospects. Now those prospects had faded, and there was opportunity (or so it was hoped) to transmute a feeble little college into a carefully planned and well-supported university.

At any rate, late in 1817 the trustees resolved that if the legislature "at the present or any future session, should fix an University at Lexington or its vicinity, this Board will enter into any friendly arrangement with any persons properly authorized which, in its opinion, it can, consistently with its duty, & the obligations of its charter, to apply the funds & property of the College in aid of the University, so as to promote, in the most eligible & effectual manner, the general objects of literature."

The trustees renewed the offer in midsummer of 1818, unanimously declaring it desirable that the university be located at Lexington. All Washington College's property was to be turned over to the university, provided that the latter be placed in or near Lexington, that the College's faculty members be taken care of, and that the College remain in operation until the university should begin to function.

But the Sage of Monticello, carefully guiding the emergence of the university, had no intention of permitting it to be located so far from his eye and in the midst of a Presbyterian area. His intimate advisers were aware of the conflict they would encounter from the Presbyterians of Virginia. Joseph C. Cabell told Jefferson early in 1816 that if the legislature should favor his idea of a university "you will see the Presbyterians about Lexington, and the Scotch-Irish about Staunton, striving to draw it away from Albemarle, and the whole western delegation . . . will threaten to divide the State unless this institution shall be placed beyond the Blue Ridge." Staunton coveted the state capital, while Washington College at Lexington would become, in Cabell's unique phrase, "the bantling of the Federalists."

Lexington, of course, lost the battle. One defensive victory did go to Washington College; an effort to divert the funds of the Cincinnati from the College to the new university was unsuccessful. And the little institution in the valley continued to exist in independence and poverty. In 1821 it joined with Hampden-Sydney in a fruitless petition to the legislature for an appropriation of state funds.

The question arose as to the effect of the new university upon the fortunes of Washington College. The Reverend Henry Ruffner, professor-elect of languages at the College, speculated in a letter to George Baxter in December of 1818: "Should the projected state university assume (as we fear it will) a character unfavourable to religion in general, or our denomination of Christians in particular, then I doubt not W[ashington] College will obtain a more powerful patronage than it has received heretofore: but should the Univy. not seem to deserve the decided opposition of a considerable portion of the state, the other seminary must dwindle into insignificance, unless upheld by enforcement of a regular & salutary, but not very rigid, discipline, & by the *abilities* and persevering *zeal* of its professors." Ruffner concluded that with favorable conditions the College could become the principal support of the Presbyterian church in Virginia.

While undoubtedly the university drew to itself students who might otherwise have attended the colleges of the state, Washington College's lack of prosperity seems to have stemmed more from internal causes during the twenties and thirties. After the University of Virginia had established an enviable reputation as the most eminent southern institution of higher learning, alumni of Washington College pursued advanced degrees there; and by 1860 the College advertised that among other things it prepared students for the University of Virginia. During the fifties graduates of the University began to appear on the faculty of the College.

TOWARD THE CLOSE of the Baxter administration the College's poverty was alleviated, in prospect at least, by a bequest from "Jockey" John Robinson. Its ultimate value has been placed at nearly $50,000 and it has been called the largest legacy received by a college below the Potomac up to that time. As with the Washington and Cincinnati gifts, however, some time passed before the full value was available to the institution.

A sketch of Robinson was published in the *Princeton Magazine* in

1850 by Dr. Archibald Alexander, who had been personally acquainted with him. According to this account Robinson was born about 1754 in County Armagh, Northern Ireland. Orphaned and apprenticed to a weaver, after a few years he migrated to America and made his way to Rockbridge County where he plied his trade from house to house, from loom to loom. He was described as a jovial young man of even temper and good humor.

He accumulated enough money to buy a "poor horse," and soon discovered a talent far more profitable than weaving. He improved the condition of his animal, then took it to Lexington on court day and exchanged it for a larger and younger mount plus a sum of money. After another successful deal he abandoned the loom for the business of a jockey—a word which then designated a horse-trader. He gained a reputation for honesty, a trait not popularly associated with that particular calling, and after a few years became a man of some wealth.

Robinson added to his fortune by speculating in certificates that had been issued to Revolutionary War soldiers in compensation for their services. As the true worth of the certificates was doubtful, many holders sold them for less than face value; and many purchasers made great profits when the federal government, as a part of "the Hamilton System," redeemed the paper in full.

To complete his climb from weaver's apprentice to Southern gentleman, it remained only for Robinson to become an owner of land and slaves. He purchased the beautiful 400-acre Hart's Bottom farm (now the site of the city of Buena Vista) from General John Bowyer, and acquired lands on the Cow Pasture River, Buffalo Creek, and elsewhere. Possession of Hart's Bottom must have given him special satisfaction; for as a young immigrant he had found a haven at the home of General Bowyer.

As a planter Robinson was not entirely happy or successful. He was inexperienced in farm management, had difficulty with the slaves he bought to work Hart's Bottom, was harassed by crop failures, and plagued by ill health. Yet he apparently remained wealthy and solvent, willing and able to aid the College and the community.

Although he was an Ulsterman transplanted to Rockbridge County, Robinson was not a Presbyterian. One writer years later said Robinson was, or had been, a Roman Catholic. But, in fact, he was a member of no church and rarely if ever entered one. The trustees of Washington College overlooked his religious shortcomings when they elected him to membership on their board in 1819.

Another occupation in which Robinson took pride and enjoyed success was whiskey distilling. This was a common activity among the early inhabitants of the valley which was considered quite respectable, and according to at least one authority was engaged in by Presbyterian elders. At any rate, a barrel of Robinson's "fruited," "ropy" whiskey was involved in an incident at the College that created a stir at the time and aroused controversy among those who have sought to relate the facts of the case.

Varying accounts have been given by George Baxter's daughter Louisa; William Henry Ruffner, son of the Rev. Henry Ruffner; and Colonel J. T. L. Preston, alumnus of Washington College and a founder and faculty member of the Virginia Military Institute. It seems definite that Robinson sent a barrel of whiskey to the campus; that some citizens imbibed too freely of the contents; and that the spree was ended by intentional dumping or axing of the barrel. The versions differ on almost everything else, including the occasion for the celebration. Colonel Preston said it was the laying of the corner- stone in 1824 of the Washington College center building, which Robinson had financed wholly or in part. Miss Baxter said it was the writing of Robinson's will in 1825, leaving his entire estate to the College. Who was responsible for the unseemly revelry, who took active part, who got inebriated and how much, and who spilled the remaining whiskey are matters of uncertainty. But it must have been some party.

Robinson died June 25, 1826. The bachelor with no relatives and no church received an impressive funeral. In the procession through the main street of Lexington moved, in order, the faculty of the College and the clergy, coffin and bearers, the College trustees, members of the College debating societies, "ladies," "citizens," and servants of the de- ceased. The body was buried on the campus. Twenty-nine years later it was exhumed and reinterred with an appropriate monument, now passed daily by hundreds of students who know but little of "Jockey" John Robinson, benefactor of the institution.

Among items listed in the inventory of Robinson's estate, and there- fore part of the endowment of Washington College, were 3 stills and 74 slaves. A quantity of whiskey was on hand, and two citizens jointly purchased 1,000 gallons at 36 and 37 cents per gallon.

Before the benefit of the legacy could be realized years were re- quired for court proceedings, sale of lands, and disposal of slaves under conditions that would keep families together. Finally the whole estate was "made available as an endowment for $46,500." Some of the slaves apparently were too old and infirm to be sold. Records show that in 1859 the College paid a doctor's account for attending two aged Ne- groes, and one man was cared for by the institution as late as 1878.

Dissension in the College family and negative attitudes in the community added to the troubles of the Baxter period. In 1819 there was friction in the Board of Trustees over the manner in which Henry Ruffner had been appointed to a professorship. Only a portion of the board seems to have had a part in the process. The trustees then resolved that the whole membership must be given ample notice of any future election to the faculty and that a two-thirds majority should be necessary for the appointment. At the same time the board ruled that no professor should be elected to fill an office of trustee. This action appears to have been a slap at Edward Graham. When he had been named to the faculty in 1813 he was a member and secretary of the board and a practicing attorney in Lexington.

During the 1820's a number of ungentle criticisms of the College appeared in letters to the Lexington *Intelligencer*. The claim was even made that the faculty members were overpaid, on the basis of the amount of time they spent teaching. The professors were accused of devoting too much effort to religious activities and tending their farms, and too little to the students. The confinement of "government and professorships" to "persons of one religious sect" was described as creating "a jealousy among all the other denominations, against the College itself." A prime cause of complaint was that professors could control the College funds because two of them (Baxter and Graham) also were trustees, and several other trustees were closely related to the teachers.

Within the College itself there were clashes of opinion and personality, which seem to have involved Edward Graham in particular. Graham had trouble with Henry Ruffner and with trustees James McDowell and Samuel McDowell Reid.

Matters came to a climax in 1829 when the trustees undertook an investigation into the causes of the College's decline. The investigators also were asked to report means by which public support could be restored to the institution. At the same time, President Baxter and Professor Ruffner served notice that they would resign at the close of the summer session.

In its report the investigating committee blamed Graham's unpopularity for a large part of the College's difficulties, and his resignation was requested. Graham continued to serve the Board of Trustees as member and clerk for more than a decade, and taught for several years at nearby Ann Smith Academy for girls. He died in 1841.

George Baxter immediately received an appointment to a professorship in Union Theological Seminary, then located at Hampden-Sydney, and served in that office until his death in 1843. Although his thirty-year tenure at the academy and College had been far from happy and ended in bitterness and disappointment, his place in the institution's early history ranks second only to that of the Reverend William Graham. Moreover, his own reputation spread beyond the borders of Virginia. He received several honorary degrees, including a doctorate of divinity from the University of North Carolina in 1812. He rejected several calls from other institutions to accept presidencies at salaries better than he could hope for in Lexington.

In June of 1829 the trustees offered the presidency to Dr. Philip Lindsley, president of the University of Nashville, graduate and former faculty member of Princeton. Dr. Lindsley, a foremost thinker on educational problems of his time, declined the invitation. The trustees thereupon appointed Henry Ruffner, who had been re-elected to the faculty at the June meeting, to serve as acting president for 1829–1830. He was assisted by the youthful Landon C. Garland, years later first chancellor of Vanderbilt University.

Elizabeth Graham, a student at Ann Smith Academy and daughter of the displaced Edward Graham, noted with vexation the new order at the College: "The most important change which has taken place there is, that the students are roused up in the morning by a horn before five o'clock, and Mr. Ruffner meets them in the hall at five and has prayers. . . ." She continued unsympathetically: "Mr. Ruffner knows that it is necessary to do something to appear like reform. They accused the former president of indolence and he is determined they should not blame him for that. He stays at College almost constantly during the day, and visits the rooms once or twice every night before bedtime." Miss Graham spoke most favorably of the impression that Landon Garland had made upon students and others.

After much investigation the trustees in 1830 found a man for the presidency who would present a sharp contrast to the orthodox American college president, but who like his predecessors failed to accomplish what was most desired in Lexington—the stimulation of the growth and prosperity of Washington College.

Chapter
VI

Marshall and Vethake:
Innovation and Restoration

Louis Marshall, one of the ten brothers of the renowned Chief Justice John Marshall, was the next man called upon to guide the College's destiny. In a brief administration he introduced radical departures in educational methods that aroused new faculty discontent, apparently discouraged students, and brought on another crisis for the institution.

Born in Fauquier County, Virginia, in 1773, Louis was some eighteen years younger than John. In 1785 Louis removed to Kentucky and afterward studied medicine in Philadelphia, Edinburgh, and Paris. According to a history of the Marshall family by William M. Paxton he was imprisoned in France during the Reign of Terror, narrowly escaped death, and was released through the efforts of his brothers John and James. He is said to have fought several duels "not without fatal results to his adversaries." Whatever the facts may have been, Marshall never discussed his Parisian experiences in his later life.

Returning to Kentucky he became a successful physician, but abandoned medical practice to form a private school at "Buckpond" in Woodford County. As a young man, says Paxton, he was "tinctured with infidelity" in religious matters; but he overcame his doubts, joined the Presbyterian Church, and entertained strong theological convictions which he sometimes defended with more obstinacy than reason.

The trustees of Washington College at first rejected Marshall's nomination as president, the negative votes apparently prompted by "inferential evidence of his deficiency in . . . prudence both of speech and of habit." Six days later, however, the board elected him over the Reverend Dr. McClelland of New Brunswick, New Jersey. Marshall was undoubtedly helped by his relationship to several large and influential Rockbridge County families—the Prestons, McDowells, McClungs, Reids, Paxtons, and Taylors. Trustee James McDowell, Jr., was especially active in behalf of his candidacy. Marshall accepted the position and arrived in Lexington in October of 1830.

Immediately the new president proposed a complete reorganization of government and instruction. The trustees approved the plan over Henry Ruffner's opposition. Unfortunately we have nothing from Marshall's pen on the subject and must rely for information upon the account of William H. Ruffner, who reflected his father's viewpoint. The younger Ruffner described the scheme as "pregnant with revolution." He wrote that because of Marshall's violent reaction to any dissent, "War, of course, was inevitable."

Marshall's educational unorthodoxy rivaled and probably exceeded that displayed in recent decades at the University of Chicago and St. John's College in Maryland. Every semblance of the old curriculum was discarded and the way cleared for complete freedom of the student. Classes were abolished save for voluntary association by two or more pupils, and even then instructional sessions lasted only as long as the students wished. Ruffner wrote that "each student was to have the privilege of striking for the goal [degree] by any route or at any rate of speed that was most agreeable to himself." Faculty members were to make themselves available to their students "at all hours" to aid them in the preparation of their work, and to hear recitations individually or in groups as the young men might determine.

The program included changes in disciplinary matters also. While some of the severe regulations were retained, such as the early morning roll call, Dr. Marshall advocated reliance upon persuasion rather than force. He illustrated this theory of individualism by attempting to be "one of the boys," participating in students' games, bandying epithets with them, and meeting them on their own terms.

Dr. Ruffner's son tells us that his father, after stating his objections to the trustees, acquiesced in the plan for the sake of harmony, nevertheless predicting that the experiment would fail in a short time. Ruffner, who had surrendered the teaching of languages to Marshall and taken over mathematics himself, believed the system "peculiarly unsuited" to instruction in the latter subject. Landon C. Garland had originally supported Marshall's proposal but became disillusioned and made no pretense of following the new scheme in the teaching of physics and chemistry.

As a historian of the institution, William H. Ruffner described his father's dogged attempt to adhere to the spirit and letter of the policy that he opposed:

> He took his stand at a high desk in his class room at five o'clock in the morning, and there he stood until night, and sometimes until bedtime with only necessary brief absences, placing himself unreservedly at the service of his ten or twelve students: who came singly or in pairs at any hour to receive assistance, or to recite, one in this branch of mathematics, and another in that—an unorganized lot of irregulars that had neither the advantages of tutorship on the one hand nor of classification on the other.

Yet, we are told, Henry Ruffner's performance in the department of mathematics did not meet with the president's approval.

William H. Ruffner has given us a possibly exaggerated and certainly an unsympathetic picture of Louis Marshall as a teacher: "At this period he had no fondness for study, and writing was his abomination! Moreover the weight of nearly three-score years and the bulkiness of his physique were naturally inclining him to sedentary habits and easy postures!" Dr. Marshall did not assume the Spartan attitude of his colleague in the mathematics department, for his classroom was furnished with a bed and an easy chair. "As likely as not," continues W. H. Ruffner, "the visitor would find him during recitation lolling on his bed, pipe in mouth, spectacles on nose, and book in hand, drilling some boys on Latin forms and constructions, less frequently in Greek, the tobacco smoke in the room rivalling in density a London fog." This meant nothing to the eccentric old president who was a law unto himself.

Although he was the first regularly appointed rector or president of the institution who was not a licensed minister, Dr. Marshall was an aggressive evangelist. In that respect, as in certain others, he endorsed the usual activities and ideas dominant in the Lexington community—the American Colonization Society project, the work of the American Bible Society, and the crusade for temperance. (He detested whiskey with "an unslumbering hatred.") He often preached to the students on his favorite Biblical subject, prophecy, working up to a climax on the imminent and definitely fixed day of destruction.

At the time of Marshall's arrival in 1830 the collegiate students had numbered only nineteen. The following year had brought a slight turn upward; but after 1832 attendance again fell off sharply, and the school declined alarmingly. The trustees ordered an inquiry into the possibility of changing the curriculum. Dr. Marshall was directed to report in writing "a detailed view of the state of the College" including fiscal operations. No such report has been found in the files of Washington and Lee University. In the summer of 1834, however, the challenged educational experiment was abruptly abandoned.

In the spring of the same year Marshall had experienced such personal financial trouble that he feared he would have to mortgage his farm, and he complained privately that he was old and unable to provide for his family. Soon afterward he left for Kentucky, never to return, without bothering to resign or to explain. He was reported to have been "disgusted" because the trustees had withheld a portion of his salary. After his departure the board ordered the treasurer to pay Dr. Marshall $800 "in full for his services as president of this college." He died in Kentucky in 1866.

AGAIN the trustees fell back upon the faithful Henry Ruffner to carry on as acting president. With Professor Joseph W. Farnum, an able teacher who had succeeded Landon C. Garland in the Robinson chair of natural philosophy, Ruffner attempted to preserve the nearly expired College.

The venerable institution was in even worse condition than it had been in 1829 after the resignations of George A. Baxter and Edward Graham. Critics and friends now engaged in a public appraisal of conditions, that continued with varying degrees of intensity and bitterness from September of 1834 until the end of that year. A battery of writers, in letters to the Lexington *Union*, analyzed the troubles of the College that for many years had been suffering a "chronic distemper." The correspondence was signed largely with such pseudonyms as "Fuscus," "Hampden," "Q," "An Observer," and "Meliboeus."

"Fuscus," identified as Phil Ewing, opened the attack by complaining of the indifference of the townsmen to the school, and calling for "radical work" to restore the College to its former reputation.

"Hampden" (J. Reid Jordan) declared that only three or four students of college rank were enrolled, with eight to ten in the grammar class. The old and well-endowed institution had sunk "in every respect below the dignity of an ordinary grammar school," and stood almost empty although capable of accommodating a hundred students. The ugly, dilapidated buildings were falling down (the center building resembled "the Dutchman's barn"), the once fairly adequate library had been scattered, and laboratory equipment had become valueless. "Reckless and culpable mismanagement" by trustees and faculty, past and present, was to blame. Marshall's tenure had ended in a spirit of mutual disgust and hostility between president and trustees. "Hampden" recommended that the College be turned over to the state legislature to preserve it from annihilation.

Promptly "Q," believed to have been Professor Ruffner, answered the "partial, exaggerated, and false" charges. Instead of only three or four students there were at least twice that number at the time of writing, and enrollment would eventually exceed fourteen or fifteen in addition to the grammar school. Low registration had been caused by conditions not under the control of the faculty. "Q" also denied that the buildings were in as bad shape as the critic had pretended.

"Fuscus" returned with a rather moderate communication contending that the College needed publicity, doubting that a transfer of control to the state would help, and calling upon the "Rip Van Winkles" of the board to awaken. In another letter he pointed to the flourishing status of Amherst College and the newly founded Randolph-Macon College which boasted nearly 200 students.

Some interesting suggestions were made in the correspondence, such as establishment of a military professorship, a school of engineering or a professorship of law, the abolition of fees, and the restoration of rigid discipline. All the critics were agreed on one thing: that Washington College did not occupy the position in the educational life of the state and nation to which its endowment and location entitled it.

The discussion attracted the notice of an engaging alumnus of Washington College and former citizen of Lexington, William Alexander Caruthers, class of 1819. This brilliant Virginian had studied medicine in Philadelphia, practiced his profession for some years at Lexington, and in the 1830's had moved to New York where he moved among the literary circles of the metropolis. He was the author of an urbane novel, *Kentuckian in New York*, and several historical novels.

Caruthers wrote public letters filled with sound observations and constructive suggestions. He excused from blame any one set of men in the alleged mismanagement of the College. He urged that the "Dutch barn" be converted into "the semblance of a beautiful Grecian Temple," and offered to obtain in New York an architect who might accomplish the transformation. He supported criticism of the library, which he said had never been adequate. He advocated using the commencement ceremony as a means of gaining favorable publicity by judiciously conferring honorary degrees and inviting prominent alumni to speak. The appointment of eminent professors also would bring prestige to the school, he suggested, and he recommended that the next president should be "an accomplished gentleman and distinguished scholar." He specifically nominated Colonel Sylvanus Thayer, superintendent of the United States Military Academy from 1817 to 1833. (Caruthers did not explain how a moribund college could attract and pay these distinguished scholars.) In other letters he opposed turning over the school to the state, recommended a maximum age limit of 35 years for election to the board of trustees, proposed that trustees should be dropped for absence at three consecutive meetings, and admonished the townspeople to cease their gossiping about the College.

Responding to criticism and the desperate situation, the trustees in December of 1834 received a detailed report from a committee of their members. The committee had concluded that "the foundation of the prosperity of this institution must be laid in a high Collegiate and literary reputation—united with a character of strict moral and religious discipline—and cheapness of education." The report noted that eastern Virginia supplied a large number of students to the University of Virginia and three colleges in that area, but that the western part of the state was materially poorer and Lexington was not well known across the Alleghenies. The lower South and Southwest were mentioned as potential fields of patronage although the increase in colleges there afforded formidable competition. To draw students from a distance Washington College would have to offer inducements including "the scientific and literary character of the professors." The Marshall program of instruction was deplored and a return to the "classification" system was advocated. Another factor contributing to the College's decline, according to the committee, was the fact that students had not been boarding on campus, and therefore were subject to various temptations to dissipation and extravagance in the town.

TURNING TO THE CHOICE OF A NEW PRESIDENT, the trustees again passed over Henry Ruffner and elected Henry Vethake, an economist and mathematician whom Dr. Caruthers had warmly endorsed. His term was to be even shorter than Marshall's had been.

Born in British Guiana of Prussian parents, Vethake had been brought to the United States at the age of four. At sixteen he was graduated from Columbia College, and from 1813 served in various professorships at Queen's College (Rutgers), Dickinson, and Princeton —where Professor John Maclean described him as one of the ablest and most popular members of the faculty. Sectarian disputes, faculty conflicts, and student riots, which plagued American colleges during ante-bellum decades, had something to do with his peregrinations. In the early 1830's he became an educational reformer at the University of New York, championing an elective system and a curriculum aimed at making men useful.

Vethake's principal interest was economics and two years after leaving Washington College he was to bring out a comprehensive two-volume work, *The Principles of Political Economy.* He was an orthodox free trader, who stressed the idea of "diminishing returns," opposed government interference in the economy, was critical of trade unions, and feared that humanitarian policies would cripple capitalists. He acknowledged however the importance of rising discontent among the "working classes" and noted with some concern the refusal of the privileged groups to make concessions. He ventured the opinion that "the larger portion of the civilized world may be . . . tending to a revolutionary state." He believed that "an organic change in government can be for a long time delayed, by the timely correction of abuses." But if government clings tenaciously to acknowledged evils, it certainly prepares the way for its speedy downfall. Doubtless Dr. Vethake described his own position when he said:

> The true conservative is he who is ready at all times to correct what is wrong in the existing system of administration, who makes every exertion to diffuse knowledge, religion, and morality, among his fellow-citizens, and who is willing to extend a larger share of political power to them, as they become fitted to employ it for their own and the public welfare.

Stepping outside his own field of study he took a conciliatory position in the controversy of that day between fundamentalist Christianity and the relatively new science of geology. Far from discrediting or even challenging Genesis, he declared, the geologist "has incontrovertibly established a most remarkable coincidence between the order in which fossil remains to be found embedded in the different strata of the crust of the earth are arranged, and that of the products assigned by Moses to the successive days of creation." This coincidence was so complete that geology could be hailed as an auxiliary of religion; it confirmed "with beautiful arrangement" the Mosaic story of creation. The "days" were geologic periods: in England clergymen had set themselves to studying geology as an adjunct to theology. Thus Dr. Vethake found against the notion that any "science" or branch of learning was dangerous to religion. His advice was to investigate seeming inconsistencies, in order to discover the harmony of the universe.

Dr. Vethake was sworn in as president on February 21, 1835. In his inaugural address he reviewed the basic principles of collegiate education. While showing a breadth of mind in respect to the curriculum, he did not deviate far from the accepted ideas then prevalent in American colleges. He championed the classical course and favored mental discipline. Likewise he held traditional beliefs on student discipline. All this made for easier cooperation between Dr. Vethake and Professor Ruffner.

Vethake was unable to offer much classroom instruction in his primary field, economics, as few of his students were sufficiently advanced in that kind of work to profit by his teaching. He performed very ably, however, in mathematics. Instruction in languages was turned back to Professor Ruffner.

The learned Vethake remained at Washington College less than two academic sessions. During his short sojourn he was roughly attacked by a dismissed student. A professor of science, Farnum, heard the scuffle, seized a pair of tongs, and rushed to the aid of the president, whom he found on the floor. Farnum fell to and sent the husky assailant reeling. Subsequently this youth and a party of friends sought to waylay the slender young science teacher as he walked to his room in Lexington's Eagle Hotel. This second attack was frustrated but affected the decision of both president and professor to leave the College.

For the second time in two years the presiding officer of the institution departed suddenly without formal notice to the board. On September 15, 1836, the trustees received a letter from a Mr. E. Backus of Detroit, which city Dr. Vethake and his wife had visited, informing them that Vethake intended to accept a professorship at the University of Pennsylvania, and that he resigned the presidency of Washington College.

The board thereupon unanimously resolved that no teacher was to be allowed to resign save at the close of a session, and that in every case the professor must give six months' notice. Seven years had passed with several hiatuses and presidents. In the fall of 1836 the old College was seemingly back in the slough of despond.

Chapter
VII

Henry Ruffner's
Troubled Years

THE TRUSTEES had twice passed over Henry Ruffner in their selection
of a president for the College; but in October of 1836 they unanimously elected the "old residenter" to that office. The vote occasioned
some surprise, as Ruffner's opinions and personality had engendered
animosities in the village and on campus during his seventeen years on
the faculty. Probably the board members were disturbed over the
unsatisfactory results of bringing in outsiders Marshall and Vethake,
and were determined to entrust the helm to one they knew. If so,
Ruffner was their only choice; for at that time he *was* the College. A
vacancy existed in the chair of languages, and Professor Farnum, the
science teacher, was on leave of absence. This time, therefore, a new
administration brought no transition or change of policy.

During most of Ruffner's twelve-year regime the College enjoyed
some growth and prosperity; but a decline set in toward the end. His
tenure was plagued by controversy including strained relations with
the newly created Virginia Military Institute. The College became
enmeshed in a tempestuous community dispute centered about the
pastor of the Lexington Presbyterian Church. The College's governance
was subjected to much public criticism, at least some of which appears
to have been deliberately exploited for political purposes. Dr. Ruffner,

moreover, incurred opposition because of his anti-slavery and pro-Union views, the former of which especially was passing out of vogue in Virginia at this period. The quarrels and disagreements finally forced him to end his long and faithful service by resigning in 1848.

HENRY RUFFNER WAS BORN IN 1790 in Shenandoah County, Virginia, of a German-Swiss family which has been described as "big-bodied and heavy-fisted." In 1793 the Ruffners moved to the Kanawha, a wild frontier country in western Virginia, where they became landholders and pioneers in education and religion. Henry attended Washington College and was graduated in 1813. After several years of theological study and travel he was licensed as a Presbyterian minister and worked for a time as missionary in the Kanawha country. In 1819 he married Sarah Lyle, daughter of Captain William Lyle, a farmer living near Lexington who was a trustee of Washington College for many years.

Also in 1819 he was elected professor of languages at the College, beginning a three-decade affiliation during which he functioned in several professorships, three times as acting president, and finally as president. From 1819 to 1831 he preached regularly at Timber Ridge Presbyterian Church; he often "supplied" at the Lexington Presbyterian Church and at rural churches; and no mean polemicist, he composed a number of religious articles and tracts.

Ruffner had wide interests and notable talents. He was to some extent a novelist, a short-story writer, a historian, an agriculturist, a student of politics, slavery, and political economy, and a travel writer. His best-known literary work probably was the novel *Judith Bensaddi*, which appeared in the *Southern Literary Messenger* for July, 1839. Supposedly based on the experience of actual persons, it has been called perhaps the first appearance in American fiction of the "Jewish problem."

As an early exponent of popular education in Virginia Dr. Ruffner could be ranked next to Thomas Jefferson. In "Outlines of a plan for the improvement of Common Schools in Virginia," prepared in 1841, he portrayed the defects in the system of public education and proposed some improvements. His ideas were incorporated in a treatise on general education which he submitted to an educational convention in Lexington in the same year, and which long afterward earned him encomiums from educators and historians. He pointed out that the two-fold program of the legislature had included the establishment of a university at a cost of about $800,000, "where the rich may now educate their sons at an expense *not very much greater* than at the Colleges which have cost the State nothing," and a yearly appropriation of

$70,000 for the counties to pay for schooling of the poor. The entire effort was divided between those attending a "grand" university and those who must beg a minimum of education as paupers. Despite twenty years of common-school support he belived as much ignorance existed as before. "There is but one effective remedy," Ruffner declared, "—*a system of district schools, supported by a tax on property*."

Dr. Ruffner's ideas on higher education were summarized in his inaugural address on February 22, 1837. Some of the disciplinary problems that troubled his own and other colleges he attributed to the "leveling spirit of corrupted democracy." In this regard, mingling with the villagers of Lexington, he believed, was a mixed blessing for the students. Discipline must be enforced but not with excessive rigor: "Much depends on the manner and spirit, in which the faculty administer the government."

At Washington College, he continued, character development formed the central purpose of education. Christian religion was all-pervasive in this work. He insisted, however, that no catechism, creed, or formulary would be employed in the religious exercises, and that prayers offered would be in terms common to all Christians. Washington College was designed for the education of youth of all Christian denominations, and offered the same opportunities to all moral, qualified young men. If the students "are to be drenched with the bitter waters of sectarian bigotry; they must go somewhere else; we eschew the task."

He discussed the course of study at the College: Latin and Greek, the badges of learned men; mathematics, "this mighty science," and "excellent discipline for the intellectual powers"; and the moral studies, which in American colleges were assigned a relatively brief time. Referring to the latter he declared: "It is to these sciences, acting as handmaidens to religion, that we must look to the deliverance of mankind, from the moral evils which afflict them in both their public and private relations."

With a weather eye toward the Jacksonian democracy of universal suffrage and power in the majority, he maintained that American institutions of learning, from the lowest school to the university, must train "virtuous and intelligent citizens" as well as patriotic and wise leaders. If Americans would avoid that degeneracy which had destroyed previous popular governments, they "must shed the influence of science and religion over the whole community; and beware of the popular vice and ignorance, which will banish the wise and modest statesman from our public councils, and subject this blessed country to the misrule of a tumultuous populace, instigated by brawling demagogues."

Ruffner held to the Jeffersonian ideal of a society in which the yeomanry would play a dominant part, but he contended that the yeomen must have the knowledge and discernment that would guide them to wise decisions and would protect them from "deceptious demagogues." He expounded his ideas in this area in an address to the Rockbridge Agricultural Society in 1839. While he realized that farmers were too busy to become profound students, he believed that they could obtain enough scientific knowledge to "strip the sheep's clothing from the political wolves who profess to be the peculiar friends of the people, especially of the numerous class of voters, and who try to make themselves great men by inflaming the passions of the majority against the minority." He also demonstrated that science was conducive to wealth and showed convincingly the relationship of science to agriculture.

The Ruffner administration came during a period of agonizing reappraisal for Virginians on their views concerning slavery and the Union. It has long been known that the great men of the state in the eighteenth century were in varying degrees hostile to slavery. The turning point in the road was reached in the constitutional convention of 1831–1832, with the decision to retain the peculiar institution—to "retreat from Monticello." But Virginia west of the Blue Ridge continued to be skeptical of the benefits of slavery.

During the quarter century that preceded the Civil War there grew up in Virginia a concern with the relative decline of the proud old commonwealth, a self-criticism and a desire to remedy this malaise of society. In 1847 Lexington's Franklin Society, an institution that provided for the discussion of important current issues, devoted much time to the closely associated topics of the division of the state and the removal of slavery from western Virginia. Townsmen and professors of the College and of the Virginia Military Institute expressed themselves frankly and at length, over a number of weeks. Among the proponents of the projected division and of excluding slavery was President Ruffner, whose argument made such a profound impression upon his hearers that a committee of them called for its publication.

Dr. Ruffner's approach to the problem of slavery was primarily economic, motivated by a desire to infuse "life, energy, and prosperity into the sluggish and almost stagnant business of Virginia, East and West." This was, of course, the thesis applied to the entire Southern region some years later by Hinton R. Helper in his famous work, *The Impending Crisis of the South.*

Views expressed in the "Ruffner Pamphlet," as it came to be known, were no doubt contrary to those held by most Virginians in the late forties and fifties. The statement excited adverse comment at the time of its publication, and both its author and the College were attacked in some quarters. It aroused even greater furor more than a decade later when one of its sponsors, Lexington's John Letcher, was Democratic nominee for governor in the 1858 contest. By then sentiment regarding slavery had veered from the Ruffner doctrines even in Rockbridge. "Honest John" lamely attempted to excuse his apparent endorsement of near-abolitionism by accusing Ruffner of altering his Franklin Society presentation in the written version.

The slavery issue even caused suppression of the history of Washington College, which Dr. Ruffner began preparing in the early forties at the behest of the newly formed alumni association. He slowly completed the manuscript and after surrendering the presidency in 1848 continued to polish the work, expecting its publication in a year or two. But John R. Thompson, editor of the *Southern Literary Messenger*, told Dr. Ruffner that he could not print it because of the author's views on slavery. Consequently the history of the College, the first official account to be written, was delayed forty years, finally appearing in the Washington and Lee *Historical Papers*.

After his resignation and removal to his lands in Kanawha, Ruffner interested himself in the gradual elimination of slavery from neighboring Kentucky. He wrote an article on the subject for Kentucky newspapers which he said was "rather longer than my Address to West Virginians, and dissects . . . Calhoun's Nullifying-Proslavery-Statistical Fallacies & Absurdities completely, and I trust effectually. . . ." He remained a stout Unionist to the end, condemning bitterly the "secession mania" and the "desperate revolutionary demagogues," and predicting ruin for Virginia in civil war.

EARLY IN THE RUFFNER ADMINISTRATION questions arose concerning the new Virigina Military Institute. Members of the College family were among initial advocates of a military school in Lexington, but there was apparently a good deal of misunderstanding as to its proper functions, purpose, and relation to the College. As V.M.I. developed into a clearly separate collegiate institution the Washington College trustees tended to view it as more of a rival than a partner in educational and cultural service to the valley. Even sectarianism cropped up when the institute brought the first sizable number of Episcopalians into Rockbridge.

The subject of military training in Lexington was discussed in the

Franklin Society in the early thirties, and in the summer of 1835 a series of newspaper letters signed "Cives" suggested the conversion of the Lexington state arsenal into a military institution of higher learning for worthy but indigent youth. It was argued that cadets would protect the arsenal better than the existing soldier guard and that the town could claim the title "Athens of Western Virginia" with the additional educational facility.

The proposal touched off a local debate. "A Citizen of Lexington" publicly opposed the idea on the grounds of economy and the pressing need for elementary education, maintaining that a manual labor school would be more desirable. He inveighed against the "morbid, vicious rage for military *glory*, which unfortunately pervades our population. . . ." He recommended that if "a set of heroes" must be bred the state should establish military professorships at the university and each of the four colleges in Virginia.

Outstanding supporters of the military school at Lexington included President Ruffner of Washington College; Edward Graham, alumnus, trustee, and former faculty member; alumnus John T. L. Preston, who was to become a prominent faculty member at V.M.I.; and several other trustees and alumni.

The 1836 legislature passed a bill "reorganizing the Lexington arsenal and establishing a Military school in connection with Washington College." The act proposed to transfer the Cincinnati fund from the College to the new institution. The Lexington *Gazette* expressed the editorial viewpoint that the lawmakers had "assumed an authority over the Cincinnati fund and Washington College, which cannot be justified." No action was taken to implement the act, which was soon repealed. However, a board of visitors for the military school seems to have come into being, and met in Lexington in August of 1837. Trustees of Washington College, undoubtedly fearing loss of control of their institution, appointed a committee to confer with the visitors and instructed the committee to proceed with caution.

In April of 1838 the legislature passed another bill to reorganize the arsenal and establish a military school in connection with it and Washington College. It was not until June of 1839 that trustees and visitors accepted the articles of agreement and cooperation. The first article provided that all classes, lectures, and exercises of each school were to be open to students and cadets; and each faculty was to adopt regulations to keep discipline. Each institution was to maintain distinct organization to prevent "collision of authorities in the maintenance of order and discipline. . . ." The trustees seized an opportunity to "carry into effect the design of the Cincinnati donation" by guardedly providing for the appointment of the military professor of the Institute "as their Cincinnati professor of military science & appropriate that department such portion of the Cincinnati fund as they shall deem equitable."

The problem of working out cooperation between schools of different control, one public and one private, was a delicate one; and apprehension as to future difficulties and rivalry was evident. A reciprocal provision stated that nothing in the arrangement should "be construed to prohibit the college from forming a class or classes among its own students for the study of any branches of science taught in the institute, & any new classes hereafter formed in the college shall have the same privileges of instruction at the institute as the classes now existing." The trustees proposed to limit the number of cadets but the suggestion was withdrawn at the request of the visitors. The relationship between the institutions, however, was at the outset cordial and well implemented.

The legislature at last enacted a definitive statute establishing the Virginia Military Institute, and Colonel Francis H. Smith was appointed its commandant. The act did not attempt to transfer the Cincinnati fund, and shortly the Washington College trustees elected Smith the Cincinnati Professor of the College. A uniform was subsequently prescribed for the College students in the Cincinnati class. During the first session of V.M.I., 1839–1840, the College opened its facilities to the new school and the June examinations of the cadets were held in the College's Philosophical Hall. Throughout the ante-bellum period students and cadets, trustees and visitors, and the faculties intermingled in processions and on such formal occasions of celebrations, holidays, and commencements. Several trustees of Washington College also were members of the V.M.I. board of visitors.

Formal separation of the two institutions was nevertheless inevitable. The process was accompanied by extrinsic expressions on denominational relations stemming from the introduction of a nucleus of Episcopalians into an almost solidly Presbyterian community, which led to the founding of the Episcopal Church in Lexington in 1844. At the laying of the cornerstone of the new Lexington Presbyterian edifice in the same year the Reverend Benjamin Mosby Smith, recently appointed a trustee of the College, asserted that his church did not employ state institutions as a means of building up its denomination. He afterward admitted that the remark was aimed at V.M.I. Early in 1845 the cadets publicly expressed complete confidence in Colonel Smith's management of their school, denying that it was under sectarian influence. A statement in Lexington newspapers declared that "it is well known that the corps (except the communicants of the several churches) march to all the churches in Lexington in rotation." (Methodist and Baptist churches had previously been established in the town.)

In 1845—termed by the historian of V.M.I. a "year of agony indeed"—the controversy became public. George D. Armstrong, a Presbyterian clergyman and professor of chemistry and natural science, accepted the role of champion of Washington College, in legislative lobbying and in open debate. He stated his case in a letter to the Richmond *Whig* of March 6, 1845, that ran to nine columns of small type. The essence of the argument had been previously presented to a legislative committee. Armstrong noted that for several weeks a number of communications had appeared in that newspaper in reference to the differences between the two Lexington institutions. The writers, he contended, had mistaken the real points at issue and had placed the College in the position of aggressor, "moved thereto by *sectarian jealousy.*" Armstrong denied that "sectarianism" had anything to do with the situation.

Instead he declared that the dispute had its origins "in the attempt which is making to convert the Virginia Military Institute into *an independent college open to general patronage in Virginia.*" He questioned whether the law which established the institute had authorized it to become a full-fledged college, and if it had, whether the action was sound policy. In the examination of the first of these propositions, he declared, he had been aided by "a lawyer of no mean eminence," not a resident of Lexington. Armstrong contended that the main idea had been to convert the arsenal into a military school, to substitute for the "old guard" young men to be compensated in education rather than wages; and in any event it had not been intended to enlarge the school beyond forty cadets.

It was unthinkable that the legislature could be so unjust to the College, "an established institution of credit and usefulness . . . as to create a rival seminary at its gates, with unlimited powers of competition, & armed with the peculiar facilities of military fascination, to make that competition ruinous." Referring to the terms of the Cincinnati gift, Armstrong observed that Washington College would be forced upon receiving the funds to become likewise "*an independent Military College open for general patronage in Virginia.*"

Echoing President Ruffner's views, Armstrong urged the state to solve the problems of elementary education before founding more colleges, which he held to be unneeded. He could foresee only ruination or lingering death for the two colleges trying to coexist in the village of Lexington. The writer emotionally demanded of the people of Virginia whether they wished to destroy Washington College, which "dates its origin in the days of our Revolution. . . ." and was one of the few "able to support itself without state aid. . . ." Professor Armstrong believed that the College and the institute could flourish in harmony only by returning to the original intentions of the founders and laws of 1836 and 1839, and by utilizing V.M.I. as a normal school for the training of teachers in the common schools.

A few weeks later Colonel Smith replied to Armstrong, emphasizing the point that the controversy had started with Washington College. "Without the least previous complaint made to the Board of Visitors," he wrote in the Richmond *Whig*, "or notice given to the Faculty of the Institute, legislative interference was invoked last winter by Washington College; the affairs of the schools were investigated by the Committee of Schools and Colleges, at the suggestion of the Rev. George D. Armstrong, the Agent of the College, when the Committee asked to be discharged from the further consideration of the complaint by a vote of *seven* to *two*." Details of the whole affair had been published by Armstrong. From the beginning in 1839, Colonel Smith declared, the institute had never changed nor concealed the policy advocated by the board of visitors and approved by the legislature. He proclaimed the limits of the institute to be "usefulness to the State." If Washington College persisted in the controversy, it was upon the ground that Virginia owed "more to that College than to her own Military and Educational interests, both of which it is the express design of the Virginia Military Institute to promote." Smith also denied that his school cost the state more than the guard of soldiers had at the old arsenal.

He held Armstrong's terms of compromise to be worthy of careful thought by Virginians, though he personally considered them impracticable. He interpreted Armstrong's views as "evidently that a STATE institution is to be rendered subservient to a DENOMINATIONAL college. . . ." Moreover, figures demonstrated that the two colleges could prosper together.

Meanwhile, the Franklin Society in Lexington debated during February and March, 1845, the topic "Should the Legislature take any action with regard to the present management of the Virginia Military Institute." A contemporary observer, James B. Dorman, summed up the history of the dispute for his diary: "The Trustees & Faculty of Washington College alarmed at the rapid growth of the Institute, which together with the ambitious views of the Superintendant, seemed to bode them no good—sent Profr Armstrong to Richmond for the purpose of having its sphere of action circumscribed." After noting that Colonels Smith and Preston had effectively replied to Dr. Armstrong, and that the affair had excited much interest in Lexington, the diarist added: "The Presbyterians and merchants bear most inveterate ill-will against Col. Smith—the one class because partly through his instrumentality they have lost the patronage of the Institute & the other because he is a zealous Episcopalian." (The reference to the merchants concerned the institute's system of state purchases.) But Dorman believed that V.M.I. should be developed rather than restricted.

President Ruffner suggested a merger of the institutions which he presented to the College trustees at their meeting in June of 1845. The plan "was promptly and decisively, yet courteously, disapproved as impracticable and inexpedient." The proposal called for a joint petition to the legislature by the authorities of the schools for a new charter combining College and military school under the title "The Washington Institute of Virginia." Officials of the existing schools were to be retained; the governing boards were to be consolidated; the property and funds, except the arsenal, were to be vested in the new corporation; the Washington Institute was to possess distinct collegiate and "academical" departments; and "a military system of police and discipline [would] pervade the whole."

In July of 1845 the College trustees announced that in the following February they would cease the practice of appointing a professor of military science from V.M.I., electing a full-time teacher of the subject from their own faculty. Correspondence between Colonel Smith and Armstrong formally severed the tie that had existed between the institutions through the Cincinnati professorship, and also continued the debate into 1846. Smith protested the trustees' action in providing "within themselves, for instruction in the only Department *peculiar* to the Institute." He also engaged in criticism of Armstrong's teaching methods and the extensiveness of his academic field.

The institute at once requested augmented state appropriations and an increase to sixty-four in the number of cadets. Armstrong wrote to the delegate from Rockbridge County, calling the application of the institute "part and parcel of an effort to convert it into a College which shall be a rival of Washington College, of such a character that the rivalry between them must eventually result in the downfall of one or the other of them." He contended also that a larger appropriation for V.M.I. would be unjust to all other colleges in Virginia, and urged again that the money go to common school education. Whether or not the College's opposition had anything to do with it, the V.M.I. bid for additional funds was lost in the legislature.

Some efforts were made at patching up the quarrel. Several distinguished citizens of Lexington addressed an identical communication to trustees and visitors deploring the display of jealousy between "some friends" of each institution and urging a remedy in the "connection" already outlined by Henry Ruffner. Conferences were held between committees representing the trustees and the visitors. A suggested compromise included provisions that the professor of military tactics at V.M.I. would be appointed adjunct Cincinnati Professor at the College; that military instruction at the latter would be limited to fortification and gunnery; and that V.M.I. would offer no work in Latin "beyond Cicero."

The trustees, however, at last concluded that the connection of the preceding years had failed to produce anticipated benefits, and that the College's financial condition did not justify a payment of $300 per year for the Cincinnati professorship. They proposed that their students be permitted to attend V.M.I. for military instruction at a charge of $10 apiece, but the institute declined this request. A tenuous agreement was made providing that if a class of thirty students should be formed, who should pay $10 each in advance and consent to subject themselves to ordinary military discipline and to attend drills, V.M.I. would supply instruction in military tactics. But such a class was never formed and the two institutions went their separate ways.

Cordial relations were resumed, however, when the college trustees adopted friendly resolutions in 1849 and the institute visitors responded in kind. The latter expressed delight in the restoration of "entire harmony," and said the only rivalry they desired between Virginia's institutions was "a generous emulation."

MEANWHILE, according to William Henry Ruffner, the College after "eight or nine years of general prosperity" was "suffering something of a relapse." Enrollment had fallen off about 25 per cent. "Parties were forming, even among the alumni . . . so that from one cause or another a disagreeable condition of affairs existed, which demanded action on the part of the college authorities."

During the summer of 1846 "a series of rabid articles" appeared in the Lexington *Valley Star*, a Democratic newspaper which had been established in 1839 by John Letcher. Articles signed "Common Sense" assailed "the management of Washington College, the men, trustees & professors & their insufficiency." "Ergo" wrote in defense of the College against such an "elaborate exaggeration," and "X" warmly supported "Common Sense." The bitterness engendered several street encounters involving very strong epithets if not physical blows.

The furor subsided as summer waned, but the College was drawn into an even more violent dispute that rocked Lexington during 1847 and 1848. The altercation is known in local tradition as "the Skinner War," as its central character was Dr. John Skinner, pastor of the town's large Presbyterian church. Dr. Skinner had come to his charge some years before, fresh from ecclesiastical controversies in his native Scotland. He established himself as a laborious worker, an excellent pulpit orator, and a sympathetic pastor. Some of his personal characteristics, such as a typical Scottish willingness to imbibe "a little speerit" on occasion, endeared him to some of his flock; but he would pour vials of wrath upon those who disagreed with him. A contemporary diarist recorded hearing Skinner engage in over three hours of "wicked excoriation" of one opponent, "who sat by him" during the diatribe.

Skinner's popularity declined, at least with a portion of his congregation, and "the people complained that there was a dearth of gospel in his preaching." A committee of eight privately intimated to him that his usefulness in Lexington had ended. His reply was "caustic, personal & defiant." The Lexington Presbytery considered the matter in August of 1847 and, after Dr. Skinner had spoken in his own defense for more than five hours, they "accepted" his resignation. He refused to concede defeat, however, and determined to appeal to higher church authority.

Several of Dr. Skinner's accusers were Washington College men: President Ruffner, professors Armstrong and Philo Calhoun, and trustees Samuel McD. Reid, John Alexander, John B. Lyle, and Alfred Leyburn. Dr. Skinner assailed these men and others in speeches and correspondence which he later published in a series of pamphlets. The arguments also brought out animosity between the accused pastor and two V.M.I. faculty members: Colonel Francis H. Smith, the Episcopalian who countenanced "balls" (dancing); and Major John T. L. Preston, a member of Dr. Skinner's congregation. The contumacious Scotsman accused Ruffner, Armstrong, and Calhoun—all Presbyterian clergymen—of interfering with his ministry, and denounced them for preaching in the Episcopal Church without his permission. He charged that the professors' action had implied that Washington College, "a true and genuine Institution of true-blue Presbyterianism," was not indeed a school of that denomination.

In November of 1847 the presbytery tried Dr. Skinner on charges of slander and libel against various officers and members of the church. Ruffner, Armstrong, and Preston constituted the committee of prosecution. The presbytery found the defendant guilty and suspended him from the ministry. This decision, and still another depriving him of his pastorate, were appealed to the general assembly, which restored him to the ministry but upheld his severance from the Lexington "bene-fice."

Dr. Skinner was not without partisans, who included editor James Gardner Paxton of the *Valley Star*, a newspaper which had already attacked the management of Washington College and was to do so again. Student opinion was divided. A letter signed by thirty-three students expressed support of Skinner and was accompanied by a "small sum" to be used "for the attainment of justice." Students testi-fied on both sides at the libel and slander trial, and expressed conflict-ing estimates of the attitude of their fellows in general. Most of the testimony, however, exculpated President Ruffner and the professors from exciting discontent with their pastor.

The matter of a congregation's dissatisfaction with its minister was thus escalated into a quarrel that not only involved the local educa-tional institutions, but affected politics and emphasized socio-economic cleavages. On Skinner's side were many of the humbler people of his church, a large proportion of the "country people," and, according to one account, "all the foreign element in town and Presbytery" and the "irreligious element." These groups were apparently numerous enough to elect the Democrat Paxton and James B. Dorman, Whig, to the legislature over anti-Skinner Whigs.

PAXTON'S CANDIDACY WAS AIDED also by a renewal of criticisms of Wash-ington College in the *Valley Star*, led by that old enemy of the insti-tution, "Common Sense." This gadfly found nothing good in the College except a few admittedly handsome buildings. He directed a withering assault upon President Ruffner, criticized all other members of the faculty—who now numbered four—and accused the trustees of mismanagement, incompetence, timorousness, and negligence. Paxton in his campaign for office promised that should the matter of mis-management at Washington College be brought before the legislature, he would demand a thorough investigation of the disposition of the large benefactions it had received.

The governance and effectiveness of a private college would seem to be, some would hold today, a peculiar issue to be dragged into a contest for public office; but the Paxton faction contended that the trustees were responsible to public opinion; and that as the faculty was responsible to the trustees, even the way in which an instructor con-ducted his classes was a suitable topic for the voters to consider.

Defenders of the College mounted a counterattack, with trustee Ben-jamin Mosby Smith in the role of official spokesman for the much-provoked management. But the *Valley Star* withheld the pro-College letters from publication until after Paxton had been elected over his Whig opponent by a narrow margin of 386 to 314.

With the newspaper bombardment reaching crescendo at the conclusion of the academic year 1847–1848, President Ruffner submitted his resignation, which the trustees promptly accepted. The four professors inquired whether the board desired their resignations also, as intimated in a local newspaper; but the trustees took no action on the matter in either the June or August meetings of 1848. With a few final salvos, including a prediction that difficulty would be encountered in finding a distinguished new president, the *Valley Star* abandoned its attack upon the College. "Common Sense" was heard no more for several years. Editor Paxton, his seat in the legislature assured, abruptly turned to the torrid politics of the presidential election of 1848, and the storm at Lexington had passed.

The new president, George Junkin, escaped the violent assaults that had beset Ruffner, and the College moved largely unchanged and almost imperceptibly into the last decade of its ante-bellum existence. The Ruffner years were years of agony and dissension; but they were also years of expansion—the faculty grew from three to five members, including the president—and years during which the pattern of the ante-bellum College became firmly fixed.

Chapter
VIII

Environs of Academe

DURING the first half of the nineteenth century, and beyond, an intimate relationship existed between "Old Lexington" and "the College,"
as townsmen then and later called the school. The people were never
unmindful of the influence of Washington College (and V.M.I., after
1839) upon the prestige and economy of the community. Because of
the interdependence of "town" and "gown," and because the pattern
of the College had become well set during the generation preceding
1861, it seems appropriate at this point to view the setting in which the
institution existed.

FOUNDED IN 1776 and named for the Massachusetts village where min-
utemen first clashed with redcoats, Lexington had attained some importance as a county seat and market center of an agricultural region
by the time William Graham's school was moved to its outskirts in the
1780's. By 1785 the town boasted a brick courthouse, with Main Street
and several "back" streets laid out. In the spring of 1796 a severe fire,
breaking out when practically everyone was in church, destroyed
many buildings. The legislature authorized a lottery to raise $25,000
for reconstruction. (Although it was not used at that time, such a form

of financing was employed intermittently through the 1830's for public works.) The community recovered well enough from the fire, however, so that a visitor from New York in 1805 recorded in his diary: "Lexington a handsome little village, good buildings."

The classification "little village" remained applicable for many years and Lexington has to this day not exceeded the dimensions of a small town. Factors that promote the growth of cities—such as high-employment industry, location at a junction of busy routes of trade or communication, presence of a major governmental establishment—have never been present in the "Athens of Western Virginia." The economy has always been based on farming and local commerce, aided by infusion through the educational institutions. In the early days nearly all the townsmen, including clergymen and teachers, were farmers. Slave labor was used to some extent in agriculture, and a number of Rockbridge County residents became fairly prosperous; but the citizens remained essentially yeomen and even the largest estates did not compare with the great plantations of the tidewater and the lower South.

The town grew slowly and in 1850 the population was only 1,743—1,105 whites, 86 free Negroes, and 552 slaves. In Rockbridge County there were some 16,000 inhabitants including slightly more than 4,000 slaves. Most of the county people, presumably, lived on farms. In the fifties Lexington had the essential community business establishments, such as J. L. Deaver's Lexington Cheap Shoe Store; a drug store purchased by J. T. McCrum & Co. in 1857 from Dr. R. T. Marshall; Aaron Kahn's Clothing Bazaar; J. D. Humphries' Cigar Store; William Kahle's cabinet shop, which had wrought the Washington statue at the College; Dr. John W. Paine's bookstore; and Potter's Cheap Cash Store and Oyster House. Some of the names are still carried more than a hundred years later. The wayfarer had his choice of the Exchange Hotel on lower Main Street or William Jordan's Lexington Hotel. Professional services were rendered by five or six physicians, at least one dentist, and a dozen or so lawyers. The medical doctors had such difficulties in collecting their bills during the fifties that they went on strike.

The Lexington *Gazette*, with optimism and exaggeration, boasted in 1852 of the town's city-like appearance and future aspirations: "A stranger looking out in the morning, might imagine himself in 'Broadway,' or a city market street. . . . With the crowd of stages, loaded with passengers . . . wagons and carts, horses and mules, men, women and children, white and black and *loafers*, there is some of a crowd, and considerable 'noise and confusion'. . . . To the neighboring *villages*,

we now give timely warning to get out of the way." But such prophe-
cies were not soon to be realized.

The absence of a bank hampered financial transactions until the
Lexington Savings Institution was established in 1853 and the Bank of
Rockbridge during the depth of the 1856–1857 depression. Money was
chronically scarce, and acutely so during "hard times" such as the
twenties and fifties of the last century.

Another major obstacle to urban development was the difficulty of
transportation between Lexington and the world outside the valley—
and for that matter, even within the valley. The Richmond *Republican*
spoke in 1849 of the need for good roads and avenues to market at
Lexington, adding hopefully that there was prospect of a canal's being
built to Jordan's Point on the North River.

In 1853 the Richmond *Dispatch* praised the beauty of Lexington's
setting, but pointed out that the town would grow more rapidly were
it not cut off from improvements "in the way of railroads, canals, and
even good turnpikes which many other places possess." Hardly a
splinter was left of an old "plank road" from Lexington to Greenville,
and travelers waxed eloquent on the subject of the roads connecting
the place with rail lines. A trip over the Goshen road was recommended "to put a man's liver in order." The *Dispatch* hoped that the
"ancient burgh," imprisoned as it was among the mountains, would
soon find outlet to the busy world.

An outlet had indeed been in the making since 1850 when the legislature incorporated the North River Navigation Company and appropriated $100,000 of which $40,000 was to be raised by private subscription. The *Gazette* had predicted "A New Era for Rockbridge." The
canal would help the county develop its resources, connect with the
Valley Junction Turnpike, bring a stream of visitors to town, and
perhaps foster the exploitation of iron ore in the area. The project
moved slowly, and it was not until November 15, 1860, that the first
packet boat to traverse the North River Canal reached Lexington,
establishing a regular line of boats between the village and Richmond.
Although subject to blockages by freshets and freezes the canal furnished the most important mode of transportation until the arrival of
the railroad in the eighties.

LEXINGTON thus remained the tiny metropolis of a rural area—but with a
peculiar distinction as an educational center. The dominance of the
educational institutions in the aspect of the village may be inferred
from a description by a visitor at mid-century. Standing on the heights

near Governor McDowell's residence "Col Alto" he thought that "few finer subjects can be found for an artist's pencil than the well built village." He described the "long, graceful crescent of hills, topped with handsome private residences, a fine Female Academy, the colonnade of Washington College, and the castle-like Military Institute, with the Jump, North, and House Mountains as a background, and in the intertwining forests the ivy-covered ruin of 'Liberty Hall Academy.'" The observer compared the beauty of Lexington's setting with vistas he had seen on a recent trip to Europe.

The impressive Washington College colonnade had taken shape in the forties, as had the appearance of "College Hill," with the building of four residences for occupation by the president and three professors who then constituted the faculty. A contemporary description said the four residences were similar in internal arrangements, size, and external appearance, except as necessary to "give a pleasing variety to the whole." Two of the homes were placed on the eastern and two on the western side of the center college group. In the same building program, wings were added to the center building, and Grecian porches to all the academic structures. The residences also were in classical architectural style. According to the *Gazette* the plan was to present "a front, uniform in design, between 800 and 900 feet in length," which would accommodate the faculty and their families, about 150 students, together with furnishing a chapel, two society halls with attached libraries, four large lecture rooms, a room for the College library, and one for the laboratory.

IN ADDITION to the three institutions whose appearance so pleased the traveler quoted above, there were a half-dozen privately operated schools in Lexington about this time, none of which continued long in existence. The "fine Female Academy" was, of course, the Ann Smith Academy, a pioneer in the education of young women in Virginia. It had been founded in 1807 with a committee of superintendence composed of prominent townsmen. As was to be expected, the group included several trustees and alumni of Washington Academy, and Edward Graham was treasurer. A charter was obtained from the legislature in 1808. Among the first subscribers was Thomas Jefferson, who gave twenty-five dollars.

Miss Smith, who had conducted similar schools successfully for years in Maryland and "George-Town," but had retired to the upper country for reasons of health, had generously tendered her services gratis for one year. She would live and board with the students. Board, lodging, fire, candles, beds, and washing were available at $50 for a five-month session. Tuition was fixed at $10 a session. The usual branches of English education were to be taught, including English grammar, geography, rhetoric, drawing, and needlework. In addition, for those prepared, a competent knowledge of natural philosophy would be imparted by Edward Graham.

Despite the patronage of some leading Rockbridge families, the seminary's beginning was not auspicious and enrollment was disappointing for the first few years. In 1812 the headmistress departed, according to a letter by Thomas L. Preston, one of the governing committee, in "violence of temper" which "outraged the most ordinary dictates of prudence." Her resignation seems to have been the outgrowth of an infatuation with a handsome young Frenchman bearing the engaging name of Hyacinthe Crusolles, who had been employed as a teacher. Preston related that Miss Smith had written Crusolles indiscreet missives, which he had vainly displayed. The same source reported that she had attempted to inveigle the Frenchman into accompanying her to Fredericksburg, but that he refused.

More serious than the loss of the headmistress was the school's financial condition. In 1812 and again in 1821 the trustees urgently appealed for state funds, but without success. Their petition to the legislature in the latter year declared that enrollment in the preceding session had risen to 49 (exceeding that of Washington College). The pupils' ages ranged from 10 to "upwards" of 20, averaging about 13 to 16. Studies usually taught were reading, writing, arithmetic, "english grammer," geography, "use of the Globes," natural philosophy, chemistry, astronomy, belles-lettres, "french," instrumental music, painting, and embroidery. The teaching staff ordinarily consisted of three persons.

The school was closed in 1821 for one year and possibly longer. It was advertised for sale, but John Robinson came forward to pay off the entire debt. Two pupils, Betsy Alexander and Sallie Lyle, conducted the academy for a time, and Miss Susan Goosley announced the opening of a session in November of 1823. Parents living at a distance were advised that they could send their daughters with Washington College students as traveling companions! A Mrs. Nicholls and two daughters took over from Miss Goosley in 1826, and Edward Graham with his daughter assumed operation in 1830. Others to head the academy in the next three decades included a Mr. and Mrs. Chapin, Robert Bradshaw, Edward G. Caruthers and Mrs. Caruthers, Mrs. E. Nottingham, and William N. Page.

During these years the academy received praise for its instruction in fundamentals; for the faithfulness, competence, morality, and piety of

its teachers; and for the fact that the teachers were ". . . *all* members of
the Presbyterian church. . . ." Some objection was raised, however, to
certain of the teachers as "too gay and volatile," and one visitor adversely criticized commencement exercises in rhetoric and philosophy
"by those who were to be neither orators nor professors in later life."
Young ladies boarding in the school were required to wear prescribed
uniforms, at least during one period in the thirties, "in order to repress
extravagance." Ann Smith students had access to Lexington society,
with reservations. The *Valley Star* observed in 1842: "They are not
cooped up like nuns, as in many other schools, but are permitted to
accept invitations from the ladies of the town, and to be out in good
weather, under the care of one or more of their teachers." Yet one of
the students in 1846, Miss Ellen Massie, facetiously used the word
"nunnery" in dating her letters.

The academy gave hundreds of young women educational opportunities that they could probably not otherwise have obtained. But the
unprosperous institution, overshadowed by two men's colleges, was
not destined to be what it might have been in another location: a
Virginia women's college of the type exemplified by Mary Baldwin,
Hollins, Randolph-Macon, and Sweet Briar. It struggled for some years
after the Civil War and finally succumbed.

NOWHERE DID TOWN AND GOWN merge more thoroughly and to greater
mutual advantage than in Lexington's Franklin Society and Library
Company, which was founded in 1811 and chartered in 1816. It was
intimately associated with Washington College from the first. Intended
to be a debating society with weekly meetings, it began to assemble a
library, first through subscriptions to five newspapers (discontinued in
1813) and later by purchase of books and subscriptions to periodicals.
The library was to be financed through the sale of stock, each member
taking at least one share. The society bought five shares and placed
them at the disposal of the College, so that students might use the
library without fee. A student desiring to take out a book had to
request the society's president for one of the shareholders' tickets assigned to the College; the librarian closely guarded the scarce and
expensive volumes in his keeping.

Franklin Hall, erected to house the organization's meeting room and
library, early proved to be a drain on the resources of the members
(although "Jockey" John Robinson donated two hundred dollars).
Book purchases had to be curtailed. Thereafter, however, the Society
prospered; and its continuity may be indicated by the fact that one

man, John W. Fuller, served as librarian and guardian of the organization from 1830 to 1876.

The period 1840–1861 has been called the Golden Age of this cultural institution, "when everyone in town who was anyone belonged to it and attended its meetings with interest." At the Franklin during that exciting era all the important national, state, and local issues were debated. Franklin Hall in ante-bellum years, as well as in a brief renaissance during the 1870's, was the intellectual center and to an extent the social center of the town. There professors of the two local colleges mingled in debates with intelligent and well-informed people of the community including preachers, politicians, lawyers, merchants, editors, and farmers. The establishment of the Virginia Military Institute had its origins in Franklin Society debates of the early 1830's, Henry Ruffner's critique of slavery in western Virginia was enunciated first in the Franklin, and there a debate raged about the proposed division of the commonwealth.

Surviving the looting by Union soldiers during Hunter's Raid in 1864, the Society was revived; it entered a brief spurt of prosperity in the seventies, but fell into the doldrums in the eighties. The decline and death of the old Franklin have been attributed to the advent of the railroad to Lexington and to the increased popularity of the daily newspaper. In 1891, when debates no longer were held, the stockholders transferred their society's library and property for preservation to Washington and Lee University, with the stipulation that a scholarship be established for worthy Rockbridge students.

LEXINGTON CITIZENS were keenly aware of the political issues of their times. The College, the institute, and the Franklin Society served to heighten their understanding and increase their interest in this area. In party matters Rockbridge County generally followed national trends until the eve of secession. Although the county had gone for John Quincy Adams, Jackson and Van Buren carried Rockbridge in 1832 and 1836 respectively. Whereas Colonel James McDowell had been a Federalist, his son and namesake became a Jacksonian and won a seat in Congress and the governorship. The political pendulum swung toward the Whigs about 1840 and that party remained predominant in the vicinity until its dissolution in the 1850's. A state Whig convention was held in Lexington in the late forties and in 1851 President Fillmore visited the town accompanied by the Virginia leader of the party, Alexander H. H. Stuart of Staunton. Some remarked that the President was electioneering.

The Lexington *Gazette,* which made its appearance in the thirties, was a faithful party organ of the Whigs and their successor throughout the ante-bellum period. The *Valley Star,* established in 1839, served a similar function for the Democrats. These weeklies superseded the earlier *News-Letter, Intelligencer,* and *Union* as local media for news and opinion.

Attitudes on more specific issues than party allegiance reflected geographic, historical, and economic factors. Proximity of the frontier brought an early interest in expansionism. Land speculation in the developing Kentucky region affected many in Lexington at the end of the eighteenth century, including William Graham. Several decades later the people of Lexington and Rockbridge became "Texas conscious." Any basic sympathies they may have had were enhanced by the exploits of Rockbridger Sam Houston and the death of Samuel ("Bigfoot") Wallace, a native, fighting the Mexicans. At a Fourth of July celebration in 1836 near Lexington many toasts were offered to these heroes and to the "Texians" generally.

LEXINGTONIANS, in common with most Virginians, exhibited a broadminded attitude toward Negroes until reason gave way to emotion under the abolitionist attack. The connection of John Chavis with the community and College has been noted. In 1817 a Sunday School was organized and, according to Edward Graham, it was attended by "upwards of sixty whites and seventy blacks." In 1819 John Erskine, "a man of colour," appeared in the pulpit of the Lexington Presbyterian Church. The *News-Letter* commented sympathetically that he had been a slave, whose freedom had been purchased by the South Carolina clergy. A movement was afoot to raise funds to buy the freedom of his wife and family. During the twenties Negro and white children attended school together "behind Parson Davidson's place." The *Intelligencer,* successor to the *News-Letter,* carried much matter attacking slavery. In the 1830's the Reverend Andrew Reed, visiting Lexington, worshipped at the local African church.

In the mid-thirties, however, a violent reaction to abolitionism set in. The *Gazette,* itself critical of slavery, could call the *Liberator* a "crazy abolition paper" on occasion; and the rise of the abolitionists was the most disturbing question before the readers of the *Gazette.* In the summer of 1835 an abolitionist was reported to be skulking about town, the citizenry became thoroughly aroused, and "Judge Lynch" almost acted. In the following year Rockbridge legislative delegate C. P. Dorman took strong ground against this fearsome group and called for a "Virginia front" in meeting the issue.

In the decade before Sumter, townsmen were agitated by the slavery issue in various forms. At the turn of 1850–1851 the *Gazette* mentioned rumors of an intended servile insurrection and planned attack on the town. The newspaper regarded the stories as a hoax but conceded that some excitement had occurred. The *Gazette* in 1854 complained of the public whipping of naked Negro men slaves in the town jail yard; but in 1859 took a wary view of the numbers of aimless free Negroes congregated in Lexington.

Leaders of the town held to the idea of African colonization as late as the early fifties, but the problem of the free Negro caused troubled comment. In general, after the Ruffner pamphlet, there was almost no serious attack on slavery in Lexington. Yet there was no demand for aggressive expansion of slave soil.

The John Brown raid startled this conservative, Union-loving, slave-holding but moderate community—as, of course, it did all of Virginia and the South. The *Gazette* inquired apprehensively "whither is it all tending?" and replied to its own question: "To rebellion and civil war, to the overthrow of the Constitution and to the dissolution of the Union." The affair was brought home to the townspeople by the dispatch of a detachment of V.M.I. cadets to Charles Town to guard against any possible attempt to free Brown; and subsequently by a letter written from Charles Town by Major J. T. L. Preston vividly describing Brown's hanging.

TRENDS AND CHANGES of lesser importance were visible in Lexington in the ante-bellum decades. One was the rise of the temperance movement in an area where distilling whiskey had once been common on the farms. The Reverend Andrew Reed expressed pleasure in the thirties that the number of "spirit stores" in town had been reduced from nine to one. The Rockbridge Central Temperance Society was established in the late twenties and Edward Graham was in the chair when it celebrated its seventh annual meeting in 1835. In 1847 the "Sons of Temperance" was organized. The *Gazette* commended the group, noted that intemperance was generally believed to be on the decline, but observed that strangers had reported seeing as much intemperance in Lexington as anywhere.

At the same time there may have been some relaxation in the attitude on dancing. At any rate, in 1848 lessons in "fashionable dancing" were offered by a Mr. Hoffman, whose repertoire included "Boyd's, Rober-son's, and Brackett's Cotillions (all full setts)," as well as the Circassian

Dance, the Spanish Dance, and the Italian, German, and Hop waltzes. Hoffman carried a recommendation from the faculty of the University of Virginia.

In such a community did the ante-bellum Washington College have its existence. The closest interrelationship between town and gown subsisted during the era before secession. The "College" belonged to Lexington, its leading citizens served as trustees and sometimes as professors (the latter, by virtue of their position, became leading citizens); and the Presbyterian Church pervaded all. During General Robert E. Lee's time more outside influences were permitted to play on the institution; but during his successor's years local pressures were reasserted; and it was far into the twentieth century (perhaps even to 1930) before the grip of Lexington upon the affairs of the College was relaxed and finally largely surrendered.

Chapter
IX

Pattern of the
Ante-Bellum College

THROUGHOUT THE DECADES BEFORE SUMTER, Washington College retained an educational pattern dominated by the classics and suffused with religion. In this it was typical of the small, church-related Southern school of its time. With the passage of years increased attention was given to scientific fields in which new knowledge was developing; and "practical" subjects began to make their appearance. Instruction in modern foreign languages was available only on a non-credit basis. English grammar was taught and composition and public speaking were emphasized; but the literature of the native tongue seems to have been neglected in the classroom. To be sure, ever since William Graham's day the library had contained classics in English and in translation from European languages. Yet the students probably had little time to read these works and apparently less encouragement to do so. In 1851 President George Junkin declared: "No good *student* can be a great reader at College; desultory reading, especially of novels, is a great resort of idlers—a mere apology to conscience for indisposition to mental exertion." With all respect to Dr. Junkin, one may suspect that general reading is a common characteristic of the best students in modern colleges.

A MAJOR WEAKNESS of American education during the nineteenth century was in the preparation of students for college. As Henry Ruffner pointed out, the state of Virginia in the early decades of the century divided its support of education mainly between the university on the one hand and minimal common-school instruction on the other. The private academies, for the most part small and short-lived, were inadequate for the task of preparing even the small percentage of the youth that aspired to college-level study. Colleges and universities themselves often were obliged to provide preparatory courses. Washington College thus maintained a grammar school even long beyond the Civil War (and for a time a "manual labor" school existed). Student rosters that have survived list numbers of "irregulars," not yet qualified for college classes leading to the bachelor's degree.

An ante-bellum student apparently could enter college with no knowledge of physical or biological science, or of his country's history and government, and with only rudimentary instruction in his own language and in mathematics. But he had to be proficient in the classics. The grammar school curriculum in 1826, according to a Washington College catalogue of that year, consisted almost entirely of courses in Latin and Greek, including prosody, with such adjuncts as "Classical Dictionary" and "Maps of Ancient Geography." The only other courses were "Elements of English Grammar" and "Elementary rules of arithmetic." Catalogues from 1839 and 1851 indicate that the College admission requirements remained essentially unchanged, although it was specified that the student's knowledge of English grammar must be "competent."

The college student of the forties and fifties spent perhaps a third or a fourth of his time on classical studies. He would read some works of Demosthenes, Euripides, Herodotus, Homer, Sophocles, Xenophon, Cicero, Horace, Juvenal, Livy, Pliny, Tactitus, and Terence, and at least part of the Greek Testament. He would have become familiar with Caesar, Ovid, and Vergil in his preparatory courses. (The 1826 catalogue does not give as much detail, but the proportion of the curriculum devoted to the classics was presumably at least as great as in later years.)

The mathematics courses covered roughly the fields embraced in mid-twentieth century in secondary school and the first year or two of college (before the advent of "modern mathematics")—such as algebra, geometry, trigonometry, logarithms, analytic geometry, and conic sections. Differential and integral equations, listed in 1839 as extra and not required subjects, were in the regular program in 1851. Applications of mathematics included mensuration, surveying, navigation, and civil engineering.

In the physical sciences or "natural philosophy" the students were introduced to chemistry, astronomy, electricity, magnetism, heat mechanics, hydrostatics, pneumatics, and optics. By 1851 "practical mechanics" and "mathematical mechanics" were being taught. Lectures were offered in botany, geology, and mineralogy.

A "rhetorical course" embraced, at least in 1839–1840, "philosophical grammar," logic, rhetoric and criticism, and elements of history. An "ethical course" covered what now would be dispersed among departments of political science, economics, philosophy, and psychology. The offerings comprised "mental philosophy" and "moral and political philosophy." The latter area included study of the Constitution, the law of nations, and political economy.

The inattention to English, in contrast to the usual present-day curricula even in undergraduate professional schools, is quite striking. The 1851 catalogue, in fact, does not indicate any subject that would now be taught under that heading except possibly a course in "elocution" in the second year. Exercises in composition and declamation, however, were required of all classes; and the debating societies also provided a means of acquiring facility in the organization and presentation of ideas.

Sundays were only partial holidays, for the students were then lectured on theological subjects.

Practical training was offered alongside the classical and philosophical instruction. A two-year agricultural course and a three-year course in civil engineering were available. The former, designed to produce intelligent farmers, did not even require a knowledge of classical languages for admission. The 1839 catalogue listed a course of studies in a "School for English Teachers," to train teachers for the common schools of Virginia, then in so deplorable a condition. The Cincinnati course of 1838–1839, offered in conjunction with V.M.I., enabled students to enroll for French, English, military engineering (including that all-important fortification and gunnery) and to drill in uniform at the institute. Instruction in French, German, Spanish, and Italian was available at the college, but without credit toward graduation.

No marked changes are evident in the curricular offerings by the close of the fifties. After the arrival of Professor John L. Campbell in 1851, mineralogy was taught to juniors and geology to seniors. On the whole, however, innovations were few, and the outlines of the curriculum remained largely what they had been throughout the Ruffner and Junkin administrations. Some changes in textbooks were made, of course, notably the substitution of E. P. Smith's *Political Economy* for that of Wayland, whose views on slavery came to be deemed unsound.

The objectives of education and the function of the undergraduate college are live topics of debate in our times. Apparently the discussion has been going on a long while, as indicated by the publication of *An Apology for Collegiate Education* by President George Junkin in 1851. Some of Junkin's generalizations have a familiar ring, in tone if not in diction. He defined education broadly as all life itself. The purpose of the College was "to wake up the mind, to create intellect, as it were to guide its activities under general laws, and so give to man an impulse in the direction of his endless course." Although the communication of factual knowledge was certainly one objective, it was subordinate "to *the end which is to cultivate and enlarge the intellect and moral facilities.*"

Less in accord with present-day thinking were Junkin's views on the relationship of the various fields of instruction and their influence upon the student. Latin and Greek were the foremost studies of the curriculum conducive to mental development. Next he placed the science of number and quantity—knowledge of the mathematics developed analytical powers. Mental and moral sciences were placed at the end of the student's course after, as Dr. Junkin believed, a boy's intellectual strength had been gained. Logic, that "prophylactic against sophistry," and rhetoric (a highly practical study) were much esteemed by Junkin. Metaphysics came at the pinnacle of the curriculum.

The physical sciences were not properly college studies, but belonged to professional training: "They are not *the* business of a course of mental drilling, preparatory to professional studies; but they are the business of life. . . ." Natural scientists would be surprised at Dr. Junkin's treatment of botany, which science, he held, tended to create habits of loose thought and expression. He considered it an undoubted fact that "the physical sciences are popular with such students as are unwilling to grapple with the more difficult subjects of languages, mathematics and mental and moral science." (A lazy student today is not likely to find a science major an "easy" program.)

Although political economy had been in the curriculum for some time, Dr. Junkin was unhappy with it. "Its introduction is a *conge de lire* to utilitarianism of the lowest order. It never can have place among the liberal arts on any other principle, for it is professedly occupied with utility and wealth. It is mammon, the meanest of the terrestrial, seeking a throne among the celestials." With entire accuracy Dr. Junkin added that the "dismal science" opened wide fields for investigation, offered numerous discussion topics, and a "a vast field for controversies." He was not meaning to be complimentary; but educators today would generally hold that social sciences, raising open-ended questions, "train the mind" at least as well as parsing and declining ancient languages. Moreover, while the argument about the place of "practical" or "applied" subjects in a liberal arts college continues to rage, economics has been accepted as a liberal discipline.

The moral sciences closed the circle of knowledge, and at Washington College morals were learned "by induction and by supernatural information." Nobody could doubt where Dr. Junkin stood. "The family, school or college which does not base the principle of its moral discipline on the doctrine of a deity and his perfections, will raise men capable of governing only by brute force: other foundations no man can lay."

Dr. Junkin believed that the curriculum could be mastered by a youth of "moderate" talents, and by a good student easily. He was worried, in fact, that the young men were not kept busy enough, and would fall victims to the "pestiferous influence of idleness." He suggested the study of modern languages to improve each shining hour otherwise unfilled. We have noted his aversion to general reading for this or any other purpose; and the good doctor would assuredly have been appalled at the thought of students spending time on extracurricular activities such as athletics and campus politics, even to help develop well-rounded-out personalities.

Some surprise may be occasioned by Dr. Junkin's observation that a youth could master the curriculum by the time he reached eighteen— the age at which his great-great-grandson would be just entering college. Perhaps the oldtime discipline and air of seriousness brought about mental maturity much sooner than the methods and conditions in contemporary schools. On the other hand, the content of the curriculum did not compare with that of a twentieth-century college except probably in the classics. At any rate, the ante-bellum student would have reached college earlier because his period of preparation was far shorter than the present average twelve years of elementary and secondary school.

Dr. Junkin remarked also that after completing the college course a student could go to the university and in another three years be ready for service. He denounced the doctrine of expediency "which twists and turns to the materialistic utilitarianism of the age, and cuts down and fritters away the College course . . . so that the Bachelor's degree may be conferred on young men preparing for professional life, who are unable to pursue a full course of liberal education." Thus he conceived of higher education as consisting of a completely liberal education in college followed by professional training in a university. As the modern graduate school of liberal arts had not yet been developed, Dr. Junkin did not have to wrestle with the problem of the college's relation to that kind of institution, a problem sorely vexing in the mid-twentieth century.

Examinations in the ante-bellum college were elaborate and formal occasions. Usually at the close of an examination period, which had been open to the public, the local editor commended the zeal and industry of professors and students. In 1852 the trustees set up a five-man board of examiners, comprising trustees and others who were paid two dollars a day for their services and eight cents a mile for travel. Examinations were partly written, blackboard, and oral. The period lasted six days, from 9 A.M. to 10 P.M. The examiners obviously earned their compensation. It is not to be expected that any one student was quizzed throughout the entire period, but several references indicate that the questioning was exacting and thorough. In underclass examinations in the classics, for example, portions of ancient authors were selected at random for translation, English sentences were assigned to be written in Latin and Greek, and testing in the principles of the classic languages was minute and critical. Yet in 1851 the examination grade was equal in value to only one-tenth of a student's recitation grade. We may infer that day-to-day assignments were demanding, and may wonder if Dr. Junkin's fears of idleness may not have been a bit exaggerated.

COMMENCEMENT EXERCISES were brief and simple during the early part of the period, with young men "speaking pieces," but during the latter thirties they became more extensive and complex. Local reports glowed with comment on excellent student speeches and on occasion a presidential address was "a gem." In 1839 the "finals" were concluded "with an unusually large assemblage of Ladies and Gentlemen at the Eagle Hotel—made doubly joyous by the presence of the Instructors and Pupils of Ann Smith Academy." For a time the commencements were joined with those of Ann Smith and V.M.I. Thus in 1840 students, faculties, and trustees of the three institutions filed through the town in "commencement procession," led by a volunteer band and followed by Lexington citizens.

A significant event of the period was the formation of the Alumni Association of Washington College on June 25, 1840. It was organized by twenty-two graduates including President Ruffner, John Echols, J. T. L. Preston, Charles P. Dorman, Jacob Fuller, and Samuel McDowell Reid. Its constitution provided for admission of all graduates upon application, and others who had studied at least two years prior to 1840 with honorable standing.

Among the principal purposes of the body, in addition to the usual objectives, were the compilation of a catalogue of graduates of the College and the preparation by Dr. Ruffner of a history of the institution. A year later it was reported that a start had been made on the alumni list, but that work had been much hampered by "defects in the record anterior to 1815." In 1842 the annual alumni meeting appointed a committee "to collect all pamphlets or other publications illustrative of the history of Washington College," as well as to assemble materials bearing upon the history of western Virginia. A "year's indulgence" was granted to Dr. Ruffner, who had begun his history of the school from its beginnings as an academy. As has been noted, Dr. Ruffner needed far more than a year for the completion of his history, which was as yet unpublished when he surrendered the presidency in 1848. The society also brought speakers to the campus at commencement, prominent alumni such as Dr. Archibald Alexander, and purchased a stone block which formed a portion of the Washington Monument, inscribed "The Only College endowed by the Father of his Country."

An effort was made in 1854 which, if it had been successful, would have given the alumni virtual control of the College. In a meeting of the society in Franklin Hall on July 4, E. J. H. McCampbell introduced a resolution for appointment of a committee to request the legislature to incorporate the organization. The body was to be empowered "to elect all Trustees of this Institution, and also to elect one Member of the said Board annually, instead of the oldest Trustee then in said Board, which said Trustee's duties shall cease, on the qualification of his said successor thus elected." The resolution was referred to a committee which was to report at the next annual meeting, but nothing further was heard on the proposal. Subsequent suggestions of a similar kind, although not as far-reaching, were to be made in 1873 and 1901–1902.

THE FACULTY REMAINED SMALL in the forties and fifties, comprising the president and two, three, or four professors, with occasional assistants and instructors. The presidents served as full-time professors; the teaching of Doctors Ruffner and Junkin was indeed more important than their administrative work. About 1837 the faculty consisted of President Ruffner and Professors George D. Armstrong, Philo Calhoun, and George E. Dabney. The turnover was not great until the early fifties when there were several resignations. All professors appointed at that time remained for several decades except for Junius M.

Fishburn, whose untimely death in 1858 cut short a promising career after a few years in the teaching of Latin and modern languages.

After 1854 the faculty included, besides Fishburn, Professors Alexander L. Nelson (mathematics), whose service ran to 1906, a record not likely to be surpassed; John Lyle Campbell (natural sciences, especially geology and chemistry), who taught from 1851 to 1886; James J. White (Greek), who became a personage in the years between 1852 and his death in 1893; and Carter J. Harris who occupied the Latin chair from 1858 to 1893. Thus two of the four professors, or forty per cent of the faculty with the president included, taught the classics.

Professors' salaries ranged from $750 to $1,000 per year, with the use of a house and one-fifth of the tuition fees. The president was paid $1,200. In view of the small enrollment and low tuition fee, professorial incomes were probably not much enhanced by the tuition-splitting device.

What manner of men were these old-time professors?

In colonial times and the early decades of the Republic a great proportion of the most learned men in America were clergymen. The education of future clergymen was an important function of the colleges and, conversely, many educators were clergymen—at Washington College, Presbyterian clergymen. We have noted that during the forties President Ruffner, Professor Armstrong, and Professor Calhoun were Presbyterian ministers on the faculty at the same time.

A change was under way, however. Emphasis was shifting to the preparation of lawyers and physicians. Separate theological schools were undertaking a growing share in the training of the clergy. The value of liberal education for laymen was more and more recognized, as a prerequisite for professional study or for other advantages. College teaching was gaining professional status in its own right. Also, the roles of teacher and preacher were sometimes seen as conflicting. A case in point was the criticism leveled at the Washington College faculty members during the forties for participation in religious activities. When Armstrong received a call to the College in 1837, his only qualm in accepting the professorship was that he might become so much absorbed in the pursuit of science that he would "forget his higher duties to his maker." In the fifties only President Junkin was a clergyman, and his professors were all laymen.

The ante-bellum professors were usually native Virginians, although some were transplanted—such as Armstrong, from New Jersey. A few were alumni of Washington College. Most had had the training of the day for their vocation, the M.A. degree, the University of Virginia being the principal source. A tutor at the close of the period, E. A.

Ludwig, held the Ph.D. But this was long before that degree became a common requirement for college professors. In fact, it was not until after 1860 that American universities began to offer regular doctoral curricula. Professor Fishburn spent a year of study in Germany in 1855–1856. Upon his return to Washington College he began a new edition of Livy and the preparation of a Latin grammar, into which he planned to incorporate the best German scholarship; but he died within two years.

In politics the faculty members tended to be Whig, so long as that party existed. They believed in such reforms as African colonization and all supported the common-school movement. The clergymen were ardent workers in temperance and Bible society causes and active preachers in college and outside pulpits.

Factors that the trustees weighed in seeking faculty members are indicated in correspondence concerning the appointment of a Cincinnati Professor of Mathematics in 1848, after the resignation of Professor Benjamin S. Ewell from the position. Under consideration was Major (afterward Confederate General) Daniel H. Hill. Trustee James Morrison wrote to his fellow Presbyterian-clergyman-trustee, Francis McFarland, of Hill's high character and brilliant attainments in the army. Moreover, he came from a Presbyterian family and was well connected. Morrison stressed that Hill's moral and religious character, together with his scholarship, were the matters most to be regarded. His connections with the South should bring students to the College. Morrison noted that Hill's only rival for the chair was an Episcopal minister, and observed: "I trust we will not have an Episcopalian introduced into our faculty."

Hill, a West Point graduate who had distinguished himself in the Mexican War, was named to the professorship but was not happy in it. He deplored the unmilitary atmosphere, compared the College unfavorably with V.M.I., and privately derided the people of Lexington as "Presbyterians of the old school, remarkable for their piety, bigotry, hospitality and intolerance." Yet when he left in 1854 it was to join the faculty of civilian, Presbyterian Davidson College. After the Civil War, General Hill served as president of the University of Arkansas and of the Middle Georgia Military and Agricultural School.

Space forbids extensive individual description of the old-time teachers; but brief sketches may be given of three who served far into the post-bellum era and stamped deep impressions upon the College and its students—Alexander Lockhart Nelson, John Lyle Campbell, and James J. White.

Nelson was born in Augusta County in 1827. He received the A.B.

from Washington College in 1849 and after teaching at the University of Virginia returned to his alma mater in 1854 as Major Hill's successor in the Cincinnati professorship. He taught over a period of fifty-two years, under five presidents. A strong personality, "Ole Alec" was long remembered by those who sat in his classes. He took an active part in the civic, religious, business, and agricultural life of Lexington and environs. He was a deacon of the Lexington Presbyterian Church at the time Stonewall Jackson was active, and later became a ruling elder. He sang in the choir, taught in the Sunday School, and became superintendent of the Sunday School. At the commencement of 1904 the alumni honored their teacher with "a massive silver service" to mark his semicentennial year in the faculty.

Professor John Lyle Campbell became well known for his work in geology and chemistry and for a book on scientific agriculture. His sons Henry Donald and John L., Jr., were to render important service to Washington and Lee, the former as professor of Geology and dean, the latter as treasurer. A member of a pioneer Rockbridge County family, he was graduated from Washington College in 1843. After teaching for a time at Staunton and serving as principal of the Richmond Academy in Kentucky he returned to the College in 1851 as Robinson Professor of Physical Science.

Campbell was tireless in his studies and research, attempting to keep abreast of "the rapid developments continually making in Chemistry, Mineralogy, Geology & Astronomy, [which] render my department extremely laborious. . . ." Toward this end he sought intercourse with colleagues at distant places, but found that one month of professional travel cost more than he could save for that purpose in two years. It has been said that he used his vacations for thirty years for geological surveys and collection of specimens. Such friends as the Reverend Henry Brown, student A. Donald Robertson, and Professor Fishburn also gathered specimens for him, the latter during his year of study in Europe. In the summer of 1860 Campbell, William Henry Ruffner, and Dr. E. A. Ludwig (who was ignorant of geology) conducted a geological survey in the Valley of Virginia, one of the richest areas in illustrative geology in America. From the material gathered Campbell constructed a map and section that he described as embracing "a very considerable variety of formations, as well as peculiarities of stratification; also a considerable number of palaeontological and lithological characteristics, as all will have the advantage of being readily accessible to most of my pupils."

The teaching of natural sciences, then as now, required continual outlays for new equipment. In the fifties Campbell obtained the trustees' approval for the purchase of "Electro-magnetic" apparatus, which he had been borrowing from V.M.I., and "the telegraph." He planned to take the latter on a trip to southwest Virginia, where its display would advertise Washington College.

As the war clouds lowered Professor Campbell served as an editor of the agricultural department of the Lexington *Gazette,* conducted under the auspices of the Rockbridge County Agricultural and Mechanical Society. At the close of the war he was editing the *Gazette* and running a bookstore, but he surrendered those "outside" activities by order of the trustees. After the war he filled the difficult post of first Superintendent of Public Schools of Rockbridge County. At his death in 1886 his faculty colleagues noted that he had become an authority in the field of geology, especially of the Virginia mountain area, and well said: "It is to be regretted that a retiring modesty, the exacting claims of routine work, and failing health prevented Professor Campbell from a fuller publication of the results of his studies and labors. *A Treatise on Agriculture* for the use of his classes, articles in scientific Journals, and reports on the Geological and Mineral Resources of the James River Valley, and other railroad lines and mineral districts, are the chief products of his pen."

Of similar stature in the faculty of old-time Washington College was Professor James Jones White (1828–1894), who held the chair of Greek for forty-one years. Born in Nottoway County, Virginia, he was the son of the Reverend Dr. William S. White, who served as pastor of the Lexington Presbyterian Church for a quarter-century. He was in the class of 1851 at the University of Virginia where his father had been chaplain before moving to Lexington. In 1852 the son was elected to the Washington College faculty. His mentor at the university had been Professor Gessner Harrison, a noted classicist of that day. Allying himself with one of the leading Rockbridge County families through marriage in 1858 to Maria Louisa Reid, daughter of Samuel McDowell Reid, Professor White became a personage in his own right in both college and community. At his spacious home in Lexington he dispensed hospitality to students and visitors. As he once put it he had given his life to the institution; and indeed, he served on the faculty until the year before his death. His wise and kindly understanding of youth endeared him to generations of college men.

A REVIEW of the ante-bellum Washington College would be incomplete without reference to the trustees; for those gentlemen played an integral part in the operation of the institution. In the early days of the nineteenth century, members' duties included administering discipline to students and paying money out of their own pockets for the needs of the struggling academy and College. As late as 1861 the rules called for a trustees' committee to attend examinations and report the results to the full board.

Such direct participation in the daily affairs of the College was, of course, in strong contrast to the current functions exercised by the governing board of Washington and Lee, which is concerned primarily with general policies and the solvency of the University. The circumstances, however, are scarcely comparable. As the University student body today represents a broad geographic and economic cross-section of the United States, present and recent board members have included residents of a great area from Ohio to Florida, from New York to Louisiana. But old Washington College was basically a local institution. Most of its students were from western Virginia. The old-time trustee, like his prototype of the earliest days, was likely to be a Virginian, a resident of Lexington or vicinity, and a Presbyterian (a clergyman or an elder). Often his roots went back to Liberty Hall.

Although in some instances of localized or otherwise limited control the governing boards of modern colleges and universities continue to take a strong hand in day-to-day affairs, it is doubtful that any of them regularly administer examinations or punishment. How many trustees could hear examinations in Mathematical Methods of Statistics, Sophocles, Anthropology Today, and Literature of the Augustan Age, all in one week?

As with most boards of trustees, there was wide variation in the degree of interest and activity of the members. Sometimes when prominent persons were elected to membership their attendance was highly irregular, necessitating frequent changes in composition of the board, especially before 1840. The actual governance of old Washington College tended to devolve into the hands of a few, who usually lived near enough to maintain almost continuous contact. The term "local board" was an expressive one in the era to 1861. Although critics assailed the management as "a clique," it is a truism that those who were able and willing to spend their time and energy in the affairs of the College assumed power.

Perhaps the outstanding example of a trustee who gave unstintedly of his efforts was Samuel McDowell Reid, who served from 1819 to 1869 and handled financial affairs until 1861. Son of Andrew Reid, also a trustee, he was educated at Washington Academy, studied law at Staunton, served in the War of 1812, farmed at nearby "Mulberry Hill," and from 1831 to 1857 was Clerk of Rockbridge County Court, an office previously held by his father. He had been a founder of the Graham Philosophical Society at the Academy and of the Franklin Society of Lexington. The "Squire of Rockbridge County" served as a delegate in the legislature and as a director of the James River and Kanawha Company.

Another ante-bellum trustee deserving of notice was the Reverend Dr. Benjamin Mosby Smith, who was elected to the board in 1842 at the age of twenty-nine. The fact that he was a son-in-law of the Reverend James Morrison, trustee (1819–1865) and pastor of the New Providence Church, may have influenced his election; but his assiduous service of fifty-one years proved the merit of the choice. A graduate of Hampden-Sydney, Dr. Smith became a leading clergyman in the Southern Presbyterian Church, serving as pastor at a number of Virginia churches and as Professor of Oriental Literature at Union Theological Seminary. He published religious books and engaged in voluminous correspondence with men throughout the nation on domestic, educational, and religious subjects. Like Henry Ruffner, he was one of the first among public men in Virginia to advocate a general system of public education.

The Reverend Dr. William Brown was the son of the Reverend Samuel Brown, pastor of New Providence Church (1796–1818). He was graduated from Washington College in 1831, afterward studying theology at Princeton under Archibald Alexander and also at Union Theological Seminary. For many years Dr. Brown was pastor of the Old Stone Church in Augusta County, and from 1860 to 1879 he was editor of the *Central Presbyterian* at Richmond. He was a master of controversial writing, capable of the severest invective—"an inheritance from a brave and pious ancestry."

Major William M. Tate of Augusta County served on the board from 1856 to 1889, was active in the Civil War, and was a founder of the Augusta Female Academy, later Mary Baldwin College. A farmer who was born on a farm near Staunton, he was apparently something of a rarity among the trustees since he was neither a clergyman, a lawyer, nor the son of a clergyman or board member. He was qualified, however, in that he was a Scotch-Irishman "without mixture of any kind," had had early connections with Archibald Alexander, interested himself in education and religion, was a ruling elder of the Hebron Presbyterian Church, and was noted for his familiarity with the Bible. It was said that in his later years he scarcely read anything else.

Judge Francis T. Anderson, a graduate of Washington College in 1828, studied law in Staunton and became an eminent attorney and judge of the Supreme Court of Appeals of Virginia (1860–1882). "A consistent Presbyterian," he was elected a trustee in 1853 and Rector of the University in 1879, in which post he died in 1887.

Another prominent Virginian chosen a trustee in the fifties was the Reverend Joseph R. Wilson, pastor of the Presbyterian Church at Staunton, and father of Woodrow Wilson. But he moved to Augusta, Georgia, before qualifying to serve on the board.

The trustees thus briefly described may be cited as typical of the important members of the governing body during the late ante-bellum years, many of whom served for years after Appomattox, undoubtedly coloring the temper and policy of the institution far into the second half of the century.

AN ESPECIAL CONCERN of the trustees in every age is that of finances. The struggling Washington College barely maintained an existence during the thirties and forties despite occasional misleading newspaper accounts that declared it to be richly endowed. Of the early major financial gifts elsewhere recounted, not all yielded income immediately and some were delayed for years in being realized. Various devices were suggested to the trustees, some of them chimerical and others of the shoestring character.

In 1837 Joseph Morrison of Pennsylvania proposed to the president and trustees of Washington College that they unite with other American colleges and universities in a petition asking Congress to appropriate a township of public lands to each institution of higher learning in the country. Congress had set aside lands for such purposes in the new states, and Morrison's idea was to extend the practice to the colleges of the old states. Nothing came of his proposal nor of an effort in 1843 to join other Virginia Colleges in an application to the general assembly for pecuniary aid.

Washington College finances were somewhat improved during the forties by realization at last of the Cincinnati endowment. In June of 1849 invested funds totaled $97,776.17, of which the Cincinnati fund accounted for $22,976. The treasurer's report for the year closing at that time showed receipts of $10,730.60 and disbursements of $10,-235.41, leaving a black-ink balance of $495.19.

Early in President Junkin's administration an attempt was made to increase the College's income by a somewhat devious and complicated scheme for the sale of scholarships. It was apparently a countermove to an "invasion" by Hampden-Sydney of territory west of the Blue Ridge by selling scholarships in Montgomery and Winchester presbyteries. Dr. Junkin believed that area to be Washington College's preserve.

In the spring of 1849 the trustees agreed upon two classes of scholarships. The first allowed an individual, for a subscription of $80, to place one scholar in the College for twenty years, two for ten years, or otherwise in proportion. The second permitted an organization, such as Odd Fellows or a division of the Sons of Temperance, to establish a perpetual scholarship for $300. The plan was scheduled to get under way when 250 scholarships could be obtained, with the numerical ceiling fixed at 800!

The tuition fee at the time was $30. (It was raised to $40 in 1853–1854 and $50 in 1860–1861.) Thus twenty years of instruction were offered at the price of less than than three years' fees; and if a twenty-year scholarship were fully utilized it would provide only $4.00 per year to the College treasury.

When Henry Ruffner, in retirement, heard of the scheme he wrote to Professor George E. Dabney questioning such economics, and expressing the opinion that nobody who could pay $80 would enter a student without purchasing a scholarship. Perhaps, however, the canny Scotch-Irish inhabitants of the valley were wary about buying anything priced too cheap; for by 1859 the scholarship fund was officially stated to be very small. (Despite the lack of success in this venture, exigencies of post-bellum Washington College dictated a resumption of the sale of scholarships, with similarly disappointing results. As late as 1930 one lad presented coupons in his family's possession and was enabled to validate them.)

A clear, brief account of the College's finances in 1859 showed that revenues were derived from five main sources: (1) the Washington donation, then listed at $50,000; (2) the Cincinnati fund which sustained the Cincinnati Professor; (3) the John Robinson bequest; (4) the scholarship fund, admittedly meager; and (5) tuition and other college fees, of variable amounts, which were appropriated to the professors.

To COMPLETE THE PICTURE of old Washington College it is necessary to sketch the situation regarding the institution's relation to the Presbyterian Church. Enough has been written here to demonstrate that from its origins the College had been presided over by Presbyterian rectors, trustees, presidents, and professors. It had been attended largely by Presbyterian students, and the surrounding region remained populated by that denomination. The College rented pews in the Lexington Presbyterian Church for its students. Yet no explicit authority could be found in the charter of 1782, or in subsequent emendations of that document, vesting control in church courts. From this condition arose persistent controversy between those alumni and friends of the College who believed in de facto Presbyterian control and those, on the other hand, who pointed to the lack of legal authority for sectarian domination.

For example, a writer in the Lynchburg *Virginian* signing himself "A Baptist" sought in the spring of 1845 to present the merits of the College to the public and to deny that it was a Presbyterian school. He cited the legislative College of Washington Act of 1796, George Washington's benefaction, the Cincinnati donation, and churchless John Robinson's bequest as indicating the purpose of serving the public good without reference to religious sects. This "Baptist" calculated that money collected through Presbyterian influence did not exceed $12,000, while funds available from other sources surpassed $107,000.

In the course of his argument the "Baptist" quoted President Ruffner to the effect that Washington College was not and had not been a Presbyterian institution. Dr. Ruffner responded with "A Card to the Public" in which he sought to clarify his position. He pointed out that although the charter made no reference to a religious denomination, it did assign control to a board of trustees who were in fact mostly Presbyterians, and who had maintained a majority of Presbyterians in board and faculty. He declared however that peculiar Presbyterian doctrines were not propagated in the classrooms, no special privileges were permitted to Presbyterian students, and proselytizing of students was forbidden. Dr. Ruffner concluded: "All denominations may enjoy equally and indiscriminately the benefits of education, in this seminary without inconvenience on account of their ecclesiastical preferences, Washington College is not, and ought not to be, a Presbyterian institution." President Junkin, however, later took a strong Presbyterian stand, despite the expression by William Henry Ruffner, Professor G. D. Armstrong, and the Reverend William S. White of "opinions . . . to Dr. Junkin ag[ains]t propriety of declaring Washington College publicly a Presbyterian College."

In 1854 Judge John W. Brockenbrough, an Episcopalian on the Board of Trustees, sought to place the body on record as recognizing an obligation to consider the appointment of a faculty member on merit alone "without any reference to the question whether he is a Presbyterian, Episcopalian, Baptist, or Methodist." The Brockenbrough resolution was tabled. Five months later the trustees took it up again, but adopted substitute declarations denying the practice and disclaiming the principle of giving "an undue estimate to the peculiar religious views of candidates for professorships." The trustees proclaimed that "while the former history and present relations of the institution have rendered the employment of gentlemen in communion with the Presbyterian Church highly proper & agreeable to the community, they do not consider the Board bound to make selections of its professors exclusively from that Church."

Yet for the remainder of the ante-bellum period the Board selected only Presbyterian faculty members.

Presbyterianism was thus in complete de facto control at Washington College. It should be noted, however, that Jeffersonian liberal thought on religious matters, which may have induced advocates of sectarian institutions to be content with secular charters and policies before 1830, was generally supplanted by orthodoxy in Virginia during the forties and fifties. A writer in the Richmond *Mail* in 1854 pointed out that William and Mary College was headed by an Episcopal bishop, Hampden-Sydney and Randolph-Macon were well-known church colleges, while Bethany was "that seminarium of pure Campbellitism." The trend was evident even at the University of Virginia. A newspaper editor who visited Charlottesville in 1860 commented: "The University is now very flourishing, since it has gotten rid of the infidel Professors whom Mr. Jefferson took care to bring into it at first."

A glance at an eminent institution with whose history Washington and Lee's was often entwined suggests that Princeton faced the sectarian problem, and met it in much the same manner. Charges against Princeton were turned back with "indignant disclaimers." "Yet," continues Thomas J. Wertenbaker in his history of that university, "year after year, decade after decade, Presbyterian ministers constituted a majority in the board of trustees, leavened with a group of men distinguished in public life. . . ." The lay members were carefully scrutinized before appointment—the ideal Princeton trustee being "the Presbyterian giver."

Future storms over sectarianism lay ahead in the post-bellum era and in the early years of the twentieth century.

Chapter

X

Young America at College

IN AN EARLIER CHAPTER an account was presented of the life of the academy student, approximately up to the time of the War of 1812. As the transition from academy to College was largely nominal, in the years immediately following, the story appears to be much the same. Students were few, governed by two or three teachers including the president. By present-day standards life at old Washington College was hard, if not grim.

Student John Coles Rutherfoord of Richmond in 1840 wrote to his father John Rutherfoord (acting governor of Virginia 1841–1842) that he rose each morning at daylight. The regional historian Joseph Addison Waddell of Staunton later remembered "Professor Henry," the janitor, a free Negro who afterward went to Liberia, making daily rounds before dawn, rousing the students by blowing a tin horn. He recalled compulsory early-morning chapel services in a spacious, dimly lighted room, conducted by a professor who kept his hands in his pockets to avoid freezing. The dismal matutinal ordeal was relieved in 1849 when the time for chapel was set at 8:40, a schedule that was maintained until near the close of the century. Waddell recollected also compulsory Sunday afternoon Bible classes, one in English and one in Greek. The latter, in which the lads read a chapter of the New Testament, he described as "dull, uninteresting, and uninforming."

Minute regulations continued to govern conduct; and members of the faculty, headed by the president, acted as police officers, patrolling the grounds and inspecting students' quarters. In 1850 President Junkin distributed the supervision and inspection of the buildings among the faculty. Professor Philo Calhoun's employment of carpet slippers in the performance of his assignments and the contrasting use of heavy boots by Professor Benjamin S. Ewell became a campus legend.

It is problematical how the efforts to enforce stern discipline were reflected in educational attitudes and processes. Student William M. Willson of Brownsburg, Virginia, wrote his Aunt Lizzie in 1856 that at Washington College it was "study all the time without any cessation whatever." He was especially critical of Professor Fishburn who apparently sought to apply teaching principles he had learned in Germany, which Willson considered "too thorough to suit 'Young America.'" Fifteen years earlier young Rutherfoord had suffered a decline in health which his father attributed at least partly to the confining studies. Student Rutherfoord roomed and boarded with Mr. and Mrs. John W. Brockenbrough, friends of his father's. He found he could study better at the Brockenbroughs' than at the College, where idle boys circulated all day from room to room, "preventing those who are disposed to be studious from being so." The modern dormitory or fraternity house resident might find a familiar ring in Rutherfoord's plaint: "They never seem to think of knocking at your door, but in, they walk, throw themselves unceremoniously on your bed, and if you do not interfere, they will cut up your books, break your combs, and destroy or deface every thing they can lay their hands upon." As for the living quarters: "All the rooms I have seen, present the appearance of Dog-kennels—so defaced have they already become with Tobacco juice, mud, water-melon-seed, & &."

But Rutherfoord was an unusual student and his judgment of his less scholarly fellows may have been a bit severe. He was preparing to enter the University of Virginia to earn the M.A., then the highest degree conferred in America in academic fields. At least once he attained first place in all his studies. He enrolled in the Cincinnati class at V.M.I. and although the group drilled "a longer time than the regular cadets" he reported, "I begin to like it very much." He gave up the intention of receiving tutoring in mathematics from a V.M.I. professor, however, because he would have had to forgo his "evening recess," the only time students legitimately devoted to amusements. His Aunt Betsy had promised him a gold watch if he should resist the lure of tobacco; and after some months at college he boasted that he had "as yet learnt no such expensive habits of chewing and smoking."

Following the permissive interlude of the Marshall administration

the trustees again formulated a Draconian set of laws for the governance of the students, as rigorous as the former code. Of interest is
Chapter VIII of the *Rules, Regulations, etc. . . . . . of Washington
College* entitled "Of Religious Worship and Moral Conduct": "Every
student shall enjoy that right which is natural to all men, and which is
so fully guaranteed to its citizens by the laws of this state:—to worship
their Creator according to the dictates of their own consciences; and
all sectarian influence is hereby prohibited." Immediately following
this a provision stated that all students should attend prayers at the
College, morning and evening, and behave themselves while so doing.
Each student was required to attend divine services on the Sabbath,
and that day was to be observed in the puritanical sense. Students were
to abstain from participation in amusements and sports, and were to
"attend to such duties as the faculty may assign" them on Sundays.

Collegians must not "play at cards, dice, or any game of hazard,
make bets, be intoxicated, or be guilty of immoral conduct." The
young men were expressly forbidden to attend balls or dances of any
kind during the session. Another much-violated section prohibited the
possession or use of firearms or any kind of weapon in the vicinity of
the College. (Later this was altered to ten miles' distance.) Participation in a duel, either as principal, second, or in any manner whatsoever
would merit expulsion. Nor could a student visit "a tavern or tippling
house" without permission from a professor. (One may imagine how a
request for such approval would be received.) It also was unlawful for
the young men to transport or possess on the premises wine, ardent
spirits, or gunpowder; nor could a student living on campus "make any
entertainment" without permission from a faculty member. And the
youths were legally prevented from insulting, assaulting, and quarrel-
ing with one another, while "contumacy" and absences were to be
dealt with accordingly.

Chapter IX, "Of Punishments," asserted that the penalties were
moral, directed to the student's sense of duty, and to his principles of
honor and shame. The degrees were private reprehension, reprehension
before the faculty, admonition before the offender's class, then before
all students; suspension, dismissal, and expulsion. The faculty could
impose all save the last category which was the duty of the trustees.

The faculty supervised the boarding of students which, as we have
seen, was a fruitful source of trouble in the academy period. Times for
meals and recreation were fixed at one hour at breakfast, two at noon,
and two or three in the evening. "At all other hours they are required
to be in their rooms; unless specifically permitted by some member of

the Faculty to be absent. . . ." However, the hours on Saturdays and Sundays "when the students shall be required to keep their rooms, are left to the discretion of the Faculty."

With remarkable lack of psychological insight the president and professors attempted the enforcement of this stringent code, which by its character invited infractions. They were no more successful than their academy predecessors. Disciplinary cases dot the trustees' records and, after 1841, the faculty minutes. Although there was but one re-petition of an assault upon the president, such as Dr. Baxter had suffered in 1812, there were outbreaks of violence and willful disobedi-ence. Something of a riot occurred, for example, on October 15, 1816, significantly the night after examinations. The trustees found that cer-tain students had violated decorum and common propriety, and had been guilty of highly disorderly conduct "particularly intended as an expression of disrespect & contempt of the Trustees. . . ." All rioters were excluded from College until apologies were offered and pledges of future good behavior given.

In 1817 Professor Edward Graham wrote his son that the students were behaving themselves better than usual, and that potential mischief-makers were deterred by lack of leadership. He presented a different picture in 1825, however, in a communication to a local citizen who had interested himself in a case involving Richard T. Gibson of Georgia, the ward of his brother-in-law. Graham contended that dur-ing the previous two years "a considerable spirit of disorder manifested itself among the students. . . ." The faculty had been harassed by cumulative misdeeds, but had attributed most of them to "that thoughtless levity incident to youth," and had hoped for a change for the better. Instead, things became worse; and when the circuit court arrived at Lexington a large number of students, expecting a criminal prosecution against one or more of their number, retired to nearby woods and caves where they remained hidden for two days. The fac-ulty, reluctant to take action against all those involved, decided to make an example of "the chief culprit," whom they determined to be young Gibson. Graham declared that in addition to committing several minor offenses Gibson had been "a member of a drinking party at Hopkins' tavern & he was the person chiefly concerned in the grand bon-fire which was made of Mr. Moody's work-bench."

There were other examples of group action by students to protect their fellows or protest disciplinary action which they considered un-reasonable. The Lexington *Gazette* in 1837 related an incident that began when some students, "out of a mischievous spirit, barred the

Professors out of one of the Recitation Rooms." The faculty called the roll and required each student to "confess his guilt or aver his innocence. . . ." According to this account a majority of the young men, "with a manly spirit worthy of Virginians, peremptorily refused to answer the question put to them, upon the very plain and satisfactory ground, that no man is bound to criminate himself." The faculty ceased the inquisition, but asserted that they would repeat it and dismiss every student who refused to comply if other means failed to identify the guilty party in future cases of great criminality. The writer in the *Gazette* protested such use of power and declared that college discipline should "nourish the spirit of freedom, instead of breaking our young men to the yoke and preparing them for slaves. . . ." But the faculty of Washington College, like that of other institutions in America, was not ready for such advanced doctrine.

The *Gazette* in 1858 reported mass protest over the dismissal of two students who had been found intoxicated in a dormitory room. A petition requesting revocation of the penalty was signed by many collegians, but rejected by the faculty. A few days later, again on the night after the close of examinations, a large group of disguised students "boisterously" marched through the town. Returning to the College, they burned effigies of Professors Fishburn and Campbell, who had discovered the inebriated youths while investigating noise that was disturbing the examinations. Several students, after reflection, explained and apologized to the faculty. They had merely demonstrated against the official acts of the teachers and had not meant to insult them personally. The faculty unanimously resolved to dismiss all those known to have taken part in the demonstration, and next day the indicated action was taken against three offenders. Forty-five students then signed a statement implicating themselves in an offense for which only three had been punished, and declaring that if they were not sent away they would give the faculty other cause to dismiss them. Next a student committee of three expressed regret at their conduct and requested reinstatement of those dismissed. Meanwhile the rebellion had induced a number of collegians to absent themselves from classes, and twenty were dismissed for "*continued resistance*" to authority. Many of those sent off subsequently apologized and were restored.

The record sometimes leaves us wondering as to the seriousness of an incident or even its particular circumstances. In 1844, for instance, a "riot" broke out in College buildings. Two students were summarily dismissed. The penalty was severe but the number of culprits appears small for a riot. In the fifties a tug-of-war between faculty and students disturbed the institution.

For the most part the records indicate relatively minor infractions. A "rencontre" took place on Christmas Eve of 1825 between students George W. Mathews and John Breckinridge, who were suspended by the board but shortly afterward reinstated in "pledge" to abstain from "profane swearing, from intoxication, & from making any unnecessary noise. . . ." One may hope that the latter restriction was not too rigidly construed. Apparently the trustees were fearful of students' involvement in graver misdeeds, for through the late twenties they ordered the faculty to inform the collegians that a summons to the grand jury would be considered "a high offense and treated accordingly."

Even the liberal regime of Dr. Marshall experienced student outbreaks. Thomas Massie of Nelson County described an episode in August of 1831 of the kind afterward called a "calathump": "A party of students went out the other knight [sic], and played on some quills, tinpans, & some other noisy instruments, & made but a very little noise. The next day they were called up about it & two of them were sent off from College, & I would not be at all surprised, if they were to send away some more of them because they have had Prayer meetings five or six times for the students & . . . because they could not convert any of them, they will send them off . . . for little or nothing."

IN THE FORTIES, after the faculty had superseded the trustees as the high court of justice, the professors assembled weekly for the dreary task of going over their rolls and meting out punishment. Drinking, disorderly conduct, attending a circus, remaining on House Mountain "without leave," and various petty delinquencies were among the crimes alleged. Malefactors included scions of some well-known Lexington and Virginia families. It did not seem to mean much in those days *who* one was, so far as the Washington College faculty was concerned. Trustees' sons, and even the president's own son William Henry Ruffner, were subjected to disciplinary action. The minutes of April 2, 1841, record that Dr. Ruffner retired "from motives of delicacy" when his son's case came up. The faculty members "examined, & reprimanded William H. Ruffner and Alexander McN. Glasgow for a fight which took place within the College buildings some nights before." Young Ruffner, afterward one of Virginia's most distinguished educators, was placed on probation for a month. Shortly thereafter he was again in difficulty because of absences.

A number of these young men were in trouble from time to time because of their penchant for bringing firearms into college. Alexander McN. Glasgow was dismissed by the faculty in 1841 for "participation in firing a large cracker at college," but was readmitted within a few weeks. James Bruce McClelland was placed "on special probation" for throwing a brickbat against the door of a room in which the faculty was meeting.

During the fifties, reviewing the status of students, the professors found time for some remarkably petty details. In 1850, for example, they ordered George A. Baxter to remove his dog, as a College rule forbade canines on campus. The faculty could be gracious on occasion, though, as in May of 1853 when they granted permission for the students to have "a party" at commencement—on condition that there would be "no 'liquor' & no dancing."

Despite the harshness of the penalties, the rules were violated not only often but sometimes with little or no attempt at concealment. A letter from David E. Moore in 1817 told of his having attended "frolicks" the two previous nights. Nancy Graham wrote her brother in 1818 that "a great dancing party" had been staged, but the boys could persuade only about a dozen ladies to attend, and those newcomers. In 1840 John Coles Rutherfoord wrote of the pleasure he found in hunting partridges with his dog Byron. As he lived in a private residence, the ban on guns and dogs may not have applied to him; or maybe this model student just took the same cavalier attitude toward the restrictions that his classmates did. The puritanical laws remained in effect in the fifties, though they were not well enforced. The military-minded Professor D. H. Hill believed the solution to problems of student conduct lay in sterner discipline and effective enforcement.

There is no reason to believe that Washington College students acted much differently from their contemporaries at other institutions, and perhaps they did not go to the extremes reached on some campuses. The University of Virginia had its riots or near-riots, one involving the killing of a professor. In 1854 a V.M.I. cadet was killed by a student of the Lexington Law School. A Washington College student, William G. Booker, was shot and killed on April 1, 1856; but the faculty understood the circumstances as accidental and no disciplinary action was taken.

As PREVIOUSLY OBSERVED, infractions of rules become matters of record while observances seldom receive formal notice. Yet despite sporadic rowdyism and some chronic recalcitrance, Washington College students could display and even promote propriety and decorum. In 1842 John H. McCue informed his friend John Coles Rutherfoord, who had transferred to the University of Virginia, that students at the College had "succeeded in raising one of the greatest temperance Societies that you have ever heard of. Between 50 & 60 students signed the Temperance pledge." McCue added complacently: "Such an institution will be of inestimable value to Old Was [sic] College which was once branded with the stain of intemperance." He described the effect of the organization as "wonderful"—he had not seen even one intoxicated student since the creation of the group. In 1849 "The Temperance Crusaders" held a celebration. A procession formed at the College and marched to the Presbyterian church, where the Reverend J. McKendree Riley spoke. The *Valley Star* was "pleased to know that the order embraces nearly all the Students." A "reading room" was set aside in the center building for the Crusaders. In his annual report of 1850 President Junkin commended the organization and remarked on the sobriety of the students. The use of profanity by collegians, of which he had complained in 1850, by 1857 had been almost "abrogated," along with card playing. But virtue's triumph was not complete, for Dr. Junkin mentioned incidents of drunkenness, some of the offenders being sons of trustees or members of other prominent Virginia families.

Student letters contain only scattered references to basic principles or major issues, so that a pattern of attitudes is difficult to reconstruct from these sources. There is little mention of politics, although debates in the literary societies indicated an alertness of public affairs. Student sentiment seems to have veered somewhat to the Democrats in the fifties, while the faculty remained staunchly Whig. In 1817 John F. Caruthers complained that the students were "very Corrupt in their religious principles." The following year David Moore, who had been reading Hume's *History of England*, expressed disgust with "the continual disputes between the religious sects & between the Pope & King the superstition & religious fanaticism that so completely clouded the minds of the human race in those ages of darkness & ignorance," and "most universal contempt for all religious sects whatever for it has always been my oppinion that any subject which is liable to so many changes & schisms as religion has, must be built upon a rotten foundation."

As American college students during the ante-bellum period aspired more and more to careers in lay professions, especially the law, and a smaller percentage looked toward the ministry, it is likely that interest in religious doctrine subsided. We have noted Joseph Waddell's reminiscence of boredom in the Sunday afternoon Bible class. On one occasion the students absented themselves from that class en masse, giving the excuse that they had assumed they were relieved from attendance because preaching was scheduled in the Baptist church.

Under such circumstances compulsory chapel attendance must have become irksome, and in later years it was made voluntary.

AMERICAN COLLEGE FRATERNITIES were founded as early as the 1820's and proliferated in the forties, but they did not reach Washington College until 1855. Their existence became known publicly when the Lexington *Gazette* commented on their activities in the late spring of 1857. The "Annual Symposium" of the Phi Kappa Psi, held at "the Lexington House," was an entertainment of "unusual elegance," attended by members from a distance. "We learn that handsome speeches were made, toasts drank, &c.," the *Gazette* continued, "and from the continued popping of champagne which came upon the night breeze" the editors' mouths were made to water. A few days before, the "Beta, Theta, Pi Society," established in 1856, had held its "anniversary supper at the Exchange Hotel. . . ."

Dr. Junkin took notice of the "secret societies" in his annual report of 1857. He observed that they wound up the year with a "Symposium"—"a drinking festival" in violation of several College laws. (The students contended that by holding their meetings outside College buildings they evaded the law.) President Junkin found that in other institutions fraternities had "produced most disastrous consequences." The secret ties overrode all others, those to the college, to literary societies, and classmate friendships. He conceded that they had not done much harm thus far at Washington College; but he felt they would "undermine" college government and he wished to "exclude these excrescences" altogether.

Having heard these words, the trustees solemnly resolved that "no student of this College shall be permitted to hold a connexion with any Society whose character is not approved by the Faculty." But there is no evidence that the order of the board was obeyed. Indeed, Howard McCutchan told "Bill" Willson in October of 1859 that a new secret society had been initiated, called the Delta Delta. The coming of the Civil War terminated fraternity activities at Washington College, but in the enlarged enrollment of General Lee's years they were resumed and multiplied.

ANOTHER INCHOATE EXTRACURRICULAR ACTIVITY of the period was collegiate journalism. The first ephemeral venture into this field was the *College Omnibus*. A prospectus appeared in the Lexington *Gazette* in March of 1847 and shortly afterward one or two numbers were printed. An "Ode to the Moon" and a dismissal interview with President Ruffner were among the items in the *Omnibus*.

More sensational was the first (and last) issue of *The Wreath*, published March 18, 1848, with the slogan "The Dew Drops of Genius Sparkle on our Wreath." Appearing thus in the midst of the "Skinner War," one article signed "Stayrographus" poured ridicule upon faculty members, "most noble *Festuses*." The writer warned the beardless youths to support their professors, right or wrong, and eschew Skinner and all his works. With heavy satire, students were enjoined to praise the philanthropy of the "most noble trustees," and to "swear that all Professors' sermons are strictly *Orthodox* and evangelical." If students followed the *ipse dixit* of the *"powers that be,"* they would have no fear of "Greek Roots and Chemical Analyses." The "good boys" would receive the patronizing smiles of the *"great big men"* and young ladies of the town, and the "special favor and patronage of the *elderly* maiden Ladies, (rather numerous 'tis true—but bless their souls very influential with the powers that be). . . ."

Other material in the *Wreath* was sophomoric enough, essays on patriotism, references to the glories of the Mexican War, and poems to young women. But a letter in dialect, "To the Revrind Henry Ruffner D. D. Doctor of Divinity and President of Washington Colledg," wounded the faculty. This crude article chided Dr. Ruffner for his famous pamphlet on slavery, alluded to suggestions that he resign, but advised him to ignore the critics and hold on; for possibly now that the trustees had secured the "Sinsinnaty" fund they would raise his salary —because, after all, "the salary's the thing. . . ."

Faculty reaction was swift but surprisingly mild. Resolutions by Professor George D. Armstrong calling for severe disciplinary action was tabled. Student Samuel Augustus Merritt, soon to receive the A.B. degree, afterward a member of the California legislature and a member of Congress from Utah, admitted authorship of the first offensive article, offering a complete and acceptable apology. Charles H. Stewart, valedictorian of the class of 1848; Madison S. Crockett, subsequently a Virginia legislator and editor; and Samuel Houston Letcher, later a lawyer, editor, and Confederate officer, stated in writing that they had made "every possible exertion" to discover the author of the letter to Dr. Ruffner. They assumed the responsibility themselves. This the faculty agreed to accept, at the same time advising the discontinuation of *The Wreath*. With the passing of that journal no student publication appeared until after the Civil War, when the *Southern Collegian* was founded.

A PROFOUND INFLUENCE in the life of Washington College students was exerted by the literary and debating societies, of which there were two—the Graham Philanthropic Society and the Washington Literary Society. These groups did much to fill the gaps in the curriculum in the areas of literature and social sciences. They maintained libraries and sponsored prominent speakers, but their most significant activity was the weekly debate session—from 9 A.M. to 1 P.M. on Saturdays during most of the ante-bellum period. From the War of 1812, through the Mexican and Civil Wars, through Reconstruction and indeed to World War I and beyond, students thrashed out in society halls the foremost national, state, and local issues. The organizations also served social purposes. They resembled fraternities in some respects and their public functions drew attendance from the elite of the community.

As early as the last decade of the eighteenth century some sort of literary or debating society had existed in the academy, as well as in town. A "Union Society" had preceded the establishment of the better-known Franklin Society in Lexington, and these provided models for the organizations which emerged at Washington Academy.

The Graham Philanthropic Society was founded in 1809, according to conclusive evidence, although it was not until the spring of 1810 that John D. Paxton, on behalf of the society, officially apprised the trustees of its existence. Paxton identified the "express purpose" of the "Institution" as "Improvement in literature." Toward that end the members had set aside a fund for the purchase of books; and one day of each week during the session had been appointed for the discussion of morals, politics, literature, and other subjects.

A letter dated in 1810 mentions a "rival" of the Graham. Though it is not known to what group this referred, it is likely to have been the Washington Literary Society which was organized in 1812, adopting a constitution and detailed rules of procedure and conduct in 1814.

Although the two societies cooperated often, they competed for members and prestige somewhat after the manner of social fraternities. A student could belong to only one. According to John Coles Rutherfoord, upon affiliation "you take an oath, never to divulge to a member of the other Society, any of the proceedings of that Society to which you belong." As professors and other nonmembers appear to have been commonly present at meetings, it is uncertain what the oath of secrecy covered. It also is unclear whether membership was open to any interested student or was available only by election. At any rate, not all students belonged to a society.

At each meeting the question for debate at the next meeting was decided upon and the participants chosen. Fines were assessed against members for failure to speak when assigned to do so, for violation of the constitution, and for other transgressions. In the early Washington Society seven debaters on each side were appointed, and at the conclusion of the debate the house voted. The earliest debate topic of that society of which we have record was that of March 6, 1814: "Whether it was more advantageous 'for a young man to read Ancient or Modern History first.'" As may be expected, the upholders of the prior study of classical history won a resounding victory, by a vote of 11 to 1.

Sometimes the young intellectual gladiators chose topics of interest to their future lives, such as whether the married state was more conducive to happiness than single blessedness. At other times ethical problems were discussed; and interspersed with these were historical questions such as the fate of Mary Queen of Scots, and of phases of Napoleon's career. But more frequently debates dealt with state, local, or national issues. Among them were the suffrage in Virginia, internal improvement in state and nation, and the Bank of the United States. Subjects before the Washington Society in 1848 included: "Does prevalence of the Catholic faith tend to the Subversion of Republicanism?"—doubtless a reflection of the nativist sentiment of the forties; and "Is the War with Mexico just and politic?"—a question then agitating partisans while Generals Scott and Taylor fought on Mexican soil, and one that historians have not answered after more than a hundred years.

With increasing frequency in the late forties and the fifties the societies debated on slavery and related matters. On May 13, 1848, the proposition: "Would it be politic to emancipate the slaves of the United States?" was rejected 14 to 5. Mindful of the significance of the large territorial acquisitions through the Mexican War and the Treaty of Guadalupe Hidalgo, the young debaters discussed: "Has Congress the right to legislate on the subject of Slavery in the Territories?" On April 28, 1849, they considered: "Is it probable that the abolition question will at some future day cause a dissolution of the Union?" and later in the year: "Is slavery consistent with religion and morality?"

That the young gentlemen were in touch with other domestic and foreign issues of the epoch is apparent from the debate subjects of the fifties. The "late" revolutions in Europe, the matter of "European intervention in the political affairs of the Western Continent" (the Monroe Doctrine had not yet been clearly defined), indicate that foreign policy was not neglected. The Lexington *Gazette* noted William H. Baylor's allusion to unfortunate, fallen Hungary in his Graham P. Anniversary address of 1850, performed in "a touching and eloquent style." The Washington debaters in the spring of 1852 argued: "If France, Russia, and Austria should combine against England, would it be good policy for the United States to assist her?"—a question which indicates that even then American isolation was a debatable matter.

Other topics included territorial annexation (with special reference to Cuba); moral and economic aspects of slavery; immigration and naturalization laws (during the years 1853–1855 when Know-Nothingism raged); colonization of Negroes; the Brooks-Sumner brawl in Congress; the possible election of John C. Frémont to the Presidency as a potential cause of Southern secession; the Pacific railroad; the Kansas issue; the John Brown raid; the dismemberment of the Democratic party (March, 1860); and, of course, in 1860–1861, the momentous issues of Virginia's attitude toward secession.

ALUMNI, faculty members, and townsmen attended the literary society meetings as participants in their proceedings. On special occasions alumni or public figures addressed the societies. Thus E. C. Burks delivered an oration in commemoration of President Harrison before the Graham P. on May 14, 1841. Burks eloquently depicted the impact upon the tranquil village when, on April 6, the stagecoach reached it with the "melancholy intelligence" of the President's death. Burks extolled Harrison, a native Virginian, voiced a paean to the state, and warned students that the older generation was passing. They would soon be on the stage themselves, and he earnestly hoped they would acquit themselves well. During the forties James B. Dorman frequented the halls of the Graham P. Society, recording his impressions in his diary. On September 7, 1842, he heard an extemporaneous address by Senator William C. Preston of South Carolina, which contained good advice to youth. "Never before did I see such eloquence, wisdom and vivacity conjoined. . . ." On Washington's Birthday, 1847, he listened to a discourse by F. W. Gilmer and various talks by students on the theme "Whether Virginia is upon the decline." Among other speakers were Professor George E. Dabney, future governor "Honest John" Letcher, and Dorman himself.

Many Virginians of the period seem to have been disturbed over the question of their state's decline. As early as April, 1826, John A. Smith of Lunenburg County delivered a critique of Virginia in the Hall of Washington College. Deploring the retrogression of his state he predicted that unless the legislature did something for the valley and western Virginia, the commonwealth would be divided. In June of 1850 John R. Thompson, editor of the *Southern Literary Messenger*, spoke to the societies on the topic "Education and Literature in Virginia." The young men were treated to a searching criticism of the state's decline in influence as well as its feeble literary productions. He explained the latter by the widespread "morbid desire for political eminence," which was the greatest evil ever to curse the commonwealth. Thompson declared that this must be checked. He denounced northern newspapers and periodicals, tainted as they were with abolitionism. The young men at Washington College were challenged to produce a literature of the South's own, "informed with the conservative spirit, the love of order and justice, that constitutes the most striking characteristic of the southern mind."

Especially poignant in the light of later events was the development of this theme by student Alfred H. Jackson of Weston, Virginia, in the valedictory address at commencement in 1857. Everywhere, he declared, one heard of Virginia's deterioration—in wealth, population, and civilization. Men had come to believe it because of repeated assertion; but Jackson vigorously dissented. He urged his classmates not to "go west." The commonwealth needed new Jeffersons, Randolphs, and Henrys: let the members of the class of 1857 remain in the state to aid its growth. The young gentleman from western Virginia then gazed clearly into the crystal ball: "And remember, that if it ever comes to pass that the difficulties between the North and the South are to be settled by the sword, this will be the battleground; so, if you are patriotically inclined, you can have an opportunity of dying for the rights of the South, not in Kansas—but in Virginia. . . ."

Colonel Alfred H. Jackson, C.S.A., died August 2, 1863, from wounds received in battle.

Special celebrations of the literary societies were prominent events for the College and for Lexington. According to one account, the Graham P. Society for some years commemorated December 19, the birthday of the Reverend William Graham, for whom the group was named; but for reasons of schedule convenience shifted to January 19, a date made doubly appropriate when General R. E. Lee's name was added to that of Graham in the society's title. George Washington's Birthday became the anniversary of the organization bearing his name. The two society anniversaries were observed in formal fashion and were eagerly anticipated as opportunities for breaking the tedium of the long collegiate year.

The fact that Washington's Birthday was honored throughout the College and the land caused the date to be perhaps the highlight of the year. In the morning a parade moved from the College to the Presbyterian church, where orators from each of the societies declaimed and debated. In the procession were the College faculty, the trustees, members of the literary societies, the faculty and cadets of the Virginia Military Institute, the young ladies of the Ann Smith Academy, townspeople, and "strangers." At night the Washington Society Hall (after the construction of the Washington College building in 1826), "brilliantly" illuminated with candles, accommodated the "youth and beauty of the town," who assembled to listen and to cheer on their favorites among the speakers of the Washington Literary Society exercises. In the audience on such occasions were the belles of Lexington and the fair pupils of the Ann Smith Academy. Present at the Washington celebration of 1860 (and perhaps at those for some years before) was Thomas J. Jackson, Professor of Natural History at V.M.I.

Rivaling Washington's Birthday as an event at the College was the annual celebration of the literary societies at commencement, which before the Civil War came in July. Though the exact practice varied, usually the combined organizations were addressed by distinguished professional men or political figures, whose effusions were often printed in pamphlet form.

One may follow through these literary society debates and addresses the political and social history of the United States and of Virginia. Whatever judgment may be held of the classical curriculum at Washington College and elsewhere, it is obvious that the students received in the literary societies a broad acquaintance with the contemporary world. There can be no doubt that their education in such sweeping yet inadequate courses as Mental and Moral Philosophy was inevitably supplemented by their participation in literary society work.

The meetings of the societies were interrupted in April of 1861, to be resumed sporadically during the war. It was not until the R. E. Lee era, however, that, sharing the new prosperity of Washington College, the Washington Literary Society and the Graham Philanthropic Society enjoyed renewed efflorescence. In subsequent pages we shall examine the later history and eventual decline of literary societies at Washington and Lee.

In the Shadow
of Irrepressible Conflict

IN THE SUMMER OF 1848 the trustees faced the problem of replacing the controversial President Henry Ruffner, whose resignation had ended a turbulent regime. The Lexington *Valley Star* had predicted difficulty in finding a distinguished man to head the College which had been so beset by dissension and criticism.

At its August meeting the board elected the famous William Holmes McGuffey, professor of moral philosophy at the University of Virginia, to the presidency of Washington College. Dr. McGuffey, a clergyman, "a Presbyterian of the straitest sect," a noted exponent of total abstinence from alcohol, and a man whose presence in the University of Virginia faculty exemplified a departure from Jeffersonian ideals in higher education, is best known to posterity as the prolific author of school readers whose moral maxims influenced the minds of several generations of Americans. Dr. McGuffey, however, decided to remain at Charlottesville "from a conviction of duty."

THE TRUSTEES next offered the post to Dr. George Junkin, also a Presbyterian clergyman, founder and president of Lafayette College and former president of Miami University at Oxford, Ohio. Dr. Junkin accepted the call and thus refuted the *Valley Star*'s prognostication. Certainly no previous head of the institution had attained such eminence in education before coming to Lexington.

Dr. Junkin's decision was prompted largely, perhaps primarily, by circumstances that represented an antithesis to the experience of his immediate predecessor. Whereas Dr. Ruffner's opposition to slavery had been a principal factor in his abdication and departure westward, Dr. Junkin had incurred troubles in Ohio and Pennsylvania for his advocacy of the peculiar institution.

But the new President was as stoutly pro-Union as the previous one. And although Unionism was acceptable in western Virginia in 1848, Dr. Junkin's persistence in that doctrine was to bring turmoil to the closing months of his administration, ending in his resignation and precipitate flight back to Pennsylvania.

George Junkin was born in 1790 in Pennsylvania of Scotch-Irish descent. His father had come to America in 1756 and had served with Lafayette at Brandywine. Young George received his academic education at Jefferson College, Canonsburg, Pennsylvania, and studied theology in New York with Dr. John M. Mason, one of the country's great pulpit orators. According to a family source "he became a teacher in the first Sunday School ever established in that city." As a pastor he settled in central Pennsylvania where his activity resulted in the establishment of pioneer temperance societies and Sunday schools, a journal called *The Religious Farmer*, and the founding of a classical academy which was one of the best-known schools of its period. Junkin was active in the earliest efforts for a public school system in Pennsylvania, spending much time in Harrisburg promoting the campaign. When this fight was won he established the first normal school in the state.

In 1830 George Junkin assumed charge of an academy in the Philadelphia suburb of Germantown. This school's activities were removed to Lafayette College, at Easton, which existed on paper only. Dr. Junkin became first president of the college and brought it into being as a functioning institution. He was especially interested in training young men for the gospel ministry and missionary work. Among his protégés were missionaries to India and Hawaii.

From 1841 to 1844 he was president of Miami University "where he was thrown into the whirl of the abolition storm. . . ." He delivered a formidable defense of slavery before the Synod of Cincinnati which John C. Calhoun, the paladin of Southern rights, declared the finest pro-slavery argument he had seen. That comment is significant not only because of its source but because the published portion of Junkin's presentation, which Calhoun had read, dealt only with Biblical arguments and covered just a fraction of Junkin's eight-hour delivery. The entire speech contained a slashing attack on the abolitionists, an examination of slavery in view of political philosophy and moral and municipal law, and warm endorsement of the "Divine plan" of African colonization.

Because of the intensity of this controversy Dr. Junkin returned to Lafayette College as president. But difficulties developed there and he was induced by Dr. Archibald Alexander, the Princeton divine and former pupil of William Graham, to accept the call to Washington College. A half century after his days at Liberty Hall Dr. Alexander retained an active interest in his alma mater.

At the age of fifty-eight, rather beyond the usual point for beginning a college presidency, Dr. Junkin faced the task of infusing energy into an old institution and harmonizing discordant elements among townsmen and alumni. He plunged zealously into the educational, religious, and civic activities of his new home community. Following in Dr. Ruffner's footsteps and continuing his own earlier efforts he earnestly advocated a public school system in Virginia. He fitted easily into such organizations as the Rockbridge Bible Society, the Temperance Society, the Franklin Society, and the local Colonization Society. Often called upon to occupy the Lexington Presbyterian Church's pulpit, he regularly preached at Ben Salem and other rural churches. An unsympathetic hearer of his preaching recorded in his diary that although Dr. Junkin had a strong, philosophical mentality there was ". . . too much *mimicry*, want of dignity. . . . [he] sometimes screams out of his falsetto voice. . . ."

Dr. Junkin was a man of decided opinions and strong convictions. His Unionism was as fervent as his religious ardor and his belief in slavery. A revealing summation of his views was contained in an address at Rutgers College in July of 1856 in the presence of the governor of New Jersey. His remarks were extensively reported in the Lexington *Gazette*, indicating the adherence to such ideas in the valley just five years before First Manassas.

The speaker drove home his point that union was the basic cause and essential of American character, greatness, and glories to come. "In 1790 we became one people." The United States government was the "fruit of the Divine skill . . . ," in which were "enshrined the hopes of bleeding, groaning humanity." This *"chef d'oeuvre* of the Almighty Architect" should not be torn to shreds. "The master idea of every American head and heart, is union—and it was never deeper seated than in this distracted hour. Who wants to dissolve the Union?"

Dr. Junkin cleaved to the doctrine of "manifest destiny" in extreme terms. He foresaw the expansion of the country from the equator to the North Pole. He "thought it likely that Americans should be compelled, by the law of charity to throw the broad folds of the stars and stripes over the poverty-stricken and priest-ridden republics on their Southern borders, to protect them from themselves and from suicide." He predicted that Great Britain eventually would call upon the United States to save her from despotic Continental foes, flinging "her American possessions, and perhaps herself, too, under our protection." Subsequent history has shown that although Dr. Junkin's crystal ball was a bit clouded, it was not opaque.

Dr. Junkin forecast the obeisance of all nations to the United States. With our resources, our mechanical advances, our predominance in merchant marine ("The Pacific trade we cannot . . . avoid monopolizing"), and our "perfect religious liberty and missionary zeal," we were thus early prepared to assume world leadership.

But all this grand future depended upon the maintenance of America's position through preservation of the Union; and for that a solution of the slavery problem was necessary. The solution lay in African colonization. Dr. Junkin saw God's design in bringing three million Negroes to America where, he declared, they had attained a higher civilization than that of France! Surely He did not intend these people as an instrument "to tear down the temple of liberty and extinguish the hopes of the world." Rather they should be returned to Africa, to convert that continent to Christianity and civilization. Dr. Junkin urged that every state request Congress to propose a Constitutional amendment authorizing Congress to appropriate five million dollars annually for removal to Africa of such Negroes as were or should become willing to go. The process must be initiated in the Southern states. Denying power over slavery to the national government, he would leave the matter to individual consciences. This plan "would free a half million Negroes from real bondage—would civilize untold millions in the forests of Africa—would save the Union."

While Northern abolitionists and Southern ultras would surely have rejected such proposals, if indeed they ever heard of them, one may be sure at least that students in Dr. Junkin's Moral and Mental Philosophy courses at Washington College heard these sometimes unorthodox sentiments.

Another dissent from general opinion was expressed in an address at Franklin Hall in 1855, advocating abolition of usury laws. Such legislation, Dr. Junkin averred, tended to eliminate honest men from the business of money-lending, oppressed small capitalists, created a monied aristocracy, and forced capital from the state. It was a denial of man's rights to prevent him from getting as much as he could for his money.

Junkin's outspokenness was demonstrated at his first public appearance in Lexington, in his inaugural address on Washington's Birthday, 1849. With his subject "Christianity the Patron of Literature" he expounded the doctrine that schools were religious institutions and his inauguration was a religious ceremony. In support of his thesis he invoked writings of eminent American jurists, Chief Justice John Marshall and Associate Justice Joseph Story of the United States Supreme Court and Chief Justice James Kent of the New York Supreme Court. Since the fourth century A.D., he declared, "it was the Church that, in the face of persecution, reared aloft these beacon lights [schools] to guide the nations through the darkness of time." He pointed out that most American colleges had been established by religious authority, and drew the inferences "That college government must, necessarily, be the same in substance as church government;" and that "the Bible must occupy the foreground in every prosperous college." The watchword of the College must be, he concluded, *"The sword of the Lord, and of Washington."* Thus he took a firm stand in the running controversy over the question whether the College was or ought to be Presbyterian.

Despite the misgivings of a few observers Dr. Junkin managed the College's affairs in such a way that only sporadic criticism was heard prior to 1853. The institution thereafter proceeded on an unspectacular course. Nevertheless, the revival and intensification of the sectional-slavery dispute after 1854 was occasionally reflected in the concerns of the College.

WASHINGTON COLLEGE, as judged by its trustees, faculty, and president, was predominantly pro-Whig (or American or Constitutional Unionist), was moderate in regard to the sectional controversy, mildly pro-slavery, and vigorously pro-Union. In general, however, abolitionists were abhorred and condemned, and members of the faculty, including the president, were slaveholders.

Meanwhile, the attendance of Southern students at Eastern colleges was drawing criticism. A resolution adopted at a Southern-rights meeting at Buckingham Courthouse, Virginia, in 1854 called upon the people "to patronize, in preference to all others, our State Literary institutions. . . ." Taking favorable notice of this resolve the Lexington *Gazette* complained that Southern students had suffered indignities and discrimination at Eastern colleges, including dismissal for defending the practices of their home states. The *Gazette* expressed fear of "the destructive *isms*" to be encountered in the East, and criticized Southerners who believed their sons must leave the region to obtain a good education.

Repression of expression by colleges was by no means one-sided. In 1855 the Reverend W. J. Baird arrived in Lexington to lecture the students on the topic "Europe," which hardly seemed germane to the slavery issue. But the faculty learned that Dr. Baird had been one of the signers of a petition to Congress against passage of the Kansas-Nebraska bill which established the doctrines of popular sovereignty and federal non-intervention in the territories. In an informal meeting the faculty condemned any "combination of Clergy for political purposes," and "as Southern men, administering the affairs of a Southern Institution" forbade the students to attend the Baird lectures and declined the use of the chapel for Dr. Baird's appearance. Some days later the faculty heard that "the imputation of abolitionism against Dr. Baird . . . is without foundation."

Despite this incident a measure of intellectual freedom obtained at Washington College throughout the fifties, especially in the literary societies, which debated every issue of importance in national, state, and local life, including slavery. Yet as the decade waned increasing pressure came to be exerted on colleges to eliminate books and professors considered dangerous. The Lexington *Gazette* in 1857 noted with approval that the trustees of Mississippi College had unanimously condemned the teachings of Francis Wayland in his *Moral Science,* and had requested the faculty to discontinue using the book as a text. The newspaper observed complacently that Dr. Junkin had long since discarded the volume "which abounds in heresies, and is especially worthy of the unqualified condemnation of the South, since it is deeply tainted with abolition sentiments and sophistry." The *Gazette* called Dr. Junkin "the loyal advocate of Southern interests and rights."

A highly favorable opinion of Dr. Junkin's teaching was expressed in a letter by student William M. Willson in March of 1859:

> We are studying the Constitution of the U.S. with old Doc. now. He makes it more interesting than anything we have had with him yet. The way he does pitch into the politicians is a caution to every one, especially the Democrats. He just dissects them atom by atom and scatters them to the four winds. He would make a noble President. I believe I will nominate him for 1860.

Dr. Junkin was even briefly cast in the role of near martyr to the Southern cause. In another letter written in the same month Willson related a plot to poison the Junkin family by putting arsenic in their milk. Members of the family became violently ill. The Junkin cook, Fanny, was implicated and tried before the mayor. Throughout the ante-bellum period Southerners were disturbed from time to time by real or imagined attempts at poisoning, arson, or servile uprisings. Southern-rights newspapers exploited such reports to demonstrate the depravity of the abolitionists who were blamed for instigating the schemes. The Junkin incident was not mentioned in the local press although notice of it appeared in the Richmond *Dispatch*. In the absence of more conclusive evidence the actual circumstances cannot be determined.

THE SESSION 1860–1861 opened as usual, with prospects excellent. Professor John Lyle Campbell was preparing for "a grand 'Semi-Centenary Rally' " of alumni at commencement of 1861, which he placed "within a few months of the 50th anniversary of the organization of the Institution into *College proper*, as 'Washington College.' " His planning seems to have been a bit premature as the designation of college was made in 1813.

Also during 1860–1861 Dr. Junkin filled many columns of the Lexington *Gazette* with a series of economic articles. In these he espoused the economic ideas of Henry C. Carey, from whose *Examples of Social Science* he often quoted, interlarding them with explanatory comments of his own. Carey's book provided material for an attack on "the radical unsoundness, tyranny, and oppression of the British trade system—falsely called *free*," together with support for an American protective tariff. These ideas placed Dr. Junkin in that wing of the Bell-Everett (Constitutional Union) party whose economic views coincided with those of the Republicans. When young Milton Wylie Humphreys arrived in Lexington to enter Washington College in the fall of 1860 he was impressed by "an immense flag-pole with an enormous flag on it bearing the legend 'Bell and Everett.' " The prominent position of the flagpole symbolized political sentiment in Lexington and Rockbridge County. It seems safe to say that President Junkin and his faculty voted for Bell, candidate of conservatism and compromise, who carried Virginia and two other border slave states in the presidential election.

THUS UP TO AND INCLUDING THE ELECTION OF 1860 the president and faculty of the College acted in harmony with the overwhelming majority of Rockbridge County and, indeed, in accord with dominant opinion in Virginia. Lincoln's victory was distasteful to nearly all and abhorrent to many Virginians. Yet the state showed no disposition to follow South Carolina's lead in secession, and probably a majority hoped for a satisfactory adjustment that would hold the Union intact.

But the crisis and uncertainty were felt in Lexington and the College, as they were throughout the slave states. As emotions rose, divisions that had appeared only as differences of opinion came to be viewed in terms of good and evil. Student Humphreys, a western Virginian "bitterly opposed" to secession and with "a great pride in my country," wrote in his memoirs of attending political rallies at which the speeches were invariably pro-Union. After the election a series of mass meetings were held in the courthouse, concerned with the course of the Old Dominion in the event of failure of compromise, and with the question of calling a state convention.

One of Judge John W. Brockenbrough's law students years afterward recreated a picture of Dr. Junkin addressing a mixed audience of citizens and students. ". . . the queer figure (he always wore a pigeon-tailed coat), the exact image of the title page of the London 'Punch,' and in the face of jeers, catcalls and hisses of the students defiantly shouted in his shrill, squeaking voice the hated word 'Union'. . . ." Professor James J. White described a "pow-wow" at the courthouse in January which lasted for several hours, winding up in "a regular Tammany row." Dr. Junkin was among the speakers, as were Judge Brockenbrough and Colonel James W. Massie, the principal champions of Southern rights in the community.

Dr. Junkin's anxiety over the impending breach is illustrated by two public letters he wrote during this period. The first was addressed to Governor-elect Curtin of Pennsylvania on December 12, 1860, under the title "A Voice from a Pennsylvanian in the Heart of Virginia." He opposed secession on the one hand but urged his native state to co-operate in the enforcement of federal fugitive slave laws. He declared that the fire-eaters of the lower South used "personal liberty laws" as a pretext for secession. These were statutes that a number of free states had adopted to prevent the recovery of runaway slaves.

In his second letter, dated January 8, 1861, and printed in the *Gazette*, he sought to clarify the position of Pennsylvania. He used copious extracts from a recent message of Governor Packer which, he believed, proved the fallacy of secession. Moreover, Pennsylvania had never had a personal liberty law. He warned his Virginia readers that the object of the secessionists of the lower South was disunion, and added: ". . . be not deceived by a name, disunion, by armed force is treason." Also by January he had reached No. 35 in a series of newspaper articles, "The Virginia School." He quoted with approval President Jackson's proclamation of 1832 describing nullification as an "impractical absurdity" and asserting the supremacy of a sovereign and indivisible government. He condemned the "heresy of a great Southern confederacy" which had been conceived in the brain of John C. Calhoun. Throughout January and February he engaged in a newspaper duel with Colonel Massie. Dr. Junkin denied that there had ever been such a thing as an independent, sovereign state in the Union.

Other thoughtful, observant men in Lexington feared that some incident would precipitate conflict. When South Carolina shore batteries on January 9 repulsed the *Star of the West*, sent by President Buchanan with reinforcements and provisions for Fort Sumter, Professor J. L. Campbell told a friend that the event "will set the whole country on fire, north and south." He expressed apprehension that secessionist sentiment was gaining ground in Rockbridge. On the same day student Frank Willson wrote a relative that the rifle company in Lexington had voted 25 to 17 to refuse a call by the governor if he should issue one. Although not much of a secessionist, Willson thought this was a disgrace to the sons of "West Augusta."

While President and faculty dreaded disaster, students of Washington College felt the stimulation of adventure. Young Willson assured his aunt that she would not believe the state of excitement that prevailed. He estimated that "unfortunately nearly one half of the students are disunionists." The proportion was to grow rapidly.

In his letter Willson told of the appearance of a secessionist flag over the College. "Flag incidents" occurred during that fateful winter also at several other institutions including Princeton, the University of Virginia, and V.M.I. This was the first in a series at Washington College that was to lead directly to the departure of the tormented Dr. Junkin.

The banner, bearing the word "disunion" and one star, had by night been ". . . raised on the roof of the college endowed by the father of his country, yea: even over his head. . . ." Willson related that ". . . the sight of the flag the next morning fairly made Dr. Junkin pale with rage, he threatened to cane the traitorous fellow if he could find him."

One of the participants was H. Rutherford Morrison, son of a trustee, the Reverend James Morrison. He wrote his sister that "I am a disunionist now, and am in favor of immediate secession on the part of Virginia. . . ." After noting political turmoil he described how he and six other boys had made and hoisted the flag which was "blue with one blood red star in the middle and DISUNION painted in large letters above it. . . ." The division among students was indicated by Morrison's account that "a part" of them had threatened to pull down the flag, "but we told them that if they tried it there would be a war. . . ."

Dr. Junkin ordered servants to remove the offensive bunting but the students, anticipating this, had concealed the ladders. When a ladder was brought from town, high winds prevented its use for the rest of the day. That night the secessionists guarded the flag against molestation by Unionist students. When the banner was finally brought down the president sentenced it to be burned and invited sundry townsmen to be present; but the resourceful youths filched it from his room. With relish Morrison related Dr. Junkin's fury, "bulging" into rooms (including Morrison's) without knocking and "squealing" for the flag he did not locate.

Dates in Morrison's letter placed the occurrence about December 10, or some ten days before the South Carolina ordinance of secession was adopted. The youth of conservative western Virginia thus displayed sentiments comparable to those of the more radical Southerners in other areas at that time.

Despite his annoyance in December, Dr. Junkin could report on January 19 that the College was quiet. And he confided to his old friend, trustee Francis McFarland, that although they lived in fearful times he remained serene in the knowledge that as "the Lord reigneth" the issue would be settled properly. He reiterated his Jacksonian conviction that the Union must be preserved and hoped "no one will be hung, tho' a few deserve it." On the same date Professor White expressed to his father-in-law, trustee S. McD. Reid, the desire that the Old Dominion might sit as umpire between the contestants: "If so, glorious is her mission." In February student Frank Willson ventured the naive opinion that Virginia should secede and stand aloof from both "ungrateful northerners and headstrong southerners."

Students and cadets observed Washington's Birthday as usual in the Presbyterian church, and the *Gazette* reported that all the addresses of the young men "to a greater or less extent partook of strong Southern rights sentiments." But Dr. J. W. Paine wrote to trustee Reid: "The College speeches were conservative . . . the speeches of the Cadets were both strong disunion speeches and were both applauded and hissed." That night at the Washington Literary Society the topic debated was: "Should Virginia unite her destiny with the Southern States?" The vote was 43 to 8 for the affirmative.

As events moved toward a climax about thirty of the more ardent students sought faculty authorization for a military unit, "the Southern Blues," which they had formed in March. But the faculty declined to be responsible for the muskets; and while they would not prohibit it, they advised against the utility of a military class, which would bring to the premises "a rabble crowd." Student T. M. Turner, a member of the Blues, doubted the unit's success in view of the faculty's attitude. Reluctant James Willson thought of joining for the sake of the exercise, but had no wish to go to war and was deterred by the four-dollar cost of the uniform.

Dr. Junkin fought doggedly on, in the classroom as well as outside. In his lectures on the Constitution to the seniors, as he afterwards wrote, "I wished, by a fair and honest exposition, to convince my young friends that Union preceded *Independence*, and even the *Articles of Confederation*; much more the present *Constitution*; that neither the Continental Congress nor the Articles of Confederation created and constituted a Government." His stated object was "to rivet the conviction in the minds of these dear young men, that *Union* was always the master thought in the minds of American patriots; that Union was the basis of all their actions; that without *Union* there could be no *freedom*, no *national government*, no *independence*." His logic inexorably carried him to the conclusion that " 'secession' is the essence of all immorality; it neutralizes the highest obligations."

But during the course of his lectures Dr. Junkin "observed a growing restlessness among the students." He heard himself "called a 'Pennsylvania Abolitionist,' and saw written on the column opposite his recitation room door 'Lincoln Junkin.' "

The confrontation between secessionist students and Unionist president was aggravated by a recurrence of flag incidents. Dr. Junkin's narrative continues:

> About the close of March, a Palmetto flag was placed on the centre building of the college, surmounting the wooden statue of Washington, on whose head they had nailed a fool's cap. In this process, led on by a Georgia student, the copper lightening-rod was bent, and subsequently broken off. . . . This flag I ordered the servants to take down and bring to me. I was asked what I would do with it, and replied 'burn it after evening prayer.' But whilst I was at dinner, they procured a ladder, climbed into a window of my lecture room, and took the flag away.

The students, not to be so easily disposed of, resumed the game of flag-hoisting a week later. When Dr. Junkin learned that the flag was back he took quick action:

> I immediately ordered the servants to take it down, and at an hour when all except the Freshmen were at their recitations; these stood about as spectators, and asked what I was going to do with it. I answered, "I'll show you." I ordered the servants to hold the but [sic] of the flag pole firmly, and throw the top over the chapel roof, which is a story lower than the centre building. When the

flag came within reach, I stepped up and took some matches out of my pocket, set it on fire, and when it blazed up told the servants to throw the pole out from the building, and whilst it flamed up, I said "*So perish* all efforts to dissolve this glorious Union!"

Milton W. Humphreys recalled that students tore "ribbands" from the burned flag, which they wore as insignia in defiance of their president, and that the Kahle statue of Washington, atop the center building, was draped in mourning.

Dr. Junkin's account, published while the war raged, records with grim satisfaction that some of the young men involved in erecting these flags died at First Bull Run, on July 21, 1861:

> Two of them were killed by one cannon shot, and a third (and he the leader) perished from excessive overexertion in carrying his wounded companion three miles to the railroad car. . . . and thus, to a melancholy and fearful extent, has the malediction prophetic been accomplished. . . . from all I have heard, I am painfully impressed with the belief that more than fifty per cent of all those misguided youth who were active in rebelling against me have paid the forfeit of their folly by the sacrifice of their lives. This is cause of unfeigned sorrow; for a very large proportion of them were youth of remarkable promise for talents, diligence in study, purity of moral and religious character; who, but for these bloody fallacies would have lived long and adorned the higher walks of professional life.

More potentially dangerous than the flag-raisings was the display of secessionist sentiment by students and cadets in a community where Unionist sympathies continued strong. On Saturday, April 13, the day Fort Sumter surrendered after a bloodless bombardment, a sanguinary clash on the streets of Lexington was narrowly avoided. Student T. M. Turner, an eyewitness, wrote his father that "although it ended in a Mechanic [workman] being knocked down and a cadet getting his nose smashed, [it] came very nearly being a serious affair." The cadets, exasperated by alleged ill-treatment of one or two of the corps, armed themselves "to the teeth" and rushed to town where they were opposed by "the Mechanics," who had knives, pistols, and axes. Some College students joined the cadets and a number of citizens arrayed themselves with the workmen. According to Turner the town rifle company, instead of clearing the streets of the mob and the "Mechanics," sided with them. Colonel Francis H. Smith, Superintendent of V.M.I., arrived on the scene just in time to prevent a collision. "If a single shot had been fired on either side the indiscriminate massacre that w[ould] have followed is awful to think of."

A SCANT THREE DAYS LATER, upon receipt of the news of Fort Sumter, followed by Lincoln's insurrection proclamation and call for troops—sharply rejected by Governor Letcher—community opinion shifted completely. Lawyer James D. Davidson, the town's foremost Unionist, wrote to James B. Dorman: "Just at this moment the Union pole, raised on yesterday, with the Eagle upon it, has been cut down by those who raised it. . . ." Davidson conceded defeat. Events had brought at least an apparent unanimity of opinion to the people of Rockbridge as complete as that produced by Pearl Harbor in the United States eighty years later. As for Virginia as a whole, on April 17 the convention which had been two months in meeting voted 103 to 46 for secession.

Dr. Junkin's position was now untenable. One morning he again espied the "disunion flag" waving above the Washington statue. He told his faculty colleagues "that this thing must be stopped;" but a professor responded that he had shortly before received a petition in the matter, signed by most of the students.

Addressed to the faculty, it read:*

It being our unanimous opinion that we, as a portion of the young men of Virginia, should signify our approbation of the recent action of our State Convention, and our willingness, if need be, to sustain the same in the trying scenes that may ensue, we have hoisted a Southern flag over the College, as the best exponent of our views. It is now our unanimous desire, that the flag should continue to float; and we, therefore, respectfully request, that you will not suffer it to be taken down. There can be no opposition to it from any quarter *now*, save from the enemies of Virginia, and we know that the people of this vicinity are loyal to the old Mother State, and that they have no desire to interfere with it.

Dr. Junkin took the display of the flag as a personal insult. A faculty member who had conferred with the students regarding their motives assured the president that the only intent had been to indicate approval of the convention's action. Unconvinced, Dr. Junkin tersely informed his associates that the decision rested with them. If they should grant the prayer of the students, "he would never give another Lecture or hear another recitation . . . until the flag was taken down; and, if the

---

* *Faculty Record* (manuscript) indicates that the faculty met in morning and afternoon sessions, and that the student petition anticipated imminent action by the Virginia Convention in adopting an ordinance of secession.

Faculty did not have it removed *at once*, he would . . . hand in his resignation—that was his ultimatum. . . ." After considerable discussion the faculty that afternoon unanimously adopted a resolution exculpating the students from desire to violate College laws or offer indignity to anyone, brushed aside Dr. Junkin's ultimatum, and concluded for *"the present"* to permit the flag to remain.

Dr. Junkin meanwhile met his eleven o'clock class, inquired if the flag was still afloat and was told that it was. His narrative is eloquent: " 'Then gentlemen,' said I, 'I am under the necessity of assuring you that I cannot submit to this kind of coercion,' and dismissed them. One student rushed toward the door, shouting, 'Thank God for that! thank God for that!' (Killed at Bull Run, as I learned shortly after from a Richmond paper.)" At noon he put the same question to his senior class. Receiving an affirmative reply he dismissed them with these words: ". . . I never will hear a recitation or deliver a lecture under a rebel flag."

Within twenty hours of the faculty decision Dr. Junkin submitted his resignation to a specially called meeting of the trustees. Some of the eight members present made kind remarks. Dr. Junkin shook hands with each one and several "were overpowered with tender emotions," as was Junkin himself. No customary resolution, however, was recorded in the trustees' minutes, praising the outgoing official and lamenting his departure.

Dr. Junkin realized that if he continued to reside in Rockbridge "absolute silence, or a voice in favor of secession, must be the price of his personal safety. The price was too great for him to pay." He hastened to dispose of his property and pay his debts. Ordinary means of conveyance being unavailable, he purchased a carriage which he drove the 350 miles to Oxford, Chester County, Pennsylvania. His books and furniture he abandoned to the tender mercies of "Mr. Benjamin's confiscation law, as expounded by himself." He crossed the Potomac at Williamsport, Maryland, "having driven the last thirty-five miles from Winchester, without stopping to feed horses." Tradition has it, though, that he paused long enough at the river to shake the dust of Virginia forever from his horses' hooves.

Behind in Virginia remained two sons, both Presbyterian ministers, and his daughter Margaret—distinguished in her own right as a poet— wife of Colonel J. T. L. Preston of V.M.I. Another daughter, Eleanor, had been the wife of Thomas J. Jackson but had died in 1854. The conflict was indeed a "civil war" for Dr. Junkin and his family.

During the war Dr. Junkin, then in his seventies, showed remarkable energy visiting encampments and prisons, distributing tracts and books, and preaching. Especially concerned for the welfare of Southern prisoners, he is reported to have gone to the field of Gettysburg immediately after the battle. In the hospital he met a dozen of his old Washington College students and preached to them. A witness described the scene that followed his sermon: "As they gathered around him, apparently most glad to meet him again, he took from his pocket the old class-book, and commenced to call the roll, and rehearsed the history of each member, showing how all had suffered more or less in consequence of their resistance to the best government which God had ever given to man."

Toward the close of his life he was again chosen president of Lafayette College. This appointment he did not accept, and death came to him in 1868. In 1925 his body was reinterred in the Lexington cemetery hard by the grave and monument of his son-in-law "Stonewall" Jackson.

WITH WAR AN ACTUALITY, the remainder of the 1860–1861 session at Washington College was filled with excitement and confusion. The College company was organized with Professor A. L. Nelson as captain and Professor James J. White as first lieutenant. Professors J. L. Campbell and C. J. Harris were active in a county ratification meeting on April 27 that approved the state secession ordinance.

Two Rockbridge companies were soon ordered out. Student T. M. Turner chafed at the relative inactivity of the student unit which remained in town. In mid-May he wrote his father:

". . . all is disorganization here and we do a little drilling and then pretend to study a little, so nothing atall [sic] is done either one way or the other and I think it wd. be far better for me to be at home than up here as a sort of dead expense. . . . Our company is already below fifty, as I understand, and they still continue to drop off one by one and there is no hope of its recruiting . . . and the sooner I get out of this crowd of boys and join some substantial company the better."

Turner apparently represented the general feelings of the students, for they petitioned the faculty for suspension of academic instruction and concentration on military instruction. This the faculty "respectfully declined"; but at the end of the month College exercises, except morning chapel, were suspended temporarily "in order to give ample time for the rapid drilling of the military company, which is expected to be called into service very soon." Twelve seniors were recommended for graduation and thus released for military service. Virginians all, they were with two exceptions members of General Joseph E. Johnston's army at the time of the award of their A.B. degrees.

Turner and his impatient fellows could now devote their time to soldiering. The Lexington *Gazette* commended the "handsome and well-drilled company, consisting of students of Washington College," directing attention to the fact that it was accepting recruits from outside. Professor White had succeeded Professor Nelson as captain, the *Gazette* noted, with the prediction: "We expect to have a good account from the Liberty Hall boys, who have, for some time past, been 'spilin' for a fight.' "

The faculty on June 1 ordered the resumption of lectures for students who remained; every possible facility was to be made available for military science; and no examinations were to be held at the close of the session. Almost immediately the Liberty Hall Volunteers were called into service by the governor and they departed for the front on June 8. Lectures and recitations, which had suffered grievously, were again suspended.

Professor John L. Campbell, in a letter to the *Central Presbyterian*, elucidated (with patriotic and historical exaggeration) the meaning of the title "Liberty Hall Volunteers":

> This is not the first company sent out by this venerable Institution, to defend the rights and soil of Virginia. When the fierce and bloody Tarleton, of revolutionary notoriety, was spreading terror throughout the Old Dominion, and threatened to penetrate even to the beautiful hills of West Augusta, Liberty Hall, (now Washington College) sent forth its band of youthful soldiers, under command of the venerable and distinguished Graham, to dispute the right of an invading foe to set his polluting foot upon their native soil. We have every reason to know that the spirit of Liberty Hall still pervades the hearts of Virginia's noble youth."

Chapter

XII

War at
Washington College

ALTHOUGH MANY Southern institutions of higher learning closed their doors during the Civil War, Washington College struggled on with its work of education. It operated, however, within altered and restricted dimensions, as military service called away most of its students and many youths who otherwise would have become students.

THE LIBERTY HALL VOLUNTEERS fought as a unit from First Manassas to Appomattox. Their story epitomized that of the Confederacy itself —the beginning in hopeful enthusiasm, the shock of learning war's realities, the prolonged and despairing effort against growing odds, and the steady attrition leading inevitably to catastrophe.

On the Saturday morning that the company marched away from Lexington a large crowd of townsmen was present to wish the boys Godspeed. A beautiful flag was presented to the unit from the ladies of Falling Spring congregation. The Reverend John Miller delivered a presentation address and after a few appropriate remarks the Reverend William S. White of the Lexington Presbyterian Church uttered a "fervent prayer." Then the young soldiers, according to the *Gazette*, ". . . well equipped, admirably uniformed . . . went off in fine spirits, determined to give the Yankees particular fits whenever, and wherever they have the pleasure of an introduction to them."

With Harper's Ferry as their destination the volunteers lay over for a while in Staunton, proceeded to Gordonsville and Strasburg on a train a quarter of a mile long, and moved on to Winchester in wagons. A *Gazette* correspondent, writing from Strasburg, reported that the company ". . . was the admiration of all who saw them, being perfect in *drill* and discipline." Members of the unit wrote frequent letters to their hometown paper, describing their journey. The ladies of Staunton sent the boys pies, cakes, and other presents. One youth observed on the way that even a slave had shouted to them to "go and kill dem Yankees." But another correspondent commented on the coldness of their reception at Martinsburg, seat of a county which had returned a 700 majority for Union (and later became part of the state of West Virginia). The unit was incorporated into Thomas J. Jackson's brigade as Company J, 4th Virginia Volunteers. Three other Rockbridge County companies also were in the brigade, which moved to Manassas to await the expected Federal attack.

Six weeks and a day after they had left Lexington the impatient collegians, "those more than brave young men," as Stonewall Jackson called them, had the chance they had so eagerly anticipated. They were in the thickest of the fighting in the first full-scale battle of the war. So was the 27th Virginia Regiment in which served a number of Washington College men. The bloody clash was described for the home people in letters written immediately afterward.

Lt. R. A. Glasgow, '53, wrote an account which glowed with pride as he detailed the gallantry of the College company, but conveyed sad news of heavy casualties. He and others told of the cannon ball and shell that killed Benjamin A. Bradley, Charles W. Bell, and "Squire" Paxton's son William L., all of the class of 1861 and natives of Rockbridge. Other members of the class fatally wounded included William B. Ott and H. L. Wilson, Jr., in a charge on the enemy batteries, and Cyrus D. Strickler and Calvin Utz. Frederick Davidson, '57, William N. Page, Jr., '60, and John J. Fry, '57, were among older alumni killed. Two future rectors of the board of trustees, G. B. Strickler, '67, and William A. Anderson, '61, were wounded.

Glasgow told of his regiment's successful charge against an enemy battery supported by New York Zouaves. The "Red breeches" fled, leaving the field strewn with dead. Glasgow expressed a hope, held by many Southerners after First Manassas, that the Federal rout would teach the North the folly of a crusade against the Confederacy. A member of the Liberty Hall Volunteers who wrote an eloquent description of the engagement likewise believed it to be a second Water-loo. He told of the "proud moments for our boys" when they beheld the flag given them by the ladies of Falling Spring waving "in triumph over the field."

Hugh A. White, '58, who had quit theological studies to join the army, wrote his father a vivid report of the battle in which he had fought beside his brother, the captain of the company. He expressed his gratitude to God for the victory but would gladly have exchanged the soldier's role for that of a preacher. In a letter to his brother George he said: "It is a great victory; but may I never pass through such a scene again. Death and hell may rejoice on the battle-field, but let man be silent. May God, who has won this victory for us, now give us peace."

The psychological result of the battle proved to be salutary for the North but unfortunate for the South, which became overconfident. The Union high command, which had unwillingly committed a half-trained army to battle because of political and popular pressure, now devoted the remainder of 1861 to reorganization and planning for attacks in the following year.

At the end of 1861 the Washington College company was assigned as bodyguard to General Stonewall Jackson. It continued in that function until after the Battle of Antietam (September, 1862), when its numbers were much reduced by casualties. The Liberty Hall boys served throughout the brilliant "Valley campaign" in which Jackson's swiftly executed marches bewildered his adversaries. At the conclusion of that campaign Jackson joined General Lee in the defense of Richmond in the summer of 1862. The College company participated in the battles around the Confederate capital which culminated in the severe encounter at Malvern Hill, July 1, 1862. Up to this point a number of alumni in the College company and elsewhere had been killed, wounded, or captured. Captain H. Ruffner Morrison, '58, and Lt. J. N. Lyle, '61, had been taken prisoner at the Battle of Kernstown in April, 1862. Members of the Rockbridge Artillery wounded in the fighting around Front Royal and Winchester included John H. Moore, '56, David E. Moore, '60, Frank Preston, '60, and Calvin M. Dold, '62. Lt. R. A. Glasgow, '53, of the Rockbridge Greys, 4th Virginia Regiment, contracted typhoid fever during fierce mountain campaigning and died in Augusta County.

Second Manassas (August 28–30, 1862) dealt harsh blows to Rock-bridge in the deaths of the youthful Captain Hugh A. White, '58, "leader of our heroic band of College boys"; William C. Preston '61, of the Liberty Hall Volunteers, son of Col. John T. L. Preston of V.M.I.

and stepson of Dr. George Junkin's daughter Margaret; and Henry R. Paine, '52, professor of Greek in the University of Mississippi and member of the Rockbridge Artillery. The valiant Lt. G. B. Strickler, who succeeded his devoted friend Hugh White as captain of the Liberty Hall company, was wounded for the second time.

General Stonewall Jackson himself related that White "fell, sword in hands, gallantly cheering on his men, and leading them to victory in repelling the last attack of the enemy upon that bloody field." Margaret Junkin Preston recorded in her war journal the grief of her household and those of her neighbors: "Alas! what sorrow reigns over the land! there is a universal wail of woe. . . . It is like the death of the first born in Egypt. Who thinks or cares for victory now!"

In a letter to his minister father a few days before the battle, Captain White had written that although he had become inured to war's hardships and even to its cruelties, he retained his deep religious faith and confidence that God would give victory to the Southern cause. In this final letter he observed: "When Lincoln presides, with Halleck as military chief in Washington, and Pope as the first commander in the field, how can they triumph over our leaders, who are as distinguished for their piety as they are for their bravery and skill."

Chantilly, Antietam, Fredericksburg, and in the spring of 1863 Chancellorsville, all saw the dwindling Liberty Hall boys in action. Chancellorsville cost the Confederacy an unparalleled loss in officers, and the impact upon Lexington was the most violent of the war. Dr. Strickler afterwards wrote that the College company "went into this battle with twenty-eight men, and lost nineteen killed and wounded." News of the encounter arrived in Lexington slowly and piecemeal. Several days passed before the worst was known, and the suspense added to the anguish. "Of the mothers in this town," Margaret Preston wrote in her war journal during the ordeal, "almost all of them have sons in this battle; not one lays her head on her pillow this night, sure that her sons are not slain. . . . God pity the tortured hearts that will pant through this night!" An arrival of mail on Sunday even caused church services to be interrupted.

Washington College alumni killed included Brigadier General Frank Paxton, '46, and Captain Greenlee Davidson, '55. Paxton, who received a degree also from Yale and graduated in law from the University of Virginia, practiced law and engaged in business enterprises and was president of Rockbridge County's first bank. A member of the local minority of ardent States' righters, he joined the Rockbridge Rifles at the earliest opportunity as first lieutenant. He served with gallantry and in intimate association with General Jackson from war's beginning until his death. General Lee cited his "conspicuous courage" at Chancellorsville. Captain Davidson, of the "Letcher Artillery," also had demonstrated remarkable courage in all campaigns. The Richmond *Enquirer* and Columbia (S.C.) *Guardian* had editorially commended his efficiency and bravery under fire at Malvern Hill.

At last, a week after the battle, General Jackson's death was confirmed. Everybody in Lexington was in tears, wrote Mrs. Preston, who in despair cried out in her journal: "Alas! Alas! When is the end to be?"

During the subsequent increasingly sanguinary fighting the Liberty Hall Company suffered grievous losses, while again and again the ranks were refilled through recruiting and replacement. In a charge at Gettysburg one was killed, four wounded, and sixteen were captured, the latter including Captain G. B. Strickler. Casualties were heavy at Mine Run. In the wilderness on May 12 an enemy assault all but wiped out the unit. Afterward the company joined in General Early's defense of Lynchburg, and served in his valley campaign of 1864. At the end of that year it was transferred to the defenses around Petersburg and participated in the heavy fighting of the closing phase of the war. The depleted company marched with General Lee's army towards Appomattox and was present at the surrender. According to A. T. Barclay and William A. Anderson the Liberty Hall Volunteers constituted "the only distinctively college company that served as such throughout the entire war."

One other tragic loss was the death in Lexington of Lt. Col. Alfred Henry Jackson of the 31st Virginia Regiment. As valedictorian of the class of 1857 he had referred to the possibility of young Virginians' being called upon to defend their homeland; and when "vandal hordes" burst into western Virginia he raised a company which saw service in that region during 1861. Appointed to the staff of his illustrious kinsman Stonewall Jackson, he chafed at the inactivity of staff work and rejoined his old unit as a private. He rose rapidly to a lieutenant colonelcy, served in the Valley campaign, and was severely wounded at Cedar Mountain August 9, 1862. Disabled for many months, he visited Lexington where he died August 2, 1863.

OF COURSE the overwhelming majority of Washington College alumni fought in the Confederate army or were Confederate sympathizers. Yet some were enrolled in the Federal army. For obvious reasons these latter sons of Washington College have not been celebrated locally by markers or plaques and probably not all of them are known. It would be appropriate here, however, to note some examples of those who served their country on the Union side. Albert Ludwig, who was at college in 1860–1861 and must have keenly felt the rise of secessionism among his fellows, was killed at Hatcher's Run in February, 1865. William Redford Sharp '50 was surgeon of the 15th New Jersey Regiment and John M. Godown '49 was a lieutenant in the 12th Indiana Regiment.

As noted in reference to the Junkins, the war brought additional agonies to some families through division of loyalties. A striking illustration was the experience of the Davidsons of Rockbridge County, who had close ties to Washington College. Two members of the family had removed to the Middle West in the generation before the war. One of these, Alexander H. Davidson, '35, had settled in Indianapolis. He maintained close contact with his Rockbridge relatives including his father, the Reverend Andrew B. Davidson, '07, trustee of the College 1815–1857, and his brother, James D. Davidson, '28, also a longtime and influential trustee. In the late fifties Alexander's son Dorman attended V.M.I., and his son Preston enrolled at Washington College for the session 1860–1861. In December of 1859, noting the trend toward sectional collision, Alexander wrote his brother James: "I want them [his sons] to understand the manners and customs and form attachments for Virginia and the South,—& the signs of the times portend such a result,—I expect to stand by my native State and I want my children to stand with me."

After Fort Sumter, however, Alexander Davidson's mood changed. A man of Southern birth among neighbors highly afflicted with war fever, he sought to remain neutral. He feared repercussions if Preston should volunteer for Confederate service, and instructed his brother James D. to prevent Preston from doing so. He wrote that he had refused to allow his son Dorman to depart for United States service with the Indiana company of which Dorman had been a member and officer for several years. It is unclear how, or for how long, a father's remonstrance could have had any effect in such a situation as Dorman's. And whether or not his injunction could have prevailed on Preston, it arrived too late. His letter apparently crossed one from Preston, informing his parent that he was on the verge of leaving for Harper's Ferry. Alexander frantically wrote his brother again, inquiring whether there was any way to gain Preston's release, and imploring James to intercede with Governor Letcher, a close friend of the family. He intimated that Preston would be mobbed or tried for treason if he should return to Indiana. The father could write to his son only indirectly, via Lexington, for fear of revealing Preston's activities to the fiercely excited Indiana people. Later the solicitous Alexander sent ten dollars in "Wheeling" currency for Preston's use. Subsequent communication from Alexander to his brother expressed concern for Preston's well-being, and ceased after a letter in late July inquiring as to his son's fate at Manassas. He added pithily: "I enclose a letter to P. If he is living forward it to him."

Preston was indeed living, though severely wounded at Manassas, and served throughout the war from which he emerged as captain. At the close of the conflict he told his uncle that he would come South to reside, as he thought it unsafe to go to Indiana—although he eventually returned to that state and died there in 1914. Meanwhile, Alexander H. Davidson, Washington College, '35, had joined the Union army, and attained the rank of brigadier general!

AFTER THE LIBERTY HALL VOLUNTEERS had departed in June of 1861 the Washington College trustees were faced with the age-old problem of higher education in time of war. A resolution on August 20 expressed the board's belief that continued instruction at the College was of importance to the long-range interests of the country, and directed the professors to distribute their work so that all classes should be provided for. The trustees also authorized a committee to prepare an address to the proper authorities requesting release from military service of those students of the College who had not completed their courses. Such a suggestion could hardly have been received favorably in view of the Confederacy's problems of manpower and of survival itself.

In the same month the Lexington *Gazette* editorially urged that operation of the local schools, with the possible exception of the College, be resumed. Even for the latter, the newspaper observed, there might be enough students to make it feasible to open the doors in the fall.

College faculty members performed various homefront services throughout the war. For example, Professor John Lyle Campbell, soon after Manassas, accepted appointment as voluntary commissary for army hospitals. He publicly appealed for bedding, clothing, food, tableware, and other articles, as well as for money. Professor White, who was forced by illness to resign his commission and return to Lexington in October, 1861, was busy in soldiers' relief work. On his departure from military service Captain White's associates memorialized his bravery, thoughtfulness, disinterestedness, cheerful endurance, and "especially . . . his heroic conduct on the memorable 21st of July, on Manassas' Plains, when, drawing his sword and throwing away the sheath, he marched, at the head of his little band, triumphantly through the bloody struggle; his Christian qualities among other incidents, in standing by the graves of our fallen comrades, and, in the midst of a drenching rain, with uncovered head, pouring forth a fervent prayer to God."

The session of 1861–1862 opened for those who could avail themselves of some sort of education, college or preparatory, with the antebellum faculty of four—Professors Campbell, Harris, Nelson, and White. The uncertain outlook for the College prompted two professors to advertise early in the fall that they would organize classes of young ladies and girls, or of young boys not yet prepared for college. The College's affairs were managed throughout the war by faculty members who, in the absence of a president and in default of frequent board meetings, assumed responsibilities not ordinarily theirs. Professor Nelson served as *ad interim* treasurer. The faculty resolved on October 28, 1861, that the students on hand be required to attend *"military drill,* as often as Prof. Nelson may think expedient." Professor Campbell early in 1862 was placed in charge of the Bible class, comprising all students living within a mile of the College, which met for recitation each Sunday morning.

Liability of professors for military service under recent Virginia legislation concerned the faculty and trustees in March of 1862 and the state attorney general, John Randolph Tucker, was asked for an opinion. Tucker replied that in his view the exemption provided in the charter of 1782 had been suspended in 1796 and no longer existed. No member of the faculty, however, seems to have been affected by the draft.

From time to time College facilities were put to military use, partially or tentatively. In April of 1862 a detachment of four hundred soldiers en route from Lynchburg to Staunton was quartered in the buildings. Two months later the *Gazette* noted that military authorities had taken partial possession of Washington College in the expectation of establishing a hospital there. Late in 1862 a group of the trustees informally leased the College buildings to Dr. Hunter McGuire for use as an army hospital. This was done apparently without the approval of the faculty, who questioned the authority of "local" trustees to take such action. The faculty requested Dr. McGuire to remove some Negroes, who had been domiciled at the College without faculty consent, to one of the dormitories. On January 1, 1863, the main building was ordered locked, and by faculty authority Professor White was given the keys, to be held until a legal call was made for them.

While Washington College was apparently hardest hit, the other Lexington educational institutions suffered also from war's effects. The *Gazette* remarked that V.M.I., "with all the 'pomp and circumstance of glorious war' about it," had been unable to retain half its enrollment through the 1861–1862 session. The neglect of education had even affected Ann Smith Academy. The local newspaper could not understand such inaction and urged townsmen to bestir themselves. After all, Lexington was secure, "undisturbed by the 'din of clashing arms.'" As the summer of 1862 waned with no sign of an educational awakening the *Gazette* sadly observed the fate of old Washington College, offering to open a Preparatory Department, at the same time continuing the regular course of instruction for those few of its students who for one reason or another had been unable to enter the army.

The College somehow struggled through the 1862–1863 session. An advertisement early in 1863 emphasized the institution's sheltered position, and urged students to bring with them such textbooks as they might have on hand. Occasionally the records indicate an item of student life as in March, 1863, when certain older students asked permission to organize a debating society. The two literary societies had been suspended for the duration of war. The faculty granted the students' plea under conditions that the proposed group adjourn promptly at 10 P.M., and that no boys under fourteen years of age or non-college people could participate.

Faculty members felt the pinch of the vicious spiral of inflation that helped to destroy the Confederacy, although the possession of farms and gardens alleviated their situations. Professor John L. Campbell, who had taken the position of agricultural editor of the *Gazette*, plaintively inquired in the newspaper, "how do *preachers* and *teachers* afford to prosecute their professions 'at old prices'?" In July of 1863 the faculty recommended an increase in tuition fees to $115 and the trustees, meeting in full session for the first time in nearly two years, approved.

The *Gazette* editorialized that Washington College had been as successful in the 1862–1863 session as circumstances permitted. Its enrollment of sixty was largely in the preparatory department, as nobody was allowed to remain after reaching the age of eighteen. The newspaper endorsed this policy: "Public sentiment in this patriotic State is utterly opposed to allowing any institution to become a retreat for those who are disposed to shun the dangers and hardships of the camp and the battlefield; or as a place where timid fathers and mothers can purchase cheap exemption for their darling boys. . . ." This College had its representative company in the field and a large number of gallant officers throughout the Confederate forces. The old school which occupied a distinguished place in the first American Revolution loomed still more important in the second. The editorial noted that the College trustees had provided for a new chair, adjunct to that of mathematics, for instruction in military science.

As 1863 wore on, the war itself pressed ever closer to Washington College and Lexington, so that the assumed security from military invasion gave way to excited reports of the approach of enemy raiding parties. The *Gazette* reported in late August that two Home Guard companies had been called out to reinforce Col. W. L. ("Mudwall") Jackson, who was falling back toward Rockbridge from the west; but the companies returned home when news came that the enemy had retired to Lewisburg.

On the night of November 5 word arrived that a Union force was nearing Warm Springs, about thirty miles northwest of Lexington. Couriers were dispatched to assemble a regiment of Home Guard and the next day Rockbridge men streamed into town. The regiment included the College company, commanded by Capt. A. L. Nelson, and the V.M.I. corps of cadets. The regiment proceeded to Millboro but was diverted southward when information indicated that the enemy had turned in the direction of Covington. General John D. Imboden, '43, however, checked the Union advance and dismissed the Home Guard with a stirring address to the "Citizen Soldiers of Rockbridge."

Again on December 12 an extraordinary meeting of the faculty caused college to be suspended until the 29th because the Home Guard had been ordered out for a week or more.

IT WAS NOT UNTIL JUNE OF 1864, however, that the actual blow fell in the form of the locally famous raid of General David Hunter. This general, though born in the District of Columbia of Pennsylvania and New Jersey parentage, a West Point graduate and professional soldier, was mistakenly believed by Virginians to be a renegade son of the Old Dominion. Earlier abolitionist proclivity and the raising of a Negro regiment had added to the hatred against him, and President Davis had proclaimed him an outlaw. After the looting and burning by his army in such towns as Staunton and Lexington he was accorded a place in Confederate demonology alongside such figures as Generals William T. Sherman and Benjamin F. Butler.

Hunter was ordered to move against Lynchburg in an effort to

annoy and weaken General Lee's army. He sought to approach his
objective by a circuitous route through the valley to Buchanan, then
southeastward through the Blue Ridge to Liberty (now Bedford). On
June 10 Hunter swept into Rockbridge County and advanced on Lexington in two columns via the Fairfield and Brownsburg roads. His
army of 18,000 to 20,000 was opposed only by the token resistance of
1,200 to 1,500 men under General John McCausland. Just the previous
month the V.M.I. cadet corps had left to join General Breckinridge's
army and to distinguish itself at the Battle of Newmarket.

The Confederates burned the North River bridge at Lexington after
retreating across it, forcing part of Hunter's army to swing westward
and approach from the Kerr's Creek road. By harassing Hunter's
movements General McCausland may have helped to save Lynchburg,
but his efforts incurred reprisal against Lexington; for Hunter, fearing
the presence of sharpshooters, ordered his artillery to shell the town.
This act has been severely criticized by southerners but Hunter defended it by accusing McCausland of an ". . . unsoldierly and inhuman
attempt . . . to defend an indefensible position. . . . by screening himself
behind the private dwellings of women and children. . . ."

Hunter's army entered Lexington on Saturday, June 11, and remained until early the following Tuesday. The commanding general
seized for his quarters the residence of General Smith of V.M.I. while
other Union generals occupied the homes of the Reverend William S.
White, Jacob Fuller, and Samuel McD. Reid. Virginia Military Institute and the home of former Governor Letcher were burned. Reid's
farm "Mulberry Hill" suffered heavily, Samuel F. Jordan's "Buena
Vista" furnace was severely impaired, and a woolen factory on
Whistle Creek was damaged. Considerable mischief was visited upon
the property of the people: edibles, slaves, horses, wagons, cattle,
sheep, and hogs were appropriated, fences destroyed, and crops ruined.

Captain Matthew X. White '55, son of a prominent citizen, was
summarily shot by Hunter's men on the pretext that he was a bush-
whacker, and a "wayfarer," one David Creigh of Lewisburg, Virginia,
was hanged. Col. Angus W. McDonald, commandant of the Lexington
post, fled town but was apprehended and treated with severity.

Washington College was a conspicuous object of vandalism. The
libraries of the literary societies and the College were robbed of half
their volumes and the remainder were "miserably defaced." Carpets,
curtains, pictures, and furniture were torn up or mutilated, or given
away indiscriminately to the Negroes of the town. Everything of value
in Professor Campbell's laboratory was destroyed. The excellent mineral and geological "cabinet" was stripped of its best specimens. The

Yankees even pelted the Kahle statue of Washington above the College's center building, believing it to be a likeness of Jefferson Davis! Many high officers, according to eyewitnesses, "rode past and looked on with seeming satisfaction while the savage scene was enacted."

Shavings were said to have been gathered to set the College afire, but the arsonist's hand was stayed. Several varying stories have gained circulation in regard to this point. It appears certain that one or more trustees and perhaps other citizens interceded either with Hunter directly or with one of his ranking officers. A faculty report identified trustee David E. Moore as pleading to save the College. According to David Hunter Strother, a "Virginia Yankee" officer and kinsman of the commanding general, a trustee reported to him that soldiers were sacking the institution and asked that a guard be dispatched to protect it.

It should be pointed out that several Union officers voiced their disapproval of the destruction. It is a remarkable circumstance that two future presidents of the United States, Col. Rutherford B. Hayes and Lt. William McKinley, were in Lexington with Hunter. Hayes wrote to his wife: "This is a fine town. . . . Many fine people . . . but some things done here are not right. General Hunter will be as odious as Butler or Pope to the Rebels and not gain our good opinion either." Another critic was Capt. Henry Algernon duPont, later a United States senator.

WE MAY NOTE HERE an epilogue to Hunter's Raid. Efforts to obtain restitution for the damage done to the College were begun as soon as the war was over. A petition by the trustees was submitted to Congress in 1865 but it received short shrift from the "Radical" Republicans, who stifled President Andrew Johnson's efforts to obtain a speedy and generous restoration of the South to the nation's councils. In January of 1876 Rep. John Randolph Tucker introduced a bill to compensate the College but the political climate was still unfavorable. Finally in 1894, with Congress under Democratic control, Senator John W. Daniel of Virginia (LL.D., 1883) obtained Senate passage of a bill providing payment of $17,484 to the University "for the injury of its buildings, apparatus, libraries and other property destroyed during the late war by Union soldiers without authority." Among supporters of the measure was the distinguished Senator George F. Hoar of Massachusetts.

In 1895 the bill was debated in the House where it was sponsored by Rep. Harry St. George Tucker, alumnus and trustee. Tucker skillfully brought forward several Republican members and Union veterans to speak on behalf of the measure, among them Reps. J. P. Dolliver of Iowa, Powers of Vermont, Daniel E. Sickles of New York (a former Union general), and Robert R. Hitt of Illinois. Sickles reminded his listeners of his own efforts, while in command of the Department of the Carolinas, in supervising the restoration of religious and other buildings for which purpose he had spent $18,000. Hitt pointed out that the College had educated thirty members of the House of Representatives.

The most powerful opponent was Rep. Thomas B. ("Tsar") Reed of Maine, who had no liking for the school which by then bore the name of the "rebel general," and opposed "granting compensation of every kind of injury that took place and a great deal of injury that did not take place during the southern rebellion." Others to question or oppose the bill included Reps. Loud and Nelson Dingley of Maine, and W. P. Hepburn of Iowa, all Republicans, and A. M. Dockery of Missouri, Democrat. Proponents carefully avoided reference to the Liberty Hall Volunteers, but Hepburn interrupted Hitt with a question that came close to embarrassing the sponsors: "Is it not a fact that during the war that institution forgot its purpose as an educational institution and sent a battalion of troops into the war to fight the battles of the Confederacy." Hitt denied that it was true, whereupon Hepburn inquired if the Virginia Military Institute were not part of Washington and Lee University. Despite the extensiveness of the debate, Tucker managed to rush the bill through a vote without a roll call; and the *Rockbridge County News* observed that only two Republicans, one of whom was Reed, had had the "nerve" to stand up in opposition. The sum of $17,484 does not seem large by present-day standards; but it was more than welcome to the hard-pressed Washington and Lee of the nineties. It also was a symbol of the progress of sectional reconciliation.*

RETURNING TO THE GLOOMY SUMMER OF 1864, we find both local institutions of higher learning bravely setting themselves to the task of rehabilitation. For a time Washington College was used as a wayside hospital. The trustees lost no time in extending assistance to the physi-

---

* V.M.I., "The West Point of the Confederacy," did not obtain this kind of tangible forgiveness until 1915 when another Democratic Congress voted the Institute an indemnity of $100,000 because of Hunter's Raid. The bill was sponsored by Rep. H. D. Flood, an alumnus of Washington and Lee.

cally destroyed institute. Four lecture rooms and the chapel of the College were assigned for use by V.M.I. in the ensuing academic year and faculty members of the institute were to be quartered in College buildings.

An advertisement in the *Gazette* on July 29 stated that Washington College would reopen in 1864–1865 largely to serve students under eighteen years old and disabled soldiers. It is evident that not many came, even of these. On November 21 Professors Nelson and Harris were authorized to lease out such parts of the buildings as were unused. The faculty continued on occasion to assemble for consideration of the minutiae of student discipline; and some of the teachers, through lack of occupation at college and perhaps to supplement their inflation-ridden salaries, sought other work. Professor Campbell, for example, on February 1 assumed the full editorship of the struggling Lexington *Gazette*.

News of battle casualties continued to bring grief to the College and community. On October 12 the people read of the death of Capt. Livingston Massie of the Rockbridge Artillery, a distinguished graduate of the class of 1857, killed at Sparta in September. A few days later the town was plunged into deep mourning by the announcement of the death of Lt. Col. Alexander Swift Pendleton, mortally wounded at Fisher's Hill on September 22. "Sandie" Pendleton, son of Gen. William Nelson Pendleton, rector of Grace Memorial Episcopal Church of Lexington, had graduated first in the Washington College class of 1857, winning the Robinson gold medal and delivering the Cincinnati Oration. He had been a student instructor in mathematics and Latin and for two years after graduation had taught at the College. In 1859 he had entered the University of Virginia and had almost completed work for the A.M. degree when the outbreak of war forever terminated his studies. He served on the staff of Stonewall Jackson, whom he so resembled in piety that it became proverbial among their associates to say that a person "prays as much as Gen. Jackson or Sandie Pendleton." His courage also caught the imagination of his fellow soldiers and one account records that as he rode into battle "his old classmates and other students of Washington College, who nearly made up the battery, were so much struck by it [his gallantry], that they rent the air with their huzzas for Sandie."

FROM THE FILES of the Lexington *Gazette* for 1864–1865 may be obtained a picture of the sagging morale of government and people. The newspaper columns contained unsparing criticism of the Confederate government and its agents; an occasional attempt at cheerfulness or reference to placing reliance on Providence; expressions of a concern for peace, giving way to a suggestion for using Negro troops in a desperate effort to rally all the South's resources for survival; stories describing the destitution of the famous Stonewall Brigade, and the quick response to appeals for aid from the Natural Bridge Ladies Society; a resolution by the Second Rockbridge Artillery at the end of February that the war must go on; and organization of a citizens' committee in March to procure supplies.

At last the suspense and foreboding were ended with the news of Appomattox. Citizens of Rockbridge County organized to set up a provisional local government and create a police force. Mercifully, the crops were good.

In the midst of such conditions the feeble session of Washington College closed in June of 1865. The faculty reported that work had been largely confined to the preparatory department, with numbers varying from 30 to 45; recommended the award of an A.B. degree to Alamby M. Miller; and turned to the physical needs of the institution. Various minor repairs were authorized and a College servant was engaged.

In July a regiment of Pennsylvania troops arrived and established a "Military Post" which would aid the citizens in "preserving law and order" until civil officials should be duly installed. The provost guard was quartered in one of the Washington College buildings. The regimental officers were described as gentlemanlike and courteous in their relations with citizens, to whom they granted much freedom. The *Gazette*, with what was perhaps wishful thinking, asserted that these Federal officers realized the undesirability and difficulty of holding, for any length of time, intelligent, freedom-loving people under military subjugation. Large numbers of "our most respectable citizens have already . . . [taken] the Oath of Allegiance." Physicians were at their posts, and lawyers awaited the reopening of the courts. The "New Order" had become an actuality at Lexington.

BOOK
TWO

*The Lee Era
and the University
1865–1930*

Chapter XIII

General Lee Revitalizes Washington College

THE DISCOURAGEMENT that pervaded the South must have been quite evident when the trustees met on June 21, 1865, and contemplated the prospects of the dilapidated College. Several vacancies on the board were noted and it was determined to investigate the chaotic condition of finances. The trustees, however, recorded a firm statement of intention to reopen the institution in September. They further agreed to meet in August to elect a president.

Accordingly the trustees convened on August 3. They proceeded to reorganize through adoption of new rules, and a committee was instructed to request the military forces occupying Lexington to evacuate Washington College buildings forthwith. Then, on the following day, the board took the step that led to transformation of the institution from a small regional school with strong ethnic identification to one of the prestige colleges of the nation. Upon nomination by Bolivar Christian, General Robert E. Lee was immediately and unanimously elected to the presidency.

The Lexington *Gazette* described the unusually full attendance and enthusiasm of the trustees, who were determined that the reverses of the war should not "bring down the elevated character [the College] has so long borne." And: "When the question of electing a President came up, such considerations were presented as led to the belief that General R. E. Lee would most probably accept the position, if it were tendered to him."

Although the trustees' confidence proved justified, there is no record to indicate the reasons for it or the origin of the inspired idea to tender the presidency to General Lee. Few generals had served as college presidents. Indeed, until the appointment of Eisenhower at Columbia University in 1948 none other of the celebrity of Lee undertook educational work. Lee's ability as a student had been evidenced by his second standing at West Point, and he had served as superintendent of the military academy. But he had not otherwise been associated with the academic world and was not a man of wide intellectual interests, although he had mastered an effective style of writing. The trustees, like all other Southerners, certainly felt R. E. Lee's charisma; and they knew that his dedication to principle and duty would be an inspiration to students and faculty alike. Yet we must wonder how they could have been so audacious as to ask the South's hero to come to them, with no preliminary contact to learn whether he would even consider doing so.

Greenlee D. Letcher, son of trustee and Governor John Letcher, has reported that as a youth he understood his father had suggested to Bolivar Christian that General Lee be offered the presidency. He offered this information as tradition rather than as history. It is known, however, that on August 2, two days before the board's formal action, Letcher wrote to General Lee regarding the position at Washington College and urged him to accept. General Lee could not, of course, in this short time have received the communication and replied before his election.

After their momentous decision the trustees dispatched their newly elected Rector, Judge John W. Brockenbrough, to press General Lee for his acceptance. He left on borrowed funds and, according to Professor A. L. Nelson, in a borrowed suit. The words of the interview at General Lee's temporary residence (near Cartersville, Cumberland County, Virginia) have not been preserved. But shortly afterward, en route home aboard the canal packet boat *Jefferson*, the ebullient Brockenbrough poured out his arguments in a letter to the general.

The judge admitted that a foremost motive of the trustees in their choice was the advancement of the "venerable College." Yet they felt that in "discharging the comparatively humble functions of President of our College new lustre" would be added to General Lee's fame, and that he would appear in a new light to his admiring countrymen. By coming to Washington College he would demonstrate confidence in the future. What could make him more useful to his state than to devote his scientific attainments to the service of its young men, "and to guide that youth in the paths of virtue, knowledge & religion," not more by precept than by example?

Having followed the fortunes of Washington College we are aware of its untoward circumstances in August of 1865. Yet as Judge Brockenbrough stated his case, the College's prospects were relatively hopeful. The University of Virginia, the Virginia Military Institute, Hampden-Sydney, and William and Mary were prostrate, and would be for years to come. Washington College alone possessed an endowment; and the general had but to "stretch forth his powerful arm to rescue it, too, from impending destruction." "You alone can fill its halls, by attracting to them not the youth of Virginia alone but of all the Southern & some even of the Northern States."

Before reaching a decision General Lee subjected himself to soul-searching, and received advice through correspondence and personal conferences. On August 24 he set to paper his now-famous letter of acceptance, which has often been reprinted. Actually it was mostly a statement of reservations. Telling the trustees of his own fears of inadequacy for the position he warned that his strength was not great, adding that he could not consent to teach "in regular courses of instruction." With characteristic modesty and thoughtfulness he pointed to his exclusion from the terms of the Amnesty Proclamation of May 29, which might draw upon the College the wrath of extreme northern critics. "I think it the duty of every citizen," he wrote, "to do all in his power to aid in the restoration of peace and harmony, and in no way to oppose the policy of the State or General Governments directed to that object. It is particularly incumbent on those charged with the instruction of the young to set them an example of submission to authority, and I could not consent to be the cause of animadversion' upon the College." If the board members, however, should "take a different view" and think his services would be "advantageous to the College and country," he would "yield to your judgment and accept."

The jubilant trustees, of course, had already rendered their judgment. At a called meeting on August 31 they agreed to General Lee's conditions; denied that his exclusion from the Amnesty Proclamation would draw upon the College "a feeling of hostility"; and declared that "his connection with the Institution will greatly promote its prosperity, and advance the general interests of education." They concurred in General Lee's observations regarding responsibilities of citizenship and educational authority. The board's views and actions were expressed in six resolutions adopted with "unanimity and enthusiasm," which were transmitted to General Lee with an exuberant letter by Judge Brockenbrough. In the letter, which bore the excited salutation "General!", the Rector welcomed the new President to Lexington on or before September 20.

Judge Brockenbrough also composed a circular informing the American public of General Lee's accession to the presidency of Washington College, which event he believed was destined to "mark the commencement of a new era in its history." The circular, which was printed in the Lexington *Gazette*, included General Lee's letter of acceptance and the trustees' resolutions, and closed with a paean to the hero: "In dedicating his future life to the holy work of educating the youth of the country, General Lee presents a new and interesting phase of his grand and heroic character, a character than which no more perfect model exists among living men."

Comment by the press and by individuals was voluminous and continued for several months. Lee's acceptance was "hailed with universal satisfaction," declared the Staunton *Spectator*. By taking this comparatively humble position Lee won new title to the love of his countrymen. Confederate General Isaac R. Trimble prophesied for the College under Lee a foremost rank in higher education and believed that it might help to destroy sectional feeling and prejudice. He accurately predicted that northern youth would find their way to the general's College and urged advertising in the North "inviting the young to come & learn what the South really is, an ignorance *of which has been the source of* all our troubles." The Richmond *Whig* remarked: "And now that grand old Chieftain . . . betakes him to as noble a work as ever engaged the attention of men . . . by the exercise of his genius, and by his virtues, and his high moral character, to inspire the sons of his well-loved Virginia with a taste for literature and a love for what is great and good." Many a southern newspaper and some northern journals echoed the sentiments of the *Whig;* but some of the latter did not. In any event, the eyes of the world soon turned to the remote campus of Washington College.

VILLAGERS AND COLLEGE PEOPLE assumed an air of expectancy in awaiting the arrival of the great man soon to become one of them. The old Washington College buildings were refurbished so that to one onlooker they appeared to be "quite charming." General Lee rode into town quietly and alone on "Traveller" on September 18, and was introduced by Rector Brockenbrough to the trustees at their meeting on the 20th.

It had been proposed to stage President Lee's inauguration at the College chapel, to extend invitations throughout the nation, to provide a brass band, and to have "young girls robed in white, and bearing chaplets of flowers, to sing songs of welcome; to have congratulatory speeches, to make it a grand holiday." But at the express wish of General Lee the exercises were planned as the acme of simplicity, "an exact and barren compliance with the required formula of taking the oath by the new President, and nothing more. . . ."

On the morning of October 2, the first day of the new session, the brief ceremonies took place in a recitation room in the presence of the trustees, faculty, students, clergymen of Lexington, a magistrate, and the county clerk. The Reverend William S. White offered "an impressive and fitting" prayer in which he besought divine blessing for the President of the United States. Judge Brockenbrough then announced the subject of the meeting. Bursting with pride and emotion, the voluble rector found it difficult to restrain himself within the prohibition of speeches, and approached the dignity of an eloquent address. He adverted to the seriousness as well as the joyfulness of the hour, eulogized General Lee, and congratulated the trustees and students, present and future, on the president.

President R. E. Lee stood with folded arms, gazing into the speaker's eyes. Squire William White, Justice of the Rockbridge County Court, then administered the oath of office, employing the quaint text provided in the charter of Liberty Hall. It enjoined the President to administer the institution's affairs without "favor, affection, or partiality." General Lee signed the oath, which was turned over to the county clerk for perpetual safekeeping, and the Rector handed the president the keys of the College. After the customary handshaking General Lee passed into the room that had been assigned to his use. The Great Era had begun.

As the news of General Lee's college presidency penetrated into the back country of the South, ex-Confederates and younger boys and their parents poured inquiries into Washington College. It can almost be said that the whole South wrote to General Lee in his final serene years, not only about education, but on a variety of topics; and some northern correspondents wrote in. General John T. Morgan of Alabama put it thus in 1868: "Eight millions of people turn their eyes to Lexington seeking instruction and paternal advice in the severe trials they have to undergo. They read in the example of their General . . . the lessons of patience, moderation, fortitude, and earnest devotion to the requirements of duty, which are the only safe guides to them in their troubles. His history, his present labors, and his calm confidence in the future kindle the flames of hope in the hearts of millions, that else would be all darkness. Their prayers to Heaven are constantly burthened with blessings on his venerated Head."

Obviously a number of the writers knew but one thing about Washington College—that General Lee was its head. Some simply addressed their letters to "General Lee's College," and were not even certain of its location. Other variations included "Virginia University," "Virginia Military Academy," and "Bob Lee University." The President was addressed in many styles, among them "His Excellency," "Principle," and "R. E. Lea."

Pathetic in the incoming letters was the recurring, plaintive note of poverty that must have touched the general, because often the requests were far afield and impossible. Sometimes the writers were able actually to come to college, but as often not. Communications told of wealth destroyed, children orphaned, and soldiers maimed by the war. Epistles came from such farflung areas as Montana Territory, California, Indiana, Iowa, Mexico, and Brazil. Persons sending sons to the College frequently solicited General Lee's personal attention to the youths. A number of others asked advice about the education and upbringing of their sons. One unusual missive came from the Prussian consul at New Orleans, J. Kruttschnitt, who mentioned that Judah P. Benjamin was his brother-in-law and said he was sending one of his sons to Washington College in the fall of 1867. His two boys, Julius and E. B., came and distinguished themselves at college and in life.

The hope of some that the institution would attract large numbers of Northern students was disappointed during the Lee years. But students flocked from the Southern states in such numbers that in 1868 enrollment reached the unheard-of figure of 411.

WHILE GENERAL LEE's name proved to be a priceless asset to Washington College, it was true as he had feared that his connection with the College would bring down upon it the "censure of a portion of the country." During his administration certain Northern observers and Radical Republicans intermittently assailed Washington College and its President. Political tension engendered by the quarrel between the Radical Republicans and President Andrew Johnson for control of Reconstruction policy made such attacks inevitable. Voices in the anti-Lee chorus included those of the English reformer John Bright, Senator Sumner, the fiery abolitionist Wendell Phillips, the Indiana Radical

George W. Julian, future Vice-President Schuyler Colfax, the Phila-delphia *Press*, the New York *Tribune*, the Boston *Transcript*, and the Louisville *Journal*.

The chorus sometimes sang far off key. The *Press*, the *Journal*, and Julian, confusing Washington College with V.M.I., were especially indignant over such matters as turning over government firearms to the rebel general and permitting him to instruct the young in gunnery. The *Tribune* waxed furious over the acquittal of a student in Judge Brockenbrough's law school who had been charged with the killing of a Negro—an affair in which General Lee was no more concerned than was Horace Greeley.

In the tense setting of Reconstruction and Freedmen's Bureau acti-vity, however, it was inevitable that Washington College students should become involved in "incidents." In March of 1867 the faculty noted that five students had disturbed the "colored school." The fac-ulty clerk was instructed to express formal regret to that school's authorities and to assure them that the faculty stood ready to prevent recurrences. An Alabama student who assumed principal responsibility was dismissed. The others, a Georgian and three Texans, were "ad-monished" and bound over to keep the peace. President Lee issued a public statement calling attention to that disturbance and to disorderly conduct by students at the Lexington post office, which had delayed mail delivery. He condemned such acts and enjoined students to avoid the area of the Negro schools—and also the post office!

A more serious incident occurred in May of 1868 when a Negro, Caesar Griffin, shot and seriously wounded one of Judge Brocken-brough's sons and was nearly lynched by students. Mrs. Brocken-brough and one of her sons had been returning home from a family visit about 11 P.M. when they encountered a group of Negroes near their residence. All moved to permit Mrs. Brockenbrough to pass ex-cept Griffin, who uttered some offensive expressions. After the mother and son had entered their home Frank Brockenbrough and his elder brother, a student, returned to "the gate." Brandishing a stick or switch, Frank hurdled the fence and approached Griffin, who fired a pistol at him.

Frank's brother aroused a crowd of students who searched for Griffin and apprehended him. Some threatened to lynch him. A news-paper story circulated at the time, and Lee's biographer Douglas Southall Freeman, reported that General Lee himself dissuaded the enraged youths. Actually the threat was quelled by Captain Harry Estill, an assistant professor at Washington College.

Lieutenant Wagner, United States military commissioner in Lexington, called General Lee's attention to continuing rumors of trouble and possible lynching. The president learned to his satisfaction that the rumors were false, at least as far as they concerned students, and so informed the officer. A company of soldiers, however, patrolled the town for a while. Young Brockenbrough recovered and the crisis blew over.

During the presidential year 1868 General Lee was made to serve partisan purposes. Some examples of vindictive prose may be cited from the columns of the *Independent*, a religious and philanthropic journal published in New York. On March 12 an editorial bitterly criticized a recent meeting in New York for the purpose of promoting subscriptions to Washington College. Among the speakers had been the Reverend Henry Ward Beecher, a staunch Unionist but willing, like General Lee, to practice the Christian virtue of forgiveness. The *Independent*, however, could view Beecher only as insensible to "treason." The writer took Lee to task on various counts, even holding him "largely responsible for the cruelties of Libby, Salisbury, and Andersonville," and demanded proof of Lee's and his students' "repentance."

The *Independent* appended the story of a "loyal" clergyman's interview with students from "General Lee's College" whom he met on a railroad train. The reverend gentleman described them as dressed in uniform, although he had been (correctly) unaware that Lee's school was military until informed by them that they did indeed wear uniforms and that they drilled. Probably the students, if such they were, had been pulling the clergyman's leg. Another statement from a minister printed in the *Independent* reported that "loyal" sons were insulted at "rebel" schools.

The old abolitionist William Lloyd Garrison, writing in the *Independent*, endorsed the criticism of the New York meeting on behalf of Washington College, which deserved "no encouragement whatever at the North." Garrison fiercely lashed the South as "still bitterly disloyal in spirit and conduct; still wishing to rule in hell rather than serve in heaven." Like that journal's editor, Garrison called upon Lee to recant, to admit that the North was "right" and the South was "wrong."

A clipping from a weekly newspaper, sent to General Lee in April of 1868, proclaimed that "facts" were being circulated to prove that Washington College was one of "the most virulent rebel institutions of the land—a school for the propagation of hatred to the Government and its loyal people."

Among Northern critics of Washington College's fund-raising was

General Neal Dow of Portland, Maine. Everybody knew, Dow asserted, that Lee had been placed at the direction of Washington College for "the express purpose of making it a great centre of Southern training in hate of the North and of the Union, that the virus of rebellion might be *surely* perpetuated through all the South."

Controversy swirled about Washington College through several numbers of the *Independent.* Julia Anne Shearman, a Northern school teacher who had spent some time in Lexington, supported critics of the institution. She had gone south to aid the Southern people, but found they "would accept no sympathy that was not founded on the acknowledgment that right was, and always had been, on their side." Apparently the "southern people" whom she desired to help were the emancipated slaves. Miss Shearman related that she had been continually insulted, she found herself "calathumped," and her school was pelted with brickbats and threatened with arson. A protest to General Lee over some insults by a group of students had elicited no reply.

In the same issue the Reverend T. H. Pearne of Knoxville, Tennessee, warned that by giving money to Washington College the North not only forged "implements for another and bloodier conflict. . . ." but it also whetted "the knives wherewith to cut the throats of the givers."

An anonymous letter in the *Independent,* purportedly from a resident of Lexington, declared professors and students at the College were unanimously "thoroughly rebel in sentiment, and act accordingly." The writer rehearsed the well-known story of E. C. Johnston, a Union army veteran who had come to Lexington in the fall of 1865 as agent for the American Missionary Association to establish Negro schools. According to the letter "seventy-five young sprigs of chivalry" from Washington College had threatened Johnston with tar and feathers and even hanging. Told to get out of town within ten days, Johnston had suffered vile abuse, and departed Lexington under student threats to "calathump" him further.

Johnston himself, from his refuge at Covington, Virginia, reviewed his case for the *Independent.* He recalled that as he was skating on North River a youth had called him by that "fighting epithet," an "s.o.b." Johnston admitted that he had threatened to shoot should the insult be repeated. A crowd of students gathered about him and insulted him. He appealed for military protection but General Lee, Judge Brockenbrough, Mayor Ruff, and John Letcher persuaded federal authorities not to send troops. Never had he lived in such a town where drunken students roamed the streets at night, firing pistols and uttering threats.

An unidentified officer in the Freedmen's Bureau and of the United States Army, stationed at Lynchburg, contradicted in the New York *Tribune* the charges published in the *Independent*, especially in the Johnston case. The officer defended General Lee, who had acted vigorously, and charged that Johnston had drawn a pistol on a twelve-year-old boy.

A blistering attack upon Lexington and Washington College, entitled "The Southern Athens," appeared in the Boston *Evening Traveller* on the eve of the presidential election of 1868. The town was depicted as a place of "smallness, meanness, filthiness, poverty, and decay." The four hundred students of Washington College all partook "of rebel proclivities." Roaming the streets at night, discharging firearms and terrorizing women both black and white, students cursed the United States and its officials. The mayor confessed his helplessness (though Mayor Ruff denied this), while civilians would or could do nothing. General Lee had only "the least control of these students possible, and is a perfect nonentity, except as to the drawing of his salary." Disloyalty was the chief characteristic of the institution: ". . . the truth is, that it is a perfect hot bed of rampant secessionism, prejudice and narrow-mindedness." It horrified the reporter that "the arch traitor Lee [was] placed over [students] to instruct them in more treason." The V.M.I. cadets and "pistol-toting" collegians together constituted an armed force of eight hundred. The account must have given Bostonians goose pimples, as it was no doubt intended to do in the political aura of a national election. The tirade concluded with a reaffirmation of Garrison's and Dow's warnings that sending money to the College from the North was simply "paying traitors to teach their damnable treason to the flower of southern youth." In the view of the Lexington *Gazette* the article illustrated how Radical Republicans systematically "kept up and increased Northern prejudice against us," but it exceeded all in "deliberate misrepresentation, malice, and meanness."

Such attacks on Lee and his College by no means represented unanimous Northern opinion; and their violence perhaps stemmed in part from Republican apprehension over the postwar popularity of the general, North and South. The Evansville (Indiana) *Daily Sentinel on the Border*, as early as June of 1867, urged General Lee's nomination for President of the United States by the Democrats in 1868. The New York *Herald* also endorsed such a nomination and even expressed the opinion that Lee might defeat Grant in the election. The Mobile *Register* in April hoisted General Lee's name to its masthead as a presidential candidate. Less surprising was the proposal by the Lynchburg *Republican* that Lee might consent to run for governor. But with

Grant's election, the Radical Republicans became ensconced in power for some years. General Lee did indeed visit the White House on May 1, 1869, where he conferred on Virginia affairs for nearly an hour with President Grant, leading the New York *Tribune* to conclude prematurely that the end of "rebel" resistance was at hand.

Hostile or partially hostile stories about General Lee and the College, with varying degrees of accuracy, appeared now and then for the next several years. In 1869 the Radical Republican Richmond *State Journal* reported a conversation of highly rebellious character on a railroad train (naturally) involving a professor in "General Lee's Military Institute." That newspaper, which should have known better, proceeded to moralize on a situation which permitted General Lee to train youth in arms. Later in the year the New York *Sun* ran an article of more than three columns of fine print on "General Lee's College." It was largely factual and not altogether unfavorable; but the reporter found what he had probably been sent to find—"a Nursery of Secession Doctrines," a veritable network of ex-Confederates among faculty and students, and unrepentant Calhounites biding their time until an explosion should take place in the West.

Harper's Weekly carried an attack upon Lee in the summer of 1869, and other criticisms appeared as the College and its president continued to bear "the brunt of radical malice." The College nevertheless managed to attract Northern financial help. And because of his leadership General Lee drew to Lexington "the stars of the rising generation," the young men whom the New York *World* called "the representative boys" of the South. More than this, General Lee increased and broadened his faculty and curriculum and virtually established a university from what had been a static, old-fashioned, classical college of the Old South. First of all, since students are always the most important element of an institution of learning, we may now examine students and their life in General Lee's years, and his influence upon them.

BIOGRAPHERS HAVE HAD DIFFICULTY in recreating a living figure of Lee the man. Professor David Donald has called his very perfection "boring." Lee's incredible self-mastery indeed limited the indulgences that are sometimes called "human"; and anecdotes describing moments of levity are rare. One of these was contained in a letter from Miss Mary Pendleton to her sister, recounting a visit to the Lee home in Lexington. The hosts showed their guests some gifts recently received from Scotland, including "a superb Afghan" and "a 'teapot warmer' . . . shaped much like an ancient helmet." The general related that "when the box arrived [his daughter] Mildred was practicing and he put this strange cap-like article on his head, the Afghan around his shoulders, and went in where she was, dancing to the music she was playing." Idolatry, however, is uncomfortable with frivolity, and Miss Pendleton hastened to enjoin her sister: "Forgive *our hero*, exhibiting himself in such a costume, and acting in so childish a manner. But he is a 'grand old man,' and certainly would become any costume and any way in which he might choose to act."

Yet if General Lee exhibited the utmost in dignity, his kindness and consideration were proverbial. His students, judging by unpublished manuscripts and other evidence, perceived a warm personality and a sincere dedication to their welfare. They responded accordingly.

Most students agreed with John S. Mizner, who in 1866 urged a friend to come to Washington College, and to bring along as many of his neighbors as he could. General Lee he described as "one of the kindest men" he had ever seen, and added, "no one can help liking him." Similarly Hugh A. Moran, a young Kentuckian whose letters mirrored college life vividly and in detail, reported: "No one can help liking General Lee he is so polite and gentlemanly. He talks to a boy just as if he were his own son." The general cultivated his students, taking care to learn their names and details about them. When Charles A. Graves returned to college in September, 1866, Lee cordially welcomed him and remarked that if Graves had done anything improper during the past session, the President had not heard of it. Recollections of a "certain callythump" occurred to Graves, but he held his tongue in the august presence. Moran wrote that Lee received each matriculate, examined all reports, knew what every boy was about, and did not tolerate laggards. A characteristic student attitude of the late sixties was expressed by Ossian Huggins, who found the curriculum so difficult that he feared he could not win a degree. Nevertheless, he would settle for "a good certificate with General Lee's name attached, which will be worth *more* than a degree from most colleges."

Students often visited the Lee residence and were entertained there. Moran described such an event on Christmas night of 1868. This student had presented the President with a cheese from a box of condiments that he had received from home, and General Lee had invited Moran and his friends to call. The youth and two companions appeared at the President's house where they saw Mrs. Lee and the Misses Mildred and Agnes Lee. Although he had expected it to be a rather stiff occasion, Moran was agreeably surprised.

Of the many changes in the College during the Lee regime, probably none was more significant or lasting than the permanent imprint of the general's own character upon the institution. A gentlemanly, lofty code of conduct replaced the narrow regulation of an earlier era. The disciplinary system of Washington College during the Lee years has been widely praised, especially the emphasis upon honor and self-respect of students. The president's kindly but firm relations with students has favorably impressed all who have written about those years.

Yet even General Lee, confronted by the influx of young men who crowded the town to capacity, faced disturbing corrective problems. The faculty disapproved, as previously noted, students' jeering of teachers of the Freedmen's Bureau school, and in November of 1866 the faculty formally called attention to misconduct apparently intended to annoy townsmen.

Some of the evidence regarding conduct is conflicting. Hugh Moran told his father with satisfaction of the students' exemplary behavior during the Christmas holidays of 1867. When someone remarked to General Lee that the students of the University of Virginia had been unruly in the same period, Moran quoted the old hero: "Well, *my boys* behaved very well, didn't they?" But following that same Christmas week stories injurious to the reputation of the College reached the ears of trustee John Echols of Staunton, who warned that such reports, always exaggerated and in greater ratio according to the distance they traveled, would harm the institution. Senator Randall L. Gibson of Louisiana, who had relatives in the student body, cautioned Professor Johnston along the same line. The faculty records contain illustrations of disciplinary action, but the infractions seem to have tended toward boisterousness and, at the worst, a few instances of intoxication.

On the other hand, there were many serious-minded men at the College in the post-Civil War years. Veterans returning from wars have been conspicuously determined in their pursuit of education. Writing on that subject in the student magazine the *Collegian*, a veteran of four years in the Army of Northern Virginia observed that the young men had accepted the situation, and had striven diligently to master their studies. According to him, Southern college presidents had unanimously praised the studiousness and deportment of students. The purposeful tone at Washington College impressed Hugh Moran; there he found "*more* study and *less* mischief" than at any other place of which he had heard.

One such veteran was Milton Wylie Humphreys, who had studied at Washington College in 1860–1861 and returned in 1866, to become perhaps the most brilliant student in the history of Washington and

Lee. Winner of the M.A. degree and Cincinnati Orator in 1869, he afterward studied at the University of Leipzig where he took the Ph.D. and dazzled German savants with his knowledge. He returned to Washington and Lee for a year and then served as professor of classics at Vanderbilt University, the University of Texas, and the University of Virginia until his retirement in 1912. Dr. Humphreys has left a revealing manuscript autobiography in which he presented an unequalled picture of General Lee, the faculty members, and students.

The shift from rigid rules of discipline to a gentlemen's code of conduct was accompanied by a broadening of social life and a relaxation of religious requirements. These trends reflected the needs of a student body generally more sophisticated and more diverse in background than the small homogeneous groups of prewar times. Dancing became openly countenanced, while social fraternities were tolerated if not officially sanctioned. The forbidding Calvinist spirit receded, chapel services were placed on a voluntary basis, and the institution, while no less Christian in objectives, betrayed less sectarianism during these years.

A lively interest in the fair sex is indicated in student letters. Young Moran complained in 1867 that he could "get nowhere" with the girls of a prominent Lexington family, because the local citizenry thought there was nobody else "half so good as Virginians." He apparently made some progress, though, as two years later he punningly observed to his mother that some of the "mighty nice" girls living near the College could probably "be persuaded to *change their state.*"

After Moran's graduation his friend Alston Boyd briefed him on social affairs at college. Two of Boyd's "colleagues" were preparing to attend the second "students hop" of the season, something new on campus. Nearly all "ladies' men" had formed a "Social Club," the object of which was periodic hops.

Although dancing was permitted, it does not seem to have gained immediate general approval. An account of the Ball of 1869 in the Lexington *Gazette* failed to record the presence of a single faculty member, and added that few of the ladies present were "to the manor born." Yet the writer was dazzled by the brilliant scene, the fair ladies and the "gallant brave" who marched into the room at ten o'clock, the quadrille, and the waltz. After the customary supper, pleasure was "chased with flying feet until sunrise."

Alston Boyd wrote a friend in 1870 of fraternity matters, the establishment of the Delta Delta Chi, which *he* thought generally acknowledged to be the best in the United States. He also reported the consternation caused by a visiting young lady who attended church wearing three fraternity badges. This was "pinning" indeed!

The church remained a center of social life. In 1870 Joe Graves, a pre-ministerial student, observed to his father that two factors were essential for large church attendance—a "good" minister and a number of "pretty ladies." In his view, the Lexington Presbyterian Church possessed both requisites. It would be interesting to know how Graves' views on this matter afterward influenced the performance of his duties as a Presbyterian clergyman.

"Theates," writing to the *Gazette* in 1869, complained that only two social and public entertainments were available in town—the church and literary society celebrations. The young ladies were devout, attending church on week days as well as on Sundays, except when lacking a beau, which however was infrequent because of the disproportion of seven hundred young men to one hundred young ladies. This ratio occasioned rivalry, and engagements had to be made weeks in advance: "It is necessary for a ladies' man to have his book of Church engagements, which he keeps, as an English sporting lord, his betting book. To make up your book for the season is to achieve a triumph." But the overwhelming majority of students went to church without dates. After service they gathered in front for parting glances, or to gain exchanges in walks to and from church. Sabbath calling at this time was not customary in town.

Students sought recreation by excursions to House Mountain or the Peaks of Otter, and in summer trips to the surrounding watering places. According to one report authorities generally allowed students one holiday when ice skating was good. Such was the case on December 14, 1868, when nearly all students and cadets appeared on the North River, joined in the evening by numerous ladies.

THE OUTLINES of a new era were thus becoming fixed for the remainder of the Victorian epoch, and a broad base was being established in a clientele from the Southern states. Great plans and accomplishments of the R. E. Lee years, "the Augustan Age" of Washington and Lee's history, remain for consideration.

General Lee's
"Practical Reconstruction"

AFTER GENERAL LEE had been in office nearly a full session, his leadership expressed itself in a new program and an enlarged faculty through which could be implemented the president's ideas of higher education for the South in general and for his College in particular. His basic objectives were to retain the features of the older, classical Washington College, while adding and expanding instruction in practical, applied subjects. Specifically he recommended the introduction of applied mathematics, natural and experimental philosophy, and modern languages.

Lee's concepts were incorporated in a "Report of the Faculty" submitted to the trustees in April of 1867, accompanied by a plan of reorganization signed by the President and professors. The immediate election of a professor of modern languages was especially urged. The report declared that "young men, who have not had the advantage of pretty thorough training in Languages & Mathematics, rarely succeed in the study of Physical Sciences & the other subjects usually embraced in a College or University Education." Furthermore, as the war had interrupted the studies of "the large majority of young men who come here," very many of them "have not had the time & means necessary to acquire a competent knowledge of the Latin & Greek." Hence a demand to study those modern languages which could be learned rapidly and would be of immediate practical use. The shadow of the future may be discerned in those comments.

This important document also requested the elevation of standards of graduation to encourage rivalry among students, and the creation of "distinctions" in the departments, at the same time offering degrees for average students. The faculty suggested discontinuance of a four-year curriculum because the young men entered college unevenly prepared. For example, fifty-four students were currently enrolled in freshman Latin and only fourteen or fifteen in freshman Greek. (Preparatory courses were provided for those insufficiently qualified.)

The trustees, in a three-day meeting which the local *Gazette* called "the most important one . . . since the foundation of the College," implemented the faculty recommendations by adopting a new curriculum that led to the A.B., Ph.B., and M.A. degrees. Nine "schools" (departments) were set up: Latin, Greek, Mathematics, Chemistry, Moral Philosophy, Natural Philosophy, Applied Mathematics, Practical Chemistry, and Modern Languages. The latter was to include French, German, Spanish, and Italian, "and for the present" English Philology and Modern History.

Thus English and history, two essential disciplines in a modern liberal arts college, but neglected in the ante-bellum curriculum, finally sneaked into Washington College through a side door. A century later we may wonder at the combination of these subjects and their inclusion with European languages. It must be remembered, however, that historical writings formed a large part of the literary material covered in the traditional study of the classical languages. It was therefore not entirely illogical to consider history written in English as part of the literature of the language. And, after all, English *is* a modern language.

Satisfactory performance in a completed course was to be graded "proficient" or "graduate." The A.B. degree was to be conferred upon students rated "proficient" in Latin, Greek, mathematics, chemistry, moral philosophy, and natural philosophy. The M.A. was to be awarded to graduates in those schools plus applied mathematics, English philology, and two modern languages.

Having thus adopted sweeping reforms of the curriculum, the trustees elected four new professors: William Allan, Applied Mathematics; Edward S. Joynes, Modern Languages; Richard S. McCulloch, Natural and Experimental Philosophy; and the Reverend James A. Lafevre (who declined), Moral Philosophy. Allan had graduated with honors from the University of Virginia and had served as ordnance officer of Stonewall Jackson's corps. Joynes also had graduated with distinction from the University of Virginia, had taught as assistant professor there for three years, and had studied for three more years in German and French universities. Returning to America he served as professor of Greek and German at the College of William and Mary. McCulloch had filled, with distinction, chairs at Princeton, Jefferson, and Columbia colleges, resigning from the latter to enter the Confederate army.

In 1867 some modifications were made in the new program; and in the spring of 1868 "Paper 'B' " of faculty recommendations emphasized that Washington College should attempt to offer "the broadest and most thorough development to the practical and industrial Sciences of the Age." The lack of such was held to be the greatest defect in Southern higher education. The faculty urged the establishment of a scientific school embracing all major branches of theoretical and applied science and technology, including those pertaining to manufacturing, mining, agriculture, and commerce. All this would cost $200,000 or more, but the faculty was eager to appeal to the public for funds.

Colonel William Allan, in a private communication, held that Washington College had "adopted all the good" of the system at the University of Virginia and had "added much from others." In Latin, for instance, the number of recitations or lectures per week was double that at the University. Every student was examined at least once a week and "in the large majority of cases much oftener." Students were carefully placed according to ability, and had to demonstrate competence on periodic examinations or be turned back. The Lee faculty kept students alert by requiring "real class standing for graduation," thus breaking up "that spasmodic studying which was often done" at the university.

In 1866 the Lexington Law School, which Judge Brockenbrough had founded in 1849 and had operated alone, was formally annexed to Washington College. The relationship was cautious and tentative for the first few years, subject to periodic reconsideration and renewal by the trustees. As head of the school Judge Brockenbrough reported to President Lee; but the law division continued as a quasi-independent unit, and its students were not even permitted to use the library or buildings of the College. The story of the law school is treated separately in Chapter XXIV.

A school of Civil and Mining Engineering was activated during the Lee administration but it did not approach the comprehensiveness that the faculty had recommended. A Students' Business School also was established in connection with the College. It was the hope of General

Lee and the faculty that this would develop into a full-fledged school of commerce; but that dream was not to be realized until 1906.

New chairs were created in the later years of General Lee's presidency. In 1869 the board authorized a distinct chair of English Language and Literature, separating that subject from the chair of History, but adding Political Economy and International Law to the latter. The "social sciences" were here at last, and topics formerly discussed only in the debating societies and "bull sessions" became matter for the classroom.

One of General Lee's most cherished projects, the establishment of a school of agriculture, failed despite the president's personal efforts to obtain the financial basis for it. The means were sought through provisions of the Morrill Land Grant Act of 1862, by which the federal government gave each state thirty thousand acres of the public domain for support of schools of agriculture and the mechanical arts. Assignment of the land or its proceeds to specific institutions was left to the states. Soon after his arrival in Lexington General Lee committed to State Senator D. S. G. Cabell a petition of Washington College to the General Assembly, and requested Cabell to present it to the Senate at a favorable opportunity. The trustees designated General Lee and Bolivar Christian to represent the College before the legislature's Committee of Schools and Colleges. Lee departed for Richmond by stage, accompanied by General Francis H. Smith of V.M.I. who sought the land for his own institution. The two men must have been somewhat uncomfortable under the circumstances but, as gentlemen and good soldiers, they could conceal whatever feelings their rivalry might have engendered.

Neither institution received a commitment; and the Washington College trustees requested President Lee to renew the application to the next legislature, soliciting a portion of the land fund for endowment of chairs for applied science. At the close of 1866 they were still seeking part of the fund, as well as payment of interest on state debt due to the College. But the matter of the land fund persisted well beyond General Lee's death. Finally, in 1872, Virginia gave one-third of its Morrill grant to Negro education and two-thirds to the "Preston & Olin Academy," a small Methodist school in the southwestern part of the state, from which would grow the large and flourishing Virginia Polytechnic Institute.

ONE OF GENERAL LEE'S MOST INTERESTING INNOVATIONS was a venture for the education of young printer-journalists. Twenty-five scholarships were offered to students nominated by Southern typographical unions. In addition to opportunities for general education, the young men were given instruction in typography, stenography, and book-keeping. The scholarship men worked in the office of J. J. Lafferty & Company, publishers of the Lexington *Gazette*. Editor Lafferty was authorized to give instruction in stenography and in 1869 was named Superintendent of Instruction in typography.

In its accent on printing and mechanical production the program differed markedly from present-day journalism curricula. The latter are designed primarily to prepare students for work on metropolitan papers or with news services—or even in radio and television—where most of them will seldom or never set foot in a composing room. The Lee plan, however, reflected the needs of its times. Local journalism was more important and influential than it is in these days of syndicated columns and news networks. Most Southern newspapers were, like the *Gazette*, published in printing offices, with printer and editor the same man. Such a situation is still found among weeklies and some small dailies, where newspaper publishing and job printing are combined in one plant. But new production processes and "canned" editorials and features have changed even that picture.

A professional view of the program was expressed by the *Gazette:*

> So far as we know, on the part of our literary institutions, this is the first recognition of the claims of the printer, which has assumed anything like practical form. Should the idea of the trustees be carried into operation, opportunity will be offered young men who propose to enter printing offices, of acquiring not simply a plain education in elementary studies, but of securing accurate and extensive scholarship, which will not only be of great service to them in their business life, but must also be of incalculable advantage to the country, in thus securing a larger proportion of highly educated men in the printing offices all over the land.

An interesting comment came from John Plaxton, secretary of the Nashville, Tennessee, Typographical Union No. 20. This step by Washington College was one in the right direction "toward raising American Journalism from the slough of venality, corruption, and party subserviency into which it has too notoriously fallen. . . ."

Yet the announcement of the program drew much ridicule from the nation's press. The abuse seems to have been based on the false notion, widely disseminated, that journalism was to be taught as a humanity rather than a profession. The Charleston *News*, for example, reported a "general titter" caused by the proposed "Department of Current Literature." The Louisville *Courier-Journal* satirized the hypothetical chair, and nominated Horace Greeley as its first professor.

To recruit students the College sent letters to typographical unions, inviting applications or recommendations. One applicant from St. Louis, which apparently was recognized as "southern" enough, said that he believed himself capable of setting 1,000 ems of type per hour and thus could earn his board in two or three hours of work per day. Another signed himself "pressman" for the Brandon (Mississippi) *Republican* "(Strictly Democratic)." Spokesmen for the unions, though, sometimes expressed doubt that their nominees could meet Washington College's scholastic requirements.

General Lee's death dealt a severe blow to the journalism program before it had hardly gone beyond the blueprint stage. Few references to it appear in the records after October of 1870 and it was quietly dropped in the declining seventies. It remained for President Henry Louis Smith to implement General Lee's germinal idea and to expand it along modern lines during the nineteen-twenties.

DESPITE HIS INTRODUCTION OF INNOVATIONS, General Lee faithfully performed the obsolescent presidential function of attending examinations. On one occasion he sat next to student Hugh A. Moran, who wrote his father: "The old fellow had a book looking on, and tried to look wise; but I flattered myself that he did not know much about it." While in earlier times even the trustees had taken part in the administration of examinations, the diversity of the curriculum and the size of the student body now made it impracticable for any individual to "know much about it" at every examination.

Progress in the R. E. Lee regime brought acclaim from North as well as South. The New York *Herald* hailed the practical education program as likely to jolt "old fogy schools just as General Lee did old fogy generals." Western newspapers praised the program and caused hopes to rise that students from such states as Iowa, Illinois, Indiana, and Ohio would be drawn to Lexington. The issues of the *Gazette* during the late sixties teem with articles on the development of Washington College, its exciting new curriculum, and its munificence in distributing scholarships, as well as friendly letters heralding the new day.

One harsh critic of the College during these years was General Smith of V.M.I. Publicly he observed the necessary amenities, and representatives of the two Lexington institutions continued to participate jointly in formal occasions. But privately Smith expressed disapproval of developments at Washington College both generally and in detail. For instance, he told Matthew Fontaine Maury that the College was "floundering," without definite plans, and grasped at every new suggestion that might attract students. When despite all this the College remained below V.M.I. in numbers, agents were sent out to "drum up students." Smith complained of articles in the *Gazette* favorable to the College's New Program, "very dextrously worded," which grudgingly acknowledged what V.M.I. was doing "& twaddle from beginning to end."

Although details of General Lee's plans may be questioned, especially regarding their suitability to a liberal arts college, the basic ideas must be acknowledged as indicating a keen perception of the region's needs. His program of practical reconstruction through education for economic life foreshadowed the "New South." Some old comrades-in-arms concurred in his objectives. General Wade Hampton praised the efforts of Washington College in a speech at the Georgia State Fair at the end of the sixties. General Jubal A. Early stated the matter even more explicitly in an address at Lee Chapel on January 19, 1872, entitled "What Old Fogyism Did For Us." "Old Jube" declared that it was the material superiority of the North, a condition that Southerners held in contempt, which had brought about Confederate defeat. It was that nation of "brokers and builders" that had "crushed our liberty, desolated our lands and butchered the bravest and noblest of our kindred." Pointing to Japanese progress in western ways, Early concluded that the South must learn to esteem "in war or peace, the improvements which science, art, enterprise or industry have produced."

WHILE GENERAL LEE and his faculty were developing their projects of practical education, the trustees and their representatives were busily at work to strengthen the financial base of Washington College. The plight of the institution at war's end was reported by a trustees' committee on July 1, 1865. Solvent investments amounted to only a little more than $90,000. Worthless investments, including Confederate bonds and currency and several stock items, totaled over $21,000. A balance of less than $1,200 cash was on hand and professors' salaries were in arrears. Arrangements were made to borrow $5,600 to pay back salaries and those to fall due on January 1, as well as interest owed individuals. Another $2,000 was to be borrowed for building repairs and "philosophical apparatus." The board planned to petition the legislature, requesting payment on the state debt owed to literary institutions.

After General Lee's election to the presidency several agents were sent out to solicit funds. Among them were the Reverends Samuel D.

Stuart and E. P. Walton, and General William N. Pendleton. Members of the board and President Lee himself, to some extent, wrote letters during the fund drive.

The campaign was carried boldly to the North and even to England. The agents met many disappointments and elicited sharp rebukes for asking Northerners to support the institution headed by the arch-rebel and traitor. Yet a number of Yankees, such as Henry Ward Beecher and Samuel J. Tilden of New York, were above such malice and contributed to the College. As previously noted, Beecher spoke at a fundraising meeting. Thomas A. Scott, president of the Pennsylvania Railroad who had been Assistant Secretary of War under President Lincoln, made a series of gifts aggregating $60,000 during the R. E. Lee administration. Rathmell Wilson, a famous scientist of Philadelphia, sent a collection of several thousand books "to repair in some measure the effect produced by its [the northern army's] excessive destructiveness." W. W. Corcoran, distinguished Washington philanthropist, made numerous gifts including an invaluable collection of books and cash donations amounting to about $30,000.

Interest stimulated by the solicitation and by Lee's presence also brought some major benefactions that were not received until after the general's death. Principal contributions of the McCormick family, Mr. and Mrs. Warren Newcomb of New Orleans, and George Peabody of Massachusetts were of this kind.

Although the largest support came from the North, local people subscribed generously in response to the appeals. The venerable William S. White spoke on behalf of the College from the pulpit of the Lexington Presbyterian Church. Benefits, musicals, literary entertainments were presented in various border and Southern cities. An example of this activity was the public meeting in the Staunton Court House on November 27, 1865, at which was read a letter from General Lee to Colonel M. G. Harman, explaining the objects of the fund drive. Several prominent persons spoke and a committee was created, composed of three women from each church congregation in Augusta County. In 1866 trustee Christian and Professor Allan canvassed Kentucky in search of support. The Reverend Mr. Walton worked in such scattered cities as Philadelphia, St. Louis, Memphis, and Houston. The Reverend Mr. Stuart solicited in New York and Washington, among other cities, but his most noteworthy effort (even if not the most rewarding) was on a trip to England in 1866.

General Lee's sensitivity in financial matters placed him in a delicate position. He wished to avoid any suggestion that the solicitation was for his benefit, and he advised Stuart that his name should be omitted from the heading of a subscription list. Yet it was obvious that only General Lee's presence made Washington College's case different from that of other impoverished institutions. This was pointed out by several persons, especially in England. Fund-raising in that country on behalf of an American college would have ordinarily appeared to be absurd, in view of the relative wealth and resources of the United States. But among Southern expatriates and Confederate sympathizers, the idea of contributing to *General Lee's* college would presumably have appeared reasonable. And so agents spoke in terms of an "R. E. Lee Endowment," and the trustees authorized the use of the phrase.

Walton's efforts were far from successful. He was making some headway in Philadelphia when the newspapers printed scathing attacks upon Stuart's English mission, demanding to know why Englishmen should interest themselves in "an American traitor." Because the midterm elections of 1866 were in progress, such assaults frightened away those Democrats who had aided Walton. At year's end he reported that "universal depression prevails throughout the South." In the following spring he moved on to cultivate Texas. He sent home newspaper clippings that contained encomiums to the "matchless Lee" and plugs for Washington College, but little cash was forthcoming. In fact, he had to borrow money for his own needs, and was in trouble with his board bill. He ran into difficulty in soliciting Republicans. One Radical Republican was reported to have told Walton that he would give no money unless Negroes were admitted, thus anticipating the official attitude of the federal government by almost a century.

THUS IT WAS that in the spring of 1866 Stuart sailed for England to solicit admirers of the Confederate chieftain. Several prominent noblemen aided Stuart and made small contributions; but the agent ran into opposition, much of it from ex-Confederates and British sympathizers with the Lost Cause. One of the most critical and prominent of the latter group was Francis A. Lawley of the London *Times*, who had been his paper's Richmond correspondent during the war. Lawley protested that "the wealth of America is so boundless, & her prospects so exuberant, that public institutions such as Washington College should, rightly speaking, owe their origin to American, & exclusively American, sources of supply." He contended that General Lee would have been embarrassed if he had known of the solicitation of funds as tribute to him, and would be humiliated by the failure of the effort. Stuart's methods and personality seem to have aroused resentment. A. Dudley Mann, erstwhile Confederate diplomat then resident in France, criticized ministers of the Gospel out of their sphere, and called for a severe rebuke to Stuart which, however, should emanate from Lexington. It disgusted one Southerner "to see Southern men and the Southern cause *exploited* by such humbugs as our Revd. friend."

Other negative factors hampered Stuart's work. Britain was beset by a severe financial crisis. Claims by the United States against Great Britain for damage done by the *Alabama* and other British-built commerce destroyers affected attitudes of Englishmen. Stuart's publicity also attracted the attention of a group calling itself the "Committee of the Holders of 7% Cotton Bonds of the Southern States of America lately Confederated." The committee adopted a resolution that if a satisfactory arrangement for settlement of the loan should be made "by the Southern States of America, or otherwise, that bonds to the amount of £10,000 be handed over to the authorities of Washington College." In the face of such handicaps, and opposition ranging from bitter to facetious, Stuart returned to America.

WHILE THE GENERAL SOLICITATION was a failure, contacts with a few wealthy and public-spirited individuals proved rewarding. The examples of Cyrus McCormick and George Peabody may be mentioned.

The approach to McCormick, a native of Rockbridge County then residing in Chicago and New York, was not left to agents but was undertaken by the president and rector. Early in his administration General Lee sketched his educational proposals for the man who himself exemplified the application of science to agriculture and industry. The practical program would be requisite to the needs of the nation and would "enable those young men who do not desire to devote themselves to special professions, requiring specific studies after graduating to enter at once upon active pursuits of life." With delicate directness Lee wrote: "To you who are so conversant with the necessities of the country, & its vast undeveloped resources; the benefit of applying scientific knowledge & research, to agriculture, mining, manufacturing, architecture, &c to the construction of ordinary roads, R. Roads, canals, bridges &c, will be at once apparent: & it is hoped will elicit your approval."

Judge Brockenbrough, with his usual verbal effervescence, wrote McCormick a lengthy epistle which opened by describing the condition of the College as it had emerged from "the late horrid & revolting war," a victim of "Vandal" Hunter and his "myrmidons." He told of the financial need, the general local response, and the greater remaining requirements. He described the plans for five new "schools" with emphasis upon agriculture and the mechanic arts. The new and distinguished president had confidence that the real friends of the South among Northern people would not permit such a good cause to perish for lack of one or two hundred thousand dollars. Coming to the point, Judge Brockenbrough declared the need to erect immediately a large and "elegant" building for the new schools of agriculture and the mechanic arts. He urged: "Can you come down with a *good round sum* to build up a school with which your name will be associated in all time to come?"

The Rector mentioned also the desire of the trustees to raise General Lee's salary of $1,500 to $5,000.

On New Year's Day of 1866 McCormick replied to Judge Brockenbrough. He expressed some apprehension at the scope of plans for expansion of the College and pleaded that his financial circumstances were not so favorable as the Rector imagined, but said he would give $10,000 and would "reserve the privilege" of contributing more when the College program should mature.

Promptly the trustees created "The McCormick Professorship of Experimental Philosophy & Practical Mechanics," the College's third endowed chair. Professor Richard S. McCulloch was appointed to the chair and during 1866 McCormick added to its endowment. In various communications he expressed interest in the College and praise of President Lee. In 1869 he was elected a trustee. He was uncertain about accepting the position but asked that the place be kept open for him, and sent $5,000 as an earnest to the endowed chair. He never got around to attending trustees' meetings and does not seem to have visited Lexington until 1875, when he made two gifts totaling $700. Cyrus McCormick died in 1884, having given $20,000. His widow and descendants continued his interest in the institution and the family's benefactions aggregated more than $350,000. In 1932 when Washington and Lee and Rockbridge County participated in the "Centennial of the Reaper," a statue of Cyrus McCormick by John Bren was placed on the campus—to be mistaken by some visitors for a statue of Robert E. Lee. In 1941, when the University library was renovated and enlarged, it was named for McCormick.

THE ADMIRATION FOR GENERAL LEE held by George Peabody, enormously wealthy capitalist-philanthropist, brought Washington College and its successor large additions to endowment funds. In August of 1869 it was announced that Peabody had donated $60,000 to establish an additional professorship as proposed by General Lee. Peabody died in November of the same year. Lee's own state of health prevented his attendance at the funeral; thus he was unable to make an appearance in New York which McCormick and others believed would have had "a happy effect on the political mind of the North." In his will Peabody donated to Washington College a claim against the state of Virginia for state bonds lost in the steamer *Arctic* in 1854 en route from England. Because Peabody had obtained the bonds through a firm that was indebted to Virginia some doubt existed as to the liability of the state for their redemption. Once again the trustees were forced into court to realize the value of a benefaction. Finally in 1881 a decree for the entire amount was handed down—$145,-000 for the value of the bonds, plus interest from July 1, 1854. It took seven years more for payment of the whole debt which according to an official reckoning netted $250,000 after all costs of the litigation.

This was the largest contribution to come to the College up to that time. William W. Corcoran, the Washington banker and friend of education, had been the first to suggest to Peabody a "magnificent donation" to the institution, and William H. Ruffner also had aided in obtaining the bequest. The chair of Latin was placed upon the endowment and on February 18, 1895, the centennial of Peabody's birth was celebrated on the campus with appropriate ceremonies and addresses in Lee Chapel.

GENERAL LEE'S HEALTH, never robust during his tenure at Washington College, deteriorated during the fall of 1869. The president was forced to avoid exertion and exposure to inclement weather, and was constantly in pain. By April of 1870 it was apparent that he must relinquish his administrative duties. The trustees, acting on faculty recommendation, granted him a leave of absence.

General Lee sought improved health in a tour of the South during the late spring. The enthusiastic and affectionate greetings of his people made this journey a triumph indeed. Savannah and Charleston rendered homage to the old chieftain. The Charleston *Courier* observed that "General Lee is evidently feeble"; but upon his return to Lexington the local newspaper thought him improved in health and in good humor as he received the hearty greetings of townsmen.

During the summer he was reported in excellent spirits and healthful appearance. He took another trip, as far as Baltimore, where the distinguished physician Dr. Buckler predicted the general's speedy recovery and complete cure. Later, he went to Hot Springs, Virginia, with Professor White, "the Dean."

General Lee resumed his duties at the start of the new session in September of 1870. On the evening of the twenty-eighth he walked home through a rain from a church vestry meeting. Mrs. Lee observed that he looked chilly. As the family gathered for dinner, the general attempted to say grace; but he could not speak, and slumped down into his chair. His physicians were called and he was put to bed. The attack appears to have been what now would be called thrombosis.

On the following day the board and six faculty members met and considered the misfortune "which under Providence has prevented his attendance during this session." A committee was appointed to express the board's deep regrets, and "in view of the precarious state of his health, urge upon him leave of absence from College duties of six months."

But the end came within two weeks, on the morning of October 12. As student Lucius Desha wrote an alumnus friend, "recitations ceased immediately, students were much affected and behaved in an exemplary manner during the mournful ceremonies."

Official delegations came to grief-stricken Lexington for the old hero's funeral. The procession, headed by Professor White, the chief marshal, passed through Washington Street to Franklin Hall on Jefferson Street, thence to Main Street. In front of the hotel it was joined by dignitaries of the Commonwealth and by others; and in front of the courthouse by the organized citizenry. The procession then moved on to V.M.I. where that institution's board of visitors, faculty, and cadets joined. Later the cortege, completed by the College students as a guard of honor, proceeded to the chapel. There the column halted, to permit cadets and students to file through the building and pass the remains, after which they assembled in two groups on the chapel's south side. Burial was in a brick vault sunk in the middle of the room under the chapel formerly used as a library, above and behind which the recumbent statute of General Lee by Edward V. Valentine was to be placed. (For some years the faculty appointed students in alphabetical order to stand guard at Lee's tomb, between the hours 9 A.M.-2 P.M. and 4-6 P.M. This practice continued through the seventies as late as 1878.)

Classes resumed after a week's suspension. Saddened professors and trustees immediately bethought themselves of the proper mode of memorializing their late president. A eulogy was planned for January 19, 1871, Lee's birthday, and the faculty expressed the desire that this date "always" be celebrated at the institution. The day continues to be observed with a convocation of faculty and students.

Jefferson Davis was invited to deliver the eulogy at that first occasion. What an opportunity for the dramatic! But it was not to be. The

Confederate President pleaded that on the specified date he would have to attend a meeting of the directors of the insurance company with which he was connected, and so "it compels me to decline the grateful task which the Trustees have selected me to perform; that of delivering the Eulogy upon the Life and Character of their late President, my Friend Genl Lee, at the time of the next 'Commencement' of Washington College."

Perhaps other reasons than a conflict in dates contributed to Davis' refusal; for although the trustees suggested that his eulogy might be postponed until September of 1871 he never spoke on the campus. No doubt an encomium by the President of the Confederacy upon its military hero would have given political foes of the South an opportunity to assail Davis and to wave "the bloody shirt." Davis also may have had more personal reservations. In a letter to Professor Johnston, his wartime colleague, he observed that the South's "greatest man" was Johnston's father, General Albert Sidney Johnston.

Davis adverted in his letter to an address in Memphis by General William N. Pendleton on the character and last days of General Lee, delivered for the purpose of obtaining funds to enlarge the edifice where Lee had worshipped. The ex-President touched upon a matter soon to become sensitive and controversial: "It is unfortunate that so many forms of expressing the respect felt for the deceased hero should be presented at this time." Davis mentioned four: increased funds for Washington College, the erection of a sarcophagus, enlargement of the Episcopal Church at Lexington, and the construction of a monument in Richmond.

The death of R. E. Lee naturally occasioned public statements and editorial comment throughout the country. Particularly significant were tributes in the Radical Republican Washington *Chronicle* and Richmond *State Journal*, accurately predicting that in time General Lee would belong to all America.

Although the emphasis was of course upon Lee the general rather than Lee the college president, the latter role was not minimized. An example of praise for "the Educator" was in an address by Senator McCreery of Kentucky in support of his resolution respecting the restoration of "Arlington" to Mrs. Lee. Noting that the transition from camp to classroom had been "a rare occurrence," he declared that the general had been equally eminent in either place. Lee's ambition, said the senator, had been to make of Washington College an institution of high scholastic standards, and "the seat of science and of art as well as of literature." Undismayed by the manifold problems at his College, through administrative ability, zeal, and energy, he overcame them all to create a firm and solid institution: "There it stands, the pride of Virginia!"

But for simple eloquence, few if any expressions could have surpassed that of a young Kentuckian, privately penning his feelings, speaking from his heart for his generation and fellow collegians:

> I think that our University should be built up as the best and most lasting monument to General Lee—useful as well as enduring and just such as he might have wished. I feel that the place has been more hallowed by his death than by his living presence. . . . For myself, now that he is dead, I feel that I admire and appreciate his virtues more than I did before. . . .
>
> I feel that I love him for the example he has set, and the world and the South owe him a debt of gratitude for going forward and showing the way to win victory over defeat, and if we the men of the South, prove true to our duty and stand by principle as he did, then there's a better time coming. . . .

Chapter
XV

Decline, Depressions, Discouragement, 1870–1897

THOMAS JEFFERSON wittily remarked to a Frenchman who had inquired whether or not Jefferson had replaced Benjamin Franklin as American minister to France: "No one can replace him, sir; I am only his successor." So it must have been with General R. E. Lee's successor in the presidency of Washington College—for who indeed could have replaced the South's hero?

But the trustees apparently believed the choice of the most likely successor was obvious. Before the month of October 1870 was out they announced the election of General G. W. Custis Lee, Professor of Military and Civil Engineering and Applied Mechanics at the Virginia Military Institute, and son of General R. E. Lee.

At the time the appointment appeared to be an excellent one. Not only was the name of Lee retained in the headship of the institution, but the younger man was familiar with his father's work and plans and was himself engaged in higher education. In the prime of life, Custis Lee seemed in excellent health.

The new president had been graduated with first honors (and no demerits) at West Point, had served on President Davis' staff throughout the Civil War, and since September of 1865 had been a faculty member at V.M.I. At the Institute he had performed very satisfactorily, and in 1867 had been offered the presidency of Maryland Agricultural College, which he declined.

Simultaneously with Custis Lee's election was announced the change in the name of Washington College to Washington and Lee University. Both actions were received with hearty approval by the local press and by friends. The *Virginia Gazette* warmly praised the presidential choice and found the new name altogether appropriate since it had been General R. E. Lee who had converted the College into a university.

The faculty congratulated their new leader, let him know that they had privately favored him, and pledged their support to his administration. The students at a mass meeting hailed this "Providential appointment" and endorsed the change in the institution's name. They believed Washington and Lee was entering a new era. Influential alumni added their satisfaction, while Professor William Allan took a roseate view of the school's future. He wrote Professor W. LeRoy Broun: "We have the best set of students we have ever had and every thing . . . is running smoothly. I do not think the General's death will seriously affect our prosperity." On the contrary Allan thought the accession of Custis Lee would be "the occasion of our getting a stronger hold on the public." He was certain that in internal affairs the younger Lee's "tact, ability and administrative qualities will give him success."

Before making their decision the trustees seem to have sounded out opinions regarding Custis Lee. Trustee John Echols informed Judge Brockenbrough on October 25 that he had talked with people throughout the state, who generally approved the choice. Echols himself was "satisfied" and added: "I knew that Prest. Davis during the war thought that he was fully equal intellectually to his great Father, and I shall never forget the emphatic manner in which the Prest. said to me, on one occasion, that, if it had been necessary to send Genl. R. E. Lee away from Virginia, he did not know of any man to whom he would have preferred to have entrusted the command of the army in Va. than to Genl. Custis Lee."

Davis confirmed Echols' report after receiving the "welcome intelligence" of his friend's election. He wrote William Preston Johnston: "Few have enjoyed better opportunity to know him than myself, and I may therefore be excused for expressing the opinion that whether morally or intellectually regarded the Trustees could not have made a more fortunate selection." Davis then pointed to an aspect of Lee's character that perhaps was to be the key factor in his presidency: "The only defect I found in him was his extreme diffidence in his own

Ruins of Liberty Hall Academy.

The Colonnade at Washington and Lee.

William Graham,
Rector 1782–1796.

Samuel Legrand Campbell,
Rector 1797–1799.

George Addison Baxter,
Rector 1799–1813;
President 1813–1829.

RECTORS AND PRESIDENTS
SINCE 1782

Louis Marshall,
1830–1834.

Henry Vethake,
1834–1836.

Henry Ruffner,
1836–1848.

George Junkin,
1848–1861.

Robert Edward Lee,
1865–1870.

William Lyne Wilson,
1897–1900.

George Hutcheson Denny,
1901–1911.

George Washington Custis Lee,
1871–1897.

Henry Louis Smith,
1912–1929.

Francis Pendleton Gaines,
1930–1959.

Fred Carrington Cole,
1959–1967.

Robert Edward Royall Huntley,
1968–   ; also Dean of
the School of Law 1967–1968.

The funeral procession of General R. E. Lee turns into Main Street, Lexington, Virginia, October 18

PRESIDENT R. E. LEE AND THE WASHINGTON COLLEGE FACULTY.

(General Lee in center) *Outer circle reading clockwise:* from John W. Fuller (immediately below General Lee): Thomas T. Eaton, Charles S. Dod, Jacob Fuller, Richard S. McCulloch, James J. White, John L. Kirkpatrick, Alexander L. Nelson, William Allan, E. A. Moore, Rodes Massie, Milton W. Humphreys. *Inner circle reading clockwise:* beginning with Frank Preston (slightly below left of General Lee): Harry Estill, William Preston Johnston, Carter J. Harris, John L. Campbell, Edward S. Joynes, John W. Brockenbrough, C. P. Grady.

John Randolph Tucker,
Professor of Law 1870–1873;
Dean 1893–1897.

Charles Alfred Graves,
Professor of Law 1869–1899:
Dean 1897–1899.

John W. Brockenbrough,
Founder of the Lexington
Law School;
Professor 1866–1873.

Harry St. George Tucker,
Professor of Law 1897–1901;
Dean 1899–1901;
Acting President 1900–1901.

William Reynolds Vance,
1901–1903.

Martin Parks Burks,
1903–1918.

Joseph Ragland Long,
1918–1923.

William Haywood Moreland,
1923–1944.

John Lyle Campbell,
1877–1913.

Paul McNeel Penick,
1913–1940.

Clayton Epes Williams,
1945–1960.

Earl Stansbury Mattingly,
1940–1966.

James Walter Whitehead,
1966–

Charles Porterfield Light, Jr.,
1960–1967; 1968.

UNIVERSITY DEANS

David Carlisle Humphreys,
Dean of the School of Applied
Science 1904–1921.

James Lewis Howe,
Dean of the School of Applied
Science 1921–1932.

Henry Donald Campbell,
Dean of the University
1906–1932.

Robert Henry Tucker,
Dean of the University 1932–1946;
Acting President 1930.

Lucius Junius Desha,
Dean of the University 1946–1

Glover Dunn Hancock,
Dean of the School of Commerce
and Administration 1920–1949.

James Graham Leyburn,
Dean of the University 1947–1956.

Leon Franklin Sensabaugh,
Dean of the University 1956–1

Frank Johnson Gilliam,
Dean of Students 1930–1962.

William Webb Pusey, III,
Dean of the College 1960–   ;
Acting President 1967–1968.

Lewis Whitaker Adams,
Dean of the School of Commerce
and Administration 1949–

The faculty of the late Victorian Age.

The W. and L. baseball team of 1898.

The Generals' football team of 1897.

The W. and L. Glee Club of 1898.

Editors of the *Ring-tum Phi* for 1900–1901.

SEVERAL DISTINGUISHED ALUMNI AS CHOSEN BY THE *Calyx* OF 1920. *Above left:* Thomas Nelson Page '73, writer of romantic Southern novels and stories; Ambassador to Italy 1913–1921. *Above right:* John W. Davis '92 and '95 Law, Ambassador to Great Britain, 1918–1921; Democratic candidate for President of the United States, 1924; distinguished lawyer. *Below left:* Henry D. Flood '85, Congressional leader of the Wilson Era. *Below right:* Newton Diehl Baker '94 Law, Mayor of Cleveland; Secretary of War, 1916–1921; distinguished lawyer.

THE FACULTY OF 1923–1924. *Bottom row:* Lawrence P. Haynes (Mathematics), E. E. Brett (Physical Education), Earle K. Paxton (Mathematics), Lewis Tyree (Law); *second row up:* Robert H. Tucker (Economics), Frank A. Shufeldt (Spanish), James W. Kern (Ancient Languages), R. E. Witt (Mathematics); *third row up:* William T. Lyle (Engineering), R. Granville Campbell (Political Science), Hale Houston (Engineering); *fourth row up:* William M. Brown (Education), Benjamin A. Wooten (Physics), D. B. Easter (Romance Languages), Edgar F. Shannon (English); *top row:* S. C. Ogburn (Chemistry), William Coan (Accounting), Livingston W. Smith (Mathematics).

THE FACULTY OF 1923–1924. *Clockwise from center bottom:* James A. McPeek (English), Robert W. Dickey (Electrical Engineering), C. E. Williams (Law), John A. Graham (Spanish), Homer A. Holt (Law), Forest Fletcher (Physical Education), James S. Moffatt (English), William D. Hoyt (Biology), Solly A. Hartzo (Commerce), George S. Fulbright (Public Speaking), Rupert N. Latture (Romance Languages), W. G. Bean (History), Carl E. L. Gill (Commerce), Henry H. Simms (History). *Interior circle reading clockwise from center bottom:* James R. Howerton (Philosophy), L. J. Desha (Chemistry), Thomas J. Farrar (German), Franklin L. Riley (History).

A Southern and National Shrine: The Lee Chapel.

ability, and that leaned so much to virtue's side, that most parents would be glad to have such an example before their sons."

Lee's shyness or self-distrust seems to have been recognized, but without realization of its possible effect on his fulfilling the duties of a college president in the difficult years of the later Reconstruction era. Professor Allan, in his letter to Broun, conceded that Lee's retiring nature would prevent his impressing the public, but he brushed that consideration aside as unessential. A penciled memorandum among the trustees' papers, initialed "F.T.A." (probably Francis T. Anderson), inquired into Lee's religion, referred to the "pro's and con's," and mentioned an "excess of modesty." The religious topic was given most weight. It is surprising that this scion of so famous an Episcopalian family had not joined the church; but all was made well in June, 1871, when President Lee was confirmed by Bishop Whittle in the Grace Episcopal Church at Lexington.

If there were other misgivings, they did not find expression. Nor was the bachelor status of their new president the cause of trustee apprehension, although in common with others in that category he was made the object of jocular comment through the years. The trustees fixed the salary of the president at $1,500, set aside the Lee house for Mrs. R. E. Lee's use during her lifetime, and undertook to pay her an annuity of $3,000. More than that, they assured Custis Lee that they would sustain him enthusiastically and unanimously in the futherance of his father's "great work" in extending and building up the curriculum and facilities.

Custis Lee was inaugurated as President of Washington and Lee University on February 6, 1871, in the old chapel before an audience of townspeople and students who had braved a snowstorm to witness the ceremony. The V.M.I. faculty attended the induction which was prefaced by singing, prayer, and the reading of scripture by the Reverend Dr. Pendleton of Grace Episcopal Church.

Judge Brockenbrough, who had been relatively restrained at the induction of R. E. Lee, had freer rein this time for his compulsive oratory. He devoted a portion of his address to lamenting the great chieftain's death, and followed with a discussion of the illustrious antecedents of Custis Lee. In sounding phraseology he declared that all these forebears pointed "with unerring certainty to the conviction among the ranks of living men, [that] the son of Gen. R. E. Lee was the most fit person to secure the full fruition of a policy so wisely originated and matured during the years of a nobly spent life." In his closing words Judge Brockenbrough voiced the hopes not only of the trustees but of the public as he charged Custis Lee: "Your own ripe scholarship, well-balanced mind, your hereditary devotion to duty, your thorough moral and intellectual training, are but so many guarantees of your perfect success in accomplishing the great work committed to your hands." With these words ringing in his ears Custis Lee took the oath of office, and then uttered a fourteen-line acceptance in which he asked the cooperation of trustees, faculty, and students.

THE SIGNS WERE AUSPICIOUS; and for a while it appeared that the high hopes for the new administration were justified. During his first year in office Custis Lee proposed, in a comprehensive report to the trustees, a continuation of the development of Washington and Lee University along the lines advocated by R. E. Lee. But the trustees postponed action and delayed approval because of the financial difficulties of the institution.

Although documentary proof is lacking, some investigators have held that Custis Lee keenly felt this frustration of his program, coming as it did at the outset of his regime. At any rate, thereafter he rigidly confined himself to his executive duties, with occasional stints of teaching in the engineering department. His subsequent annual reports to the trustees were punctiliously correct in setting forth factual data and statistics but were devoid of educational ideas or plans.

Following that initial effort Lee's administration was characterized by his submission of a series of resignations (which were declined), leaves of absence, periods of ill health, and repeated indulgence by the trustees. It is doubtful whether a situation comparable to that of Custis Lee and his relations with the Board of Trustees could be found in the history of American higher education. Psychosomatic medicine had not been recognized in the nineteenth century; but a modern physician would undoubtedly discern the physical effects of mind and emotion in the unhappy experience of this reticent man, overshadowed by his father, the beneficiary of an undesired nepotism.

Beginning in the late winter of 1872 Custis Lee absented himself from the campus with increasing frequency. In 1874 he submitted the first of his resignations, declaring that his health was deteriorating and that his physicians had told him he must "lead a more active life." If the trustees could not accept his resignation, he requested a year's leave without pay. On behalf of the trustees the Reverend B. M. Smith reported their pain at his wish to resign. They desired him to remain and help them effect his father's "large and liberal" plans "for the good of our beloved Virginia & the entire Southern country." But they granted his wish for a year's leave.

In June of 1876 President Lee asked and received another year of leave. He reminded the board that "you always have my resignation in your hands" and that "nothing would afford me more real gratification than the appointment of some one to the office . . . who would be of greater service to the institution than I am or can ever hope [to] be." A year later the trustees learned with regret of the continued ill-health of their president, assured him of their sympathy and of their desire that he resume his duties, and granted him conditional leave for the session 1877–1878 should his health require it.

After persuading Custis Lee to withdraw another resignation, tendered on June 25, 1878, the trustees indicated at least some uneasiness by resolving that three months' notice must be given for a resignation by president or professors to become effective at the end of an academic year. The resolution did not seem to affect Lee's future efforts to leave office.

In June of 1879 the trustees reaffirmed their full confidence in Custis Lee and expressed the hope that his health would permit him to resume his duties. For several years thereafter no presidential resignations appear in the records, and occasional highly complimentary notices concerning Lee were printed in the newspapers. Dr. Thomas T. Everett of Philadelphia, who received an honorary D. D. from Washington and Lee, indicated a favorable opinion of the president's views and administration in a communication to the Philadelphia *Progress*. G. Watson James, also a degree recipient, extolled Custis Lee in 1882 in the Richmond *State* as a "wonderful" administrator and a friend of the students, who idolized him.

But the early 1880's saw Washington and Lee reach nadir in enrollment, and on June 16, 1885, the President submitted his resignation for reasons of ill-health and "other causes" that he did not care to discuss. Again the trustees induced him to withdraw it and adverted to his able and satisfactory service. They extended to him a leave of absence from November to May, or for such time as his physician should recommend. Lee declined that offer, and also the provision of a secretary; but he was relieved of all classes except one for the session 1885–1886. He was too ill to attend commencement of 1886, and begged the trustees to believe that he was "ready and willing" to vacate his office whenever they might conclude that a change could be made for the better.

During the late eighties there appeared to be a surcease from formal resignations of the president. Yet in 1887 he wrote of his desire to separate himself from his duties and observed that several times he had tried to do that but without success. He told a friend that fate seemed to have decreed that he should remain to the end at Washington and

Lee, and added that perhaps it was best even from his own viewpoint, as he was "too good for nothing . . . to undertake anything else."

Tulane University conferred its first honorary degree (LL.D.) upon Custis Lee in June, 1887. While fulsome citations for such honors perhaps should be taken with a grain of salt, it should be noted that the president of Tulane was William Preston Johnston, former Washington and Lee professor, who awarded this degree with especial warmth: "He has borne the weight of a great name so well, that no one can think him an unworthy successor, in his last great work, to Robert E. Lee. He is as good a man, and of as royal a nature, as is alive on earth."

Six years later, however, President Lee's health had become extremely bad. In June of 1893 he informed the board of his wish to resign, transmitting the message verbally through John L. Campbell, treasurer of the University. He apparently felt too ill to submit a written statement, and Campbell had to call twice before he could see Lee to give him the trustees' reply. Again the board reacted warmly and unanimously in sending President Lee their deep and "affectionate sentiments." But these sentiments might have been partially inspired by the fact that, as trustee William McLaughlin expressed it to Campbell, Lee's resignation would have been considered disastrous. Campbell's report of his first interview with Lee during this exchange is a moving document, relating his impression of Lee's "noble forgetfulness of self, his devoted loyalty to the University, and his great desire to serve its interests at the sacrifice of his own convenience and comfort."

By the following June President Lee was able to write the trustees his thanks for their kind sentiments brought by Mr. Campbell, but he remained anxious not to burden Washington and Lee. Bluntly and pathetically he stated that he did not think he should ever be good for anything. It is not surprising that in these last years students saw Lee but rarely, although he was punctual in presiding over faculty meetings.

The academic end came for President Lee in 1896. In the spring he referred to the probable increase of expenses at the University and the likely decrease in enrollment because of the abolition of the preparatory department, and asked that his salary be reduced to place it in line with the salaries of professors. On December 29 he resigned, telling the board plainly what he had said before, that he was "utterly useless here, with but little probability of ever being useful to the University. . . ." At long last his resignation was accepted.

The trustees conferred upon Custis Lee the title of "President emeritus"; it was the first time that designation had been used at the institution. The board also offered that he should continue to live in his campus residence and voted him a yearly salary of $2,000. Lee refused the house on the ground that it should be the residence of the president of the University, and the salary because he believed the institution needed all its resources for its own work. In the summer of 1897 General G. W. Custis Lee left Lexington to reside at "Ravensworth" in Fairfax County, the old homestead of his maternal grandmother's family, the Fitzhughs.

In contrast to presidents of Washington College who had departed in bitterness and sometimes in haste, Custis Lee maintained cordial relations with the University for the rest of his life. His continuing interest was manifested by the gift of more than 500 volumes to the library, the establishment of a scholarship, and the donation in 1897 of the priceless Charles Willson Peale portraits of Washington and Lafayette. In 1898 he was elected to the Board of Trustees, but declined on the plea that he could not attend meetings and—characteristically —that he could not contribute anything if he did. In 1901 the ex-president lent Washington and Lee the valuable collection of family portraits that had hung at Mount Vernon and Arlington, and in his will gave the University title to the collection. In addition he bequeathed his interest in a certain claim against the United States government, and provided that $5,000 in cash should be used as an endowment in the improvement and protection of the Lee Chapel.

Custis Lee died at Ravensworth February 18, 1913. The Washington and Lee trustees at their June meeting adopted an eloquent resolution declaring that: "His administration witnessed periods of depression in the affairs of the University calculated to make the stoutest heart lose courage, yet at no time did he lose confidence in the work to which he had put his hand. . . ." *De mortuis nil nisi bonum.*

NOTWITHSTANDING all the fine things that had been said of Custis Lee as a man, "the perfect gentleman," it must have become painfully obvious that he was far from a success as a college president.

Hopes had been high at the beginning of his administration. While other Southern colleges and universities generally had had to struggle for survival amid the prostration that had followed the decision of Appomattox, Washington College had been relatively prosperous through its good fortune in having R. E. Lee as President. It had pulled ahead of many other regional institutions and seriously challenged the more broadly based University of Virginia. The loss of the great leader was a severe blow; but the University now was a living memorial to him, and enjoyed the momentum that his influence had given it.

Optimism continued through 1871. Trustee James D. Davidson told Cyrus McCormick in March that "Our university never had better, or as good and encouraging prospects, as now." In September it about held its own in enrollment despite reported declines at other institutions in the state, including V.M.I. and the University of Virginia. "We have opened well," declared Professor William Allan in a letter to a colleague. The board congratulated the president and faculty on the prosperity of Washington and Lee and was gratified at an actual increase in numbers of students from Rockbridge County and other parts of Virginia. But disturbances in the Southern states had sharply reduced attendance from other regions. In all, there were 286 students from nineteen states and one territory.

Enrollment declined only slightly in 1872–1873 and the trustees again highly commended the Custis Lee regime in June of 1873. It was ominous, however, that only 117 of the 263 students had paid their tuition in money. The others were on "Coupon scholarships" and the "Long Credit."

Matters became worse with the national economic crisis of 1873. President Lee's annual report for 1873–1874 listed only 78 of 226 students who paid their fees in money. In the following year 110 out of 196 were on coupon scholarships or the free list. By 1877 registration had fallen to 134 and it became necessary to solicit students throughout the South, under the direction of Professor James J. White. But the trend continued downward and in 1880 the number fell below 100 for the first time since 1865. There was some recovery through the eighties, though not fully satisfactory, and in the last few years of the Custis Lee administration, enrollment fluctuated above and below 200.

The loss of R. E. Lee's personal magnetism, the economic decline of the South, and the panics of 1873 and 1893 undoubtedly affected attendance at Washington and Lee. Various other factors were cited. Some alumni blamed apathy among their own number. One of them charged that the reactivated alumni association existed for "oyster openings" and champagne jollifications only. An unsigned article in the student magazine *Southern Collegian*, apparently written by trustee Bolivar Christian, criticized the Presbyterian domination of board and faculty, and urged enlargement of the board to include a prominent person from each Southern state. "We *must* conciliate. Colleges, like all other enterprises, must stoop to *seek* patronage."

It is paradoxical that despite the sad economic plight of the region, and the difficulties its educational institutions were experiencing generally, old colleges were being revived and new ones created in the South. Colonel William Preston Johnston in 1874 and Acting President White in 1877, analyzing the situation of Washington and Lee, both emphasized the effects of financial pressure upon enrollment, but also observed that the new and expanded colleges were drawing students away. Professor White additionally blamed the "free-school" feature adopted at the University of Virginia and the decline in elementary classical education, through which the "source of supply is thus dried up."

A writer in the *Southern Collegian* in 1877, using the pseudonym "Loudon," offered an interesting view. The adversities of the Civil War had so ingrained economy into Virginians that even though some had regained a measure of affluence they retained a closeness with money. The *nouveaux riches* by hook or by crook had to an extent supplanted the Virginia gentlemen—"the bottom rail was on top." These parvenus wished to send their sons to college, "but it must not cost them much." Therefore they sent their boys to the University of Virginia.

Early in 1878 the *Southern Collegian* expressed concern that Lexington's isolation was causing Washington and Lee to be forgotten. (The nearest railroad was twenty miles away.) Deploring conditions on the Goshen turnpike, the magazine complained: "A wretched road, traveling at the rate of three miles an hour at an exorbitant price, has doubtless kept many students from the halls of our institution." While the Goshen turnpike was probably no worse than it had been in R. E. Lee's time, access in 1878 was indeed worse because a flood the previous year had destroyed portions of the canal.

Low enrollment was partly a cause and partly a result of the University's poor financial condition, inadequacy of facilities, and general inability to provide the educational services that trustees and faculty desired. Needs for institutional development and for obtaining outside support were clearly evident.

Shortcomings of the physical plant were illustrated by the observations of a geologist who visited Lexington in the summer of 1873 and wrote of his journey in the *Atlantic Monthly*. Although pleasantly situated atop a ridge and with a most "enchanting" view, "the place offended by its dirty, unkempt look." He described "an unshapely, dingy old building" which appeared "the more forlorn" because of its contrast to the new Lee Chapel.

A procession of faculty resignations throughout the seventies reflected conditions at the University and added to its problems. Professor John Randolph Tucker was elected to Congress, but the most common reason for departure was insufficient compensation. William

Allan, Judge Brockenbrough, William Preston Johnston, R. S. McCulloch, N. A. Pratt, Edward S. Joynes, and Milton Wylie Humphreys
were others who left. Colonel Johnston resigned in 1873, but remained
in Lexington for several years. He served as agent for the University,
lectured occasionally, practiced law, taught in the law school from
1876 to 1880, and sold some historical papers in his possession to raise
cash for support of his family. Meanwhile he completed and published
a well-written but controversial biography of his father, General
Albert Sidney Johnston. He left Lexington for a short, stormy tenure
as president of Louisiana State University and a distinguished administration as president of Tulane University.

In his analysis of Washington and Lee's problems in 1874 Colonel
Johnston, judging the South "a ruined country" in material wealth,
saw the region's only hope in its moral energies, and "chief among the
agencies of redemption was education. . . ." The Southern people
expected and indeed demanded the completion of the broad program
of R. E. Lee, and that Washington and Lee become not only "the
representative University of the South," but equal to the best among
American institutions. The needed money could not come from student fees, for each student cost the University some fifty or sixty
dollars more than he paid in tuition—"an ungracious fact" from the
proclamation of which the authorities shrank. (Modern officials are not
so shrinking, as the discrepancy between income from fees and cost of
instruction is a prime argument in college and university fund-raising.)
If the trustees did not openly acknowledge that technicality, they
knew that money must be obtained by solicitation.

THERE WERE MANY SCHEMES afoot for the development of the University, most of them centering around exploiting the name of R. E. Lee.
As early as 1871 one such plan was presented to the board in considerable verbosity by Colonel Joseph W. Taylor of Alabama. Its object
was to convert the institution into the "Lee Monumental University,"
with the backing of the entire South.

The trustees endorsed the Taylor plan. In fulfillment of R. E. Lee's
program they proposed further enlargement of the curriculum to provide educational facilities "unsurpassed by any Institution in the country. . . ." They invited contributions totaling $400,000 for the inaugu-
ration of new courses and the construction of new buildings. If the
fund-raising goal should not be attained by January 1, 1876, instead of
creating a "Lee Monumental University" the money collected would
be used to establish "Lee Monumental Departments."

Taylor conjured up scholarship plans, including "perpetual" scholarships, and a system of free tuition for a number of students from each state in proportion to the ratio of contributions from the states. Taylor, naturally, was to be "General Agent" in the solicitation of funds. A board committee arranged details for compensating him on a percentage basis, and allowing him to keep $5,000 from the initial funds he obtained. But nothing came of this grand idea, one of the many paper designs and pipe dreams through Washington and Lee history. No doubt the hard times of Reconstruction, aggravated by the panic of 1873 and prolonged depression, sealed the fate of the "Lee Monumental University."

AT THE CLOSE OF THE SESSION 1873–1874, which hardly seems to have given any cause for rejoicing, the trustees strangely congratulated themselves on the excellent results of the year. Yet at the same meeting they authorized their executive committee to sell $30,000 of six per cent scrip, secured either by the University's real estate or by interest on state securities due on or after January 1, 1880. A board committee was set up to present to wealthy men "the condition of our interest-bearing endowment, which is now inadequate to support the charges upon it."

General Robert D. Lilley had been appointed fund-raising agent for the board. His efforts, like those of his predecessors in that office, seem to have been ineffective; and he indulged in misrepresentation that drew the ire of veteran trustee Benjamin Mosby Smith. Lilley's oral report to the trustees was deemed unspecific; and his tabulated statement revealed that while the treasury had received $15,000 Lilley had paid "himself for his services, in round numbers, $18,000." Dr. Smith took vigorous exception to General Lilley's circulars, particularly to a statement that "W. & L. University '*has now an endowment of $300,000*, an aggregate capital of more than half a *million dollars, and is free* from debt!'" Patently it was dishonest to talk of Washington and Lee's wealth when the trustees were offering scrip for sale. Dr. Smith also assailed the scholarship sales. After paying twenty per cent to agents and fifty dollars tuition fee for each scholarship holder, there was little left for endowment. Much had been broadcast by General Lilley of state professorships, but the public should know that they existed only on paper.

Dr. Smith expressed himself also on a key point in the University's fund-raising of that period:

> It is time that we cease "big talking" of what we *intend* and *purpose to do,* & especially, cease to *ask* or *claim patronage for our Institution,* because *named for Gen'l Lee,* or because, we retain

custody of his honored and glorious remains. While he lived it was all right to ask patronage for an Institution, over which *He* presided, for his *living presence* was a *power*, to encourage, incite, restrain, and govern youth, was worth all he cost, had he done no more than live in his house, and walk among the students. Even "a living dog, is better than a dead lion."

In 1878 Acting President White made a fruitless recruiting trip to Texas, and later in the same year Colonel Johnston was appointed agent to stimulate patronage and endowment. Meanwhile, General Lilley's services as agent were continued.

Somehow the University struggled through the eighties. At the start of the decade President Custis Lee, with enrollment hovering at the hundred mark, suggested a reduction of student fees, which were higher than those at other Virginia colleges. Lilley and White labored to stir interest in New York, largely through the alumni. Registration crept upward; but the feeble academic state of the college can be measured by the fact that only two A.B. degrees and one Ph.B. were awarded at commencement of 1883. Eleven men won the B.L. degree. The alarmed trustees in June of 1884 deplored the meager numbers taking baccalaureate degrees, the irregularity of courses, and the freedom of election permitted. They called upon the faculty to investigate and correct the evils believed to exist. In June of 1885 the board resolved that "at a time when some other Institutions of the State have, by the energy of their respective Faculties secured large accessions of students, the members of the Faculty of this University are respectfully urged to devote themselves, especially during vacations to the use of diligent efforts for securing similar results." Urging the faculty to "beat the bushes" for students was an act of desperation, which could hardly produce anything except resentment. Enrollment declined by twenty-five in 1885, and in 1886 only three A.B.'s were conferred.

A FOREBODING of the twentieth-century running debate over the relation of "scholarship" to teaching may be read into suggestions made in 1885 by the distinguished alumnus Clifton R. Breckinridge, Congressman from Arkansas and associate trustee. He feared that Washington and Lee could draw patronage from a distance only by the appointment of eminent scholars to its faculty. With an eye on Johns Hopkins he advised: "You need men who can and will write books, as well as lecture, and of sufficient merit to attract the attention of the country." Breckinridge illustrated his point by the example of William Preston Johnston, whose writings had brought him a reputation and the presidency of "one of the most promising Universities in America [Tulane]."* Breckinridge may be forgiven for failing to comprehend a distinction that is not generally recognized even today. Johns Hopkins had been established as a graduate school on the model of the German university, dedicated to research and specialized advanced study, whereas Washington and Lee represented the English tradition of a college devoted to liberal education. The Congressman could not know that the forced hybridization of the two types of institutions in single universities, a process just getting under way in his day, would cause severe stresses and strains in American higher education to the detriment of undergraduate instruction. Breckinridge may be regarded as an unwitting harbinger of the "publish or perish" doctrine.

The eighties were not entirely without favorable developments. Mrs. Warren Newcomb donated funds for the construction of a building, completed in 1882, as a memorial to her husband. By 1888 the litigation over the Peabody bequest had been settled, bringing the University a quarter million dollars in all. At the close of the dreary decade enrollment was climbing, aided by the incipient economic boom which reached its zenith (and then collapsed) in 1893. Registration then spiraled downward again and the trustees insisted on the most rigid economy.

PERHAPS A MEASURE of the desperation felt at Washington and Lee by the spring of 1896 was disclosed by the discussion in faculty and board of the issue of coeducation. This question involved attitudes deeply rooted in American historical experience. In the long-settled East and South, the older colleges had been established for men and were continuing as such. Higher education was deemed intellectually and physically strenuous for women and likely to affect the feminine graces expected of those in the upper socio-economic classes. These views were especially strong in the South where the influence of plantation life, Negro servants, and Sir Walter Scott's novels has even yet not yielded entirely to the effects of emancipation, urbanization, and Margaret Sanger. Colleges were indeed being opened for women in the

* Neither Johnston's biographer Arthur M. Shaw nor John P. Dyer, author of a recently published (1966) history of Tulane, seems to have considered Johnston's writing a major factor in his election as president of that university. Shaw had no doubt that the appointment was due principally to the influence of Johnston's cousin, close friend, and former college mate, General Randall L. Gibson, who was president of the Tulane board of administrators.

nineteenth century, providing more advanced instruction than the female seminaries and academies of the Ann Smith type had afforded. But in these the students were shielded from working association and competition with men; and in addition to academic subjects they could still find courses in genteel arts such as drawing, music, and sometimes ceramics.

In the Middle and Far West, coeducation very early became the general rule. Frontier conditions still prevailed in many areas late in the century and were still well remembered in others. Where women had worked and often fought alongside their men, it was natural for their daughters to go to school with their sons.*

At Washington and Lee little mention of coeducation had appeared publicly before Professor Addison Hogue moved in the faculty on June 1, 1896, to admit women students. A lone article in the *Southern Collegian*, in 1888, had advocated coeducation and denied that Southern women would lose "*delicacy* and *refinement*" by associating with men in college. The record regarding Hogue's motion is skeletal, but an adverse vote of seven to three suggests that there was no real likelihood for the adoption of the proposal. Hogue persisted with a second motion, to admit women from Lexington and vicinity, which lost more narrowly, six to four.

Even if coeducation had carried the faculty it seems highly improbbable that the trustees of 1896 would have seriously considered such a radical departure. The reverend trustee Dr. E. C. Gordon moved on June 17, 1896, for the appointment of a board committee to inquire into the expediency of "opening the doors of this University to women." Next day the board tabled Dr. Gordon's resolution, and nothing further was heard of the explosive issue for several years.

The enrollment situation became so serious by the fall of 1896 that the trustees called a special meeting "to consider the causes which have led to the large falling off of students this session, and to remove the causes if practicable. . . ." Professor James A. Quarles prepared a memorandum for Judge William McLaughlin, the rector, on the fluctuation of enrollments 1886–1896, which had risen to 242 but had cur-

---

* An intermediate pattern, "coordinate" colleges for men and women within the framework of a university, was introduced in 1886 when Mrs. Warren Newcomb founded Newcomb College in Tulane University as a memorial to her daughter Sophie. The arrangement has often been merely administrative rather than functionally distinct, as coordinate women's colleges have varied from geographically separate units, such as Mary Washington College of the University of Virginia, to integrated divisions such as Radcliffe whose students attend Harvard College classes.

rently dropped to 180. Quarles discounted the effect of hard times on the ground that other institutions had not similarly suffered. The decline could not be attributed to lack of excellent instruction, he averred, nor to inadequacy of facilities, which had been markedly improved in recent years. The school was in better condition than ever before to do good work and to receive larger numbers of young men. Quarles then listed what he considered the reasons for Washington and Lee's failure.

First he cited the lack of active personal supervision by the president, which had not been possible because of Custis Lee's health. Thus the institution had been without vigorous leadership. Next Quarles blamed the toleration of saloons in Lexington. (The town was to go dry within a few years.) He pointed to the rise of West Virginia University as an illustration of the proliferation in the South of excellent colleges. Quarles mentioned also the high prices in Lexington (always the cry in college towns); the dropping of preparatory classes; and increased fees in the School of Law.

Two factors listed by Quarles deserve particular attention. A Presbyterian clergyman himself, he believed that the University had followed an ambiguous course regarding religious affiliation that by 1896 had left it without a real constituency from which to draw. Since it was professedly nondenominational it had cut loose from Presbyterian traditions, causing many alumni to become lukewarm or hostile. Dr. Quarles could think of only two or three loyal friends of Washington and Lee among the Lexington Presbytery. Even alumni guided their ministerial candidates to Hampden-Sydney. Yet although the institution had "alienated the Presbyterians" it had "failed to gain the favor of other churches, by keeping the Board and the Faculty stocked with Presbyterians."

Another serious weakness was the attempt to cover too many fields. Quarles held that on a yearly budget of less than $40,000 it was impossible to do adequate work in law, the academic college, postgraduate training, and engineering. In his view Washington and Lee had means only sufficient to maintain a good undergraduate college. By implication he suggested that the Law School be dropped, in order that several professors could be added to the academic faculty. On this basis the school could compete with Southern rivals. Dr. Quarles concluded: "As it is how can we expect students to pay us $80 [tuition], when better advantages are offered elsewhere for less money?" That question has had a haunting refrain in the years since 1896.

Professors David C. Humphreys, Henry D. Campbell, and Addison Hogue also addressed themselves to the problem in a report of 1896.

They fixed a desirable enrollment at between 300 and 500; but emphasized that the faculty should not be required to recruit students. These professors considered it the first duty of faculty and trustees "to see to it that we really have superior advantages to offer." They advocated a policy which would maintain high standards and draw a student body of picked young men from the entire South. The best agents for the school were its students, who if they felt the University to be excellent and modern would commend it to others. The committee then issued a warning which, although more needful in 1896 than today, may well be kept in mind at Washington and Lee and all institutions with long and honorable histories: "There is so much of interest in our history that we must be careful not to produce an impression that our history is of more importance than the work we are doing."

The board members were thus subjected to strong arguments for new policies and methods, which only energetic leadership could put into effect. And perhaps, beneath the continued cordiality and expressions of esteem toward their president, the trustees nursed a growing disenchantment that finally moved them to accept one of his resignations.

President Lee's last annual report of June, 1897, barren and laconic as usual, listed the enrollment at 173—a loss of 50 from the past session. Thus the younger General Lee passed from office bequeathing to his successors the solution of one of the most chronic problems of the preceding twenty years—that of adequate numbers of students.

Chapter
XVI

Critics, Contentions, and Other Vexations

Besides the practical problems of enrollment and finances, the years of Custis Lee were plagued with troubles of less tangible character. Washington and Lee was thrust into an unsought rivalry with the University of Virginia; the old issue of sectarianism flared again; and plans for a gala centennial celebration were met with frustration.

While General R. E. Lee lived and served as president of Washington College it was not possible for critics within Virginia openly to attack him or his institution. Student magazines of the College and the University of Virginia printed articles of mutual friendliness in 1869. But after R. E. Lee's death critics came into the open. Hostile articles appeared in the *Virginia Educational Journal* and the *Virginia University Magazine*, ridiculing Washington and Lee as a college presuming to be a university. In June of 1871 a sharp editorial in the Richmond *Whig*, "embodying an equally outrageous one from the Petersburg *Index*," assailed the Lexington institution as (among other faults) being dependent upon "the capital of a great name" and hardly more than "a sectarian institution in the Presbyterian interest. . . ."

Trustee Bolivar Christian retorted to the *Whig* through the columns of the Staunton *Valley Virginian.* He pointed out the influence of R. E. Lee and Washington College on education in Virginia and elsewhere, and deplored that anyone should attempt to impede Lee's program which was being carried on by his son. He denied that the Episcopalian Lees should have been so foolish or knavish as to build up a Presbyterian school. Christian declared that Washington and Lee and the University of Virginia were quite similar (except for the latter's medical school), with comparable graduate requirements and qualifications for the faculty. Enrollments at Washington and Lee had sometimes been greater since 1866; more students had been educated gratuitously there than at Charlottesville; and whereas the University of Virginia had cost the commonwealth about $15,000 a year, Washington and Lee had accumulated an endowment from outside sources.

At about the same time Professor William Allan of Washington and Lee, an alumnus of the University of Virginia, addressed an alumni gathering of Virginia men at Charlottesville in favor of harmony and cooperation. Colonel Allan pointed out that the majority of his faculty colleagues at Washington and Lee were alumni of the University of Virginia.

Later in the year, however, the *Virginia University Magazine* resumed the attack, asserting that Washington and Lee drew Southern students seeking "elementary" education—a hit at the preparatory classes. The *Southern Collegian* in response regretted to observe "so many evidences of jealous and unkind feeling toward this University," and smugly observed: "In aspiring to develop a University for the whole South it does not place itself in hostility to the various State institutions." In President Grant's words, the *Collegian* intoned: "Let us have peace." But there was no immediate peace. For a brief season the Lexington and Charlottesville newspapers took up the student warfare.

The Charlottesville viewpoint was summarized in the spring of 1873 by "Gath," a correspondent of the Chicago *Post.* Visiting the University of Virginia he found it, like all Southern colleges, laboring under a severe financial handicap. The faculty there "regarded General Lee as having diverted from the collegiate revenues of Virginia by going off to Washington College, and giving it the fictitious advantage of his name." One member thought that "it was not legitimate, regarded from a scholastic point of view, for a college to build its hope on a military reputation." Apprehension over the establishment of a state agricultural college added to the concern at Charlottesville. The consensus at the University of Virginia was that the entire South could afford to maintain but one great institution. Unfortunately, "the ambition of localities has covered it, like the North, with small-fry faculties of an academic grade, which accomplish little more than to make all education beggarly. . . ."

The Lexington *Gazette* indignantly denied that General Lee had diverted the state's revenues. Washington and Lee did not get a penny from Virginia. It was not an exclusively Virginia institution but "belongs equally to the whole South." General Lee had not "gone off" to Washington College, as he had never had any connection with the University of Virginia. Furthermore, there could never be anything fictitious about General Lee. The *Southern Collegian* likewise deprecated the sentiment attributed to the University of Virgina professors.

THE UNFRIENDLY DEBATE DIED DOWN; but during the seventies the interests of the two universities conflicted over a matter involving both concrete advantage and prestige—the establishment of an astronomical observatory. Leander McCormick of Chicago, brother of Cyrus McCormick and like him a native of Rockbridge County, proposed to donate a large telescope for this purpose at one of the "Literary Institutions" of Virginia. He did not commit himself regarding the specific location; but as his early communication of the subject was only with representatives of Washington and Lee, it was widely assumed that the gift would come to Lexington. For several years, while construction of the telescope proceeded in a Northern city, agents of Washington and Lee tried unsuccessfully to raise funds for the required building and personnel. McCormick finally turned his attention to Charlottesville, and a legislative resolution decided the issue in favor of the University of Virginia. Now it was the turn of Washington and Lee's adherents to feel that something to which they had prior claim had been "diverted."

Before June of 1870 Leander McCormick had written to President R. E. Lee and other friends of Washington College asserting his deep desire "to promote the welfare and honor of our honorable State, by the erection within its limits of an Astronomical Observatory on a most liberal and extensive scale." He visited Lexington in 1870 for a conference on the project. Trustees and faculty agreed that everything should be done to secure this facility.

In the summer of 1871 drawings and plans of the telescope were in Lexington at the home of trustee James D. Davidson, long an intimate friend of the McCormick family. Davidson urged McCormick to place the observatory at Washington and Lee, an institution free from the turbulence of Radical Republican state politics, in Lexington, the

"Mecca of the South." He pictured the University of Virginia and
V.M.I. as being in peril because members of the legislature considered
them to be rich and aristocratic. A year later the New York *Tribune*
announced that McCormick was "about" to present the magnificent
telescope, largest in the world, to Washington and Lee. Other press
notices suggested that there was "no doubt of the location of the
observatory. . . ."

Nothing regarding the telescope appears in the local press or University records for the next four years. Then in 1876 General Robert
D. Lilley, planning a "Centennial" endowment meeting in Philadelphia,
urged upon Davidson that "it would have a most happy effect" if
McCormick "would only announce to the meeting that he gives his
telescope to Washington and Lee." The *Southern Collegian* announced
that the observatory would come to Lexington if a suitable building
could be constructed, and suggested theatrical benefits to help raise the
money. In June of 1877 the trustees appointed a committee to communicate with McCormick; and the New York *Times*, perhaps inspired by General Lilley, praised Washington and Lee in connection
with the matter.

But McCormick had become impatient with the failure to assure
financial support of the observatory, and made his position known in a
series of conversations with Davidson during the summer of 1877. The
gist of the discussions was contained in a letter written by McCormick
in January of 1878, requesting Davidson to present the complete facts
to the trustees so that they would understand McCormick's position. It
appears that during the conversations Davidson had reported "the finances of the Washington & Lee Institution were in very straightened
circumstances," and even that "they are in a much worse condition
than you have any idea of." McCormick had said that he wished the
telescope to go to Washington and Lee, that he indeed regretted the
unreadiness of that school's authorities to receive it. "Now Mr. Davidson," he declared, "I simply wish that you will place me right in this
matter with your Trustees, because if you shall have lost my gift, it is
certainly no fault of mine."

Soon afterward McCormick was in contact with representatives of
the University of Virginia. Authorities of that institution proposed to
obtain $30,000 by legislative appropriation, while friends undertook to
raise a sufficient amount to begin the work of mounting, equipping,
and endowing the observatory.

A resolution in the Virginia House of Delegates gratefully accepted
for the University of Virginia the proffered telescope, but represented
that because of the financial condition of the commonwealth it was
impossible immediately to erect the observatory. If McCormick would

agree, however, the telescope would be received, housed, and well taken care of until the observatory could be constructed. This proposition was obviously not all that McCormick had hoped for. But it had become necessary to move the telescope; and he apparently thought Charlottesville offered a safer present haven and a more promising future for it than Lexington did. Delegate John B. Lady of Rockbridge ventured some futile resistance to the resolution.

At the meeting of the Washington and Lee trustees in June of 1878 James D. Davidson read his correspondence with Leander McCormick. The correspondence was ordered filed and the embarrassing matter was officially closed.

PARTISANS OF WASHINGTON AND LEE were stirred also by a legislative proposal in 1876 to raise the annual appropriation of the University of Virginia from $15,000 to $30,000. The measure provided also that tuition fees, which had been similar to those in private colleges, would be waived for Virginia residents eighteen years old or over.

In Lexington the bill was deemed "a monstrosity" and "a well-prepared scheme for plundering the public treasury and ruining the colleges of the State." The local *Gazette* noted that two University of Virginia professors were in Richmond "lobbying." The Washington and Lee trustees, at a called meeting, went on record as earnestly protesting "against the passage of such a measure as unjust and injurious to the other institutions of learning in the State, founded by private enterprise, endowed by private funds, & dependent in large measure for their efficiency and success upon the patronage of their students." Delegate W. B. F. Leech of Rockbridge County, an alumnus of Washington College, sponsored an amendment to strike out the free tuition feature. He pointed out that other Virginia colleges had long waived tuition for students of good character and that Washington and Lee "has schooled, free of tuition, 464 Virginia students since the war, without any cost to the State whatever."

The *Southern Collegian* criticized the University of Virginia for seeking "pap"; but after passage of the appropriation, the magazine revived a suggestion often heard before, that state funds should be distributed to all colleges. The Old Dominion would then become to America what Germany was to the world. Richmond College proposed a conference of sister institutions to advocate a modification or repeal of the university bill. Nothing, however, came of the protests. And as we have seen, the fortunes of Washington and Lee plummeted during the late seventies.

MEANWHILE THAT SMOLDERING VOLCANO, the issue of sectarianism, burst into one of its recurrent eruptions. The board of trustees was criticized from both sides. Episcopalians deplored its predominantly Presbyterian composition; Presbyterians bemoaned its nonsectarian policies of administration, which did not coincide with their ideals for a church-related school. The unfortunate departure of Judge Brockenbrough took on denominational overtones. On the other hand, the Episcopalian William Preston Johnston was one of the trustees' most vigorous defenders. Students and alumni generally pleaded for peace.

As of 1869 the trustees comprised eighteen Presbyterians and a lone Episcopalian, Rector John W. Brockenbrough. Only four of the nine faculty members were Presbyterians; but a Calvinist atmosphere was maintained by the practice of keeping the key chair of mental and moral philosophy filled by a Presbyterian clergyman. Students were urged to attend churches of their own preference and proselytism was not fostered. Daily religious exercises on the campus were conducted by local ministers in rotation.

During the presidency of R. E. Lee the issue of sectarianism burned only beneath the surface. Such Episcopalians as Judge Brockenbrough and the Reverend William N. Pendleton, pastor of Grace Church in Lexington, had urged Lee to head the college. Dr. Pendleton had conveyed to him the trustees' assurances that "the institution would in the future be undenominational." General Lee apparently had no problems with the trustees in this area and during his first academic year he approved the appointment of the Reverend John L. Kirkpatrick, president of Davidson College, to the chair of mental and moral philosophy.

Awareness of the issue is nevertheless indicated in private communications from that period. The Reverend R. L. Dabney of Union Theological Seminary, writing to a trustee, said of Dr. Kirkpatrick's appointment: "I heard with great pleasure the wise and proper design of the Trustees, to fill this place with a Presbyterian clergyman." The veteran clerical trustee, Dr. Benjamin Mosby Smith, in a letter to William H. Ruffner argued that Washington College was indeed a Presbyterian school: ". . . thus far that it ought to be managed as to promote the views of Presbyterians, inasmuch as they founded it & gave it the first endowment." He would not object to having men of other faiths in certain chairs, such as mathematics and engineering, but in the chair of philosophy it was "all important to have a Presbyterian of decided & sound views." No one who would oppose a proper Presbyterian influence should be appointed to board or faculty. In January of 1869 Colonel Thomas H. Williamson of V.M.I. in a family letter implied that the Presbyterian supporters of Washington College were concerned at "the strong Episcopal influences, which the new President and some of his Professors have brought into the community with them."

Some mention of the subject, conciliatory in tone, appeared in the *Southern Collegian*. One writer cautioned against narrow sectarianism and approved current policies. An article signed "Episcopalian" (probably Professor Johnston) spoke favorably of the board and remarked that the mere "suggestion that a majority of its members are lawyers is sufficient guarantee *that it has not enough sectarianism to hurt*." The real issue was not who the trustees were but how they implemented their policy.

A few years after General R. E. Lee's death certain board members apparently initiated a movement to reestablish more definitely the denominational quality of Washington and Lee. The year 1873 saw the development of public controversy in proportions unlike any since the attacks of 1846 and 1848.

Difficulty arose in the spring of 1873 over the collision of financial appeals for the Grace Church (now the Robert E. Lee Memorial Episcopal Church) and those for the Lee sarcophagus. In a private letter Dr. Pendleton declared: "As Genl. Lee's friend, chiefly instrumental in getting him here, by conveying assurances from the Trustees . . . I ought never to consent to the appropriation of his remains, his fame, the wealth he has secured to Washington College, & all the influences therewith connected, by the single denomination holding the Institution, in direct violation of the agreement, that it should be wholly unsectarian, on which alone . . . he accepted the Presidency. . . ." In a letter to President Custis Lee he repeated the charge that the trustees had broken a pledge, pointing out that of six or eight members subsequently elected "Every one is the same old color, and some chosen assuredly on that account alone, because other men every way their superiors were rejected and they lugged in." Dr. Pendleton said the situation was so serious that he was praying for divine interposition. He was so pained by the "extremely grave improprieties" that his physician had "emphatically warned [him] against dwelling on the distressing subject, and forbade [his] participating in any way in publications on questions raised."

As the last sentence implies, discussion was not confined to private correspondence. Newspapers and religious journals in the summer of 1873 treated the question "Is Washington and Lee a Presbyterian institution?" Writers in the *Central Presbyterian* and Lynchburg *News* so characterized it, while in the Episcopalian *Southern Churchman* contradictory contentions were set forth. The Reverend J. William Jones, a Baptist who claimed to know the facts through intimate association with R. E. Lee, discussed the issue in the *Religious Herald*. The Lexington *Gazette* deplored the public controversy which disturbed the community where those familiar with R. E. Lee's program wished to see it fulfilled. But since the question had been raised the *Gazette* urged the trustees to clarify their position.

Into this intense disputation was injected the resignation of Judge Brockenbrough from the Law School he had founded. The previous year he had resigned from the board of trustees (and was replaced by a Presbyterian). The school was not flourishing, and the panic of 1873 augmented its problems. The trustees were forced to discriminate between the salaries of Judge Brockenbrough and John Randolph Tucker, an eminent attorney added to the faculty in 1870. They determined to retain the services of Tucker and Brockenbrough's resignation was virtually demanded. The ousted professor believed his Episcopal affiliation had been a factor in the board's decision, and stated his case in a "card" in the Richmond *Enquirer*.

An article in the Lynchburg *News* a few days later attributed much of the institution's postwar prosperity to its connection with prominent Episcopal names. "A Trustee" promptly replied in the same paper, minimizing the contributions as such. General Lee's fame was so great as to transcend sectarianism; he himself did not flaunt his church affiliations or request patronage for his coreligionists. This official spokesman contended that "one half, at least, of present means, real estate and investments together, have come from Presbyterians." Gifts from other sources had "been bestowed on an Institution, founded by Presbyterians and in equity as, decided by the courts, the Institution must retain the character conferred by the founders, who ever choose to contribute to its funds." He laid down official doctrine: "From the time Hanover Presbytery established it the purpose of its foundation has been kept in view—to afford along with intellectual instructions the elements of sound Christian culture." "Trustee" quoted "the oldest member of the board" (David E. Moore) as having often avowed: " 'this Institution by its history, is a Presbyterian Institution, and so it must remain *in order to prevent it from being sectarian.*' "

Judge Brockenbrough retorted by assailing "Trustee" for hiding behind a pseudonym, and averred that the silence of the trustees in regard to his published "card" had convicted them of guilt. Soon afterward Professor Johnston offered a defense of Washington and Lee against attacks that had appeared in the *Southern Churchman*, concealed by pseudonyms such as "Daleth" and "Warden." He identified "Warden" as Colonel Williamson of V.M.I. and contended that he had accused Washington and Lee of obtaining money under false pretenses. Johnston demanded proof of the charges.

The faculty meanwhile had read with dismay the statement by "Trustee," and requested the board to define its policy. At a called meeting on September 18, 1873, the trustees formally denied sectarian bias. They declared that there was nothing relating to sectarianism or that gave to any "denomination any preponderance or influence in the University to the exclusion or injury of any other." They appealed to history to support their contention.

Regarding appointments to the faculty the board proclaimed that fitness and usefulness provided the criteria of choice. The trustees viewed as "sufficient vindication of the policy" the success of the University and the loyal support of all concerned (drawn from various religious denominations). They closed with a sweeping statement: "It has been their effort to offer to the people of the South a University free alike from all complications of church and state, which should represent at once the highest and largest interests of Education, & the noblest remembrances of Christian Heroism and devotion." The declaration, approved by a vote of 11 to 2, appeared in Virginia newspapers and evoked reverberations for some time.

Student and faculty expressions supported the trustees' position. Professor Tucker, speaking to a campus group, scorned the idea of sectarianism at Washington and Lee. The *Southern Collegian* decried newspaper discussion of the question and incorrectly believed that the resolutions of 1873 would quiet the matter. Unfortunately, a newspaper exchange between William Preston Johnston and Colonel Williamson kept the dispute alive. Johnston claimed that one could prove the sectarian character of V.M.I., but he would refrain from doing so. Williamson described the Washington and Lee trustees as "a close corporation" of Presbyterians.

Tightrope-walking can be a dangerous exercise. By attempting to reassure their non-Presbyterian clientele of the institution's nonsectarianism, the trustees disturbed Presbyterians. At the Virginia Synod of November, 1873, the Reverend E. D. Junkin, pastor of New Providence Church in Rockbridge County, and Elder A. R. Blakey of Charlottesville asserted that Washington and Lee "had been diverted from the intentions and plans of the founders." A resolution was offered "reflecting on and regretting the recent action of the Board of Trustees of Washington and Lee." According to this, Washington and Lee's history was Presbyterian, the trustees' declaration was in conflict with the facts, and synod was requested to regret the apparent assault by the board upon "the vested rights of our Presbyterian people. . . ."

Defense of the board action was presented in synod by Elder Thomas J. Kirkpatrick, a trustee of Washington and Lee, and the Reverend John L. Kirkpatrick, the professor of philosophy. Elder Kirkpatrick (who had been absent from the meeting at which the declaration was adopted) contended that the institution still occupied the ground assumed in 1782 when the charter was requested. He recalled that George Washington and the Cincinnati had donated funds "for the public good." The trustees were "Presbyterian gentlemen, pledged to use the funds of the Institution for purposes of higher education, and not directly to promote or injure the cause of any religious denomination whatever." Professor Kirkpatrick similarly argued that in accepting the charter the "founders" consented that control "should be passed from the Presbyterian to a close corporation," and that large donations had been made on the ground that the College was nonsectarian and nondenominational. "If it be sectarian, this money ought to be returned." Yet Washington and Lee was Presbyterian in a sense, through the composition of the board of trustees, and it was doing more for the Presbyterian church than ever before. Both men pleaded for continued support of the University.

Divisions within the University family, however, were aired in synod. The Reverend W. W. Houston, alumnus of Washington College, held the trustees' declaration to be inconsistent with Presbyterian control. He demanded to know "whether they intend by that paper to deny what we believe to be the rightful preponderance of Presbyterians in the management of that institution, as it has been from the beginning till now." The Reverend William Brown, one of the two trustees who had voted against the declaration, fully ventilated his views. Pointing out that the school "was in its origin completely Presbyterian," he maintained that the charter of 1782 had confirmed rather than abrogated denominational control. He noted that the Episcopal Church had been the established church in Virginia until 1785. Dissenters had been under many restraints and no doubt welcomed incorporation as a means of protecting their property. Brown remarked that no charter mentioned denominational control; and if Presbyterians were to be uprooted at Liberty Hall, denominations could also be eliminated at Hampden-Sydney, Emory and Henry, Roanoke, Randolph-Macon, Richmond, and William and Mary.* The crux of Dr. Brown's argument was: "In point of law it is thoroughly settled . . . that when institutions are founded for eleemosynary purposes, the

---

* Each of the colleges named is still identified as church-related except William and Mary, which is under state control.

character and intent of the first donation gives complexion to that [which] comes after it, no matter from what quarter received. . . ."

Students became aroused at the public discussion of sectarianism, and this was the subject of a mass meeting on November 28, 1873. Speaker John Glenn Pitts of Baltimore expressed chagrin at seeing Washington and Lee diminished "in numbers and influence, through the scandals of unscrupulous enemies and gross misrepresentations of narrow minded men who have by some means . . . crept into the executive body." He demanded that the board silence its members who wrote in the vein of the Lynchburg *News* article signed "Trustee." Another lad, afterward an Episcopal bishop, defended the school against sectarian charges; and early in 1874 the *Southern Collegian* took to task a Charlottesville newspaper for similar writings.

The alumni association late in 1873 endorsed the board declaration as accurately representing the position and aspiration of the University. In June of 1874 William A. Anderson of Lexington addressed the association along the same line. His ambition was to make his alma mater the Oxford or Cambridge of the United States. For that objective Washington and Lee "must not only not be sectarian, it must be positively and absolutely non-sectarian." Broadening of the composition of the Board of Trustees also was suggested. The association recommended alumni representation (as the faculty had proposed in 1871). Young Anderson suggested the inclusion of certain prominent Confederates and Democrats, among them Jefferson Davis!

Trustee Bolivar Christian sought to enlist the support of Cyrus H. McCormick for the resolutions of 1873. In a letter to the industrialist he listed large benefactions from non-Presbyterians and referred to sums obtained from friends and admirers of General R. E. Lee "on assurances *published* that it was *not* a denominational college. . . ." He expressed the thought that the "war" was over at the time of writing (February, 1874).

While severe fighting had indeed died down, sporadic firing continued. The Reverend William N. Pendleton had an unpleasant discussion on the sectarian issue with trustee James D. Davidson. Both men later apologized; but Dr. Pendleton believed the board's course would alienate R. E. Lee's friends, "cause his remains to be removed, & throw the institution back to a mere Secondary College."

In the summer of 1878 an alumnus and Presbyterian clergyman, the Reverend William T. Price, publicly praised Hampden-Sydney College but included some uncomplimentary remarks about Washington and Lee. Professor John Lyle Campbell replied, characterizing George Washington, the Cincinnati, and John Robinson as the true founders, and scouting the thought that they could have desired the school to be under rigid Presbyterian control. Yet Campbell held the institution to be a reliable auxiliary of the Presbyterian denomination, "safe" because "it kept in the chair of Philosophy a Presbyterian, the peer of any member of the Synod of Virginia."

During the eighties an occasional critic voiced fears of Washington and Lee's church and spiritual relations. One such was the Reverend Daniel Blain, '58, whose grandfather of the same name and calling had been a student and associate of William Graham and George A. Baxter. In a fourteen-page epistle to the trustees in 1886 he urged the appointment of a permanent Presbyterian chaplain and an increase in religious activities including revivals. Throughout the nineties the sectarian question rarely appeared in public discussion although privately it was noted by President William L. Wilson.

An interesting sidelight on the matter of sectarianism in Southern universities during this period is provided in letters from Professor Edward S. Joynes of Washington and Lee to his friend W. LeRoy Broun in 1874 and 1875. Shopping around for a job, Joynes sought a chair at the newly founded Vanderbilt University but was shocked to find that Vanderbilt wanted only Methodist professors. He had heard that William Preston Johnson was a candidate for the chancellorship of the University of Georgia, but that Johnston's membership in the Episcopal church would hurt his chances. Joynes believed that denominationalism should be resisted "by all enlightened friends of true culture," and that state universities were especially well suited for such resistance. But in his opinion even the University of Virginia had not maintained resistance, as in a recent faculty election the Baptists had dictated the appointment!

THE CONFLICTS OF THE SEVENTIES passed into history at Washington and Lee; and entering the new decade the trustees laid plans for a centennial observance. A capably managed event of this kind could well have been used to promote the development of the University, and might at least have been a morale booster during times of low enrollment and shaky finances. As it turned out, however, the effort merely exemplified the ineffectiveness of the leadership during those years.

In June of 1880 the board appointed a committee to prepare for a celebration. Some earlier dates that might have been chosen to mark the passage of a century had gone by without significant attention. Now the trustees chose 1882 to note the hundredth anniversary of the charter of Liberty Hall Academy. A motion by trustee McLaughlin that 1885 be observed as the centennial of the first commencement was rejected. The unveiling of the Valentine recumbent statue of General R. E. Lee in the mausoleum also was planned for June of 1882; and the committee envisioned 20,000 in attendance at the dual ceremony.

Although the files of the *Southern Collegian* and Lexington *Gazette* reflect some enthusiasm for the centennial, little appears to have been done to implement the original plans. Torpor pervaded the University administration, and it became apparent by the spring of 1882 that the celebration must be postponed. On April 11 the trustees set up a committee to fix the "time and circumstance for holding the centennial. . . ." A printed circular stated the reasons for the delay: (1) the unreadiness of the mausoleum to receive the Valentine statue; (2) unavoidable delay in collection of the necessary funds; (3) unavailability of the Valley Railroad, which was under construction.

The installation of the Lee statue and the centennial celebration were next scheduled for the spring of 1883. The statue was indeed placed in the mausoleum; but that event so fully overshadowed everything else that little was heard of a centennial observance. The trustees then shifted to 1885, the "Centennial Commencement" as McLaughlin had suggested. The *Gazette's* satirist "G. Whillikens" wrote in July of 1883: "We have had the Centennial . . . Our Centennial was a big thing. There was a very few under Brigadier there. We are mightily pleased about it. We are so tickled we think of having another when the Valley Road is completed."

In 1884 the trustees created a "Centennial Commission" with a fund of $1,000 to arrange the celebration in June of 1885. An eminent divine, the Reverend Moses Drury Hoge of Richmond, was invited to deliver the oration. Lexington's foremost literary figure, Margaret Junkin Preston, was requested to prepare a commemorative poem. Mrs. Preston's brilliant *Centennial Ode* was read at Commencement of 1885 by her husband, Colonel J. T. L. Preston. The *Gazette* later reported that it received "high encomiums" from various sections of the nation; and as far away as Portland, Oregon, Judge M. P. Deady garnished his July 4 address by a quotation from the *Ode*.

But except for the poem, the centennial observance was again deferred "for several reasons." The following year Dr. Hoge delivered his "historic" address, which read today seems tame indeed. He recalled that his grandfather had been one of the Liberty Hall graduates of 1785. He called the roll of distinguished alumni: seven state governors, eleven United States senators, more than a score of congressmen, twoscore and more judges (among them Trimble of the United States Supreme Court), and a dozen or so college presidents. The historian looking for enlightenment on the early history of Washington and Lee, however, will search in vain for it in this superficial "centennial oration."

Nothing further was heard of the centennial after 1886, at the close of which "G. Whillikens" confided to fictional Josiah Simpkins: "Owin' to the dry season they didn't have any Centennial at Colledge this year." Perhaps that was as good a reason as any.

Chapter
XVII

Later Victorian
Student Life

IN EARLIER CHAPTERS were noted some basic changes in student life from the years of Liberty Hall to the administration of R. E. Lee. Strictly-business austerity faded and a more relaxed atmosphere prevailed; rigid rules of discipline gave way to a gentlemen's code of honor; outlets for youthful interests and energies were increased. These trends continued in the last three decades of the nineteenth century, and the basis was laid for modern American campus life. More and more opportunities for extracurricular activity were provided. These became steadily more highly organized.

STUDENTS THEMSELVES probably did not change much. At least, an article in the *Southern Collegian* in 1874 described some types easily recognized in our time. First there were the "bores," whose prolonged night visits kept fellow students from needed study. There were the chronic grumblers—"gripers" would be the most polite term applied today. Especially contemptible was the "fast young man" who delighted to descant upon "his dashing escapades" even though a young lady's reputation was sometimes made to suffer. Even worse than these (in the 1874 evaluation) was the popularity seeker, who would burgeon into the campus leader (the honored "B.M.O.C." of a later date).

Before the formalized enrichment of student life had developed, boredom was a common complaint. In 1870 Ossian Huggins wrote his parents that a performance by a traveling theatrical troupe had provided the only excitement enjoyed for some time. Frank Cockrell told his mother in 1877 that Lexington was "the dullest place" he ever saw. No business, no excitement, "no nothing." Cockrell longed for the "buisy" life of Dallas, Texas, itself hardly a metropolis, and commented: "I think if any one who has been accustomed to a buisy life should come to Lexington they would go mad." Sometimes student display of boredom irritated townspeople. When a group departed from the Presbyterian church in the fall of 1877 the pastor mildly rebuked them.

"Calathumps," noise-making orgies that originated in the antebellum period, continued to be indulged in. Sometimes the calathump was a deliberate effort at annoyance, as in the case of the Northern woman who came to Lexington to teach in the Negro school (Chapter XIII). This purpose persisted with the professors as the principal victims. The *Collegian* indicated in 1879 that the practice was on the wane, and argued: "Let *Calathumps* die then along with such old tricks as veiling Washington's statue, emptying classrooms of their furniture. . . ." But in 1882 the *Collegian* inquired, "Imagine oneself a Professor on Calathump night," suggesting that the end had not yet arrived.

The calathump, however, became better organized and institutionalized. It was used to celebrate "All Fool's Eve," March 31, and the *Gazette* reported in 1871 that: "Tin horns, tin pans and 'squedunks' by the hundred were brought into requisition, and their hideous music made the night resonant with sounds not to be excelled this side of the infernal regions." The following year students armed with cowbells and tin horns held the annual parade, and the *Rockbridge Citizen* complained: "To a man in bed, it sounded very much like all cow bells had been separated from their calves, and were indulging in mutual regrets." Sometimes Valentine's Day was made the occasion for a calathump. The tooters were out in full force on February 14, 1873, after town merchants had been kept busy for a week to furnish the tin horns. In 1882 the *Collegian* described the March 31 event as an old, time-honored custom, in the performance of which all students assembled at a time and place "appointed by His Majesty *Rex Calathumporum* in his Proclamation, which sets forth . . . [that] his loyal subjects are required to be equipped . . . which we cannot disclose, lest we violate that confidence reposed in us by his gracious Majesty."

Contrary to the adverse attitude on the annoyance calathump, the writer argued that this annual event was desired by the majority of the students and engendered esprit de corps. It was doubtless a letting-off of steam in the long period from Washington's Birthday on February 22 until the close of the session, during which grim interim not one holiday intervened.

On the evening of November 7, 1884, students celebrated with a calathump the election of the first Democrat to the Presidency since 1856. Professors, "white Republicans," and others were serenaded while "Old George" (the Kahle statue atop the Washington building) was draped on the "morning of the Democratic jollification." Washington stood resplendent, "a winding sheet of brightest crimson enveloping his manly form, and a crimson cap upon his head, while in his right hand he proudly upheld a floating banner, which displayed the inscription, 'Hurrah for Cleveland! Paint the Town Red!'"

Sometimes the calathump was attended by vandalism which extended to breaking into homes, and the student and local press, the faculty and administration, condemned such excesses. The custom died with the advent of more sophisticated and structured activities, but as late as April of 1898 students used this device to protest the faculty's "non-support" of athletics.

STUDENT LIFE was made more agreeable by the closeness of the faculty to the young men. A greater urbanity had penetrated "Presbyterian Lexington" during the broadening years of the Lees, and things became a bit more jolly than when shivering John S. Wise, a decade before, had had a date in a bleak "parlor," where he had been treated to "a cold red pippin on a cold white plate." Quite different, for instance, was the home of John Randolph Tucker, "Blandome," the scene of many entertainments. From time to time we may glimpse other occasions such as that reported in the *Collegian* in January of 1876. Dr. John L. Kirkpatrick, Professor of Moral Philosophy, was host to his classes together with a segment of Lexington's "youth and beauty" following the Graham-Lee Society celebration of January 19. After enjoying Dr. Kirkpatrick's "good things" the young people repaired to the parlors "where bright eyes glanced and sweet voices made melody in merry conversation," and "eyes looked love to eyes that spoke again."

During vacations and summers Washington and Lee men experienced cordial treatment by their elders at the Virginia resorts and watering places such as Hot Springs, White Sulphur Springs (West

Virginia), the Rockbridge Alum, and the Rockbridge Baths. In the summer of 1871 the *Gazette* reported that Mrs. R. E. Lee (who "had won the hearts of all") and daughter; Samuel McDowell Moore and daughter; Professor A. L. Nelson and family; and Dr. John A. Graham and family were there with students Fisher, Bateman, and Torrens. Student Brown Ayres, '75 (later a distinguished professor at Tulane University), established the *Rockbridge Baths Review* for the edification of summer guests.

Edward A. O'Neal (afterward head of the American Farm Bureau) recalled in 1900 the many kindnesses of Mrs. Harry St. George Tucker to himself and other college men, "calling for us at our lodging places when we were the escorts of the young ladies under her chaperonage." Professors continued their entertainment of the students in the "gay nineties." In 1896 fifteen students were guests of Dr. Edwin W. Fay, Professor of Latin, in his bachelor's quarters where story-telling occupied the group. Afterward all repaired to the ten-pin alley where "many marvelous scores were made." An "oyster supper" at the Lexington Hotel followed. Professor David C. Humphreys treated his mathematics classes to "progressive games" at his home. Dr. Henry A. White invited to his residence members of the West Virginia Club, his advisees, and members of the department of history—as well as a large number of the "calic."

Once in a while students relieved their tedium by out-of-town expeditions such as the train trip of ten "fashionables" to Staunton in the spring of 1887 to attend a performance by Lillie Langtry. As a member of the party described it: "After a late dinner we went to the Opera House where two stage boxes had been reserved for our use. We cut a heavy swell . . . as we were all in full dress and each wore a camellia *boutonniere*." Mme. Langtry and the fair ladies of the audience exchanged many "admiring glances" with the collegians. The manager invited the Washington and Lee men to a reception in the actress' private railroad car where "La Langtry" was reported to be more beautiful offstage than on, and graciousness itself. After a half hour of affable conversation "a delicious cold collation" was served and champagne corks "flew in profusion."

In the spring of 1890 more than a hundred Washington and Lee men, natty in blue-and-white caps and blazers, journeyed to Richmond to participate in the dedication of the Lee monument. The students were presented with a large Confederate flag and carried an impressive banner proclaiming significant dates in the school's history: 1749, 1796, 1870. The students attracted much attention and received ovations. They were repeatedly called upon to give their college yell which they obliged by doing, accompanied by the hurling of their canes, "be-decked with streaming college colors, in the air." The yell went: "Chick-a-gorunk, gorunk, goree,/Hay-oh, hi-oh, Washington and Lee."

DANCING BECAME AN ESTABLISHED FEATURE of student life during the three decades to 1900, against the slowly yielding opposition of the trustees. The diversion, profoundly disapproved before the war, was tolerated in the R. E. Lee regime. Faculty members at first avoided the balls, hops, and germans but the *Collegian* noted the presence of several professors at a hop held by the Students Social Club in the fall of 1871.

A prototype of Washington and Lee's renowned Fancy Dress Ball was held in September of 1876, and pronounced by the *Collegian* a "great success." Miss Henny Johnston went as a Quakeress, Miss Fan-nie Dold as "Winter," and Miss Mary Jordan as an American flag. Miss Annie White, who appeared as Pocahontas, "was charming, and . . . could easily have saved John Smith's life from even so savage an Indian as 'Sitting Bull.'" The "Final Ball" became a custom in the seventies. That of June, 1879, was staged in the literary society halls with music in both rooms. The *Collegian* complained that the affair was entirely too short, lasting only from 11:30 P.M. to 3 A.M.

As ever, the older generation wondered what the younger was com-ing to. The new-fangled "round dances" were especially shocking. A visitor at commencement in 1883, writing to the *Gazette*, rhetorically inquired what Henry Ruffner or George Junkin or Stonewall Jackson would think of the youth in Lexington "dancing the licentious german, or the disgusting racket?" He sorrowfully noted that "the girls did not mind being hugged and going from one pair of arms to another any more than the boys. . . ." The *Gazette* concurred, saying the time had come "for the public sentiment of the Christian people of Lexington to discountenance the lascivious dances which we are sorry to say are being introduced here."

In the following year "Alumnus," also through the *Gazette*, ex-pressed fear that the new-type dances would injure Washington and Lee's future. Parents would be antagonized by this evil and the Uni-versity, having proclaimed itself "unsectarian," would be open to the charge of worldliness as well. "Alumnus" called for a revival of the "informal and inexpensive *sociable* and *party* which once filled our homes with the light and gay and merry laughter of youth," all within the oversight of the "old folks at home." How better this entertainment than "these hops and Germans . . . protracted till the rebuking sun chases to rest the flying feet of intemperate youth."

The *Gazette*'s satirist "G. Whillikens" as usual took the opportunity for sage humor: "As long as there is music and young folks it will git into their toes." And he added: "*Girls like to be hugged, and the boys like to hug them.* The question is whether it is better to do it in the ball-room or behind the door."

The trustees, while allowing students to hold dances, maintained a position of formal disapproval by restrictions on the use of University buildings. The events took place mostly off campus until the late nineties. McCrum's Hall on Main Street seems to have been the most usual site for the hops and germans by fraternities and other organizations. A break in the trustees' resistance came with the reluctant permission to hold the Final Ball in Newcomb Hall. But a resolution in June of 1884 prohibited the use of any University building for the purpose of balls or dances during June, save for the night of commencement, and in no case should it be used for "the purpose of the German or Round Dances." In 1888 the trustees refused a student petition for a dance in Newcomb Hall, and a request by "the Cotillion Club" for use of the gymnasium for a german during commencement week of 1894 lost in the board by a 4 to 4 vote. In 1895 the trustees decided 5 to 4 to turn over to the faculty the subject of social entertainments and amusements of students, with power to grant use of the gymnasium for "regulated" social entertainments which were to be limited to two. And in 1897 the Cotillion Club held "a delightful hop" in Newcomb Hall.

Sometimes during these years the election for the coveted honor of president of the Final Ball engendered bitterness that divided the campus, and in 1895 a faculty member complained that the contest had adversely affected the work of a number of students.

OTHER FORMS of organized student activity included hare-and-hound races, ten-pin rolls (sometimes with the fair sex), and intramural tennis. Glee and banjo clubs provided outlets for those with the appropriate talents and on occasion made extensive winter tours through Kentucky, Tennessee, and Georgia. State societies were highly regarded. In 1893 the *Collegian* described the Kentucky and Missouri Clubs as especially flourishing. The former brought a famous editor from Louisville, "Marse Henry" Watterson, to lecture in Lee Chapel that year.

A PARTICULARLY IMPORTANT DEVELOPMENT of this period in the formation of the Washington and Lee pattern was the growth of the social
fraternity system. This type of organization, as has been described, had
appeared on the campus in the fifties, *sub rosa,* and been bitterly op-
posed by President Junkin. With the influx of students after the Civil
War the ante-bellum Phi Kappa Psi and Beta Theta Pi were reactivated
and a number of other fraternities were introduced. One, the Kappa
Alpha Order, was founded in 1865 by Washington College students.
By 1872 a semi-official list included Alpha Tau Omega, Beta Theta Pi,
Delta Kappa Epsilon, Delta Psi, Theta Delta Chi, Sigma Alpha Epsilon,
Sigma Chi, Phi Gamma Delta, Phi Kappa Psi, and Chi Phi. Kappa
Sigma Kappa, Sigma Alpha, and the Rainbow Club came into being
during the seventies. An honorary society, the "Eli Banana," nowadays
identified with the University of Virginia, was said to have had fifteen
members at Washington and Lee in 1879. Two chapters were established in the nineties, Phi Kappa Sigma and Delta Tau Delta.

Fraternities in the Victorian epoch held meetings in rooms rented in
town. In 1874 they met to discuss the possibility of erecting a two-
story building with a large college hall on the first floor and fraternity
lodge rooms above. Nothing came of the proposal, however, as social
fraternities and clubs were affected by the downward trend in enrollment. Thus in 1879, with eight men each, Sigma Alpha Epsilon and
Sigma Chi boasted the largest membership. Kappa Alpha, Phi Delta
Theta, and Theta Delta Chi reached the ultimate in exclusiveness with
one member apiece. Delta Kappa Epsilon, Beta Theta Pi, Delta Psi,
Theta Delta Chi, and Chi Phi passed from the scene. Of these only Beta
Theta Pi was reinstalled, and that not until after World War I.

In 1895, as the faculty was considering the establishment of chapter
houses, Professor James Lewis Howe undertook a survey of conditions
at other colleges. Responses from Williams, Amherst, and Dartmouth
brought varying opinions: fraternity houses produced social exclusiveness and extravagance; the chapters stimulated a sense of responsibility
and good citizenship; it was a good thing to inculcate the sense of
taxpaying and property-holding among young men; a few "evil"
youths might influence others. The day of impressive fraternity houses
did not dawn until after 1920; but the fraternity system became firmly
entrenched at Washington and Lee between 1865 and 1900.

STUDENTS OF THIS TRANSITIONAL PERIOD found that a campus organization provided an effective means of endeavor in spiritual matters as in
other aspects of their extracurricular life. The specific instrument was

the Young Men's Christian Association, which had been founded in London in 1844 and brought to America in 1851. Thus, despite the trend toward "unsectarianism" and the growth of social and athletic activity, effort in religious matters was probably increased rather than diminished.

A Y.M.C.A. was organized at Washington College at President R. E. Lee's suggestion in the spring of 1867, to be composed of all church members and "all moral young men who are disposed to take part in it." It became a going concern at the next session and was open to young men of Lexington as well as students. By February of 1868 the "Y" was reported to have more than fifty active members, who assisted in chapel and college prayer meeting each Sunday afternoon, as well as conducting several boarding-house prayer meetings.

Joseph A. Graves, chairman of the Y committee, sent appeals for the support of a library for the organization throughout the United States and even to England. A New York firm wrote General Lee offering the Y as many books as might be desired at half price. General Lee began the subscription with a fifty-dollar pledge. Student Hugh Moran wrote his father about obtaining payment of this pledge: "I had to go to him to get it. I did not much like the idea of *dunning* General Lee. But I went to him yesterday, and he took me with him to his house and paid it over." General Lee spent time in the library and encouraged the workers.

The Y.M.C.A. sponsored addresses by clergymen and interdenominational services. In 1869 some of the young men undertook missionary and Sabbath school work in the area surrounding Lexington. They publicly sought Sunday schools lacking teachers, or any "barren point" where a teacher or prayer would do good, and organized a Sabbath School at House Mountain. The Y declined in the seventies along with other student activities but continued to be quite active in the eighties. In 1886 Y president G. A. Wauchope described the maintenance of three mission schools, each "supplied" by two Y men who had charge of Sabbath afternoon services. The Washington and Lee Y furnished most of the male teachers in the Negro Sunday school founded in Lexington by Stonewall Jackson and later conducted by Col. J. T. L. Preston and Professor J. J. White. The Y's of Washington and Lee and V.M.I. were joint hosts to an intercollegiate conference in 1885, which was followed by a three-week series of services. President G. W. C. Lee warmly commended the Y in each of his annual reports.

The University encouraged religion also by tendering free tuition to all candidates for the Christian ministry. Another religiously related organization was the "Friends of Temperance," which appeared in 1869 and secured a large number of pledges.

No NON-ACADEMIC DEVELOPMENT of the later nineteenth century was more far-reaching in shaping the character of American college life than the rise of intercollegiate athletics. But in the early days of this movement intramural competition often generated as much interest as contests between institutions. A very popular sport at Washingon College was rowing, which took form as a competitive activity during R. E. Lee's presidency. It would be difficult to find a more symbolic reference on this subject than a paragraph in the *Gazette* of May 12, 1869, describing a race of a mile and a half over a course extending from "Clifton" (residence of Colonel Johnston) to the bend of the river and return:

> The balmy day and the interest in the contest allured many fair ladies from the city to grace and witness the scene. . . . Under the wide-spreading sycamore at 'Clifton' were General R. E. Lee (on horseback), Col. McDonald of the V.M.I., Professors White and Johnston, of Washington College, Col. Ross and others. Several 'turnouts' with ladies and children collected near this spot, among them the fine, stately 'team' of Professor White, drawing his family carriage. Higher up the stream were General Smith, of the V.M.I., Prof. Nelson, of the College, and Captain David E. Moore. Captains Henderson and Brooke, of the V.M.I., and Prof. Walker, of the College, were in skiffs.

There was the greatest military genius that America has ever produced, who had sent an incomparable army into mortal combat, and only four years since had surrendered the remnants of that army in the most poignant episode of our history. There were other officers who had fought for the Lost Cause. They were watching, and presumably taking a genuine interest in, a boat race between Washington College students that could not have any practical effect upon anything at all (except for any little bets that might have been made). If such a scene could have been enacted on North River at Lexington, Virginia, in 1869, it is no wonder that Americans a century later can forget their own cares and all the woes of the world as they shout for their teams to win.

Following that race the trustees gave official encouragement to the sport by appropriating four hundred dollars for the college boat club. (The club had owned one of the boats in the race; the other was privately owned but manned by students.) Early in 1870 the faculty ordered two boats, and two rival clubs were formed. An annual regatta between the *Harry Lee* and *Albert Sidney* clubs developed as a regular feature of commencement. So intense did club loyalties become in the nineties that, according to the *Collegian*, "mother . . . separated from daughter, husband from wife, student from sweetheart (perhaps). . . ." Flags and streamers of red (the *Harry Lee* color) and blue (*Albert Sidney*) floated from housetops, were suspended across the streets of Lexington, and waved everywhere. The town turned out to witness the races: the river banks, cliffs, and the "island" were early filled by those seeking vantage points.

In April of 1892 Governor and Mrs. Fitz Lee attended christening ceremonies for a new four-oared shell owned by the Washington and Lee Athletic Club. The president and vice-president of the association rode in the governor's carriage in a procession through town, and at the river Lee delivered an appropriate and witty speech. Little Louise Haskins then smashed a bottle of old port on the *Annie Joe*, named for Miss Annie White of Lexington, a friend to the students who was "always foremost in good works and who by her indomitable energy raised a large sum of money for the purchase of the boat."

An athletic association was formed in 1872 by seventy youths "who had not had their noses a foot from a book" in a month. Its purpose was to encourage exhibitions of track events during the fall and spring.

The trustees early indicated an interest in providing gymnastic exercises for the students and in 1866 authorized the employment of a gym instructor, but with the proviso that the funds of the college could not be levied upon for that purpose. Problems of finances and facilities continued. An insistent demand for a gymnasium and athletic field was heard during the seventies. The pressure impelled President G. W. C. Lee in 1885 to equip the "Art Gallery (in Newcomb Hall) as a temporary gymnasium." In 1889 the trustees appropriated three thousand dollars to build a gymnasium and a year later the president reported completion of a better building than had been intended. The cost had exceeded the appropriation by eight hundred dollars. Lee characteristically made up the excess from his own funds. In 1891 Dr. E. M. Schaeffer was appointed head of the Physical Education Department, instructing in "the Swedish drill," gymnastics, running, boxing, and wrestling. He gave physical examinations to students taking his classes and checked on their health, in one instance detecting a "case of commencing nervous prostration" in a youth undertaking a double course in law. He added that "several cases of tobacco poisoning" had concealed themselves from his sight until far into the session. In June of 1895 the trustees finally voted three thousand dollars for an athletic field, ending a long-standing and frequently expressed student grievance.

With University funds scarce, other means of financing were sometimes employed. Professor W. G. Brown advanced money for baths in the gymnasium. In 1892 Miss Annie White directed a student presentation of Sheridan's *The Rivals* for the benefit of the athletic association, and herself played the part of the romantic heroine Lydia. In 1895 the *Collegian* demanded the imposition of a five-dollar athletic fee on each student. The money for the athletic field apparently became available through the windfall of Congress' restitution for damages done in Hunter's raid of 1864.

The Great American Game of baseball blossomed forth as an intercollegiate sport in the sixties, with frequent games between Washington College and V.M.I. At first it was played the year around. The "Beechenbrooks" of Washington College engaged the Cadet Club in December of 1866, and again in a doubleheader in May, 1867. The latter two games ended: Cadets 34, Beechenbrooks 19; Beechenbrooks 66 (correct), Cadets 22. The defense apparently improved by March of 1869 when the student bodies of the two institutions turned out en masse to watch Washington College win 32–13.* A commentator in the *Collegian* observed that in a game of the same year: "Base-ball men speak with peculiar satisfaction of a 'catch' by Mr. E. P. Clarke, for which he received a bouquet from some of the ladies present." (!) During the spring of 1871 the varsity nines of the Lexington schools met repeatedly, with Washington and Lee winning the trophy—"an elegant bat, properly inscribed, silver mounted."

Games with the University of Virginia were being played by 1871; and if the events did not provide the best of baseball, they were notable social successes. When the "Monticello" team from Charlottesville came to meet the local "Shoo Fly" team, school boys petitioned for a holiday, Washington and Lee declared a half-holiday, boarding houses served midday dinner early, and even "the wash-women kept their suds in motion late on Tuesday night to gain time for the game." At the match political figures circulated among the crowd, beaux disported themselves in "plum colored coats and light pants," and belles abounded in "pretty linen hats," many ordered for the occasion. The game was played on the V.M.I parade ground and General "Specs" Smith served as grand marshal for the day. The "Shoo Flies" wore handsome uniforms of tight dove-colored pants, with white stockings and caps.

A note of skepticism, however, was seen in the *Gazette*'s account of the affair, pointing out that the University of Virginia could "boast of Nine *Students* who can hit a ball with a round stick better than our

---

* It should be charitably noted that in the formative years of baseball the fielders did not wear gloves, and pitching techniques developed slowly.

fellows." There was a facetious reference to that type of rivalry between two "leading *literary* institutions."*

After the game the players of both teams, their friends, and guests
enjoyed a supper for which champagne had been brought into town.
One witness called it the "jolliest" gathering he had ever seen: "Every
one seemed to be in good humor with the world, the flesh and the
d—l."

Later, when a return match was played at Charlottesville, the Washington and Lee men found hospitality unexcelled, including "cooling
mixtures" at Colonel Venable's. The home teams were hospitable even
on the playing field, as the Monticellos won in Lexington in extra
innings, 24–20, and the Shoo Flies were victors at Charlottesville, 31–18.
The reception of the Shoo Flies on their return home could only be
compared to a triumph of a later Roman emperor.

The Monticellos took a friendly three-hour match in 1875 and won a
pitcher's duel at Lexington in May of 1877, 19–17. The Virginia men
made quite an excursion of the latter visit. They arrived on Saturday
night to the sound of rousing cheers, attended church and went sight-
seeing on Sunday, and sought out the "calico," many of whom became
Virginia rooters at the game on Monday. Spirits flowed freely at the
supper afterwards.

But bitterness superseded friendly jollity in 1878 when the Washington and Lee pitcher, George Augustus Sykes, unleashed a secret
weapon at Charlottesville—the curve ball! Said the *Virginia University
Magazine:* "It has been our sad misfortune to see once in our lives one
of the above mentioned experts (curve ball pitchers), and it will ever
be our lasting impression that we were the innocent victims of as
scurvy a trick as has ever been exhibited in the annals of base ball from
its earliest foundation. . . ." Sykes, however, had much help from the
Virginia fielders, who committed fourteen errors. Next season, with
Sykes still on the Washington and Lee nine, Virginia refused to play.
Athletic relations were later resumed, but Washington and Lee's baseball fortunes ebbed along with everything else during the eighties. In
1889 Virginia defeated Washington and Lee 23–9. The losers made 23
errors, third-baseman Brown bobbling six of seven chances.

* The illustrious founder of the University of Virginia would no doubt
have shared the attitude of the *Gazette,* judging by his advice to his nephew
Peter Carr in a letter dated August 19, 1785: "Games played with the ball,
and others of that nature, are too violent for the body, and stamp no character on the mind."

DURING THE EARLY SEVENTIES football emerged as an absorbing pastime at Washington and Lee. In contrast to the jovial spirit that attended the early baseball games, however, football very soon became a source of trouble and ill-will. There was considerable vagueness about the rules. Hordes of players swarmed over the field, apparently confused about what they were supposed to do. In November of 1873 Washington and Lee defeated V.M.I. 4–2 in their first intercollegiate game. The match was probably intended to resemble soccer but there were fifty men on each side, and the ball was hit by hand as well as kicked. The *Collegian* complained that the contest might well have been called "fist" ball rather than football. In the following year, after a tie game between the local schools, the *Collegian* protested that despite an agreement limiting the number of players to 35 per side, the cadets had mustered 43. A contest with V.M.I. in 1878 concluded with hard feelings. According to a Washington and Lee source, sentiment had "become entirely too bitter and unforgiving." Intramural games continued to be played during this period between state clubs and other groups.

After a decline of interest in the eighties, football presented the faculty with serious problems in the nineties. Students expressed ire in 1890 when the faculty refused to grant the team a two-day leave to play in Charlottesville. In 1891 students violated faculty rules by employing a "trainer" or coach without consulting the faculty committee. Yet the autumnal enthusiasm for football infected members of the faculty. At the Sewanee game of 1892, characterized by brilliant, hard-fought play, one of the gravest professors was reported to have seized the hands of a young lady and to have squeezed them, "not only once, but repeatedly; and she, sweet, innocent child, could only manage in her fervor, to exclaim: 'O! Mr. Mitchell, Mr. Mitchell—the dear, dear, thing.'" As amusing as this may have been, the rest was sad: Sewanee 22, Washington and Lee 16.

Football was abandoned at mid-season of 1893 and athletics seemed at nadir. Certain faculty members and trustees wished to discourage the sport, despite student pleas for an athletic field "about which college enthusiasm and patriotism center. . . ." In 1894 not enough men came out to form a scrub eleven against which the varsity might scrimmage. In the following year students supported the faculty stand against professionalism, and an indictment of the trend in American intercollegiate athletics, especially football, appeared in the *Southern Collegian*. The author condemned the brutality of the game, the victory-at-all-costs attitude, and the employment of trickery and foul play. He declared: "Many less scrupulous institutions, finding the possession of a winning football team an effective means of advertising the fact of their existence, encourage or even aid in the securing of brawny matriculates for the sole purpose of playing foot-ball."

Difficulties reached a climax in 1897 with two of the most serious incidents in the history of Washington and Lee's relations with other institutions. These were a melee between students and V.M.I. cadets and the playing of a "ringer" in a game against the Central University of Kentucky. We have detailed accounts from the diary of William Lyne Wilson, who had been appointed President of the University earlier in that year.

The fracas with V.M.I. followed a football game on Friday, October 9, in which Washington and Lee had defeated Columbian College (the first entire game under "modern" rules that Wilson had ever seen). A group of students "in a specially hilarious mood" rather "imprudently" drove in a wagon by the V.M.I. barracks where the cadets were marching in dress parade. Some students uttered "tantalising" expressions and one of them bellowed imitation military orders through a megaphone. When the dress parade ended the cadets rushed in a body at the wagon, "throwing imprecations and stones at the occupants." The driver "whipped up" and the wagon escaped, but several students on foot were "vehemently abused." Surprisingly, there was no further trouble that day, but on the following afternoon another affray was sparked by an altercation between a student and a cadet. According to President Wilson, the cadet ordered the student from the sidewalk before the V.M.I. gate, using objectionable language, and shoved the student when the latter refused to obey. The student struck the cadet, who called for his "Brother Rats." The cadets responded in force and grabbed stones en route. Other students on the scene were attacked, two being beaten severely and another beaten "shamefully."

At about 5:30 P.M. Wilson heard the Washington College bell tolling furiously. Soon Professor Nelson came to inform him that a student mass meeting was being held "under great excitement" in the Graham Society Hall. Wilson hurried to the hall where he urged the students to investigate and ascertain the facts, and to do nothing that night. The students applauded "moderately" for they were boiling with indignation. The gentle and kindly Wilson could tell his diary that he shared their feelings.

Despite the tension, Saturday night passed without another outbreak; and on Monday Mayor Thomas E. McCorkle of Lexington sent for Wilson and Superintendent Scott Shipp of V.M.I. to learn the details of the incidents. Wilson confided to his diary that Shipp's "information as to the beginning and subsequent course of the occurrence was partial and incorrect." Deeply incensed at the attack upon a few students by a mob of two hundred, the mild-mannered Wilson called it "little less than murderous."

The mayor set a hearing for the following Thursday at which he (with the commonwealth's attorney present) heard testimony of students, cadets, and townspeople. Both Shipp and Wilson were trained in the law (the former at Washington College) and each examined witnesses in a manner to favor the cause of his own youths. Wilson thought the weight of the testimony was on the side of the students and he believed only one to be even technically blameworthy. This youth had drawn "a pistol and blackjack or sling-shot to defend himself and companions, when they were confronted by a hundred angry, cursing, threatening cadets, many of them with stones in their hands, and that only after he had been struck by several." Nevertheless, the mayor apportioned fines on students and cadets "without regard to whether the blows were struck in self defense or wanton assaults. . . ."

In his diary Wilson remarked that he and General Shipp eventually must bring about a *modus vivendi,* conducive to better relations between their institutions. This project never materialized. Athletic relations continued to be sometimes strained and were finally severed in 1904 following trouble at a baseball game. A major cause of friction was removed.

The other untoward incident of 1897 occurred when the football team "clandestinely took with them on their recent tour, a stalwart young man, formerly I believe of the police force in Lexington, passed him off as a student and played him as such in the match game at Lexington, Ky., and would have 'lined him up' at Charleston against West Virginia University . . . if Professor Humphreys had not . . . hurried to prevent it." The president, who had contributed $180 from his own pocket toward expenses of the tour, was mortified and indignant at the stain on the University, and he was not alone.

Wilson called on the carpet the football captain, manager, and a member of the athletic committee whose only excuse was that "they all do it." The faculty promptly disbanded what the *Southern Collegian* called the "best team we ever had." Wilson apologized to the Central University of Kentucky and received a courteous acknowledgment.

The protest that "they all do it," while not a moral justification, may have been pretty close to a truth. At any rate, football came in for widespread criticism during this period and the death of a University of Georgia player in a contest with the University of Virginia added to the argument against the game. Late in 1897 the Virginia state senate debated a bill to prohibit the sport in Virginia. Senator S. H. Letcher of Rockbridge defended the game, and the bill was defeated. In the closing years of the century President Wilson remarked in his annual reports that intercollegiate football and baseball presented many "grave difficulties."

YOUNG MEN who came to college in the generation following Appomattox enjoyed a period marked by absence of international tensions and freedom from wars except for the last of the frontier clashes with Indians. It was only in the spring of 1898 that alarums of that "glorious little war" (in John Hay's phrase) with Spain intruded. Several Rockbridge County men enlisted in the "West Augusta Guards" which were mustered into the United States volunteer forces, and Washington and Lee men were among the liberators of Cuba. The records, however, show but little disturbance on the campus, as the academic session ended in June and the war (virtually) by mid-July. The patriotic motif was present at the Final Ball of 1898 with the display of red, white, and blue colors. But most of the graduates of 1898 would live to see the end of their secure world and the opening of a far grimmer age with the invasion of Belgium in the summer of 1914.

Chapter
XVIII

ᏜᏝᏜᏝᏜᏝ

And Education, Too

DESPITE THE SPECTACULAR GROWTH of social and athletic activity, the Victorian students still recognized intellectual development as the principal objective in going to college. They pursued that objective not only in the classroom but through the literary societies, which had been so vigorous in ante-bellum decades and so valuable in supplementing the bare bones of the classical curriculum. These were among the first student institutions to be revived after Appomattox. In 1868 they jointly founded the *Southern Collegian* which served as a report of the societies' proceedings as well as a literary journal. A writer in the first issue expressed hope that the magazine would impress upon its readers the importance of the societies as agencies of education. Indeed, by the character of an institution's literary societies could the worth of that college be gauged. In the society was to be found "a miniature world," where give-and-take contents involved the assimilation and presentation of ideas, where valuable experience could be gained, friendships and college esprit de corps created. Truly the literary societies were the pride of the students at Washington College.

The halls of both the Washington and Graham societies had been pillaged by General Hunter's Union Army in 1864. Libraries, records, and other properties were lost. Among the missing items was George Washington's famous letter to the trustees, which had graced the walls of the Washington Society hall. Some of the lost articles were returned, and the societies and their alumni appealed to townspeople who might have come into possession of others. Gradually many of the missing records, manuscripts, and other treasures reappeared, while members bestirred themselves to recondition their halls.

Although fewer than half the students joined the societies, the increased enrollment of the R. E. Lee years brought the groups unprecedented prosperity. One account from early in 1868 placed the Graham membership at about 100 and the Washington at 76. A student's letter in November of that year gave approximately the same figures in reverse. The societies reached their zenith in the early seventies before suffering in the general decline that followed.

Procedures of the societies followed the pattern set before the war—debates, orations, and celebrations, especially those of January 19, February 22, and commencement. Students who attended these notable events appeared to enjoy themselves hugely. The celebrations continued to be important social events. In 1867, for example, the Graham Philanthropic Society celebrated its fifty-eighth anniversary on January 19 in the Methodist Episcopal Church (South) before a crowded audience. Next month the Washington celebrated its fifty-fifth anniversary with an overflowing house. On the Graham's sixtieth anniversary, classes were suspended.

A satirist wrote in the *Collegian* (March, 1869) on the social significance of the celebrations. According to him, a date to escort a beauty to such an occasion was booked as far as a year in advance. These events ranked in the same category as church-going among the authorized "amusements" in Lexington, "this moral town." The final celebrations in 1871 brought together a brilliant assemblage such as had been rarely seen in this "Athens of the South." The local *Virginia Gazette* pictured the dignified professors, the solemn divines, the sober matrons, the ebullient students, the lovely belles and their attentive escorts, "little boys" and "sweet little girls"—all out in best attire. For this entertainment Weber's "Germania Band" had been imported from Washington. It became the custom for the societies to invite outside speakers to address them at commencement, usually divines, political leaders, or educators. After completion of the Lee Chapel on the campus the society celebrations were held in that building.

Not all accounts of the events were complimentary. Sometimes proceedings were disturbed by chattering audiences or the rushing about of young pages carrying striped batons that looked like "miniature barber poles" or billets doux from admiring females. One speaker was pointedly honored by being presented with an auger.

As their fathers had done, the society debaters argued topics not likely to come up in their regular classes. At their anniversary in 1867 the Graham contestants tackled the questions: "Was the Execution of Charles the First justifiable?" Despite the alleged affiliation of so many of their ancestors the members voted 52–32 in the negative. The Washington in that year considered: "Would the independence of Ireland advance the prosperity of her people?" Subjects debated during the later sixties were diverse indeed, including: "Whether war ever advanced civilization" (Southerners had reason to feel deeply on that); "Whether Napoleon I's career profited civilization"; "the justifiableness of lying"; "Which tends more to advance a man in life, Personal Merit or Powerful Friends?" and "Is it *ever* right to marry for money?"

During the seventies debate topics inevitably included controversial questions. Among the subjects were free public schools, then being introduced into Virginia; the justification for the execution of Emperor Maximilian; and whether the victory of Germany "in the present [1870] war of races" would benefit mankind.

Meanwhile, among the topics of student orators were such great themes as "Dogmatism is an Enemy of Truth" and "The Character and Influences of the True Scholar, and his Duty to the Present Age."

During the seventies Southern problems were debated, as they still are in other forums. The Washington in 1873 considered the feasibility of removing Negroes from the South and replacing them with European immigrants. In 1875 the same society was objective enough to debate whether the Civil War would eventually prove beneficial to the South, though it is hardly surprising to learn that the question was decided in the negative. Reconstruction issues repeatedly broke into orations and debates. Etheridge of North Carolina in the Washington anniversary address of 1875 demanded: "What cry of agony is that floating on the soft air of Louisiana?" Rhetorically he identified it as "the death shriek of liberty being murdered in her own temples by ruthless and base usurpers who are too mean for hate and hardly worthy of scorn."

Northern newspapers narrowly watched Southern utterances during these years, often to prove unrepentance and make political capital; and even college literary society celebrations did not escape. When a South Carolina "Bourbon" enunciated fiery sentiments before the University of Virginia societies an observer predicted that such a speech would lose the Democrats an election in Ohio! (Some years before, the University of Georgia had been closed because of a "treasonable" speech by a student.) In 1878 the Philadelphia *Sunday Republic* was indignant about proceedings at the Graham-Lee anniversary, and suggested that Northern philanthropists who had helped Washington and Lee might be "satisfied" at the results. It seems that students had called attention to the degenerate state of national politics in the Grant era, a situation long since acknowledged by historians but not by vindictive Northerners of that day. The *Republic* may have been even more disturbed by a debate the following month in which the Graham-Lee considered whether slavery as it had existed in the South was right, and decided in the affirmative.

The question of labor versus capital was sometimes before the societies. The Reverend R. A. Holland, in an address at the commencement celebration of 1869, aroused the ire of the New York *World* as a sneer at "labor." Debates at the Washington celebration of 1878 weighed the topic "Ought Laws to be enacted restricting the Formation of Labor Union Societies?" The arguments advanced pro and con seem strikingly similar to those still brought forth regarding "right to work" legislation.

Young men "viewed with alarm" social and economic changes during the Gilded Age. On February 22, 1880, the Washington debated the proposition: "Resolved, that the present communistic tendencies are likely to result in an overthrow of the Republican form of Government in the United States." The "array of labor against capital" was cited as calling for "a strong government." The enfranchisement, education (!), and (future) social equality of Negroes were viewed as steps to communism. But student Dufour of Louisiana reassured the audience that capital and labor resembled the Siamese twins, and together would maintain American freedom.

Notwithstanding the educational and social value of the literary societies, signs of decay set in, as indicated by lack of interest and decline in membership. Factors included the interference of faculty and trustees in the awarding of society medals and the adverse effects of social fraternities, which among other things brought fraternity politics into the distribution of coveted society honors. The societies eventually (after World War I) would cease to occupy a paramount place in college life.

THE *Southern Collegian*, established by the literary societies, became a major activity in its own right. At the outset it served as a combined newspaper and literary quarterly. As time passed the latter function eclipsed the former, so that only passing mention was accorded campus happenings. Articles, essays, poems, and comment of various kinds filled the *Collegian*, much of the material being in satirical vein. A number of the student editors distinguished themselves in later life, among them Charles A. Graves, eminent professor of law at Washington and Lee and the University of Virginia; William L. Prather, president of the University of Texas; William S. Currell, president of the University of South Carolina; and the popular writer of "Old South" novels and stories, Thomas Nelson Page. Page's father became displeased at the future novelist's wasting his time in "scribbling" instead of applying himself to his Latin and Greek classes, in which Page admitted he had been trifling.

In 1899 Page commented on a copy of the *Collegian* sent to him by his friend Harry St. George Tucker of the Washington and Lee faculty. Comparing it with the magazine of his student days twenty-five years before, he observed: "It had none of the pretentious, vapid, wordy, windy papers that used sometimes to blot the pages with ink in the form of sentences." He added: ". . . there were some of the biggest fools who used to write for that paper that I have ever known and I have an extensive acquaintance with the class."

With Page's judgment on verbosity the modern reader must agree, although some able and well-written articles appeared.

The *Collegian*'s most notable exploit, however, was not much of a literary effort but a sensational hoax that attracted nationwide attention. In view of the medium, a mere student magazine of limited circulation, the repercussions appear as remarkable as those that stemmed from Orson Welles' dramatization of H. G. Wells' *War of the Worlds* over a radio network on the eve of World War II.*

In its March 8, 1873, issue the *Collegian* printed, under the heading "The Probable Destruction of the Natural Bridge," a letter purporting to have come from one. J. Parry McClure at "Fancy Hill," Virginia. The writer indicated that as the regular weekly editions of the local newspapers had been circulated he would describe the wildest excitement caused by the burning of the Natural Bridge fourteen miles south of Lexington:

> As I neared the spot, the smoke became denser and blacker, and when I got to the Hotel, I found everybody excited and everything in the wildest confusion. The negroes who occupy the deserted premises near the Bridge on the brow of the hill, had moved

* The Welles broadcast was, of course, no hoax, but it caused consternation among jittery listeners who were not aware of the nature of the program and thought they were hearing actual reports of a Martian invasion.

down to the Hotel, so great was their terror, and every one was making ready to depart at once. From below the Bridge volumes of deep black smoke were rolling continually, except when interrupted by jets of bright flame which occasionally flared up to a great height. The surface of the ground is warm for some distance around, and is steaming very visibly. The peculiar smell I noticed on Sunday last is now plainly perceptible to all. The rock on the western side of the Bridge had been cracked by the heat and large masses have fallen into Cedar Creek. As yet the arch, as well as can be seen in the intervals between the volumes of smoke, is intact. Occasionally, however, we could distinguish the crashing sound of a boulder as it dashed into the water below.

The letter also contained further statements of Negroes living nearby, and a suggestion that Professor John Lyle Campbell of Washington and Lee be asked for a scientific explanation of the phenomenon. Accordingly, the *Collegian* included such a letter represented as written by the geologist.

The *Rockbridge Citizen* of March 12 remarked that the last *Southern Collegian* had contained a highly *"scented"* and sensational treatment of "The Destruction of the Natural Bridge." But Lexington's other weekly organ, the *Gazette*, copied as straight journalism in its March 14 issue the article from the *Collegian*, purporting to be a description of the partial destruction of the bridge by "spontaneous combustion." In its next issue the *Gazette* carried a history of the prank and paid tribute shamefacedly to ". . . a bold, smart and successful hoax." A bona fide letter from the *Collegian* editors to Professor Campbell, dated March 9, explained the whole episode and hoped that he had taken no offense at the use of his name. The young men had produced no small amount of hysteria in the environs of old Rockbridge, where people wept, sighed, and even detected a distinct odor emanating from "the Bridge." Divers clergymen were reported to be profoundly disturbed.

Nor were the local folk alone in being duped. Some of the newspapers taken in were the Norfolk *Journal*, the Winchester *Times*, Baltimore *Gazette*, Mobile *Register*, and Richmond *Enquirer*. The New York *Herald* desired further particulars, the Baltimore *Sun* became wroth, and even the staid New York *Times* deigned to notice the affair. The New York *World*, alarmed by the Vesuvian propensities of the Natural Bridge, quickly calmed itself when it learned that the matter was all a joke, and that the bridge "still hovered uselessly over its ravine as usual." The Norfolk *Journal* sourly recommended that those youths responsible be soundly "birched," and one critic adverted to "Gen. Lee's bad boys." One William T. Heaton published a poem on the episode in the Parkersburg *Times*.

The *Collegian*'s "bad boys," however, enjoyed themselves immensely. The magazine's April 5 issue offered a cryptic explanation of the authorship: "It was the work of an immoral Alabamian immediately from Texas, who only tarries for a short while upon the soil that sprouted the memorable cherry tree, over which the great Virginian told the truth and astounded the Mother of States and Statesmen." The editors included William Edmonds of Texas (who reportedly could throw a curve in baseball), W. H. Tayloe of Alabama, and T. J. Kernan. But it was "Windy" Edmonds who emerged from the smoke and flames as "The Great Incendiary."

Despite this notorious success, the *Collegian* suffered from that chronic complaint of college literary magazines, paucity of student contributions. Difficulties sometimes arose also between the faculty and the literary societies over the appointment of editors. The *Southern Collegian* ran uninterruptedly, however, until World War I, was revived in the late twenties under the auspices of student "literati" (whose iconoclastic views contrasted sharply with those held by nineteenth-century editors). Later it gradually became transformed into a kind of light-humor magazine, so frequently employing risqué material that it was abolished (as a University publication) by faculty action in 1966.

MEANWHILE, the faculty continued to teach school.

Four ante-bellum professors had greeted General R. E. Lee in 1865 when he assumed the presidency of the College. To this nucleus additional faculty members were appointed to implement the expanded program of the late sixties; but by 1880 most of the newcomers had departed, leaving the faithful four, I. L. Campbell, James J. White, A. L. Nelson, and C. J. Harris (with Professor Kirkpatrick) as the core of the teaching staff. Nelson survived into the twentieth century. The other old-timers were replaced in the eighties and nineties. Washington and Lee must acknowledge a heavy debt to that stalwart quartet who labored so faithfully through most trying times.

By the mid-eighties much of the curricular accretion of R. E. Lee's expansive program had been necessarily eliminated, leaving a faculty of eight full professors aided by several assistants. Departments consisted of Latin (and Roman history); Greek (and Greek history); modern languages, English, and modern history; moral philosophy and belles-lettres; mathematics; applied mathematics; natural philosophy (physics); and chemistry and geology. Thus the curriculum appeared essentially similar to that approved in 1867 with the added identification of belles-lettres and geology. The inclusion of the former with moral philosophy rather than English will appear strange to modern readers.

Also striking was the continuation of a single department comprising modern languages, English, and modern history, as it had been constituted in 1867. Professor James A. Harrison, appointed to this comprehensive chair in 1876, set about to elevate English to a position of eminence in the curriculum. His efforts were successful but they placed a horrendous burden upon the multipurpose department until the various disciplines were finally separated.

The Mississippi-born Harrison, who gained the soubriquet of "Old Hatchet," had been educated at Bonn and Munich. He came to Washington and Lee from Randolph-Macon and served for nineteen years until called to the University of Virginia. Shortly after arrival he insisted that English should be required of all students for graduation. Elementals of English had been deemed superfluous or left to the student, causing a shameful neglect of basic rules of grammar and syntax. Dr. Harrison argued that English should be on a par with "the languages of Athens and Rome, with the science of Numbers, or with the bugs and birds of our Museum." The faculty quickly accepted the idea of compulsory English for all. Of the 109 students in college during 1881–1882, 92 were enrolled in one or another of Harrison's courses. In another session he taught 105 from a college enrollment of 132. There are references to overflowing classes in later years, although the problem was alleviated by the employment of young and inexperienced student assistants, a practice of which Harrison disapproved.

For students who had never studied English grammar or who wished to review what they had had elsewhere a special course was available. Thorough drill in composition, analysis, and punctuation, together with reading in English poets from "Shakspere" to Tennyson, constituted the main work in "junior" English. Passing this course or an examination in it was required for graduation in any study. Intermediate and senior courses concentrated upon the "historical study of the language as developed out of the Anglo-Saxon and enriched by the French and other languages." Work included Anglo-Saxon grammar and readings, and early English masterpieces from Beowulf to Chaucer. In the senior year the study of Gothic was begun "as the foundation of English and Germanic philology." Despite the historical material there were frequent exercises in English composition and emphasis was placed upon accurate usage. A "special piece of work," probably a thesis or essay, and parallel reading were required of each senior. With all of this, the catalogue for 1885–1886 announced that "English literature, specifically, and Rhetoric are taught in the Department of Moral Philosophy and Belles-Lettres."

Washington and Lee's course in English attracted wide attention in this country and England, and Harrison's scholarly reputation spread far. "The Early English Text Society" of London placed the institution on a list of colleges eligible to receive the society's annual prize for excellence of work in Old English. In 1883 Harrison prepared the "Library of Anglo-Saxon Poetry" for publication and was invited to lecture on Anglo-Saxon poetry at Johns Hopkins University.

Modern languages offered during the eighties were French and German, two classes of each, junior and senior, meeting three hours weekly. Almost every year produced a demand for instruction in Spanish and Italian.

The course in modern history covered Europe from 400 A.D. to current times and brought American history into the curriculum. Obviously it tried to cover too much ground. Professor Harrison admitted the course's inadequacy, which also was stressed in an ably written critique by a student in the *Southern Collegian* for May, 1888.

Dr. Harrison nevertheless found time to direct graduate students, and thus trained both his successor and a scholar who brought some belated relief to Harrison's heterogeneous department. Washington and Lee offered the Doctor of Philosophy degree during this epoch and up to 1912. There were few takers but several of these became excellent educators. Among them were Dr. Henry Alexander White, a Presbyterian clergyman who was appointed in 1889 to the newly created chair of history, and Dr. William S. Currell, who took Harrison's place in 1895. Dr. White himself undertook no small burden in teaching, virtually unaided, the entire field of history. He also wrote several books the while.

In 1888 Harrison suggested to the board that his chair be divided into two professorships: Teutonic languages (English and German), and Romance languages. The division was yet unrealized several years after his departure when Dr. Currell complained in 1889 that Washington and Lee remained the only college of high rank in the South requiring one professor to teach three languages. Not until 1905 were modern languages separated from English, and it was not until the arrival of Professor De la Warr B. Easter in 1910 that French and German were divided.

Older values and techniques continued to prevail in the "key" Department of Moral Philosophy (to which belles-lettres was attached until 1890). The professorship was filled by an unbroken line of Presbyterian clergymen. Dr. John L. Kirkpatrick served from 1866 until his death in 1885. Dr. John P. Strider succeeded but died in the following year. Dr. James A. Quarles rendered yeoman service to the University until his death in 1907, when Dr. James R. Howerton was appointed to the chair of philosophy, as it came to be called in the twentieth century. This department changed little. In the mid-eighties it covered "philosophy of the mind" or metaphysics; logic; ethics or moral science; and evidences of Christianity.

Durable Professor Nelson taught mathematics three hours daily six days a week, carrying a "teaching load" that would horrify modern college professors. Junior mathematics embraced algebra, geometry, and plane trigonometry. For those unprepared to enter this class a lower section was provided. The intermediate class studied spherical trigonometry, analytical geometry, and differential and integral calculus. Senior mathematics consisted of more extended attention to analytical geometry, differential and integral calculus, and the philosophy of mathematics. A Department of Applied Mathematics, in which President Custis Lee sometimes taught, was continued. It offered in the junior course descriptive geometry, topographical drawing, shades, shadows, and perspective; in the intermediate class rudiments of architecture, applied mechanics, and stone-cutting. Applied mechanics and civil engineering followed in the senior class. With a bow to the Cincinnati Society the catalogue stated that this department would teach the principles of "fortification and gunnery to students that wish it." There is no indication that anyone wished it.

A major academic development of the period was increasing specialization in the natural sciences. In the ante-bellum curriculum "natural philosophy" had embraced all science (except mathematics, which was considered among the liberal *arts*). In President R. E. Lee's program separate departments of chemistry and "applied chemistry" were established. By the eighties natural philosophy comprised only physics and mechanics. In the junior class elementary mechanics and physics were studied, all members performed experiments, and solution of problems was required. Senior students worked on analytical mechanics and one or more branches of physics (heat, light, or electricity).

An outstanding faculty member during this time was Sidney Turner Moreland, Professor of Physics from 1880 to 1898. Born in Georgia and reared in Louisiana, he began college study at the University of Mississippi. He was attracted to Washington and Lee by Colonel William Allan's presence and received the A. B. and C.E. degrees in 1874. Learning from Allan that the M.A. degree was worth an additional thousand dollars a year, he won that distinction in 1876. Moreland became a pioneer investigator in X-ray work. In time he succeeded to

Professor James J. White's preeminent position on the Washington and Lee faculty and for several years served in the newly created position of dean of the faculty. A low salary and unpromising local conditions combined to cause him to accept an invitation to the distinguished McDonogh School in Maryland in 1898. His departure was a severe loss, but was somewhat offset by the fact that his colleague David Carlisle Humphreys, whom he had trained, remained on the faculty in the applied science field, afterward becoming dean of engineering.

In the early eighties Professor John L. Campbell, who had taught the inclusive science courses before the war, was still teaching both chemistry and geology, assisted by his son Harry. The elder Campbell died in 1886 and in the same year Dr. William George Brown, a native of England and a graduate of the University of Virginia, was placed in the new Bayly Chair of General and Applied Chemistry. In 1887 Henry Donald Campbell was appointed Robinson Professor of Geology and Biology.

The divisions of chemistry as taught by Campbell and son already were much like those that persisted into recent times, at least in title—chemical physics (or physical chemistry), inorganic and organic chemistry, and physiological chemistry. Campbell senior also continued, from ante-bellum times, a course of lectures on agriculture. A brief history of chemistry was offered.

Dr. Brown was forced to resign in 1894 following differences with H. D. Campbell and questions by the trustees as to Brown's teaching effectiveness. Dr. James Lewis Howe was then called from Kentucky to fill the Bayly professorship, in which he continued until his semi-retirement in 1938. At the time of his election Howe was dean of the Hospital College of Medicine and the Louisville College of Dentistry. A native of Massachusetts and graduate of Amherst, he had won his doctorate at Göttingen in 1882. Electing a New Englander to the faculty was a new departure; but Dr. Howe's activity in Christian Endeavor and Y.M.C.A. work, and service as a Sunday school superintendent in Louisville, commended him to the trustees. And after all, he was a naturalized Kentuckian. The *Courier-Journal* in fact lamented that Louisville was losing one of its "very learned and best citizens."

Dr. Howe, who lived vigorously until his death in 1956, built up a scholarly reputation, trained professional chemists and premedical students, and served for a time as dean of the School of Applied Science until that division's discontinuance. He continued active in church work, rising to high lay offices and preaching in churches of his own and other denominations. At the same time he performed countless civic and club duties and services.

In the "practical" development of the sciences after the Civil War, biology was unrecognized as such and but a half session was devoted to geology. Apparently some instruction in botany and zoology, focused on classification, was introduced in the next few years. With H. D. Campbell's appointment in 1887 instruction in these fields was expanded. Campbell taught large and popular classes in geology, and also in biology or natural history until 1915. Emphasis in biology shifted from classification to principles of growth and the student was taught to think on vital questions. A writer in the *Collegian* in 1888 extolled the study of biology for "mental discipline" and quoted Herbert Spencer on the value of the laws of biology as applied to the state. "Social Darwinism" was long believed to be of practical value.

Elementary courses in mineralogy and zoology were studied prior to geology, while comparative zoology prepared for paleontology. Geology was divided into four segments: Dynamical geology (or geological agencies); structural geology; historical geology (especially of the United States); and practical application in searching for ores and other minerals and in civil engineering and mining. Along with scientific instruction Campbell dispensed general wisdom illustrated with anecdotes. In 1907 he was appointed to the office of dean, in which he offered kindly and sympathetic advice to students, and became well known in the Southern Association of Colleges and Schools. During his few years of retirement he served as university historian, a post in which his detailed knowledge of the institution and community stood him in good stead. For Washington and Lee men their "Dean Harry" was *sui generis*.

Instruction in the sciences advanced despite a lack of adequate and up-to-date equipment which, judging by the recorded complaints of the professors, must have been severe. Professor McCulloch made an excellent early beginning in the installation of a physics laboratory about 1870, purchasing useful optical apparatus, but there was little for heat, sound, and electricity.

Fifteen years later Professor Moreland declared that hardly any advance had been made in physics and chemistry during that interval. Vanderbilt, Texas, Tulane, and Georgia, not to mention Northern schools, exceeded Washington and Lee in laboratory work in those subjects. Applied mathematics was just as bad off. In 1885–1886 Moreland was compelled to employ his own manual labor and $75 of his personal funds in repairing the physics laboratory. He asked for a yearly appropriation of $250 for equipment!

Professor Brown in 1886–1887 requested a chemical laboratory possessing the latest improvements and arrangements "for assaying as well as for purely analytical work," and which would enable the University to offer mining engineering.

In the middle nineties Professor Humphreys, reading in the Washington and Lee *Historical Papers* of the scientific apparatus purchased by William Graham in 1776 for Liberty Hall, noted that the first item was "a small reflecting telescope." To Humphreys' knowledge that was the only telescope ever owned by the institution save a few insignificant instruments. He remarked also that a Hadley's Quadrant had been purchased at the same time, and calculated that from an expenditure of £160 astronomy had fared well. He concluded with a question: "If it was considered necessary in 1776 to have a telescope to aid in giving a liberal education, what might be said now after the great advance made in the science since that time?" But next June (1896) Humphreys had not obtained his telescope, for he was again requesting one.

Teaching of geology and natural history was facilitated, however, by the establishment of a museum which came to be named for its donor, Lewis Brooks, a bachelor recluse of Rochester, New York. Brooks' gift of $25,000 in 1875 remained anonymous until his death two years later. It was transmitted through Professor Henry A. Ward of Rochester, who has been called "Museum-maker to America," and who personally supervised the preparation of the rooms and cases. The museum, much admired in its time, was housed in the northeast wing (now Robinson Hall) of the Washington College group until 1936, when it was dismantled and its contents were stored. It comprised four "cabinets": (1) Zoological, with stuffed specimens and mounted skeletons illustrative of the divisions of the animal kingdom—mammals, birds, reptiles, fishes, etc. (2) Mineralogical, containing a valuable and beautiful assortment of specimens from the United States and other areas, with a collection of lithological specimens of all varieties of rocks employed in building and works of art. (3) Geological, setting forth in miniature the earth's history from the earliest periods, and including an excellent collection of fossil animals and plants representing flora and fauna of successive geological ages. (4) Botanical, with an herbarium of five thousand specimens, possessing everything needful for instruction in botany and vegetable physiology.

As the academic curriculum steadily took on more "modern" aspects the classics continued in their traditional form, but relinquished their position as the universal basis of a liberal education. Instruction apparently changed little from ante-bellum days. Latin students read Livy, Cicero, Vergil, Terence, Tacitus, Horace, Juvenal, and various poets, as well as texts in Roman history and literature and classical geography. Greek readings included Homer, Aeschylus, Demosthenes, Thucydides, Sophocles, and Euripides, and texts in Greek history and literature.

After Professor James J. White's death in 1893 and Professor Harris' ill health and resignation that same year, Professors Addison Hogue and Edwin W. Fay succeeded them in the chairs of Greek and Latin respectively. The former exemplified the older type of college professor. Known among students by the invidious soubriquet "Judas," this strait-laced pedagogue unsparingly condemned alcoholic beverages, frivolity, and athletics. He had been educated at Hampden-Sydney, the University of Virginia (where tradition has it that an altercation prevented him from receiving a degree), and at German universities. He had taught for some years at Hampden-Sydney and the University of Mississippi. He compiled an impressive record of publications. A local account spoke of Dr. Hogue as an accomplished "gentleman of earnest piety," and added, "He is a member of the Presbyterian church." He was married to a daughter of the late trustee Dr. Benjamin Mosby Smith. He remained in his chair until 1921 when he retired, giving over his work to Professor Kern.

More indicative of the future college professor was Dr. Fay, a native Louisianian, who had taken his Ph.D. degree from Johns Hopkins in 1890 and followed with a year's study at the University of Leipzig. He had taught at the Universities of Michigan and Texas and like Hogue was identified as a Presbyterian. In contrast to Hogue, the established pundit, Fay came to Washington and Lee a young and relatively unknown scholar. He remained only until 1899 when he was succeeded by Professor George H. Denny, who became president of the University two years later.

During this period the University offered the A.B., M.A., and Ph.D. degrees. Students were not required to study for a degree. They could pursue any courses for which they were prepared so long as they attended a total of fifteen lectures a week. In 1886, for example, aspirants to the A.B. numbered 86, and 38 registrants were not degree candidates.

For several years prior to 1888 three "schemes" for attainment of the A.B. were offered. Each involved some study in every general field of knowledge in the curriculum. Scheme "A" emphasized the classics, scheme "B" English and modern languages, scheme "C" the sciences. Rhetoric and moral philosophy were required in all schemes. English literature was required only in scheme "B," and was offered in scheme "A" as an alternative to modern history. Some Latin and Greek were necessary in all schemes. The scientific scheme required the whole courses of French and German. Scheme "A" required the whole course in one of those languages or the junior courses in both. This basic pattern of classical, "Literary," and scientific programs persisted in a number of colleges well into the twentieth century.

Throughout the years criticisms of the curriculum, degree requirements, and instructional techniques had been voiced. Emphasis upon
the practical which General R. E. Lee had introduced had not eliminated traditional insistence upon Latin, Greek, and mathematics. As
early as 1871 the Franklin Society had debated the value of the classics
in the curriculum and the programs of the eighties provided some
dilution of Latin and Greek. Finally, by the spring of 1888, faculty and
trustees dealt a fatal blow to the dominance of the classics.

In approving degree changes the trustees observed that Latin and
Greek could be "optioned out," enabling a student to win his degree
without them. They accepted this change only as an experiment, and
over the objection of the Nestor of the board, Dr. B. M. Smith; but
trends were against Dr. Smith and the experiment became a curricular
fixture.

Such was the faculty and such the curriculum of the later Victorian
epoch. Despite shortcomings the courses on the whole afforded excellent training for those able and willing to profit by the work. Perhaps
it was no accident that men schooled at Washington and Lee during
the generation after R. E. Lee's death made their mark in the world,
especially in the sphere of public affairs during the era of "the Great
War."

Specialization of the curriculum thus made some headway, science
was strengthened, and history added. Still there was much to be done,
with such subjects as economics and psychology to come into their
own in the next century. Specialization itself eventually was to come
under fire from curricular "integrationists," but such faculty members
as Harrison, Quarles, and the Campbells taught with insight and
breadth in a curriculum perforce integrated.

William Lyne Wilson,
1897–1900

W̲HEN IT BECAME KNOWN that General Custis Lee would at last be permitted to resign the presidency at Washington and Lee, several names were suggested to the trustees as candidates for the position. Among those seriously considered was Woodrow Wilson, then a professor at Princeton and a prolific writer on American history and government. He was recommended by Professor James A. Harrison of the University of Virginia, formerly of the Washington and Lee faculty, who characterized Wilson as "a brilliant speaker, writer, and scholar, whose recent works on Washington and others are universally praised and who is an immense favorite, they say, with the Princeton students." Wilson had other attributes that must have impressed the Scotch-Irish trustees. He was a native of Staunton in the valley of Virginia; was the son, grandson, and son-in-law of Presbyterian clergymen; and was himself an elder of the church.

But the board did not act on Harrison's suggestion. And while Washington and Lee from its origins, like the commonwealth of Virginia, had been something of a "cousinwealth," the trustees did not appear inclined to base their choice upon kinship. In fact they passed over other candidates recommended strongly because of genealogy. For example, the novelist alumnus Thomas Nelson Page urged the election of Colonel Thomas H. Carter, observing: "He has one of the largest family connections in the state of Virginia, by all of whom he is greatly beloved; his father and General Lee's mother were first cousins, so as to family connections I need say no more." Quite similar was a recommendation of Colonel Thomas M. Jones, a West Pointer and long-time army officer who had been engaged for many years in teaching white persons and Indians: "He is a Virginian, tracing as far back as John Smith and Powhatan."

One avowed candidate was President Henry E. Shepherd of the College of Charleston, a Confederate veteran, a Presbyterian, and as he put it, "no politician." Shepherd declared that Washington and Lee should have an enrollment of five hundred—and the implication was that he was the man to invigorate the institution. A number of testimonials arrived in behalf of Shepherd. Professor Harrison and trustee Clement D. Fishburne of Charlottesville suggested William M. Thornton, formerly chairman of the faculty of the University of Virginia. Fishburne conceded that Thornton had been criticized, but wisely noted: ". . . but what Chr. or Prest. will not be criticized if he does his duty?"

The final choice fell upon a Wilson, not Woodrow, but one better known to the public of 1897—William Lyne Wilson, former Congressman, and Postmaster General in the Cleveland cabinet. His Virginia credentials were good. A native of Middleway (now in West Virginia), he had been reared in nearby Charles Town. After a preliminary education at a local academy where he demonstrated precocity he entered Columbian College (now George Washington University) from which he was graduated in 1860 at the age of seventeen. He entered the University of Virginia but with the outbreak of war enlisted in the Twelfth Virginia Cavalry. He served under Jeb Stuart and the gallant General Turner Ashby, was captured and exchanged in 1862, re-entered military service and was with R. E. Lee at Appomattox. Returning to Columbian as assistant professor of languages he resumed the study of law and was admitted to the bar. In 1871 he began legal practice in Charles Town. As to his denominational identification he was a Baptist, and his wife's father had been pastor of the Lexington Baptist Church in 1850-1851. (He later concluded that his religious affiliation had weighed in his favor with the trustees of Washington and Lee; for he confided in his diary that while they maintained a "Presbyterian grip . . . very strong and unyielding" by appointing members of their faith to vacancies on the board and faculty, "they purposely keep the Presidency in some other denomination.")

In the fall of 1882 Wilson had served briefly as president of West

Virginia University, then a struggling, faction-ridden institution. He thus had had at least an acquaintance with the academic world as both teacher and administrator. It was his career in public service, however, that attracted the attention of the Washington and Lee trustees, even before their open search for a president.

Election to Congress had allowed Wilson to extricate himself from his difficult situation at West Virginia University. He served six terms in the House and made a reputation as a tariff reformer, but lost out in the Republican congressional landslide of 1894. He then was appointed Postmaster General for the last two years of the second Cleveland administration.

Harry St. George Tucker, member of Congress and trustee of Washington and Lee, had formed a close association with Wilson. And as early as the spring of 1896 trustee Thomas D. Ranson, an intimate friend of Tucker's, had sounded Wilson out as to whether he would care to become a professor in the School of Law. It was evident that administration officeholders would be seeking employment after March of 1897. The Democratic party was torn between the Cleveland sound-money element and the free silver advocates. The latter had wrested control of the party from Cleveland and his followers and obviously would dominate the forthcoming convention.

This trustee informed Wilson that an enlarged School of Law at Washington and Lee had become imperative. Assuring his correspondent that Tucker and enough other trustees heartily agreed with the proposal, he wrote: "We will elect you to the new chair, if you say so, and if preferable will tender you the presidency later on."

Ranson's political forebodings were fulfilled as the Democrats nominated William Jennings Bryan and the Republican William McKinley was elected. Wilson was torn between Lexington and a tempting offer to enter law practice in New York. A quiet, contemplative man, small and fragile, more like a poet than a politician, he indicated to friends that he should like time for writing and study. Yet he looked upon the prospect of Washington and Lee not as peaceful relief from the hurly-burly of Washington but as an opportunity for positive, dynamic accomplishment. His doubts were concerned with the possibility of attaining his objectives in the "retired village" of Lexington. As he afterwards wrote in a letter to *Harper's Weekly*, explaining to the public his reasons for accepting the academic post: "I was influenced, I may say captivated by the possibility of making this institution a great centre of sound learning and sound citizenship, a power to reproduce in the South some of that high thinking which made her leadership in past generations so conservative and yet national. I am sure the seed has not run out. But it needs strong and wholesome culture."

Before making his decision, however, Wilson sought counsel from his circle of eminent friends. To his surprise Isidor Straus, brother of Nathan and Oscar, suggested that Wilson would be better off with five thousand dollars a year and a house in Lexington than with ten or twelve thousand in New York.* Wilson even put the matter before President Cleveland who listened with marked interest to an account of the condition and prospects of the school, and agreed with Straus that Lexington would be better than New York. Another whose advice Wilson sought was Walter Hines Page, then on the editorial staff of the *Atlantic Monthly*. Wilson inquired of Page whether Northern friends would or could be interested in helping to build a great university at Lexington. Page, a warm advocate of progress for his native section along "New South" lines, replied with penetrating observations on the educational scene. He told Wilson that, so far as he knew, no general appeal either to North or South had ever been made to build up such an institution as Wilson had in mind. The usual appeal was "to help some church college, or some university because of its antebellum traditions, or some institution to educate negroes [,] an appeal for missionary help or for the generally impossible task of reviving (without remolding) some old institution. To build up a great school at Lexington that should have nothing of the medieval cloister life but should face present conditions and problems just as they are, would be, I think, the very noblest work a man could do. Whether it can be done in our life time, I do not know; but even to lay the foundations would be a monumental piece of work."

It had seemed to Page (a graduate of Randolph-Macon), though he conceded that he had been out of touch with Southern conditions for a decade, "that the educational activity in almost all the Southern States is . . . far too much in ecclesiastical lines and going too much into ecclesiastical control." The writer expressed his appreciation of the work of church schools, but feared that the South would "forever be behind and will loose [sic] ground if the training of the most capable men is confined to these institutions." Page felt that Wilson exemplified both national spirit and sound economic doctrine, and told him that he would surely accomplish much at Washington and Lee.

Wilson weighed the Washington and Lee offer throughout January. He read about the institution's history, and expressed surprise that so full an account had been preserved. He reflected upon the paucity of great contemporary statesmen in the Old Dominion, and upon the fact

---

* The Straus brothers, who attained distinction in business and public service, had grown up in Georgia and retained an interest in the development of the South.

that Virginia had fallen so low as to support Bryanism. He speculated on what he might accomplish at Lexington and dwelt on the disparity in wealth between North and South, the contrast between Washington and Lee with its "mere 6 or 7 hundred thousand endowment as compared to Harvard's millions of dollars and thousands of students." During the month Harry St. George Tucker visited Wilson several times and urged his acceptance, bearing written pledges of support from trustees and a promise of carte blanche in administering the institution. As Tucker had been forced to retire from Congress because of the silver issue the two men must have felt a strong bond of sympathy.

On February 3 Wilson cast the die. He wrote Tucker that he would accept the presidency of Washington and Lee, but added in his diary, "and now I am somewhat repentant of the act." The trustees on February 11 unanimously elected Wilson to the office and Tucker hastened to telegraph his friend of that action.

Some Virginia newspapers criticized Wilson as a member of a Democratic administration who had worked against a Democratic nominee for president. Most press comment, however, was favorable. Such papers as the Baltimore *Sun*, Baltimore *News*, Baltimore *American*, and Boston *Globe* lauded Washington and Lee's president-elect, and the staid Boston *Transcript* called him "Statesman and Scholar." *Harper's Weekly*, in a patronizing sort of way, commended Wilson's efforts as offering a ray of hope for the generally benighted and erring South. Since Washington and Lee was one of the "soundest" of Southern institutions, and under Wilson's leadership it could become a center of light, the magazine urged northern philanthropists to donate money to that school, in order to benefit Southern youth and to serve as a precaution for the nation's future.

In addition the educator received scores of congratulatory letters from his associates and from Virginians. Henry Villard, journalist and financier, whose son Oswald became for some years an active friend of Washington and Lee, observed that in Lexington Wilson would find "a safe anchorage" from the vicissitudes of politics, and concluded, "I have always thought the academical career the noblest of all professions." Especially welcome were letters from Virginians, which served to offset the sometimes vicious attack of free-silver newspapers. To the Virginians Wilson sometimes replied that he was "simply moving from my home in the upper valley to a new home in the same glorious valley."

Distinguished men of the world paid their tribute to Washington and Lee's new president. Lord Bryce, noted British historian and interpreter of America to his compatriots, placed him among the ablest and finest of Americans, while President Eliot of Harvard spoke of him in glowing terms. Harvard, indeed, honored Wilson by selecting him as the Phi Beta Kappa orator of 1897; and he received before and after that date honorary doctorates from various other universities.

Within the University the news of Wilson's election was received with enthusiasm by the faculty and "uproarious applause" by the students. Trustee William Henry Ruffner jubilantly wrote his daughter, adding that the town had responded "by a joyous murmur . . . so we may hope for better times." He expressed the general belief that a new day was about to dawn at the institution, indicating his hopes of Wilson: "We shall send him after Mr. Rockefeller."

INTERESTING INSIGHTS into conditions in the University and the community may be gained from Wilson's observations in his diary of visits to Lexington in March and April, before he had assumed office. The first trip he made immediately after his exit from the cabinet. It must have had a melancholy beginning for the train on which he left Washington was crowded with Republicans returning home from McKinley's inauguration. Wilson stayed overnight in Staunton, leaving next morning for Lexington on "a mixed passenger and freight train, traversing the thirty-six miles in two hours and thirty-five minutes." The new president recorded a thought expressed by generations of students: "My first impressions of my new home are that it is a very hard place to reach."

Wilson was wined and dined, and tendered a reception where he was "called out" by a serenade of students accompanied by a large crowd. On the whole, however, his visits were not reassuring. The quietude and remoteness of Lexington made him question whether he had made a mistake. He asked his diary: "Will I be able to quicken the sluggish life of the school and start it on a new career, broader, less sectarian, more national, more progressive?" A visit to President Custis Lee's darkened sick-room must have been far from inspiriting.

On his second trip to Lexington he had a lengthy confidential talk with John L. Campbell, secretary of the faculty and treasurer of the University. From him Wilson learned some things he had not previously known. These caused him to write privately: "All the information that comes to me—*since my acceptance*, strengthens my conviction that I have a heavy task before me. The School has a bad case of dry rot, and how to get new life and vigor and growth into it, again, is the question I shall have many ponderings over." He was intimately introduced to the ugly issue of sectarianism. Campbell told him that the trustees had looked with disfavor upon a highly recommended candidate for law professor as successor to John Randolph Tucker (whose death early in 1897 had been a severe blow to Wilson) because they were not satisfied as to his "religious character." A week later he heard more on the subject from Miss Mildred Lee, R. E. Lee's daughter, who confirmed what he "had begun very clearly to see" regarding the "Presbyterian grip." He indited a sentence, the substance of which has often been hurled by critics at sectarian colleges and universities: "They claim that they try only to choose the best men, but it always turns out that 'the best man' is a Presbyterian."*

Wilson was uneasy also over evidence "that the people of Lexington and other friends of the University are deeply affected with Lee worship." He shared in the admiration for R. E. Lee and did not doubt that Custis Lee possessed many of his father's qualities. But he felt that the interests of a great institution could not be "made subordinate to the personality of any one man. . . ." An example of what seemed to be "Lee worship" was the effort of the townspeople and trustees to compel Custis Lee to remain on the payroll and continue to occupy the president's house—an attempt which Wilson noted had been "thwarted only by his [Lee's] own good sense and modesty."**

Yet Wilson was fully solicitous of the comfort and feelings of Mildred and Custis Lee. He recorded a pang at the prospect of taking over their house. He wrote Miss Lee to remain in the house as long after July 1 as her convenience required, and urged on Rector McLaughlin

---

* The question of sectarianism disturbed Wilson and there are many references to it in his diary. In December of 1897 he wrote that Professor Moreland, a Methodist, was the only non-Presbyterian on the faculty, and that no large number of non-Presbyterians had been permitted in faculty or trustees "even in General Ro. Lee's day." As it pertains to the faculty the latter observation is at variance with a statement in the *Southern Collegian* in 1869 that only four of the nine professors at that time were Presbyterians. Moreover, in view of the obvious merit of such later appointees as Professors Harrison, H. A. White, Currell, Howe, H. D. Campbell, Humphreys, and Hogue, it is likely that they were indeed "the best men" available.

** The Mary Custis Lee Chapter, U.D.C. (Lexington), desired to launch a project to purchase the Lee home from the University "as a tribute from Southern women to the memory of that great and good man, General Robert E. Lee—to be set apart as sacred to the use of his family, if they will accept it, or as a Museum of the relics of our beloved Chieftain and his brave soldiers." Custis Lee, however, expressed the view that the President of Washington and Lee University should reside in the home.

the establishment of a G. W. Custis Lee professorship. Wilson implemented the suggestion with a small contribution.

The new president brought his family to Lexington early in August. He enjoyed their surprise and delight "at the size, completeness, thorough comfort and elegance of the house, and the convenience of all its appointments." Wilson recorded his and his family's appreciation of Custis Lee's characteristic thoughtfulness and consideration, together with the fact that he permitted the family portraits, many of them formerly owned by Martha Washington, to remain.

If there was any local resentment at the Wilsons' occupation of the Lee home it was not evident in the warm welcome the townspeople gave the newcomers. The stream of callers was so constant that Mrs. Wilson at first could not repay the visits.

Attending the Baptist church, Wilson noted that the congregation was ". . . apparently made up of the poorer and humbler classes of the community." This condition, however, did not deter the Wilsons from regular attendance at that church.

PRESIDENT WILSON'S INAUGURATION on September 15, 1897, was quite a contrast to the simple rites in which the Lees had been inducted. The program included three hours of ceremonies in the chapel, a banquet at which 350 persons were seated, and a reception lasting several hours. Prominent visitors who came to honor their friend Wilson included the merchant prince Isidor Straus, former Secretary of the Navy Hilary A. Herbert of Alabama, magnate Henry H. Villard, and his son Oswald Garrison Villard, then beginning his long career as editor and publisher. Governor O'Ferrall of Virginia, Washington College, '69, also was present. Speakers were Professor Henry C. Cameron of Princeton, Chancellor James H. Kirkland of Vanderbilt, and President Daniel Coit Gilman of Johns Hopkins. Greetings read at the banquet included letters from former President Cleveland and James Cardinal Gibbons.

Shortly after 10 A.M. students and alumni marched into the chapel, an orchestra rendered "a beautiful selection," the Reverend W. Strother Jones offered prayer, and Judge William McLaughlin began the formal proceedings to install in office the ninth president of the chartered existence of Washington and Lee.

Dr. Cameron, a Presbyterian clergyman, a Virginian, and a former student of Dr. Archibald Alexander, wove his speech around what he called a "threefold cord" binding Princeton to Washington and Lee: William Graham and "Light Horse Harry" Lee, who had been students at Princeton, and George Washington, victor in the Battle of Princeton in which decisive action was centered on the college campus.

Chancellor Kirkland urged emphasis on the future rather than the past and pointed out "some especial obligations" that faced educational leadership in the South. He declared that the great issues before the nation were economic, and posed questions more difficult of solution than the slavery problem. He lamented the lack of effort to collect and preserve documentary records and to study them scientifically so that a true history of the South could be compiled. Referring to the oft-made charge of intellectual inactivity in the South he urged the application of "more intelligent labor" rather than passion and self-glorification. (The historian may heartily endorse the chancellor's words of 1897, which continued to be applicable far into the twentieth century.)

His final point dealt with the need of cooperation among colleges and universities to bring about educational reforms in the South, and injected a touch of his well-known humor:

> Here the diversity in requirements for admission to college is greater, the standards of college work more varied, the number of high schools and academies smaller, the relation between schools and colleges less intimate and cordial than anywhere else in the whole United States. Educational imposters and charlatans ply their trade with brazen effrontery and laugh at exposure. The boom town that had already established a Methodist University and a Baptist one, and had the logs cut for a Presbyterian one, may not have been located in Virginia, but it was certainly in the South.

Dr. Gilman described his conception of a university, called upon the universities of America to instruct its political leaders, and in the same words as were spoken to him by President Eliot of Harvard in 1876 on the opening of the Johns Hopkins University, enjoined Mr. Wilson to carry on in his noble work.

The remarks of the visiting speakers served as preliminaries to President Wilson's formal inaugural address, the first uttered at Washington and Lee since Dr. Junkin's in 1849. His talk gives us an authoritative view of the problems faced by this institution and by Southern education generally at the close of the nineteenth century.

Wilson touched upon the sensitive question of sectarianism, which occupied so much of his thought. He declared that there could be no denominational "limitation" at Washington and Lee. He stated delicately:

Born of piety and love of education which marked the first settlers in this region, this school enjoyed the friendship and, at times, the official patronage of the church to which those settlers were so strongly attached. It can never forget that obligation, and it has endeavored to repay it by educating some of the greatest men in the annals of that church. But later friends and benefactors have been limited to no denomination, and, as these memorial portraits show, to no section of the country.

The new president called for the training of statesmen at this and other Southern schools, still engaged in slow and painful postwar recovery under the handicap of woefully inadequate financial resources. Despite their difficulties these institutions achieved highly creditable work "in the most important and immediately useful branches of education." But Wilson cited a serious omission in the curricula of contemporary Southern colleges—"the general lack of schools, or of adequate schools, in historical, economic and political studies, such as now form so large a part of the course offered in the great universities and colleges of other parts of the country." He could point nowhere in the South to anything approaching what was being done in history, political science, and economics at such centers as Johns Hopkins, Columbia, Michigan, Cornell, Harvard, Yale, Wisconsin, Williams, and Amherst. Wilson believed such studies were obligatory "if we are to perpetuate government by the people and bear our freedom unscathed. . . ."

Aware that his proposals would be misconstrued as suggestions for partisan instruction, Wilson sought to anticipate his critics:

Let it not be understood that such studies are designed to train recruits for any partisan camp, still less to mould them to the views of any teacher. I am no disbeliever in sturdy partizanship that seeks through political organization the highest good of the country; but it is to generate and develop the desire and the power of independent, original research, to foster the habits and the ability of independent judgment, to acquaint men with the origin and historic growth of our institutions, with the fundamental principles of government, and so enrich them with the results of human experience that they can decide on this or that economic doctrine, as it may advance or impair the general welfare; above all, to make them intelligent and strong leaders, not servile and ill-informed followers of popular opinion or selfish beneficiaries of popular delusions, that such education is designed.

There were toasts and more speeches at the banquet in the old gymnasium; and later in the evening President and Mrs. Wilson, assisted by their two daughters, entertained the inauguration throngs at their residence.

WITH THE CLOSE OF THE FESTIVITIES and the departure of the crowds of Confederate veterans, alumni, and distinguished guests, President Wilson faced the realities of his new position. He was deeply concerned with the low enrollment, although he noted a small increase to a total of one hundred and twenty. Only about half the students were from Virginia; and Wilson believed the Old Dominion should send many more than that to Washington and Lee. Dr. William H. Ruffner, who had been the first superintendent of public education of Virginia, provided an explanation. Public high schools were almost unknown in the commonwealth; and "if all the students prepared for college by existing classical schools of Virginia were divided up among the colleges of the state there would not be more than ten apiece annually." Dr. Ruffner urged upon Wilson the advocacy of the establishment of high schools in the county school systems.

Washington and Lee was not alone in problems of enrollment. Wilson noted that the University of Virginia had opened with a marked diminution in the number of students despite two practices which he considered undesirable—the offering of free tuition to Virginians, and admission without an entrance examination. Despite Wilson's exertions during his three years at Washington and Lee the registration remained below two hundred.

Wilson desired a cordial relationship with his students. He invited them to come see him in Newcomb Hall and at times asked groups of three or four to dine. Somewhat to his distress, his most frequent student contacts ordinarily involved the discipline of malefactors, still a presidential duty as there were no deans to take over the onerous chore. On the whole he was gratified by the good behavior, studiousness, and gentlemanly conduct of the students, and believed faculty attitudes toward discipline were too severe. President Wilson often attended undergraduate organization meetings, usually speaking a few words. In the fall of 1897 the Baptist Church prevailed upon him to teach the student Sunday school class.

As related in Chapter XVII, exuberance of football spirit caused two major vexations of Wilson's administration. The president expressed his views on this and other sports soon after taking up the reins at Washington and Lee, in a talk to the students "in the interest of their football club." Being a mature person and a wise educator he sought to impress upon them that their chief reason for attending Washington and Lee was "to train their minds." Gymnasium exercises and participation in their "ball clubs" were valuable in so far as they gave students vigorous, sound bodies, but intellectual training was always paramount.

How the youths received this doctrine is not recorded, but Wilson sighed to himself: "I could wish that they would concentrate their energies on base ball and tennis, as football is too dangerous a game, especially for youths so young and light as most of ours are." But as students were set upon football, Wilson told them he wished to see Washington and Lee have a good team and that he would help them to make it just that. In view of Wilson's feelings about football and his subsequent troubles stemming from the sport, it is ironic that the football field should have been named for him.

THE PRESIDENT's relations with his professors appear to have been cordial, in some cases intimate. He contrasted the tedium and trivialities of faculty meetings with the cabinet discussions of the business of state. Yet after commenting on one such meeting he wrote: "But to its credit I may say, no faculty could be freer of cliques and factions, and none in which the individual members more freely and independently, give vent to their opinions, always too with marked kindliness and courtesy, even with anger." Sometimes he accompanied a professor to his classroom, as with Dr. Henry A. White to inspect the maps and needs of the Department of History; or journeyed into the country to attend Oxford Church with Harry St. George Tucker and young son Albert; or visited the Tucker residence, "Col Alto," for a glass of eggnog and good-fellowship.

Now and then Wilson dined more or less in state with members of the faculty. Professor Henry A. White, whose books on Civil War history and biography had won him a considerable reputation, entertained the publisher George Haven Putnam and the Wilsons at a dinner that proved too rich for Wilson's blood. It is evident that Wilson would not have relished a certain type of twentieth-century social diversion, for he wrote: "I never did enjoy such gatherings where you flit from one person to another for scrappy conversation."

ASIDE FROM the able and conscientious performance of routine duties, Wilson accomplished three objectives at Washington and Lee. These were, in ascending order of importance: (1) introducing weekly assemblies; (2) encouraging men from the larger world of business and politics to be interested in the institution; and (3) establishing a chair of economics.

The weekly assembly was, in Wilson's view, a matter of far more significance than an observer at this point in time might surmise. He sought through that means to bring the University community together at frequent intervals and to inculcate an esprit de corps, the absence of which struck Wilson upon arrival. The faculty approved the idea in principle when Wilson presented it to them in October of 1897, although there was some objection to compulsory attendance which Wilson thought a necessary feature. Students and faculty had formerly come together in compulsory chapel services. But chapel attendance, made voluntary in 1868, had declined until the *Collegian* observed that on some mornings it was "a literal exemplification of the two or three gathered together."

Objections to compulsory chapel had rested mostly upon religious grounds. While brief prayers opened President Wilson's weekly assemblies the emphasis was otherwise. The president, a faculty member, a clergyman, or an invited visitor would speak on a subject of general interest. The sessions must have had considerable educational value to the students as the topics were often international, political, or economic issues, calculated to bring the young people abreast of current themes. They partially filled the lack of instruction in social sciences that Wilson had noted.

For example, the approach of the Spanish-American war supplied Wilson with subject matter for several talks. His expressions, in historical retrospect, appear remarkably sound and objective, in view of the jingoistic flames being fanned at the time by Theodore Roosevelt and others. After the *Maine* disaster he counseled his students to suspend judgment pending the outcome of the official U.S. Navy inquiry. He dismissed as "incredible" the charge that Spanish authorities were responsible. Speaking on a pending bill for appropriation of $50,000,-000, to be spent at the President's discretion for defense in case of war, he observed that "at the mere prospect of war—much more at its actual coming, the careful and long approved safetyworks of legislation were leveled or swept aside." An incomplete account of these assembly remarks elicited a sharp mean-spirited comment in the war-mongering New York *Sun*, which never lost an opportunity to attack Wilson. Villard's New York *Evening Post*, however, supported Wilson's views.

As conflict neared President Wilson spoke on "the history, political institutions and present position of Spain among the nations of the earth." After the declaration of war he advised students that no longer could difference of opinion exist. He explained McKinley's declaration blockading Cuban ports, international law, and the relationship of neutrals. He paid tribute to the courage and endurance manifested throughout Spanish history. He pointed out, however, that mechanized and scientific modern war, together with American quickness and enterprise, would "turn the chances decidedly in our favor—even a combat of apparently equal forces."

And so it turned out to be. Indeed, the war with Spain, opening as the academic session closed, was over by August. Although a few students left to join the colors, it scarcely affected life at Washington and Lee.

A discussion by President Wilson on the value of the study of the natural sciences, in September of 1898, illustrates a basic shift in the purview of education that had taken place over the previous half century. In signing matriculation papers, Wilson thought he discerned "some disposition to avoid chemistry, and Physics, and take easier tickets." In 1851 Dr. Junkin had expressed an opposite opinion on the relative difficulty of science studies (Chapter IX).

Whether or not the weekly assemblies brought all the results in esprit de corps that the president desired, they met regularly throughout Wilson's tenure and were continued by President Denny along similar lines.

WILSON EXPENDED TIRELESS EFFORT to interest men (and women) of wealth, influence, and intelligence in the institution and to obtain from them financial contributions. His long career as a national political leader, his attractive personality, and his patent sincerity drew a number of the more thoughtful men of large affairs to him. This group collaborated in assuring the success of a campaign that was under way when Wilson reached Lexington, to raise $50,000 for a law building as a memorial to John Randolph Tucker.

Isidor Straus, although constantly harassed by requests for charity and engaged in aiding Jewish refugees, offered Wilson $1,000 to purchase books on economics and finance. The capitalist E. C. Benedict sent a gift through ex-President Cleveland which Wilson applied to establishment of a history library. (Upon Wilson's death, a group of his distinguished friends raised a memorial fund of $100,000 to endow the professorship of economics and political science.)

While actively seeking to improve the University's financial resources, Wilson expressed concern, at least in the privacy of his diary, at the management of the endowment fund. This was handled by the executive committee of the board of trustees, a local group dominated by Rector William McLaughlin. The committee decided investments and securities honestly according to its best judgment, but necessarily with scant real information on "the safety and value of many investments." A large block of railroad bonds had become unproductive, and heavy losses had been sustained in other bonds. As an illustration he cited a holding of $67,000 in Texas and Pacific five percent bonds which were selling below par. He observed that there must be some uncertainty about them, "or some speculative element," or else a five per cent bond promptly paying interest would be selling above par. He wrote about them to Henry Villard, who after investigation replied that "if a good re-investment could be found it would be wise to sell, as the speculative element in these bonds made them too hazardous for an institution to invest its endowment funds in them." Wilson read Villard's letter to the executive committee; but McLaughlin "pooh-poohed it," saying that he had met a lawyer in Fort Worth the previous summer, who had assured him that the bonds would rise to par. Wilson was disturbed by this incident in which the opinions of one of the nation's best-informed railroad men were brushed aside by a local judge, who preferred to take the opinion of a Texas lawyer. "Unless more enlightened and trustworthy management controls our stock and bond investments," he wrote, "we are in constant danger of losing part of the endowment, and almost certain to have a part of it in default." The situation, however, was far from unique. The historian of Princeton, Thomas J. Wertenbaker, has made a classic understatement to the effect that the history of college and university endowments is "discouraging."

The death of Judge McLaughlin in August, 1898, brought a more favorable appraisal from Wilson of that "most prominent citizen of this part of Virginia." Until Wilson's arrival McLaughlin had been "the practical head of the University." The president had no criticism of his own relations with the rector, who had given signs that he desired to disengage himself entirely from the management of Washington and Lee. A childless man, an intense Scotch-Irishman, a "strong Presbyterian, though not a church member [!]," Judge McLaughlin was not popular, but in Wilson's opinion he "was a firm and upright judge, and no institution of learning is hurt by having so watchful, alert and critical a trustee as he was."

THE ACCOMPLISHMENT that was probably closest to President Wilson's heart during his brief administration was the establishment of a chair of economics, to which Dr. H. Parker Willis was appointed. Not only was that youthful scholar to launch a new department, but his zeal and ambition were expected to enliven the entire institution—to provide new blood for the static faculty. Of this Wilson wrote a revealing page in his diary:

> I am afraid this last will be our greatest undertaking. All the professors are able men . . . and conscientious instructors; but partly because of absence of leadership here for some years, partly because of our breeding in and steady selection of Presbyterians, and more yet I fancy because the Scotch-Irishman is not an enthusiastic, or enthusiasm breeding man, there is a lack of progressiveness and spirit, which is strikingly patent to myself as a newcomer.

President Wilson undertook to guarantee the payment of the new professor's salary of $1,500. One may take this as a measure of his determination to provide Washington and Lee a separate chair of economics, so that the school might assume the lead in this respect among Southern colleges.

Henry Parker Willis, a native of Wisconsin, held the Ph.D. degree from the University of Chicago, and had studied at Paris, Berlin, and Vienna. His mentor, Dr. Laughlin of Chicago, who recommended his appointment to Wilson, said of him, "He is the most intellectually honest and sincere man I know." The only fear expressed for Dr. Willis was that he would overwork himself—a fault not found excessively in the professorial tribe. A better person could hardly have been found to undertake the new program of economics. Dr. Willis proved to be a highly satisfactory teacher, an indefatigable research man and writer, and he fulfilled every expectation. Ultimately the dynamic, brilliant scholar left Washington and Lee for a career that led him to a professorship in Columbia University and repute as an adviser to Congressman Carter Glass, chairman of the House Banking and Currency Committee and an author of the Federal Reserve Act of 1913.

Wilson took more presidential initiative in the appointment of faculty members than his predecessors seem to have done, although his recommendations were still subject to approval by the trustees. Dr. Willis' selection appears to have been his own. When Professor Moreland resigned, a number of worthy applicants sought the position of professor of physics. Among these Wilson was most impressed with Dr. Walter LeConte Stevens of the Rensselaer Polytechnic Institute, who had an excellent record and had been trained in European universities. Wilson interviewed the candidate in New York for two hours. Curiously, the interview took place in a department store. It was, of course, Macy's, which was operated by Wilson's good friend, Isidor Straus, who made facilities available to him.

Despite the many complaints in his diary on the trustees' attitude toward religion, Wilson reassured the prospective teacher on this score. Stevens had somehow gained the notion that he would be compelled to participate in religious exercises at the chapel. Wilson ". . . told him that his not being a member of any Church would not be counted against him, and that if he had any peculiar views on denominational or other questions he would never encounter personal criticism or provoke opposition if he did not himself force those views upon others."

Professor Stevens' appointment provided in its sequel none of the supposed difficulties. He came to Lexington, married there and became one of the distinguished, if at times eccentric, members of the faculty.

COLLEGE PRESIDENTS are called upon for many addresses and other off-campus activities. Wilson accepted a number of such engagements despite bad health and the pressure of fund-raising efforts. In the fall of 1897 he attended a meeting of the Southern Association of Colleges and Secondary Schools in Knoxville, and was chosen president of the organization. Washington and Lee was the only Virginia member at that time. A year later, en route to the association's meeting at Athens, Georgia, Wilson was among a group of educators who arrived at 4:10 A.M. at the hamlet of Lula, Georgia, a railroad junction where they had to change trains. His grimly humorous description of the "hotel" where the group sought rest until their departure at noon would do credit to Dickens.

Following the Athens meeting Wilson journeyed to Atlanta where he addressed the Georgia legislature on the political issue of the hour, imperialism, and received a rising vote of thanks.

In March 1898 he went to Princeton to serve as a judge in a debate between Yale and Princeton, with ex-President Cleveland in the chair. The long trip wearied Wilson and he dozed during the debate. To his consternation he found that the other judges had split their votes, leaving Wilson to decide. He cast a shaky vote for Yale and the hometown audience glumly filed out. He then attended a supper in distinguished company which included former President Cleveland and future President Woodrow Wilson. It was 2 A.M. when Washington and Lee's Wilson got to bed.

In May Wilson delivered the Storrs lectures at Yale, at the conclusion of which the students gave him three cheers and the Yale yell. He spoke also at the University of Chicago, but turned down a flood of other engagements.

During 1899 Wilson's health worsened. His diary abruptly terminated in April and late in that year he obtained a leave of absence that extended through the initial months of 1900. He visited Arizona in quest of restored health, returning to his duties in the fall. Typical of the man was his refusal to accept salary while on leave, and his request that his salary be reduced from $5,000 to $4,000. This the hard-pressed trustees granted with appreciation.

Death came on October 17, 1900. Wilson was buried at Charles Town, West Virginia. The funeral cortege of Confederate veterans, students, pallbearers, faculty, trustees, and ministers of the gospel was joined at Charles Town by Grover Cleveland and Isidor Straus. Simple services at the grave were held, in accordance with the wishes of the deceased. The press rang with tributes to him and in the annual report to the trustees in June of 1901 his friend and temporary successor, Harry St. George Tucker, expressed his belief that the passing of President Wilson was a calamity to the University comparable to the death of R. E. Lee. In this judgment the historian may well concur.

Chapter
XX

Years of Transition

UPON THE DEATH of William Lyne Wilson the trustees appointed Harry St. George Tucker as acting president and set about to select a permanent head for the institution. Their effort took almost a year. A capable man was finally chosen; but in the process strong antagonisms were aroused, and Tucker and the able historian Henry A. White afterwards felt impelled to leave the University. At the root of the controversy was the old issue of sectarianism. On the brighter side, however, it can be said that after this bitter period that issue steadily subsided until it eventually ceased to be a discernible factor at Washington and Lee.

AT THE TURN OF THE CENTURY, whenever any academic post of importance became available, it seemed inevitable that the name of Professor Woodrow Wilson should come up. He had been offered a number of college and university presidencies and several prestigious professorships; and on January 9, 1901, trustee Lucian H. Cocke wrote Dr. Wilson tendering him the presidency of Washington and Lee. But the prize that Woodrow Wilson most desired was then within his grasp—the presidency of Princeton University, in which he was to be the first non-clergyman in the institution's 156-year history. Nevertheless, the fact that the trustees made the offer is evidence that they were acting in the tradition which had brought General R. E. Lee and William L. Wilson to Lexington.

During the interregnum the New York *Evening Post* said it had learned in a roundabout way that Grover Cleveland would be invited to become president of Washington and Lee. With characteristic bluntness Cleveland disposed of that rumor: he had never "heard of it, thought of it, or dreamed of it," and he did not believe anyone else ever had either.

But genuine prospects for the position were not wanting. A few days after the offer to Woodrow Wilson an inquiry by the *Rockbridge County News* elicited the jocular comment from a trustee that each member of the board had a different candidate, and probably by the June meeting would have two.

Tucker, of course, appeared to many as the most logical choice. A former trustee, he had been elected professor of law in 1897 and dean of the Law School in 1899. He had several supporters on the board. In November 1899 trustee William C. Preston, in a communication to another board member, listed some of Tucker's assets. He had done excellent work in the Law School. His age was right, he was popular, well-known, and of good habits. Most significant was his "undying love for and enthusiasm about the College." Preston had sounded out members of the Lee family and learned that Tucker's election would be satisfactory to them. Preston believed the alumni supported Tucker. In this he was certainly correct; for before the board's final decision, alumni associations in various parts of the country had almost unanimously endorsed Tucker.

Among other candidates, one of the first to be mentioned was the Reverend W. H. Marquess, president of Westminster College. He was recommended by the Reverend E. C. Gordon, a trustee residing in Missouri. Other possibilities included the Reverend G. B. Strickler, rector of the University; Professor Brown Ayres of Tulane University, a Washington and Lee alumnus; and Hilary A. Herbert, former Secretary of the Navy. Herbert, however, recommended Clifton R. Breckinridge, '71, as similar in type to William L. Wilson, whose friend he had been. Breckinridge had served in Congress and as minister to Russia. Another suggestion was Governor J. Hoge Tyler of Virginia, but Tyler told a newspaper reporter that he knew nothing of the matter. A. W. Gaines, named to the board in June of 1901, urged the election of the president of the University of Tennessee, Dr. Charles W. Dabney.

None of these candidates appears to have been considered seriously by the board as a whole. And the choice of a president was influenced largely by changes in the board membership and the division of the trustees into "clerical" and Tucker factions.

Of eight trustees elected during the period 1898–1901, two were Presbyterian ministers and four were elders. The clergyman Dr. Strickler succeeded to the rectorship on the death of Judge McLaughlin. Tucker, in a pamphlet privately published in 1915 relating to his reasons for leaving Washington and Lee, declared that a group in the board had attempted to fill three vacancies with members of the clergy between 1897 and 1900. Tucker himself had informed the board that if this were done President Wilson would resign. Actually, of five trustees elected in 1898 and 1899, two were clergymen (Robert H. Fleming and Augustus Houston Hamilton), and two were elders (Judge William P. Houston and John A. Preston). The fifth member, Lucian H. Cocke, was a Baptist. According to Tucker, Cocke's election had resulted from pressure exerted indirectly by President Wilson.

Meanwhile, three good friends of Tucker had left the board. Helm Bruce and Thomas D. Ranson resigned, and in a later letter to Ranson Tucker implied that they had been "shelled . . . out" by the "gang" that was opposed to him. William C. Preston died in 1901. Besides being a Tucker supporter Preston had vigorously opposed the suggestion that Dr. Marquess or any other clergyman be elected president.

In 1901 these vacancies were filled by the election of George Walker St. Clair of Tazewell, Virginia, John S. Munce of Richmond, and Albert Winston Gaines of Chattanooga. The first two were elders of the Presbyterian church.

Following Wilson's death, Acting President Tucker became busily engaged in behalf of the Wilson Memorial Fund. These efforts, instead of impressing the trustees favorably, had indirect negative results. Some promoters of the fund recommended that several important capitalists, among them George Foster Peabody of New York and Frank T. Howard of New Orleans, be added to the board of trustees. Also, a movement for formal alumni representation on the board seems to have been coordinated with the drive to raise the Wilson Fund and to endorse Tucker for president. The "clerical" trustees could hardly have taken kindly to any suggestions for loosening their decisive control.

An open break came at the board meeting of June 18, 1901. Clement D. Fishburne moved that the trustees proceed to the election of a president. Immediately his motion was superseded by one offered by the Reverend Messrs. Fleming and Gordon providing that action be postponed until a committee of three, headed by Rector Strickler, should gather information and be ready to present their findings at a call meeting. The lines of division may be discerned in the vote by which the postponement was adopted: six ayes (Strickler, A. T. Barclay, Gordon, Fleming, Houston, Hamilton), to four noes (William A. Glasgow, Fishburne, John A. Preston, and Cocke). The trustees then requested Tucker to continue as acting president. This he declined to do, being by this time thoroughly aroused and profoundly suspicious that the board, dominated by its clerical members, meant to integrate Washington and Lee into the system of Presbyterian education.

It was by this bold defiance of the board that Tucker lost the game, some of his friends believed—with what justification it is difficult to say. George Foster Peabody regretted Tucker's precipitate act. While Tucker has written that he had never aspired to the presidency, and permitted the use of his name in the subsequent October meeting only through a desire to thwart the supposed machinations of the clerical group, perhaps he would have been less than human had he not expected his own election by a board which he had so laboriously served.

FOLLOWING TUCKER'S REFUSAL to continue in temporary office, the clerical faction nominated Professor Henry A. White, D.D., Ph.D. Strickler urged his election. Fishburne, in a deliberate countermove, nominated George H. Denny, Professor of Latin. Before a vote was taken the rector read a long letter to the group from trustee William A. Anderson, who could not attend the meeting because he was serving in the Virginia state constitutional convention.

Anderson, an Episcopalian long associated with Washington and Lee, believed the institution was at a crisis. He traced the origins and development of the school, academy, and college to 1865. During that period the institution had been "universally regarded" as denominational because of its location in a Presbyterian region, despite the undenominational endowment from George Washington, the Cincinnati, and John Robinson. The writer discussed in some detail the "new departure" of 1865 when R. E. Lee had been brought to the presidency with assurances regarding the nondenominational character of the College. He related the broadened appeal and growth of the R. E. Lee administration, followed by efforts "looking to the re-establishment of the denominational character of the school," partly offset by the resolutions of 1873. Anderson pointed out that fund-raisers in the seventies and eighties had assured prospects that Washington and Lee was free from denominational control.

Then followed an analysis of current conditions in which he pointed out that "Today, every member of the Faculty, except one, who is a member of any church, and every officer and employee of the institution, except the colored janitor and colored laborers, and every member of this Board, except two, is a member of the Presbyterian church." This far-seeing trustee concluded his exposition with a sentence of prophecy which subsequent decades have to a degree justified:

> Washington and Lee University can never attain the measure of usefulness, and of greatness, which is the fitting destiny of an institution having the names of such illustrious founders, unless its governing body, its faculty, and its officers, are fairly representative of the faiths of the people of the vast region from which in the generations to come it may confidently expect to draw its patronage.

With these words ringing in their ears the trustees voted for an acting president. The count was 5 for Denny (Gordon, Fishburne, Houston, Preston, and Cocke) and 4 for White (Strickler, Barclay, Fleming, and Hamilton).

Glasgow, in a letter to Anderson, noted that only clergyman Gordon's refusal to vote for White had prevented the latter's election. A faculty member had spoken adversely of White to Dr. Gordon. Elders Houston and Preston likewise had voted for Denny, who was the son of a Presbyterian minister. He also was Dr. Strickler's son-in-law, a fact that gives an ironic touch to Denny's passive role as a means of thwarting the rector's plans if, indeed, those plans had been accurately represented.

THE ELECTION OF DR. DENNY brought to the fore a young and vigorous individual, who at once applied himself to his task with zeal and industry. His excellent work in the summer of 1901 commended him to many, so that by the fall he had to be considered in the matter of the permanent presidency. Dr. Denny, while attributing his election to "mere accident," attacked especially those twin problems that had baffled Wilson—finances and enrollment. Tucker, meanwhile, betook himself and his thoughts to Europe, leaving the field of action to his opponents.

Another board meeting was set for September 30. It was called at the request of Tucker supporters who mistakenly believed they commanded enough votes to elect their candidate. Shortly before the meeting there appeared two editorials that must have compelled the attention of the trustees.

On September 25 the *Central Presbyterian*, an organ of the Southern Presbyterian church published at Richmond, appeared with "A Suggestion" that Washington and Lee become "the Presbyterian University," the "capstone" of the system of higher education of Southern Presbyterianism. Colleges in this scheme would be Hampden-Sydney and King, while Fredericksburg, Fishburne's, Hoge Memorial, and Chester Springs Academies were to serve as "feeders." Appearing at the moment when some believed the Washington and Lee trustees were preparing a coup of sectarianism, that editorial seemed "timed" and a part of the campaign.

On September 28 the recently founded *Ring-tum Phi* boldly announced a warning to the trustees. The rumor was current, it said, that the board proposed to elect as president a minister of the Presbyterian faith. The student newspaper asserted: "We cannot for a moment think, however, that a board, whose predecessors as well as themselves, have shown such wisdom in their selections in the past, would be so indiscreet as to place any minister of this denomination (or any other) at the head of the institution." Should the board do this it might as well erase the "declaration of 1873," and proclaim Presbyterian control to the public.

Fourteen trustees were on hand for the meeting, including two of the three elected since the June meeting, Gaines and St. Clair.

On the first ballot the votes were almost evenly distributed: Tucker, 5 (Glasgow, Anderson, Fishburne, Cocke, Gaines); Denny, 5 (Gordon, Houston, Preston, Ingles, St. Clair); White, 4 (Strickler, Barclay, Fleming, Hamilton). On the runoff ballot the five who had voted for Tucker stood by him but Barclay, Fleming, and Hamilton shifted to Denny, giving him 8 votes and the election. No vote by Strickler was recorded.

What happened to the movement in White's behalf is not entirely clear. Although a man of ability and energy, for some reason he was not popular with certain board members. After their common defeat White and Tucker compared notes. Tucker believed that White, "an open, avowed foe," had been "double-crossed" by his supposed supporters. White had shown Tucker a letter from Strickler promising him 7 sure votes, and another when needed, which would give him 8 votes and the election. It is possible that some trustees, having seen Denny demonstrate the qualities of an energetic and efficient administrator, recognized in him also the only immediate means of restoring harmony and healing wounds.

But the wounds were deep, especially among the Tucker faction. Tucker himself showed continuing resentment through harassing tactics, and fourteen long years after the election he (privately) published his pamphlet on the reasons for his departure. A number of his friends were incensed at the board's action and remained alienated from the University for some time. Tucker believed that the clerical group, foiled in their design to elect a clergyman, had done the next thing to it in electing the son and son-in-law of Presbyterian ministers.

Tucker peremptorily demanded of the respective trustees, in writing, that they define their attitudes toward the *Central Presbyterian*'s "Suggestion." Replies from ten trustees are in the Tucker *Papers*. Several of these either curtly dismissed the inquiry or said they had not seen the article. In general, those who replied at any length expressed opposition to the suggestion. Of particular interest was the Rector's statement:

> I think Washington and Lee should remain just as it now is. So far as I know there is no purpose on the part of any members of the Board of Trustees to put it in any other relation to the Virginia Synod and to the Presbyterian institutions of the State, than that which it now occupies. Indeed, I had not heard any members of the Board mention the subject.

MORE SERIOUS to the immediate future of Washington and Lee was the effect of the election upon the completion of the Wilson Fund, and upon the friends of Wilson and Tucker. The fund represented a consolidation of efforts begun separately in 1900 by Tucker and by Herbert Welsh of Philadelphia, editor and publisher of the weekly newspaper *City and State*, crusader for varied causes including Indian rights, honesty in politics, and world peace through arbitration.

Welsh became interested in Washington and Lee, made several visits to the campus, and undertook through his newspaper to collect $100,-000 for general endowment of the University. He elicited a small but "cheerfully made" contribution and a commendation from Grover Cleveland, who wrote Welsh: "I doubt if you ever interested yourself in a nobler and more useful undertaking, than the effort to raise an endowment fund for Washington and Lee University. It has traditions and opportunities to do good that ought to commend this enterprise to every American who is alert to further the nation's welfare." A present-day university fund-raiser or "director of development" would cheerfully *pay* more than $100,000 for such a statement from a two-term President of the United States, especially one known as a "sound-money" man. Welsh urged the establishment of a great technical school at Washington and Lee and hoped for an educational balance between North and South. He noted particularly a need for assistance in economics and sciences in the South.

Toward the end of the summer, Acting President Tucker attempted to interest Cleveland in a project to endow the chair of economics that had been established through Wilson's efforts. Cleveland preferred a plan for Wilson's personal relief, which drew a comment from Tucker: "The Northern mind does not distinguish the difference of feeling. Our people do not accept gratuities." After Wilson's death and following further correspondence Cleveland agreed to assist a movement to secure a memorial endowment. At his suggestion Welsh's and Tucker's groups were merged. Tucker persuaded Cleveland to become chairman of the Wilson Memorial Fund Committee; Welsh served as secretary and treasurer. Oswald Garrison Villard tendered space in his New York *Evening Post* for friendly articles. He also suggested prominent men as members of a "strong" committee. Tucker worked with the same zeal that he had applied in raising money for Tucker Hall. He solicited friends and admirers of William L. Wilson by mail, and sent out circulars.

In addition to Villard and Welsh, prominent Americans who cooperated in the Wilson fund movement included George Foster Peabody; James C. Carter, a Wall Street attorney; William H. Baldwin, president of the Long Island Railroad; Frank T. Howard, New Orleans capitalist; and businessman Charles B. Webster. These, together with Tucker, pledged donations of $5,000 each to give the drive momentum. Others in the forefront were Isidor Straus; Abram S. Hewitt, iron manufacturer and former mayor of New York; and Harry Howard of New Orleans. Of all the great financiers probably none proved more helpful than Peabody, who placed his wide contacts at Washington and Lee's disposal.

A most unusual gift was a $2,000 donation sent from Harvard University through the interest of Major Henry Lee Higginson, Boston blueblood and Union army veteran, who had been seriously wounded fighting in Virginia. Higginson wrote Senator Henry Cabot Lodge: "I am tearing my shirt . . . to get a few remaining dollars for a professorship of economics at Washington and Lee University, to which I attach great importance." The Boston *Transcript* editorially endorsed the Wilson Fund.

Some interesting comments emanated from contributors and prospects. The capitalist John Hartness Brown wrote Tucker that he was happy to send $1,000 as he admired Washington and Lee, a "noble university" which stood for the doctrine of sound finance. A doubt that political science or economics could be taught, however, was expressed by Tom L. Johnson, street railway tycoon, iron manufacturer, single-tax advocate, and the reform mayor of Cleveland. He did not believe the universities were "going to teach Political Science in a way that will offend the ears of the well-to-do classes from whom they expect endowments." He contended that "when men teach or attempt to teach or to point out the inequalities due to monopoly and special privileges, the Professors lose their Chairs." Johnson challenged Tucker to refute the claim of Henry George, in his book *The Science of Political Economy*, to the effect that no truth and only error could be expected from college courses in economics. Johnson's statement suggests a contrast to present-day attitudes, as the most usual complaints about the teaching of economics in colleges come from conservatives alleging radicalism among the professors.

A different point of view came from Thomas A. E. Weadock of Detroit who as a Democrat regretted that those "outside our party ranks" had been responsible for much teaching and literature. The result had been distortion of history and falsification of the principles of free government, as well as of trade and commerce. It took strength and courage for a man to oppose the "vested interests" of America.

A matter of particular appeal to many Northerners at that time was the possibility of improving race relations by helping Southern colleges and universities for white students. Welsh and Villard were deeply concerned for the welfare of the Negro people and for solution of the race question. Welsh and other Northern men of goodwill believed that only "the Southern whites, after all, can bring about the solution of the race problem." Through education of Southern whites, backed by Northern philanthropy, prejudice against the Negro could be dispelled. Welsh suggested that Washington and Lee's "indirect" influence in this regard be stressed. Of course, it was necessary also to educate Negroes; and a campaign circular said that Washington and Lee endorsed the Tuskegee-Hampton program. Among contributors to the Wilson Fund was Dr. Booker T. Washington, who gave five dollars.

In his report to the trustees in June 1901 Acting President Tucker recited the history of the Wilson Fund, which at that time amounted to $65,000. He had no doubt of the ultimate realization of the full $100,000, citing Cleveland's promise to approach two prominent and wealthy men "in his own way." Baldwin, Villard, and Peabody had indicated their hope that the Wilson Fund would be but the beginning of "better things" for Washington and Lee.

But after the election of Dr. Denny as president, Tucker completely washed his hands of the Wilson Fund. He hastened to state his reasons in letters to Welsh, Villard, Straus, and others. He charged that the trustees had perpetrated "an attempted fraud" in their "new departure," had broken faith with donors, and had placed Tucker in an untenable position. He could not participate in the "getting of money under false pretenses."

Tucker's startling pronouncement placed a damper on the ardor of Northern friends of Washington and Lee. Isidor Straus feared at first that the election of Dr. Denny was a grave blunder. The successor of William L. Wilson, he believed, should have been a man of national reputation. He wrote Tucker: "I am pained to learn from your letter that the selection of this young man as the representative of the University to the world, has at its foundation a spirit of narrowness which is a complete departure from what the conception of a university is, and what our lamented friend intended Washington and Lee should be."

"This young man," however, rose admirably to the occasion. In early October he attended a meeting in New York of the Wilson Fund Committee, where Villard said that all were quite favorably impressed with the new president and his ideals, and did not fear clerical influence upon him. Indeed, Tucker himself disclaimed any differences with Denny except as to the board's future policy. He wrote Villard: "Dr. Denny himself is a young man of fine capacity and high character, my personal friend and one whose statements about the University can be confidently relied upon as containing his honest beliefs. . . ."

The new president entered into an extensive correspondence with Herbert Welsh. He assured the Philadelphian that he approved of Wilson's program and ideals regarding Southern economic and industrial education. He denied Tucker's allegations regarding a "new departure" in University policy and declared: "Our mission is the same; our policy is the same; our work is the same; our ambitions are the same." Early in November Denny asked Welsh to visit Isidor Straus and disabuse the latter's mind of the supposed "new trends."

George F. Peabody showed some hesitancy but in the end he came around and was, in Denny's words, "all right." In mid-November he expressed skepticism that Dr. Denny would carry on Wilson's program. He also seemed to believe that Tucker was more favorable to the "great work" of Booker T. Washington, in which Peabody was deeply interested, than other faculty members at Washington and Lee. A rumor had circulated that a trustee was prejudiced against aid for Negroes. Means were taken to resolve Peabody's doubts, including a visit by Professor H. Parker Willis, who found the capitalist friendly and disposed to see the fund through to completion.

Thus the interest of key Wilson Fund Committee members was retained. The campaign proceeded despite continued salvos by Tucker and some other unpleasant incidents. Two university presidents were among those involved in the skirmishing.

Damaging gossip was spread by Dr. Charles W. Dabney, president of the University of Tennessee, at a conference on Southern education held in New York in November 1901. Dr. Denny had urged Welsh to attend the conference as a representative of Washington and Lee, and some other friends of the institution were there also. Dabney told Peabody that it was well known throughout the South that Washington and Lee was destined toward a more sectarian stance. Peabody quoted to Dabney some striking phrases of Denny's which denied the validity of Tucker's views. At a dinner Dabney met Villard, who vigorously attacked statements of Dabney and Tucker and said he would appeal to Denny.

Dr. Denny was indignant over Dabney's charges. In a letter to Welsh he pointed out that, after all, a clergyman had *not* been elected president of Washington and Lee; that he had himself been nominated acting president by C. D. Fishburne, "a warm supporter of Mr. Tucker's"; and indeed, it could be said that it was Tucker's backers who had chosen Denny as acting president. He noted further that his father-in-law, Dr. Strickler, had never voted for him for any office at the University, and had never so much as mentioned the possibility of the presidency to him.

Dr. Denny heard also that Dr. Charles Duncan McIver, president of the North Carolina State Normal and Industrial College (now the University of North Carolina at Greensboro), had charged the trustees with acting to make Washington and Lee "more of a church school than heretofore." McIver promptly denied having said such a thing; and Dabney sent a letter to Denny in which he denied that he had made the remarks attributed to him.

Tucker's guerrilla warfare disturbed Dr. Denny. The president suspected that Tucker dwelt upon the sectarian issue with Isidor Straus, while with W. H. Baldwin and others interested in Negro education he emphasized alleged opposition to Booker T. Washington. At the end of January 1902, Denny learned that Frank T. Howard had sent Tucker a $2,500 check for the Wilson Fund, and that Tucker had returned the check to Howard with the statement that he was receiving no further contributions. Howard also had been informed, presumably by Tucker, that he had been rejected for membership in the board of trustees at the June 1901 meeting. It was true that Acting President Tucker had suggested Howard's name, but it had not been voted on.

Tucker's position in regard to his own obligations involved him in a prolonged correspondence with G. F. Peabody. The philanthropist disagreed entirely with Tucker's contention that he was relieved of moral and legal commitment to work for the Wilson Fund. Peabody also resented the implication that he and others were parties to a fraud, as he had been informed by Tucker. Tucker also rehearsed his role in the movement for the Wilson Fund in an exchange of letters with John G. Carlisle, Secretary of the Treasury in the second Cleveland administration, and an active worker for the memorial.

President Denny found time for the Wilson Fund although he worked hard at his administrative responsibilities and had not been relieved of his duties as professor of Latin. By personal efforts, aided by Welsh and others, he brought the fund within striking distance of completion by the spring of 1902. In March an unlooked-for gift of $1,000 came from H. P. Wilder of Boston, who had been a "popular and genial Federal officer" stationed at Charles Town, West Virginia, immediately after the Civil War. In July additional contributions by Peabody and Major Higginson, both already generous donors, sent the drive "over the top." The fund amounted to $100,553.03.

The money was transmitted to the University by an act of donation signed by Grover Cleveland as chairman of the committee. The document provided that the fund was to be used to endow the William L. Wilson Department of Economics and Political Science, and that a surplus of $20,000 might be employed to construct a building for the department, with sufficient additional money. Isidor Straus had suggested that "a clause should be inserted providing against any sectarian management of the Department." Tucker and perhaps others had expressed similar views, and the committee made its wishes on this point known to the trustees.

Resolutions adopted by the board in accepting the fund included the following: "In consideration of said donation, it is hereby agreed by the said University that the said Department shall always be conducted in accordance with the declarations contained in the resolutions adopted by the Board of Trustees on the 22nd day of September, 1865, and on the 18th day of September, 1873." To a degree this statement represented a victory for the Tucker viewpoint, and the appointment of H. Parker Willis as the first occupant of the chair was in the spirit of Tucker and Wilson.

PRESIDENT DENNY'S FIRST YEAR in office thus ended with some cause for optimism: a fund-raising drive had succeeded, and enrollment was the highest since the time of R. E. Lee. Before the close of the session 1901–1902 the two unsuccessful candidates for the presidency had resigned. Dr. White's resignation was a curt, four-line letter to Dr. Strickler on May 28. Tucker had surrendered the deanship of the School of Law, and on January 1 sent in his resignation from the faculty, to be effective July 1 "or earlier at the pleasure of the board." Severing the tie of more than thirty years with Washington and Lee was most painful, he wrote, "but the attempt in the Board to wrest the School from the broad and Catholic policy heretofore outlined by its great leaders leaves me no alternative."

For some months, therefore, Tucker had openly feuded with the board and vexed the Wilson Fund Committee while he was still on the faculty. He continued to harass the president and trustees now and then as he engaged in various occupations including work in public education, deanship of the Columbian (now George Washington) University School of Law, direction of the Jamestown tercentenary exposition, and in political campaigns for governor and Congress.

BUT TUCKER was unfortunately not the only irritant on the sectarian issue. Spokesmen of the Methodists, Baptists, and Episcopalians cried out against Washington and Lee's supposed policy. As early as October of 1901 indications of Methodist dissatisfaction appeared in several resolutions adopted by the board of stewards of the Trinity M. E. Church of Lexington and transmitted to President Denny. In January 1903 the Reverend John H. Light, Trinity's pastor, created a mild furor in the religious and secular press by the publication of a letter in the *Baltimore and Richmond Christian Advocate*. He contended that "Randolph-Macon is no more Methodist than Washington and Lee is Presbyterian—with this exception, that Methodists own and pay for their college and Washington and Lee is a private foundation under Presbyterian control." He cited the oft-quoted statistics on church affiliation of trustees and faculty.

Mr. Light, however, went farther than such critics as Tucker, for his purpose was to warn Methodists against the dangers of attending colleges controlled by other denominations. He claimed that Methodist boys had been proselyted away from their church through the exercise of influence by Washington and Lee professors. He noted the temptations to which Methodist youth would be subjected at Washington and Lee, where "the final ball is quite as much an event as the delivery of diplomas, and 'the Presidency of the Final Ball' is familiarly spoken of as one of the highest honors of the University." Mr. Light may be presumed to have had some first-hand knowledge of conditions at Washington and Lee for he had himself enrolled in some courses—tuition free.

The Baptists reacted through their organ, the *Religious Herald*. That paper did not vouch for the correctness of every detail of Mr. Light's article, but declared that it had "simply given public form to a statement which has been privately current for some time—namely, that Washington and Lee had always been non-sectarian when it was appealing for money, and that it had received large sums on that basis, while as a matter of fact it was virtually a Presbyterian school, and that a considerable party in the board was anxious to put it under the control of some Presbyterian body." This charge was a favorite one with the critics—putting the school in the hypocritical role of getting money under false pretenses.

The *Ring-tum Phi* ran several editorials and stories in an effort to refute Mr. Light's "narrow, uncalled for, and ungrateful attack." The student paper, edited by W. Jett Lauck (afterward a distinguished labor economist), indulged in some satire at the reverend gentleman's expense. It explained that history and environment had made the institution what it was, and stated that, deplorable though it might be, in Lexington "the gradations of society are laid down on the basis of church membership." If students shifted their allegiance to the Presbyterian Church it could be explained because of better entertainment, better sermons—or because of some girl! A nine-column editorial concluded that despite its detractors Washington and Lee had "stood for liberal training, fair-minded teaching, and freedom of opinion." The paper referred in one issue to the minister's attack as "Darkness from Light."

A group of twenty-eight Methodist students publicly repudiated the Light charges, especially his allegation that faculty members had brought pressure to wean them away from their church. Student Y.M.C.A. leaders also denied that denominationalism existed in the Washington and Lee branch of that organization. The Richmond *News Leader* published a detailed refutation of the Light indictment and other Virginia newspapers joined in the controversy.

On several occasions during 1903 President Denny directly or indirectly answered Washington and Lee's critics. He did so most explicitly in a letter to the Richmond *Times-Dispatch* early in March. He denied that a group of trustees had desired to place the University "in organic connection with the Presbyterian church" and contended that if church affiliation of trustees was the criterion then Yale, Columbia, and Princeton were sectarian. The *Rockbridge County News* agreed with President Denny that Washington and Lee's policy was in keeping with that of other important nonsectarian schools.

Mr. Light sent a conciliatory letter to the *Times-Dispatch*, denying any malice. Yet he observed with satisfaction that the critics had made some impression, for it "was noteworthy that the present liberalizing of the University faculty within the last five years synchronizes with a somewhat vigorous agitation that has been going on in recent years over that subject." Professor David C. Humphreys privately wrote that Mr. Light had proclaimed from the housetops what people had been saying and thinking. By the close of 1903, Humphreys reported, several trustees maintained that they had been misunderstood, declaring that they would never dream of voting for a clergyman to head Washington and Lee.

THE SECTARIAN ISSUE came up in connection with two significant moves made during the Denny administration—an attempt to introduce alumni representatives into the Board of Trustees, and an application by Washington and Lee for admission to the program of the Carnegie Foundation for the Advancement of Teaching. The former effort had considerable backing from important alumni individuals and groups. As early as 1901 a plan for alumni representation was before the board, but the question came to a climax at that body's meeting in June of 1903.

Presumably alumni representation would bring into the board persons of diverse religious faiths and from various sections of the country, chosen by the alumni for fixed terms. To forestall this the rector, Dr. Strickler, proposed a resolution stating the trustees' position on University governance:

> The consideration that controls us is the religious policy of the institution, adopted at the beginning and observed ever since. As is well known, this is not a sectarian school, that is, the peculiar tenets of no religious sect are taught in it; nor is it a denominational school, that is, it is not under the control of any church court; nor has it ever been administered in the interest of any particular denomination, as its past history and present condition plainly show; but it is a Christian school, and has always been, and was always intended to be, under the control of a Board composed of a majority of Presbyterian Christians, representing those by whom the school was originally founded and by whom its affairs

have always been managed. This control we believe we have no right to surrender; and, therefore because it would be imperilled by the proposed alumni representation, we are constrained with sincere regret to decline it.

Dr. Strickler called attention to the fact that all members of the board except one were alumni; declared that it always had been so and always would be; and promised that the institution would be managed in the usual "broad and catholic spirit." The rector asserted that the board had had assurances that the alumni had no desire to change the management of Washington and Lee, "and as in the respect mentioned their plan would probably bring about that result, we trust we may anticipate their acquiescence in the conclusion which the Board has reached." In such manner were the alumni gently but firmly told that their agitation to break into the board was to no avail. The Strickler resolution was made public in the Richmond *Times-Dispatch* and its text appeared in the *Rockbridge County News.* According to the latter newspaper, which was usually well informed concerning affairs at Washington and Lee, the resolution would have passed had it been brought to a vote. It was postponed, however, and was never voted upon. Yet it may be taken as representing the consensus of the trustees at that time.

Philanthropist Peabody was kept informed of events at Washington and Lee and received numerous communications from Tucker, especially unfavorable comment such as a critical article in the *Religious Herald.* Peabody denounced Strickler's position and statement, but argued that a board composed of a majority of Presbyterians or Episcopalians could yet be nonsectarian; and "if the Faculty are not teaching sectarianism the school is not sectarian. . . ." The wise New Yorker counseled patience. Time, he believed, was "on our side."

WASHINGTON AND LEE sought membership in the Carnegie program in 1906. This program had widespread effect on raising standards in American education, and among other things the foundation supported faculty pensions. For inclusion the Washington and Lee board of trustees was required to place itself on record explicitly stating that "no denominational test is imposed in the choice of trustees, officers or teachers, or in the admission of students, nor are distinctly denominational tenets or doctrines taught to the students." Dr. Denny informed President Pritchett of the Carnegie Foundation that "while there is now and always has been a majority of Presbyterians in our Board of Trustees, the Board has never adopted any 'denominational test' in making such selections." He recommended that the board adopt the Carnegie conditions; and this was done.

Harry St. George Tucker seized upon the board's action as an opportunity for embarrassing the Washington and Lee administration and especially Dr. Strickler. In 1903 he had sent Dr. Denny the offer of a small financial contribution conditioned upon certain provisions regarding the position of the school. And, of course, he had circulated his proposal among a number of alumni friends. Now he professed to interpret the acceptance of the Carnegie terms as an implied rejection of the Strickler resolution of 1903. He forwarded his fifty-dollar contribution, which Dr. Denny promptly returned. Tucker wrote Dr. Strickler requesting the rector's interpretation of his vote on the Carnegie matter. Dr. Strickler replied that he saw no conflict in his vote of 1906 with his resolution of 1903. Tucker, striving for vindication of his tenacious position, circulated among alumni and prominent educators the Tucker-Strickler-Denny correspondence. Doubtless to his satisfaction many of the replies, including one from President Woodrow Wilson of Princeton, entirely supported Tucker's position.

Gradually the institution emerged from the heat of the highly charged controversy, until little was heard of the old issue during the closing years of the Denny regime, less in the World War period of Dr. Henry Louis Smith, and almost nothing in modern times. As predicted by George Foster Peabody and General G. W. C. Lee, time, the great healer, has disposed of the once fiercely debated question.

The issue of sectarianism had run like a broken thread through the institution's history since the days of Dr. Baxter a hundred years before. As the *Rockbridge County News* once pointed out, the term around which so much contention centered, "sectarianism," had never been clearly defined. It meant one thing to the Tucker mind and quite something else to Dr. Strickler and his group. It all seemed to boil down to what one thought of a majority of Presbyterians on the board. Except for isolated and apparently groundless complaints such as that of Mr. Light, there is no evidence that any denominational influence was brought to bear upon students during the latter nineties and early twentieth century. And whether or not the criticism of the University had anything to do with it, the defenders of Washington and Lee's policy could point to the growing number of non-Presbyterian appointments in the faculty.

And so a generally melancholy chapter in the history of Washington and Lee comes gratefully to a close.

Chapter
XXI

The Denny Decade

WILLIAM LYNE WILSON had come to the presidency of Washington and Lee from the rough-and-tumble of political life in the national capital, so that the change was (or seemed to be) from a milieu of greater to one of lesser complexity and intensity. His successor, by contrast, moved into a challenging executive position from the relatively cloistered life of a classical scholar.

George Hutcheson Denny, a son of the manse and professor of Latin, would have been ideal to head Liberty Hall Academy a century earlier. But judged *prima facie*, he appears to have been a most unlikely person to lead an American university into the new twentieth century. In an age of rapid industrial development, with horseless carriages running around and people even trying to build flying machines, with "progress" a national fetish, could the education of young men be entrusted to a thirty-year-old classicist who had written his Ph.D. thesis on "The Subjunctive Sequence After Adjective and Substantive Predicates and Phrases"?

The answer proved to be a definite if surprising affirmative. The *Southern Collegian*, in fact, called Dr. Denny "a twentieth century man." Despite his earlier interest in ancient syntax he was fully capable of grappling with the most practical problems of running a university.

[*271*]

Through sheer intelligence and unremitting attention to duties he adjusted so quickly to new demands that the record reveals no ill effects of inexperience.

Dr. Denny worked tirelessly to close the ranks for the good of the University, and in this he was largely successful. His personal charm was a helpful asset. The *Rockbridge County News*, commenting on his election to the presidency, observed:

> He is cordial, approachable and sympathetic, and makes friends. His attractive personality and interest in the affairs of the students soon made him particularly popular among them here, and his abilities and character quickly earned for him the appreciation and esteem of his colleagues in the faculty and his fellow citizens in this community.

The students' attitude toward Dr. Denny had been demonstrated a fortnight before his election, when he was still acting president, as he was received with "loud demonstrations of welcome" at an assembly opening the 1901–1902 session. His remarks on that occasion indicated his comprehension of the realities of the times. He alluded to the moral teachings of the University and warned "against the spirit of the age which substituted expediency for righteousness, and urged the development of a patriotism that was intelligent and strong and devoid of self-seeking." And whereas his predecessor had abhorred the gridiron, Dr. Denny elicited applause "when he declared football to be the greatest of college sports."

President Denny enjoyed exceptional popularity with the students throughout his tenure; and this esteem was fully merited. He followed the example of General R. E. Lee in making it his business to know personally each student (and know about his family à la Virginia). An apocryphal story grew up that he could identify a student by his step on the stairs. The young men appreciated his hearty, direct, man-to-man manner. Without a "dean of men" Dr. Denny concerned himself with the performance and difficulties of individual youths. He was an assiduous letter-writer, and many parents received detailed communications about their sons' academic and other problems. While not always pleasant, the letters indicated that the president of the University kept an eye upon the students. He often exhorted the parents to see to it that their sons persisted to graduation.

Denny captivated his elders as well as his juniors. Endowed with a dignified bearing and striking profile, he bore himself with an air of calm confidence that enabled the thirty-year-old President to walk alongside the graybearded trustees and faculty with no seeming inappropriateness. Other institutions recognized his achievements. Furman University awarded him an honorary degree in 1902, the University of South Carolina in 1903, Washington College (Maryland) in 1905, and Tulane University in 1912. He was elected a member of the board of the Carnegie Foundation for the Advancement of Teaching in 1905; Governor Claude Swanson appointed him to the State Board of Charities of Virginia in 1908; and he represented Virginia at the Southern Commercial Congress in Atlanta in 1911.

George Denny had been born December 4, 1870, in Hanover County, Virginia, the son of the Reverend George H. Denny and Charlotte Wright Denny of Essex County. He attended public schools of Amelia County and was graduated with distinction from Hampden-Sydney College in 1891. He remained there on a fellowship in Latin and Greek and took his M.A. in 1892. He taught at and was assistant master of the old Pantops Academy near Charlottesville from 1892 to 1896. Meanwhile, he enrolled at the University of Virginia from which he received the Ph.D. degree in Latin.

DR. DENNY WAS FORMALLY INAUGURATED as president of Washington and Lee in June of 1902. It was characteristic of him that the event was lacking in the pomp and ceremonial usual to such occasions. The list of official representatives from higher education was limited to those from the five institutions most closely associated with Washington and Lee: Professor W. E. Peters of the University of Virginia (President Denny's graduate teacher); Dean Andrew Fleming West of Princeton;* and Presidents Francis Preston Venable of North Carolina, Ira Remsen of Johns Hopkins, and Richard McIlwaine of Hampden-Sydney.

Dean West alluded to the ties binding Washington and Lee with Princeton, as Professor Cameron had done at the inauguration of William L. Wilson. Others spoke briefly, bringing greetings.

In an eloquent inaugural address Dr. Denny pleaded the cause of religion in higher education. He inveighed against the skeptical contemporary age, an era whose motto he said was, "Doubt your beliefs and believe your doubts," a time which had changed the cross into an interrogation point. Noting that many people preached the idea that science was the religion of "today and tomorrow," Dr. Denny offered

* Dean West afterward was Woodrow Wilson's opponent in the contest for control of graduate studies at Princeton, the loss of which was an important factor in influencing Wilson to leave Princeton and accept the Democratic nomination for governor of New Jersey.

no objection to science itself but opposed its "guesses." There could be, he asserted, no real conflict between science and religious faith; each could operate in its own sphere, but science should not invade that of religion.

The president warned that whenever institutions of higher learning nailed to their mastheads "flags without religious color," and whenever they failed to recognize "the Eternal as the most important member of the faculty," these institutions would become dangerous factors in society. He declared that should Washington and Lee ever fall into these errors it would betray its history and the memory of its leaders Graham, Baxter, Ruffner, Junkin, Lee, and Wilson.

AMONG THE FOREMOST DIFFICULTIES facing Washington and Lee at the turn of the century were the old matters of enrollments, finances, and sectarianism. Denny attacked each of these; and while he did not solve all problems, at the end of his ten years in office he had built a more dynamic institution than college hill had seen since General R. E. Lee's time.

Enrollment expanded so dramatically during the Denny Decade that instead of having too few students the institution had more than it could properly handle. The admission of women, considered and rejected in 1896 as a means of increasing registration and income, was brought up again in 1902. The *Southern Collegian* and the *Ring-tum Phi* both advocated coeducation; but the faculty voted it down 9 to 1. Save for the admission of a few resident women students during the wartime summers of 1942–1944, when the University was all but emptied of male students, Washington and Lee has steadfastly remained a men's college.

Regardless of the merits or faults of coeducation *per se*, it was not needed in the early 1900's to boost registration. At the assembly opening his first year in office, in September of 1901, Dr. Denny expressed gratitude at the highest enrollment in twenty-five years. The president's annual reports each June showed further increases, to 278 in 1902, 308 in 1904, 335 in 1905, 375 in 1906, and 418—the highest in history—in 1907. In that year Dr. Denny warned that without a large augmentation of endowment the University had reached capacity, except in the Law School. As funds did not permit expansion of the faculty in proportion to the student body, it was necessary to employ some of the students as teaching assistants—a practice for which the Denny regime received sharp criticism. Yet numbers continued to climb: 480 was reported in 1908, and 570 in 1909. The president again declared that the limit had been reached and overcrowded conditions existed in some departments. Yet the snowballing persisted, and in his last annual report, in 1911, Dr. Denny noted a new high of 617. He again observed that the number of students had outstripped faculty, plant, and equipment; and that enrollment should be checked in order to consolidate gains and to afford the institution a breathing spell.

This was a period of general economic prosperity, with rapid development of new industries, and the number and percentage of young men going to college was growing throughout the country. But the tripling of enrollment at Washington and Lee was far out of proportion to the national rate. Dr. Denny's personality and the friendly atmosphere that he fostered must have had influence. There was another factor, however, much less complimentary to the administration.

Some critics claimed that the rise in enrollment was achieved by the admission of unqualified students. This charge was a principal reason for the refusal of the Carnegie Foundation for the Advancement of Teaching to place Washington and Lee on its "accepted list" of colleges, in 1909.

At times President Denny spoke out publicly to defend his policies. At an alumni smoker in Richmond in 1910 he "successfully disposed of those critics of the institution who claim that its educational growth has not kept pace with its numerical growth." Later in the same year, at an alumni banquet in Washington with Col. R. E. Lee, Jr., as toastmaster, he was reported to have rebutted criticism by persons motivated "by personal enmity toward himself and which is without soundness, or the interest of the university at heart, which he wished to face in a denial before the world." (The far-flung influence of Washington and Lee was illustrated at that dinner by the presence of three graduates who had attained distinction in distant parts: Senator George Earle Chamberlain of Oregon, Senator Robert Latham Owen of Oklahoma, and Representative Miles Poindexter of Washington.)

The admissions policy was certainly far from ideal; but it had been geared to the realities of a dismal shortage of properly prepared students in Virginia and presumably in other Southern states.* There were many aspirants to a college education who had sufficient native ability but had not had the opportunities for preparation. It had been the custom to admit some applicants for the privilege of taking some courses but not as degree candidates. The *Ring-tum Phi* in May of 1907 remarked: "The standard of entrance examinations has been a

* See Chapter XIX for an observation on this subject by William H. Ruffner in 1897.

very moderate one. For those who take elective courses only it amounts to about two years study in a high school; two studies having been made mandatory, English and Mathematics. For those who take the regular A.B. course the proficiency acquired by about three years in the high school completes the entrance requirement."

Despite the low entrance requirements and the upswing in numbers, Dr. Denny expressed the belief in his report for 1905–1906 that the quality of the students had improved. He privately wrote of a desire, however, to drop twenty per cent of "substandard" students, but said he could not do so because of financial reasons. The next year he concluded that the time had come to strengthen admission requirements, and the minimum number of entrance units was raised from six to eleven. In 1908 the number was raised to fourteen, the standard set by the Carnegie Foundation, and no one could become a student unless he had completed three years of high school. The president suggested that the higher standards would for a time deter further enrollment increases.

Yet it appears that the paper requirements were not implemented during the Denny administration, even after the adverse action of the Carnegie Foundation. It remained for Dr. Denny's successor, Dr. Henry Louis Smith, to prune the student body by adherence to the stated requirements.

THE REASONS FOR REJECTION of the University's application to the Carnegie Foundation were set forth privately in a letter from President Henry Smith Pritchett of the foundation to Dr. Denny. In Pritchett's possession were letters from Harry St. George Tucker, apprising the foundation of persistent efforts to transform Washington and Lee into a Presbyterian institution, and recommending " 'that it should not be admitted to the Carnegie Foundation until its absolutely non-denominational character had been made evident.' " But Pritchett's letter to Denny indicated that the decision had rested wholly upon criticisms of administrative policy and practices rather than upon the alleged persistence of sectarianism.

Prefacing his statement with the remark that he was "born of Virginia parentage," Dr. Pritchett assured President Denny that the foundation sought to render Washington and Lee the best service possible —"an honest and frank opinion."

The foundation's executive committee had made its judgment under two broad categories—admission standards and the "opportunity" of Washington and Lee. The foundation expressed dissatisfaction with its failure to find evidence of the enforcement of stated catalogue entrance requirements of eleven units for 1908–1909 and fourteen units for 1909–1910. No registration system existed, as usually found in comparable institutions, to indicate the basis upon which students were admitted. The Carnegie people recommended that the entire business of registration and admissions be placed upon "some exact basis."

According to the Carnegie investigation, of 133 students admitted during the preceding year into the College and the School of Engineering, only 107 had been graduated from any type of high school. In the Law School "a considerable portion" of entering students had not completed high school. Students were admitted from high schools unacceptable to the University of Virginia; and although the catalogue referred to a list of accredited schools, the committee could find no carefully kept list.

The committee reached the conclusion "that practically no really definite requirements are enforced." During the past four years a very large number of students had been gathered within Washington and Lee's walls—far more than could be efficiently educated. Large enrollments had been obtained through the "adoption of extremely low standards of admission." Above all, in the committee's judgment, Washington and Lee must reduce that attendance by enforcing reasonable standards, and by the improvement of the student body and the caliber as well as the facilities of instruction. Whenever Washington and Lee should adopt and enforce such standards of admission and should be prepared to offer better education, then the institution would be welcomed "to the benefits of the Carnegie Foundation."

Under the heading "opportunity," Dr. Pritchett wrote, the committee had held that Washington and Lee was really a college rather than a university, in possession of quite enough funds to enable it to conduct an excellent college similar to Haverford, Bowdoin, or Beloit. Instead of applying its resources to this end, the institution sought to maintain "the appearance" of a university through the Schools of Law and Engineering. The committee was blunt on this point: "For neither of these is there the slightest justification." At Washington and Lee's doorstep was a "polytechnical school" (V.M.I.) which emphasized engineering, but neither school's facilities could approach those of the University of Virginia.

The grounds for continuation of the Law School were found even more obscure than for engineering. The University of Virginia, the committee noted frankly, "a much stronger school than Washington and Lee can ever hope to be," was quite equal to the task of preparing all the lawyers that the commonwealth would need. In 1909 the legal profession suffered from "overproduction of ill-trained lawyers." Rather than more law schools, Virginia needed fewer, but with high standards of admission and instruction. Historical factors, however, ignored by or probably unknown to the committeemen, made it impossible for President Denny or anyone else to implement this implied recommendation from New York.

Dr. Pritchett closed with an exhortation that the institution exploit more wisely its existing resources, with fewer but better students and higher admission standards and more effectual instruction. To make of Washington and Lee another Bowdoin or Haverford in Virginia would be a noble aspiration; and the creation of such a college would furnish the best monument to the great Virginians Washington and Lee—sincerity in higher education.

The Carnegie rejection not only kept Washington and Lee from the list of approved institutions, but it denied the faculty participation in the program of retirement benefits that the foundation sponsored.

THIS BLOW TO THE UNIVERSITY'S PRESTIGE was largely offset by the establishment of a chapter of Phi Beta Kappa. The national honorary society granted a charter to the Gamma of Virginia chapter in September of 1910. The *Ring-tum Phi* noted, however, that the University of Virginia had declined to endorse the Washington and Lee petition.

On the financial front, conditions improved considerably during the Denny administration, but the President's hopes for obtaining a really substantial endowment went unfulfilled. In 1902 the University had an accumulated debt of almost $61,000, nearly fifty per cent greater than the current annual budgets. The deficits, however, were declining— from $6,900 for 1899–1900 to $4,600 for 1900–1901 and $510 for 1901–1902. At the end of the session 1902–1903 the new president achieved a black-ink margin of $1,019, thanks largely to an income of $43,309, larger than in former years.

Those figures did not include an income of $4,453.50 from the Wilson Fund, against which expenses of $3,600 were charged, yielding an additional "profit" of $853.50. Another favorable factor was an $86,000 endowment fund for the School of Law donated by Vincent L. Bradford, a Philadelphia attorney, at the turn of the century.

Several improvements to the physical plant were made in the Denny years, financed mostly by three major benefactions. A bequest of $30,-000 by Mrs. Susan P. Lees of New York permitted construction of the Lees Dormitory, now the south wing of the Freshman Dormitory. Reid Hall, listed at $36,611, was constructed through a gift by William

H. Reid of Chicago, who was put in touch with the University by Herbert Welsh. This building originally housed the Physics Department but was remodeled for occupancy by the Department of Journalism and Communications in 1964. A library was built at a cost of $55,000 of which $50,000 was donated by Andrew Carnegie. Dr. Denny's annual report of 1909 listed a heating plant at $20,646 and other improvements totaling $20,000.

In that report the President referred also to an increase in the value of invested endowment from $593,702 at the start of his administration to a current $830,683. He added that a floating debt of $21,700 had been paid off in the period.

WHILE GENERAL PROSPERITY, high enrollment, and some benefactions helped Washington and Lee financially, President Denny's careful management was important in the maintenance of balanced budgets. His practices, in fact, seem to have bordered on the penurious. Full professors were paid well enough, perhaps relatively even better than nowadays, but they were overburdened with students. Associate and assistant professors and student assistants did not fare as well. In 1906 Dr. Denny opposed a faculty committee's plan to alleviate the instructional problem because it would have cost $3,500 which, he pointed out, was equal to a five per cent return on an investment of $70,000.

Of course Dr. Denny's policies incurred opposition. In his final annual report, in 1911, he noted criticism of his financial management. People forgot Washington and Lee's lean years; they complained of too much economy and objected to accumulated "earnings." Yet the President reminded the trustees that the University's capital assets had grown by half a million dollars during the decade.

President Denny's basic philosophy of educational financing was set forth in his annual report of 1906. He asserted his belief that "too large a proportion of the income of the institution has been spent upon salaries, and too small a proportion upon its material development." He urged care, especially in the immediate future, to apply "a juster proportion of any increase in our income towards the material equipment of the institution." He advocated that chairs should be established only after endowment to support them had been obtained, and criticized the previous establishment of two new chairs "without a dollar" of endowment. He opposed the University's policy of compensating all professors alike, contending that the trustees were not obligated to increase anyone's salary but should not refrain from raising the pay of a really able teacher as funds permitted. He prophetically recognized the significance of competition from tax-supported institutions, and urged against overexpanding and attempting to do too many things. He believed Washington and Lee should be a small, compact, well-equipped educational "army"—which suggests Theodore Roosevelt's contemporary idea of the American standing army. If the University pursued this plan, and "continued to foster a distinctly moral and religious atmosphere and ideal," then he argued that the institution need not fear competition from any source.

President Denny, realizing that budget-balancing was not enough to assure the effectiveness of a twentieth-century university, evolved ambitious proposals for development. In 1905 he urged the raising of a million-dollar fund to be used "with a view to guaranteeing the comfort, the dignity, and the convenience of the work of the institution under its present organization." In the following year he spelled out a more extensive program. It contemplated six new professorships endowed at $50,000 each; a gymnasium director; six adjunct professorships supported by $180,000 endowment; six fellowships on $60,000 endowment; an administrative fund of $100,000; a fund of $780,000 for building maintenance; and $295,000 for additional buildings and equipment. Dr. Denny suggested that "a person" be enlisted in New York, one who could launch the work and establish the necessary contacts.

If Dr. Denny had real expectations for such a program he was soon disheartened. In 1907 he wrote President Pritchett of the Carnegie Foundation of his unpromising struggle in fund-raising. Dr. Denny was desperate. Should anyone offer him a million dollars on condition that Washington and Lee meet this with another half million, he confessed, he could not reach such a goal in his lifetime. He believed that he had drained the Washington and Lee constituency through his own success in accumulating a quarter million during the preceding six years. In later correspondence Dr. Denny mentioned an imperative need for five million dollars for real progress at the institution.

The president worked to keep alive the contacts established in connection with the Wilson Fund, especially those with the reformers Herbert Welsh and Oswald Garrison Villard. Through these he hoped to reach wealthy Easterners including such major philanthropists as Andrew Carnegie and John D. Rockefeller. These efforts were unavailing, however, except for the Carnegie library gift. Welsh was instrumental in bringing the Reid donation mentioned above, but his interest waned soon afterward.

Relations with Villard continued to be cordial for several years. In 1902 he addressed a University assembly on the topic "Responsibility of the College Man to his Community," and in 1906 spoke to the students on a theme dear to his heart, "Self-Criticism, North and South." On the former occasion he pointed out that members of his family had not always been welcome in the South. Sixty years earlier the state of Georgia had offered a reward for his grandfather, the abolitionist William Lloyd Garrison, dead or alive. But North and South rejoiced, he observed benignly, that those days were past, with the North standing by ready to help Southern education. Unfortunately, Villard was not long to remain a symbol of sectional reconciliation in Virginia.

Villard served as treasurer of the library fund committee which sought to raise money required to qualify for Carnegie's offer of $50,000. This effort was spiced by an incident that seems humorous in retrospect but was embarrassing to Villard at the time. The Washington and Lee librarian, Miss Anne Robertson White, better known in Lexington as "Miss Annie," made a precipitate trip to New York to see Carnegie. Unable to gain an interview, she appealed to Villard who gallantly escorted her to the presence of the great man. Miss White proceeded to criticize the architect's plans and to demand more money, to be used for training librarians. Carnegie was courteous and cordial and actually promised "a little more money." The red-faced Villard finally managed to disengage the importunate visitor from the busy philanthropist.

Recognizing Villard's labors for Washington and Lee, as well as his distinction in the world of letters and journalism, the trustees awarded him the honorary degree of Doctor of Letters in June of 1906. By that time whatever chance had existed for a solution of the Negro problem along the lines President Denny and Villard were working, had been blighted by the growth of racial bitterness and "Jim Crowism" fanned by Southern demagogues. Also it seems unlikely that the mild approach could have succeeded in the face of Villard's growing radicalism together with the more extreme views of Dr. W. E. Burghardt Du Bois and anti-Booker T. Washington Negroes.

Carter Glass's Lynchburg *News* immediately denounced the trustees. Other criticisms rained upon Washington and Lee and Villard in May and June of 1908. In March of 1909 Villard expressed a desire to inspect the new library, but with tongue in cheek asked the president if his presence in Lexington would "endanger the Denny dynasty and lead to a race riot." The *News* returned to the attack in June of that year when it condemned a national Negro conference in New York where racial intermarriage had been discussed and at which Villard had presided over a session. The paper urged that Villard's degree be revoked. More than ever it seemed "a very sacrilege upon the name and memory of Robert E. Lee that such a man as Villard should wear an honor voluntarily bestowed by a university which bears the Southern chieftain's name."

Villard retained his degree, surely one of the distinguished and courageous awards of the trustees. He published his standard biography of John Brown, sending Washington and Lee an autographed copy. He continued to admire Dr. Denny's administration until its close. Denny letters became scarcer in the Villard papers after 1909, however. The race question had severed what had been a promising relationship.

The sectarian issue was relatively quiet after the first year or two of the Denny regime, although some alumni complained to President Pritchett of the Carnegie Foundation regarding Presbyterian control at Washington and Lee. In the spring of 1908 Dr. Denny took an opportunity for an oblique refutation of the critics. He had learned of a putative removal of Hampden-Sydney College to Richmond where it was proposed to merge that institution into an interdenominational university. Dr. Denny, an alumnus, preferred an independent status for Hampden-Sydney while President James Gray McAllister favored the amalgamation of his school with Washington and Lee through removal to Lexington. Dr. Denny reported to Pritchett that the McAllister proposal had been defeated in the Hampden-Sydney board by the activity of local trustees and clergymen. The latter, according to Denny, argued that Presbyterian control would be surrendered if Hampden-Sydney should come to Lexington.

WHILE THE VILLARD RELATIONSHIP evoked expressions of sectional bitterness, the centennial celebration of R. E. Lee's birth on January 19, 1907, was made to symbolize reconciliation and goodwill. The principal speaker was Charles Francis Adams, Jr., distinguished orator and historian, who had been a gallant Union soldier and commander of a Negro regiment, whose father had been Lincoln's minister to Great Britain, and whose grandfather John Quincy Adams had championed the right of the federal government to abolish slavery. In 1902 Adams had delivered the Phi Beta Kappa address at the University of Chicago, entitled "Shall Cromwell Have a Statue?" in which he defended Lee's course in 1861. Thomas Nelson Page, spokesman *par excellence* of the Old South, a student at Washington College in Lee's time, publicly voiced his acknowledgment to Adams "for his courage, his breadth and the classic dignity of his recent address in advocacy of a monument to Lee." Adams thus appeared to be a logical choice to make the commemorative address at the centennial.

Announcement of the forthcoming event at Lexington drew nation-wide attention. The Chicago *Tribune*, which at times earlier had shown hostility toward the South, published an editorial entitled "The South Vindicated." It referred to Adams' "strong declarations favorable to national appreciation of the character and services of the great Virginian." The paper praised Lee for his refusal to become an obstructionist after Appomattox and for his services at Washington College. It was fitting, the *Tribune* concluded, that the great-grandson of the "rebel" John Adams had been selected to "appraise that other great 'rebel' Lee." Even the *Independent* of New York, which had raged so furiously at R.E. Lee and Washington College some forty years before, conceded: "The country forgives Lee and Jackson, as it does not forgive Davis."

The weather was ideal for the occasion which Dr. Denny viewed as "a notable event in the history of the country." At 11 A.M. the faculty, alumni, and senior class assembled before the Washington building and marched in procession to the Lee Chapel. The other students lined each side of the walk leading to the chapel. Inside the somewhat crowded building the faculty, with the alumni from Lee's days, sat on the rostrum. Various camps of Confederate veterans occupied the front rows of the audience, behind them were Washington and Lee seniors, and in other seats were students and visitors. The gallery accommodated members of the Daughters of the Confederacy and Sons of Confederate Veterans. Confederate, United States, and Virginia flags decorated the platform, interspersed with flowers and the Washington and Lee colors.

The Reverend Dr. G. B. Strickler, captain of the Liberty Hall Volunteers, offered prayer and the assembly sang what has been called General Lee's favorite hymn, "How Firm a Foundation."

President Denny paid a brief tribute to General Lee. The meaning of Lee's career and service to the institution has never been more concisely stated:

> To all of us it brings to memory our great President, the greatest man who has ever adorned the presidency of an institution of learning, not merely within Virginia, nor merely within the South, but—I dare also to say—within the limits of the American republic. We believe that, whatever immortality is destined to attend his great career as commander of armies, this work which engaged the last energies of his life and upon which he pronounced his final benediction, will rest like a capital upon the solid shaft of his civic and military renown.
>
> No one who reads aright the history of this institution will ever

undertake to question the fact that the life and service of Robert E. Lee is its largest asset, its richest tradition, and its noblest memory.

Dr. Denny graciously acknowledged the presence of the "stout-hearted" Confederates and other groups and proceeded to introduce "the sincere, large-minded son of Massachusetts" to the eager audience. He again rose to heights of eloquence:

> I know of no more splendid spectacle in human history, no surer evidence that Virginia is loyal to the national flag, than the spectacle that we behold today. I know of no greater or finer expression of human sympathy, of human courage of heart and of human sincerity of spirit, than the coming of a man, distinguished in the service of his country, and no longer young in years, from the capital of New England, in mid-winter, a thousand miles, to the tomb of Robert E. Lee, in order to strew fresh flowers upon his grave.

After a few more sentences on the ties between Washington and Lee and Massachusetts, Dr. Denny conferred upon Adams the honorary degree of Doctor of Laws, thus making of him "a son of Washington and Lee, and therefore, of Virginia."

It was a dramatic scene in the Lee Chapel when the distinguished representative of Massachusetts and of the victorious North stood by the tomb of the Southern chieftain, whom he had come to commemorate. Adams faced a thousand people, some harboring sentiments less generous than his own. The *Rockbridge County News* described the speaker as a vigorous man of less than medium stature, who bore well his seventy years. "His face is of a strong, somewhat reserved New England type, as would be recognized by those familiar with the published portraits of his grand-father, President John Quincy Adams, whom he is said much to resemble." The Lexington *Gazette* noted his masterful use of gestures and facial expression and observed that his "quiet, unassuming manner made a deep impression." Several sources have remarked on the excellence of delivery in the address which consumed "considerably" more than an hour.

Adams alluded to his own shifting attitude toward the subject of his address. As a Union officer he had subscribed to the community attitude toward Lee, and would have learned with pleasure of that general's death in battle. He quoted the bitter words of Senator Charles Sumner of Massachusetts in the debate of 1870 on the matter of returning "Arlington" to the Lee family. Sumner did not deign to discuss the "traitor," handing "him over to the avenging pen of history."

Adams disclaimed the role of a representative wielder of history's pen or of official spokesman of the Massachusetts Historical Society, but the facts were that he was a Massachusetts man and president of that rarefied society. Here he stood, to render judgment on the South's hero, observing that the "situation is thus to a degree dramatic."

The speaker artfully built up the dramatic tension. He declared that "the charge most commonly made against Lee in that section of the country to which I belong and with which I sympathize is that, in plain language, he was false to his flag,—educated at the national academy, an officer of the United States Army, he abjured his allegiance and bore arms against the government he had sworn to uphold. In other words he was a military traitor. I state the charge in the tersest language possible; and the facts are as stated."

A contemporary source noted that "glances of displeasure flitted across the countenance of the General's faithful soldiers." But Adams immediately relieved the tension by expressing his conviction "as the result of much patient study and most mature reflection, that under similar circumstances I would myself have done exactly what Lee did. In fact, I do not see how I, placed as he was placed, could have done otherwise."

Analyzing the historical position of the believers in state sovereignty, Adams concluded that legally and technically the South was right. But from the viewpoint of the strengthened nationalism, nourished by the rise of the national spirit and the growth of the New West, secession in 1861 was unthinkable. In deciding for his state Lee may have been technically a traitor. But Adams found that he stood before the bar of history in very respectable company indeed, including William the Silent, John Hampden, Oliver Cromwell, George Washington—"a Virginian of note"—and Adams' own Revolutionary forebears.

The remainder of the address touched upon Lee's military career and presidency of Washington College, and closed with a reaffirmation of the nobility of his character.

The spirit of good-fellowship continued throughout the day, heartily entered into by the distinguished guest. Adams had a seat of honor at the luncheon of Camp Frank Paxton, Sons of Confederate Veterans (Lexington), presided over by Matthew W. Paxton '76. William A. Anderson, attorney general of Virginia, eulogized R. E. Lee, whose memory was toasted. In reciprocation of Adams' spirit the Union army was toasted and a visitor from New York, the internationally honored artist Francis D. Millet, responded. At 5 P.M. the Mary Custis Lee Chapter, U.D.C., sponsored a reception at the residence of President and Mrs. Denny. In the evening the faculty tendered a dinner to the "Lee boys," former students of the years of R. E. Lee's presidency. Toastmaster was Mortimer N. Wisdom '73 of New Orleans. Following much old-style oratory and numerous toasts the dinner closed at 11:45. The septuagenarian Adams, who had attended everything during the thirteen-hour day, appeared in good form at the finale of this memorable occasion.

FOR SOME TIME after the centennial celebration, efforts were made to establish a memorial to Lee at the University. A campaign was begun to raise $100,000 to improve the chapel and endow a chair of history in the general's name. The movement had little success, however, and faded away as had other high hopes of this period.

Impetus for the movement came from no less a source than the President of the United States, Theodore Roosevelt, a zestful follower of developments in every phase of American life and an able historian of his country. Although he had sometimes shown himself somewhat less than generous toward the Confederacy, he rendered tribute to General Lee at the time of the centennial. He extolled Lee's character and wrote:

> It was eminently fitting that this great man, this war-torn veteran of a mighty struggle, who, at its close, simply and quietly undertook his duty as a plain, everyday citizen, bent only upon helping his people in the paths of peace and tranquility, should turn his attention toward educational work, toward bringing up in fit fashion the sons of those who had proved their faith by their endeavor in the heroic days.

President Roosevelt then suggested that General Lee's life and deeds be commemorated by the establishment "at some great representative educational institution of the South of a permanent memorial that will serve the youth of the coming years. . . ."

Roosevelt's proposal was hailed by the friends and officials of Washington and Lee as referring to "General Lee's own institution." Dr. Denny in particular expressed gratification at the President's allusion to Lee's work as a college executive. Although Roosevelt had refrained from mentioning any school by name, it was clear to Dr. Denny what he had had in mind, "since the context immediately preceding clearly indicates that this school was on his mind, and especially since it is not only a representative institution (with a larger percentage of its student body drawn from a distance than any other Southern school could boast), but it is also the only appropriate institution for the memorial proposed."

Richmond, Norfolk, Staunton, and Lynchburg newspapers endorsed a significant memorial to Lee "at his own school," and Dr. Denny reported receiving letters from all over the country interpreting Roosevelt's suggestion just as he had done. Denny learned with some astonishment, however, that a project was afoot to establish a Lee memorial at the University of Virginia. And correspondence with the novelist Thomas Nelson Page threw a new light on the subject.

Denny took the view that Washington and Lee had the same priority in regard to General Lee as the University of Virginia had in relation to its founder, Thomas Jefferson. Page, an alumnus of both universities, denied that any institution had exclusive claim to either of the great Virginians and suggested that Washington and Lee could reasonably establish a memorial to Jefferson or any other outstanding American. He dealt a telling blow to Dr. Denny. According to Page, President Roosevelt "had prepared to write a letter specifically about the University of Virginia, and it was at the suggestion of Dr. Alderman, Mr. Wilmer and myself that the suggestion was not confined to the University of Virginia, but was made Catholic enough to embrace other institutions."* Thus, Page declared:"It cannot therefore be said that he had in mind exclusively or even especially Washington and Lee." The double alumnus promised to work for both institutions, and concluded virtuously: " . . . for my real allegiance is to the whole country, and any simple efforts I may be able to make are made with the design of helping towards the education and uplifting of the young men of the South."

Meanwhile, a group of Virginia women headed by Mrs. Kate Pleasants Minor proposed to establish a chair of history at Washington and Lee as a memorial to General Lee. Dr. Denny preferred development of the chapel as a shrine to the Southern hero; and in March of 1907 a movement was launched in Richmond to raise $100,000 for the combined purposes—$25,000 to modernize the chapel, $75,000 to endow an "R. E. Lee Chair of American history." Dr. J. William Jones, a biographer of Lee, and Professor James A. Quarles of the Washington and Lee faculty were appointed special agents. Dr. Denny solicited Page's counsel but tactfully did not press the matter.

In May the Lexington *Gazette* reported that Lee Memorial literature was being disseminated, the press was favorable, and a Virginia com-

---

* Dr. Edwin Anderson Alderman was president of the University of Virginia.

mittee had been formed, headed by Dr. Denny and including Mrs. Minor, Governor Swanson, Senators John Warwick Daniel and Thomas Staples Martin, Attorney General Anderson, Mr. and Mrs. Joseph Bryan of Richmond, and others. Professor Quarles died in 1907 and the Lee Memorial movement was then headed by ex-Governor D. Clinch Heyward, '86, of South Carolina. With the announcement of Heyward's appointment a statement was issued setting one million dollars as the goal, and a nationwide organization was projected.

President Roosevelt continued to exhibit interest. In November of 1907 he entertained Dr. Denny and Governor Heyward at luncheon in Washington, and the proposed Lee Memorial was among matters discussed. On Lee's birthday in 1909 he renewed his public appeal in a letter, this time in words which explicitly pointed to Washington and Lee as the institution which he "understood" had been "chosen." He urged that a Lee Memorial committee assemble in the near future at Washington or elsewhere.

Roosevelt's protégé and successor, the genial William Howard Taft, also publicly endorsed the Washington and Lee Memorial drive. Winding up his 13,000-mile tour of the country in Richmond on November 10, 1909, he expressed desire to assure the South of its full fellowship in the Union, and spoke of waning passions regarding the Civil War. "We have reached a point, I am glad to say," he told Richmonders, "when the North can admire to the full the heroes of the South, and the South admire to the full the heroes of the North."

This loyal son of Yale referred to his Alma Mater's policy of erecting a memorial to her sons who had perished in the Civil War—Southern as well as Northern sons:

> And so it is that I venture to hope that the project suggested by my predecessor, President Roosevelt, may be alluded to by me with approval, and the expression of the hope that it is coming to fruition, to wit, that there should be a great memorial in honor of General Robert E. Lee, in the establishment of what he himself would value most highly, a great school of engineering at Washington and Lee University, and I take this opportunity to express my deep sympathy in that movement, and my desire to aid it in every way possible and proper.

President Taft thus escalated the campaign, at least in theory, to something far bigger than anyone had previously considered. According to newspaper comment he even called for four or five millions to create at Lexington "a central point and headquarters for scientific and engineering instruction for the whole country."

But despite the blessing of Presidents and the active interest of governors, senators, and other influential citizens, the movement was doomed to failure. Taft's suggestion was out of the question. Even the lesser original objective proved unattainable. The fund drive was affected by the "bankers' panic" of 1907, Governor Heyward's ill-health, and "other disturbances." Within a few years it faded into oblivion. While the Lee centennial and its aftermath failed to yield for Washington and Lee significant material gains, it would be true to say that its real importance lay in what it symbolized—the end of the road to reunion.

Dr. Denny's administration brought notable successes and some disappointments. The problem of under-enrollment was overcome, and superseded by the problem of over-enrollment. The physical plant was improved and finances were strengthened. Phi Beta Kappa acknowledged Washington and Lee's academic standards but the Carnegie Foundation rapped the University for its admission practices. The sectarian issue was pushed toward limbo.

Through it all Dr. Denny's personal popularity continued constant; and his departure in 1911 brought consternation to campus and community. Late in the summer of that year it was learned that he had been offered the presidency of the University of Alabama. Trustees exchanged expressions of alarm. At a meeting on September 8 they unanimously adopted a resolution referring to the President's "signal success" and "great work," deploring his proposed departure as a calamity to the University and to the cause of liberal education in Virginia, and assuring him of continual cordial support and cooperation in his "wise and efficient efforts." They also increased his salary. Papers were presented signed by faculty members, Lexington businessmen, the mayor and councilmen, all urging Dr. Denny to remain. A committee of four trustees visited the president to communicate the board's views and other expressions. Dr. Denny appeared to be noncommittal, however, and declined to consider a salary increase.

Soon after the opening of school student leaders prepared resolutions reciting Dr. Denny's accomplishments and urging him to continue at Washington and Lee where, they said, his work was incomplete. The resolutions were adopted at a mass meeting, at which the students decided to call upon the president and escort him to the Lee Chapel. They searched for him in vain at his office and residence and surged through the town, stopping at the Court House to give three cheers for Dr. Denny, or "Mike" as they had come to call him. At last "Mike" was found at V.M.I. where he had taken refuge from his own popularity. One may picture students *en masse*, filled with emotion, returning with their president to the chapel. With the college bell atop the Washington building clanging, the whole extraordinary atmosphere suggested that of a football weekend. Nothing approaching it for drama has ever been recorded in the institution's modern history.

Pressure came from far beyond Lexington. The *Rockbridge County News* related a visit that Dr. Denny made to Richmond in connection with his duties as president of the State Board of Charities: "His room at the Richmond Hotel was in a constant state of siege; his friends telegraphed him, wrote to him, even pursued him into the country, whither he had gone on Sunday to find retirement." Messages came from alumni throughout the nation, from United States Supreme Court justices and other jurists, and from members of both houses of Congress.

Virginia newspapers poured out editorial pleas to the Washington and Lee president. The Richmond *Times-Dispatch* directed a blunt message, "To George H. Denny . . . . Stay where you are."

Dr. Denny sought advice from his friends and colleagues. In a letter to Oswald Garrison Villard on September 1 he listed the factors pro and con. There was no doubt in his mind that from the viewpoint of patronage, traditions, and prestige, Washington and Lee appealed more strongly to the South and to the nation than did the University of Alabama. But he noted the financial limitations at Washington and Lee. As Alabama appeared to be a dynamic state in 1911, he could be assured of adequate annual appropriations for the university.

Villard told Denny that if he wished to train selected men who would serve and do honor to the South and nation he should stay on at Washington and Lee. For some years Villard had been impressed favorably with the Washington and Lee alumni. He believed this was because the small colleges accomplished more for their students and would continue to do so until the big universities recast their organizations upon British models. But such educators as Chancellor James Hampton Kirkland of Vanderbilt, President Edwin A. Alderman of the University of Virginia, and President Edwin Boone Craighead of Tulane advised Denny to accept the challenge at Alabama.

Dr. Denny had taken the Alabama offer under advisement until October 1; and he weighed the matter as long as he could. His resignation from Washington and Lee was dated September 30. He pointed out that he had declined other "calls" but had determined to go to the University of Alabama where he could render greater educational service to the people of a whole state. That was the key to his decision.

The trustees, the *Ring-tum Phi,* and other sources expressed praise for Dr. Denny and regret at his departure. But he realized his dreams of greater educational service to a state, for he built at Tuscaloosa a large modern university.

Nor did Washington and Lee and George H. Denny forget each other. On a number of occasions he returned to the campus, where he received ovations and other signs of esteem from the students. One such instance was a visit in April of 1915. He was tumultuously welcomed by the students, led by the class of 1915 and a band. Next day he addressed a University assembly, receiving an ovation from students, townspeople, and faculty. His successor, Henry Louis Smith, eloquently introduced him with flattering reference to Dr. Denny's record at Washington and Lee. Thomas McPheeters Glasgow of the law class of 1915 paid tribute to Dr. Denny's work and presented him with a cane as a token of appreciation from the senior class. Dr. Denny responded with a nostalgic address but closed by drawing some lessons of life and conduct, warning against worship of mammon.

As the years passed these visits became less frequent. Yet so devoted did the trustees remain to Dr. Denny that in the fall of 1928, when President Smith's retirement was impending, they again offered the presidency to their old favorite. There was jubilation among the students, to whom Dr. Denny had become a legend. He visited Lexington and was greeted at the railroad station by nearly a thousand students lustily singing the Washington and Lee "Swing," accompanied by a band, with several hundred sympathetic townspeople on hand. He rode triumphantly up the hill in an antique tallyho festooned with blue and white, drawn by fifty freshmen, through fireworks and cheering students aligned on each side of the street.

During this exciting visit Dr. Denny carefully examined the situation at Washington and Lee, conferred with trustees and faculty, inspected the financial books, addressed a crammed assembly at the chapel, and viewed a football game at Charlottesville (Virginia 30, Washington and Lee 7). He returned to Tuscaloosa and a week later declined to accept the presidency of Washington and Lee.

Chapter

XXII

President Smith's
Washington and Lee

DR. DENNY'S RESIGNATION set the trustees once again the task of choosing a new president; and if their hearts were heavy at the loss of a popular leader, they at least could go about their work calmly, with none of the dissension and acrimony that had accompanied the choice of William L. Wilson's successor.

During the fall and winter of 1911–1912 a number of persons were publicly mentioned as prospects. They included two Washington and Lee faculty members, Dr. John H. Latané, Professor of History, and Dr. William S. Currell, head of the English Department; Professor George A. Wauchope of the University of South Carolina; President Charles W. Dabney of the University of Cincinnati; and two alumni prominent in public life, former Governor Heyward of South Carolina and John W. Davis, then U.S. representative from West Virginia. Wauchope and Currell each held four degrees from Washington and Lee.

A trustees' committee appointed as *ad interim* executives Dean Henry Donald Campbell, to be in charge of academic, faculty, and student affairs, and his brother, University Treasurer John L. Campbell, to be in charge of business matters and to serve as chairman of the executive committee of the board of trustees.

[*292*]

On January 24, 1912, the trustees unanimously elected Dr. Henry Louis Smith, president of Davidson College, to the presidency of Washington and Lee. Although he, like his predecessor, was the son of a Presbyterian minister, and also was then head of a Presbyterian institution, his selection appears to have evoked no serious outcry of sectarianism.

Dr. Smith was born at Greensboro, North Carolina, in 1859, and thus was eleven years older than the man he succeeded. His father, the Reverend Jacob Henry Smith, was a native of Rockbridge County and had served as pastor of the Presbyterian Church of Greensboro. Henry Louis took his undergraduate work at Davidson and received his Ph.D. in physics from the University of Virginia in 1886. He was professor of physics at Davidson from 1887 to 1901, when he became president of the college. Reports had it that during his regime scholarship was emphasized and enrollments increased. Advance notices in Lexington described him as "an attractive and forceful speaker" who "was possessed of a sterling Christianity of a manly type." His brother Charles Alphonso Smith was professor of English at the University of Virginia and another brother, the Reverend Egbert Watson Smith, was secretary of foreign missions of the Presbyterian Church of the United States. All three were regarded as accomplished lecturers and preachers.

Pressure to remain at Davidson was exerted upon Dr. Smith, similar to that applied to Dr. Denny to stay in Lexington. Letters, telegrams, and petitions deluged him. Davidsonians questioned whether the new appointment constituted in truth "a wonderful promotion." The academic colleges at each campus were about the same size, and a Davidson spokesman opined that a "careful comparison of the standards of scholarship . . . shows nothing to the advantage of Washington and Lee." It was claimed that Davidson boasted a better esprit de corps because of its dormitory system. North Carolina Presbyterians pointed out that Davidson, an out-and-out Presbyterian institution, exercised a greater religious force than Washington and Lee.

Dr. Smith told the Charlotte *Observer* that he anticipated "many sleepless nights" before he could arrive at a decision; but he took only about a month and on February 26 telegraphed his acceptance to Washington and Lee. He assumed office on July 1.

The new President was formally inaugurated on May 7, 1913. Secretary of State William Jennings Bryan was invited to attend as a featured speaker. In view of the attitude toward "Bryanism" held by William Lyne Wilson and the Washington and Lee trustees of his time, along with the fact that Lexington and Rockbridge County had gone Republican in 1896 rather than accept the free-silver doctrine, the invitation to the noted spellbinder might seem as remarkable as that extended to Charles Francis Adams for the Lee Centennial. But the University and the community had made their peace with Bryan in 1908, as will be described later. In any event, he was unable to attend the inauguration. He sent as his proxy the U. S. Commissioner of Education, Dr. P. P. Claxton, whose arrival was delayed by the not unusual failure of train schedules.

The academic procession was the most august and colorful ever witnessed at the University, with delegates from sixty-four institutions. Dr. Smith's brother Alphonso and Professor Charles A. Graves, formerly of Washington and Lee, represented the University of Virginia. The venerable President Lyon G. Tyler and Professor John C. Calhoun came from the College of William and Mary. Appropriately the University of South Carolina sent Dr. G. A. Wauchope. From the University of Tennessee came President Brown Ayres, one of "General Lee's boys." The distinguished professor of English, John C. Metcalf, attended for Richmond College, and President Daniel H. Hill for North Carolina A. and M. College. General Edward West Nichols and Colonel Hunter Pendleton came over from V.M.I., while nearby Virginia women's colleges, Randolph-Macon, Hollins, and the newly established Sweet Briar, sent delegates. Phi Beta Kappa's national president, Dr. E. A. Grosvenor, represented that society.

Dr. George H. Denny was present at the urgent invitation of his successor. He spoke briefly in welcome of Dr. Smith and himself received an ovation.

In his inaugural address on "The American College of Tomorrow" President Smith made some remarks that would have been quite pertinent in a similar kind of address in subsequent decades of the century. He brought out the stresses and strains and confusion of purposes in higher education and insisted upon the importance of humanism, upon educating people rather than "transmitting knowledge." In preface to his main theme he described the position of the undergraduate liberal arts college in 1913, encroached upon from above by the universities with their graduate schools and from below by the secondary schools.

Dr. Smith distinctly disapproved the notion that college should prepare students solely for graduate work or for the learned professions —a notion that was to persist and grow through many decades among some groups of educators. The colleges in 1913 swarmed with potential businessmen. Dr. Smith declared that the "bane of our present educational system is the professional pedagogue's belief that the chief end of man is study, and therefore the chief end of study is to prepare for further study."

President Smith found the keynote of the twentieth century to be Christian leadership. He hoped to train for citizenship, and to produce "a citizen with a passion for righteousness and a self-sacrificing devotion to the public welfare." Yet in his curricular interest he stressed the practical, as General R. E. Lee had done. The core of Dr. Smith's educational program consisted in emphasis upon engineering, commerce (to an extent), and journalism.

The ideal college professor to carry out the Smith objectives would be first a man—human, magnetic, high-minded; second, an expert and inspirational teacher; and third, a scholar. The relegation of the scholar's role to third place perhaps did not please some of his professorial auditors. It would certainly be disdained by modern research-oriented academicians who judge their colleagues almost wholly by their bibliographies.

As for the students, Dr. Smith deplored "the idleness and restless shallowness of the average undergraduate." Student life was marked by a "a unique combination of social loafing, childish frivolity, degrading dissipation, and strenuous athletics; where homeopathic doses of intellectual discipline [were] administered by discouraged physicians to unwilling patients when more important activities allow. . . ." Thousands were being taught to loaf and to play ball, but colleges did not fit them for the fierce competition of professional and business life.

Yet Dr. Smith made some reassuring observations. He declared that "hard-hearted, cool-headed, far-sighted American businessmen are today investing more of their treasured millions in the American college than ever before"; more parents were sending their sons to college than at any previous time; and despite everything, somehow or other college graduates outstripped their non-collegiate rivals as competitors for the prizes of life.

The president was not averse to extracurricular activities *per se*, but he thought certain improvements were in order. Regarding sports he stated the desire to develop the individual through bodily training and exercise; but he criticized what he called the one-sided and narrow intercollegiate athletic program which he believed had been allowed to gain headway through lack of faculty sympathy and control. The social and recreational aspects of college life he desired to improve through guidance in "this world in miniature."

DR. SMITH'S VIEWS on the purposes of college education may be illustrated also by other references. In his first appearance before a University assembly he championed a course of training that would develop the well-rounded "college citizen," instead of "the goody-goody, the

mollycoddle, the textbook grind, or the childish loafer." He had no
sympathy, however, for the student who sought "roundedness" at the
expense of basic education, and who was satisfied with the "Gentlemen's grade of 'D' " (later to be inflated to "C"). He was convinced of
the overriding importance of doing well in the classroom. He emphasized this point by a ploy at an assembly in February of 1915. There he
read a statement to the effect that in order to win success in life,
knowledge of men and things was better than book learning and ab-
stract scholarship, that the best students in college did not attain the
greatest success "out in the world"; but it was the well-rounded, fair-
grade man who won the laurels in life. President Smith asked the
students how many agreed with the statement. A forest of hands went
up; but when he called for the negative, only one brave non-conformist responded. Dr. Smith then proceeded to demolish that doctrine
which he called "A Wide Spread Campus Fallacy." He cited statistics
from *Who's Who in America* and studies of the careers of honor men
in Eastern universities to demonstrate the success "in the world" of
these *cum laude* graduates.

The *Ring-tum Phi* had some fun over this incident, with an article
portraying an imaginary difference of opinion between President
Smith, praising the "crammers," and Professor Easter, defending the
"grinds."

More widespread publicity came from the syndicated columnist
"F.P.A." (Franklin P. Adams), who found amusement in Dr. Smith's
intention to recognize good scholastic performance by publishing an
honor roll—a practice now followed by many institutions.

> Washington and Lee University is the progressive little insti-
> tution. Its authorities have decided to publish in the newspapers
> at intervals during each session the names of students who have
> reached certain high standards in studies and recitations. And why
> not? Conceive the headline "Stickley wins at Solid Trig," over the
> story "Stuffy Stickley, the math shark, beat all college records
> yesterday at tackling the cotangent."

Good scholarship was to Dr. Smith a moral as well as intellectual
exercise. At the opening assembly of 1916 he challenged students to
master "the hardest and dryest" courses in order to develop leadership.
Long hours must be the rule; the eight-hour day, as specified for
railroad workers by the recently passed Adamson Act, was not for
leaders. Dr Smith pointed out four paths of leadership: warm and
friendly sympathy, enthusiasm, sense of obligation, and capacity for
unlimited drudgery. In 1919 he listed four "foes" of a college student
as excuse-making, gambling, a loafing attitude "so prevalent among the

college men of today," and "campus cowardice" or "going along with the crowd."

Dr. Smith propagated his educational ideas and program through a series of University "bulletins." His bulletins of 1918 and 1919, addressed to students wavering in their dedication to learning, drew hundreds of commendatory letters. The president was prevailed upon to publish them in 1920 under the title *Your Biggest Job: School or Business? Some Words of Counsel for Red-Blooded Young Americans Who are Getting Tired of School.* In the uncertain days following World War I Dr. Smith thus made available in book form these heart-to-heart talks in order, as he put it, to fire the ambition and stiffen the backbone of restless, red-blooded young Americans.

Another device of communication consisted of "President's Paragraphs" in the *Ring-tum Phi.* Through this means in 1924, for example, he reverted to one of his favorite ideas, that it was best to study courses that the young man found difficult and uncongenial in order to obtain "mental maturity." In another column he endorsed "cramming" because he considered rapid, concentrated study as necessary in college as in life.

Dr. Smith's Spartan attitude extended to sports and physical exercise. These must be serious pursuits and not just a means of recreation. One of his early policies was a proposal for systematic and compulsory bodily training, necessary to the development of a well-rounded man. A bulletin of 1914 proclaimed the new physical training requirements inserted into the curriculum which the Richmond *Times-Dispatch* reported had attracted attention in the North. In President's Paragraphs a decade later, under the heading "The Acid Test of Campus Activities," he approved the gymnasium and the playing field but flayed the movies, pool rooms, and other "loafers' headquarters."

Thus President Smith flung himself headlong against the current of the Jazz Age. While he advocated serious study as preparation for business leadership, college graduates found a fraternity presidency more valuable than an "A" average in landing a good job. The gymnasium and the playing field became symbolic of American culture not as means of bodily development for prospective leaders, but as arenas in which never did so many sit so long to watch so few.

DR. HENRY LOUIS SMITH lived up to the convictions that he propounded. He followed his conscience and never the herd; and in the old Southern tradition he fought as hard for a doomed cause as for a favored one. He spoke out boldly on national and state issues. An ardent Wilsonian, he supported the administration's war policies; and he also became a warm exponent of the League of Nations. Perhaps upon no public question did he express himself more forcefully than upon the issue of national prohibition, in which he deeply believed.

Eager to be known as "a cantankerous dry," Dr. Smith issued a public statement on this theme in September of 1914. As a Virginian by parentage, ancestry, and education, and a North Carolinian by birth, rearing, and residence until 1912, he branded as falsehoods propaganda circulated in Virginia to the effect that state prohibition had been a failure in Tarheelia. He contended that prohibition was based on wide popular support in the Old North state which during that period had surpassed Virginia in almost every aspect of industrial, social, and educational development. He predicted that if Virginia were "unable to shake off the blight of the saloon and the blind tiger," this disparity would widen.

In 1926 the Virginia "Dry Messiah," Bishop James Cannon, Jr., read a letter from Dr. Smith into the record of a United States Senate committee investigating the enforcement of national prohibition. The letter stated that during 1925–1926 there had been less drinking among Washington and Lee students than ever before. A faculty member had reported to Dr. Smith that the mayor had said that the Lexington police had "not located or arrested a single case of intoxication" from September to April, a remarkable record for nine hundred students, if true. Persons conversant with the situation on the campus during the spring of 1926 perhaps would not have been as optimistic as Dr. Smith, and during the later twenties much concern was expressed in Virginia at the conduct of college students on state-maintained campuses, leading to an official inquiry during Governor Byrd's administration.

Dr. Smith himself finally concluded that prohibition was not succeeding in the nation at large as he believed it had in North Carolina. In May of 1929 he sent a circular to youths about to enter college, urging them to be teetotalers. He found drinking responsible for "tragedies innumerable on every American campus," and never had things been worse! In this circular Dr. Smith referred to the "premature" triumph of "political prohibition," and denounced postwar "backwash of moral degeneration" as well as the vile poison dispensed by bootleggers.

Thus in courage and strength of character Henry Louis Smith was well worthy to hold the chair once occupied by R. E. Lee, William Lyne Wilson, and George H. Denny. But he was not the sort of official who sought or obtained popularity. Unlike Lee and Denny, he never mastered the art of knowing students by name—or even, for that matter, some professors. The stories are legion of his *faux pas* along that line.

Despite his reserve and dignity, however, Dr. Smith endeared himself to campus and community by word and act. One long-remembered incident deserves mention. On March 1, 1914, a freshman named Ernest Gary was drowned in Reid's pond near town when ice on which he was walking gave way. The president reached the scene before a student searching party had arrived. According to the *County News* "Dr. Smith, throwing off his coat and overcoat, to the trepidation of his friends, walked across the ice to the hole and took . . . the pole." With that he was able to recover the lad's body.

President Smith shone most brilliantly through his eloquence in both speaking and writing. He spoke frequently throughout the country and, though a layman, he often preached or lectured at church gatherings. In 1915 he was principal orator at the 134th anniversary celebration of Cornwallis' surrender at Yorktown. A few years later he represented Governor Westmoreland Davis in the presentation of a bronze copy of Houdon's marble statue of Washington to Great Britain "as a token of friendly relations between mother country and her oldest colony." This gift of the commonwealth was unveiled in London's Trafalgar Square June 30, 1921. Meanwhile Dr. Smith turned out a stream of pithy paragraphs in the inimitable "bulletins." Students many years later vividly recalled their impressions of this forceful man.

THE SEVENTEEN-YEAR ADMINISTRATION of Dr. Smith was marked by some noteworthy advances despite the interruption and dislocation caused by World War I. Departments of Accounting and Statistics, Education and Psychology, and Journalism were introduced. A new science building was added, a dormitory and faculty homes were constructed, and athletic facilities were expanded. A vigorous campaign for additional endowment realized nearly a million dollars, and as a result faculty salaries were increased substantially.

Dr. Smith's first major administrative act was directed against conditions that had brought adverse criticism during the previous regime —low admission standards and a resultant overcrowding. The *Ringtum Phi* heartily commended his insistence upon "strict adherence to the number of entrance requirements, which are demanded of every one entering the University." From 700 students in 1911–1912 Dr. Smith decreed that the number should be reduced to 450 in 1912–1913, and it was announced that enrollment would remain at that level until facilities could accommodate more. In September of 1914 the roll stood at 478. After the war the student body increased to 900. This normal growth was made possible not only by the expansion of the physical plant but by a doubling of the size of the faculty.

A lasting contribution of President Smith to the curriculum, and one to which he devoted much effort, was in the field of journalism. In January of 1921 the trustees approved his plan for "re-establishing" a chair of journalism and naming it "the Lee Memorial Chair of Journalism" for General R. E. Lee "who had founded the chair in 1869." According to Dr. Smith's version, based upon Professor James Melvin Lee's brief history of the origin and development of journalism as a profession in the United States, "The First School of Journalism in America" had existed at Washington College in the time of General Lee.*

While no doubt Dr. Smith, Professor Lee, and others overstated their case and stretched historical accuracy, the president won the backing of Southern editors for his idea. The Alabama Press Association had become interested in a school of journalism at Washington and Lee, and it was reported that editors of the South would assume direction of endowment-raising. The Southern Newspaper Publishers' Association at its 1922 meeting endorsed the movement in which Powell Glass of Lynchburg became active, with Verbon E. Kemp named as field agent. Dr. Smith took a vigorous part in the campaign although severe injuries suffered in an automobile accident in 1924 temporarily halted him in this as well as his other work.

Sufficient funds had been raised by the fall of 1925 to introduce Roscoe Brabazon Ellard as first Professor of Journalism, and the new department came into being. Certain professors in the older and time-honored disciplines complained (usually in private) against the new emphasis upon journalism, but the project received administrative support during the remainder of Dr. Smith's tenure. Eventually the work in journalism developed into a valuable part of the curriculum. The department has attracted students to the institution, and its various activities, such as the Southern Interscholastic Press Association annual convention, sponsored by Washington and Lee and meeting on the campus, have contributed heavily to the promotion of public relations for the University. Most important, the program has trained numerous students for journalistic careers.

* James Melvin Lee was Director of the Department of Journalism at New York University.

A PRINCIPAL PROJECT in President Smith's postwar program for development was a plan for erection of a new and much larger memorial chapel to General R. E. Lee. But this proposal died in the face of determined opposition led by local and state groups of the United Daughters of the Confederacy and joined by alumni, Confederate veterans, and Virginia newspapers.

The plan originally called for razing of the Lee chapel and construction, on the same site, of a building with a seating capacity of 1,400 and equipped with a handsome pipe organ. In addition to providing a vastly more impressive memorial it would give Washington and Lee a much-needed auditorium. It was emphasized that General Lee's office and the mausoleum, with the Valentine recumbent statue of Lee, would remain intact. But demolition of the chapel that had been built in 1867 under the eye of General Lee himself was regarded by the opposition as unconscionable desecration.

The controversy involved a little civil war within the U.D.C. itself, for the national organization strongly favored the project. The national U.D.C. convention in November of 1921 not only endorsed the plan but appropriated $100,000 to support it.

Members of Lexington's Mary Custis Lee Chapter, however, bestirred themselves in vigorous protest. They printed a brochure and wrote to influential individuals in the alumni, U.D.C., and the Lee family. Mrs. R. E. Lee, Jr., approved the chapter's stand "against the desecration proposed, of changing or moving a single 'stick, stock or stone'" in the Lee chapel. Other members of the Lee family do not seem to have become so much aroused.

The venerable rector of the University, William A. Anderson —whose wife was reported to be among the protesters—confessed to bewilderment at the depth and ferocity of the opposition, which he conceived to be motivated by hallucination and delusion, and which exceeded anything he had known in a long and active life. He expressed inability "to fathom 'the true inwardness' of their attack on the Board of Trustees and authorities of Washington and Lee. . . ."

National U.D.C. leaders, Mrs. G. Tracy Rogers and Mrs. Livingston Rowe Schuyler of New York, visited Lexington in the late summer of 1922. Thereafter they were deluged by letters of protest and lost heart at the prospect of raising funds for the reconstruction. Mrs. Rogers closed a plaintive letter to Rector Anderson with a paraphrase of Woodrow Wilson's reference to senators who had filibustered against a bill to authorize the arming of American merchant ships early in 1917: "So you see that 'little group of willful women' . . . have held up the work and are making no end of trouble."

Local U.D.C. members took their protest to a meeting of the Virginia Division of that organization in the fall of 1922. Dr. Smith informed the rector that their attendance at the meeting was necessary. Though he "would rather be dragged through a mud hole or a sewer pipe than go to Fredericksburg" he was "willing to chew gravel for a little while to beard these lionesses in their den."

At Fredericksburg the "lionesses" triumphed over Dr. Smith and voted to forward a Virginia protest to the national U.D.C. convention at Birmingham in November. After a tense debate, according to Dr. Smith, that convention "by an overwhelming vote" rejected the protest and reaffirmed the purpose of furnishing funds for the chapel reconstruction, this time $150,000.

The opposition, however, gathered strength. Newspaper attacks were spearheaded by the *Rockbridge County News*, published by Matthew W. Paxton '76. The Baltimore *Sun*, Norfolk *Virginian-Pilot*, Lynchburg *News*, and others joined in.

President Smith moved to a new position in 1923, revising his views of what could be done to make of Lee Chapel a building "more worthy architecturally of General Lee's memory." He consulted eminent architects and various state and national agencies, and there emerged a plan for "a new Memorial Chapel" consisting of additional buildings attached to the old chapel, which would remain intact.

This compromise was approved by the trustees but did not mollify the opposition, which would stand for nothing but the status quo. The sentimentality involved in the protests is indicated by a letter to the *County News* from the Virginia-born artist Marietta Minnegerode Andrews of Washington, D.C. Criticism of the architecture of the Lee Chapel, she declared, had as much point "as criticism made to a man upon his mother's countenance." "To change it would be a sacrilege, a robbery of dear inspiration, even though it were rebuilt as high as the Eifel [sic] Tower." She urged Washington and Lee to build something else for the students, but concluded: "oh, leave this dear, modest honest little chapel all untouched."

Women's clubs, groups of alumni and Confederate veterans, and various individuals uttered protests. The British dramatist John Drinkwater joined them in a letter to the New York *Times*. Drinkwater had written a play about R. E. Lee and had visited the Washington and Lee campus, which he had described as the most beautiful college setting in America. He conceded that the drawings of the proposed memorial were "sensitive in design and inspired by reverence," but he felt that if the change were carried out the old chapel with its integrity and character would be forever lost and with it "one of the most touching memorials of America's greatest historic moment." In October of 1923 the Virginia U.D.C. reaffirmed its action taken the previous year at Fredericksburg.

As with several other matters concerning Washington and Lee, this controversy reached to the highest rank of American leadership. In mid-December of 1923 former President and Mrs. Woodrow Wilson (the latter also of Old Dominion family) wrote to Dr. Smith, declaring that the changes would be "an outrageous desecration" and would bring serious discredit upon the University and the Commonwealth. The Wilsons' letter pained and injured Dr. Smith. He replied to his revered leader, pleading with him to listen to both sides. On the other hand alumnus and trustee John W. Davis, who was to be the Democrats' unsuccessful presidential nominee in 1924, staunchly defended the Smith proposal.

At length on Lee's birthday in 1924 the University trustees, meeting with four U.D.C. officials who expressed opposition to the changes, adopted a resolution "that, in the opinion of the board it is inexpedient to proceed further with the plans heretofore proposed *and discussed in relation to Lee Chapel.*" It was further stated that if the wishes of the U.D.C. were adhered to, that organization would aid with funds toward the erection of a building at Washington and Lee on another site.

It was reported that after this meeting President Smith and Rector Anderson left the room slowly arm in arm, as if to support each other in their personal Appomattox. The Lynchburg *News*, felicitating the board upon its surrender, warned that the little chapel should stand untouched: "Lay not hand upon it—change it not either in interior or exterior appearance—for it is a holy thing!"

Nothing further was ever heard either from Washington and Lee or from the U.D.C. concerning an auditorium elsewhere on the campus, and well past mid-century the University still managed somehow to get along without such a building.

There remains a happy epilogue. Through the years the chapel had deteriorated (a fact noted in President Denny's time as well as in Dr. Smith's), necessitating major structural repairs and much-needed modernization. These were made possible in 1961 by a grant of $370,000 from the Ford Motor Company Fund, as the president of the fund, Henry Ford II, declared, "to help preserve one of the South's landmarks." Fireproofed and air-conditioned (to aid in the preservation of the chapel's priceless art collection as well as mementoes in the museum), the renovated building was reopened in 1963 largely as it had been in General Lee's time. President Fred Cole of Washington and Lee said that it would "be built to last forever." Thus in conclusion it can be asserted that truly the Lee Chapel now and for all time to come belongs to the nation.

THE GREATEST KUDOS that Dr. Smith received during his years as president of Washington and Lee concerned an idea that was not related to the University, but which made a unique contribution to the American and Allied war effort in 1918. This was a suggestion for sending President Wilson's speeches and other documents behind the German lines in small balloons, timed to descend at varying distances. The north temperate air drifts, Dr. Smith pointed out, would carry the balloons in the desired direction. The plan was set forth in a communication to the New York *Times* appearing in the issue of February 24. The article was sent to President Wilson, who referred it to George Creel, director of the Committee on Public Information. Creel forwarded it to the Army War College. Dr. Smith thus anticipated the propagandists of World War II who sought to weaken enemy morale through radio broadcasts.

In June of 1918 Dr. Smith received a $250 prize, a share of an award offered by the National Security League. Years afterward William G. Holman of Greensboro, North Carolina, recalled a conference with President Wilson, William Jennings Bryan, and John Garland Pollard of Virginia. At the close of the meeting Wilson referred to Dr. Smith as "a great man" who had done more than any other living person to bring the war to an end. Holman quoted Wilson: "As soon as the German army and people got the information contained in these balloons, the soldiers began surrendering all over Germany. The Kaiser fled and the war was at an end." While possibly this went too far in oversimplifying the great forces brought to bear upon the Central Powers in 1918, George Creel wrote Dr. Smith in later years praising his balloon idea, which the propagandists used to acquaint the German population with "America's war aims and peace aims as defined by Woodrow Wilson" and also to inform them of their army's defeats on the Western front.

MOST OF DR. SMITH'S OBJECTIVES at Washington and Lee were achieved or attempted in his first twelve years in office. After his automobile accident near Rock Springs, Wyoming, on a summer tour in 1924, the remainder of his presidency was anticlimatic. He retired in 1929 as the country was approaching the Great Depression.

The date seems symbolic. Dr. Smith had spoken out for virtues and values that were being largely disregarded. Americans in the twenties showed much interest in "making whoopee" and in get-rich-quick schemes but little "passion for righteousness and . . . self-sacrificing devotion to the public welfare." They would make heroes of gang-sters, blandly let their country shirk its natural role of leadership, and accept Calvin Coolidge's dictum that "the business of America is busi-ness" as a sufficient statement of national aspiration. Perhaps in his retirement Henry Louis Smith reflected on his position as a Jeremiah as he saw the economy collapse at home, governments topple abroad, totalitarianism run rampant, and the great nations move into another and more devastating world war.

Chapter
XXIII

Twentieth-Century Collegians
in Peace and War

AS THE NEW CENTURY DAWNED the stream of college life continued largely unbroken and unchanged. Victorian students' activities have been described above; the artificial chronological transition from the nineteenth to the twentieth century brought no visible break at Washington and Lee.

Artificial or not, the turning of a cycle is a natural takeoff point for an educator addressing students, and it may be significant that the speaker at Lee's birthday assembly in January of 1900 suggested "Some Contributions which College Men Should Make to the New Century." President Charles F. Thwing of Western Reserve University declared that college men should do battle for the people, as the new century would be a "human century." Science had been the rallying cry of the nineteenth century, but since the twentieth was to be "a century of man," its slogan would be "sociology." College men should aid in needed adjustments between the individual and the community; and in this process Dr. Thwing urged the college-trained men to enter business. His advice to Southern graduates of 1900 was that they become manufacturers or merchants, applying their brains to material problems. With most of the century now passed into history, the need for adjustment between the individual and the community remains a primary problem; but there have been some differences of opinion on the relation of business to social objectives.

MUCH OF THE FROTH AND SUPERFICIALITY of nineteenth-century college life, however, was continued. Some of the less sophisticated types of activity, however, happily disappeared. Halloween parades were finally abandoned in 1913. Warfare between freshmen and sophomores, a legacy from an earlier day, raged until 1910. On occasion the two classes battled throughout a day around "Old George." Vandalism sometimes accompanied these encounters; and in 1903 it could be reported that nobody had been "seriously injured." When this form of barbarism was abolished the *Ring-tum Phi* approved.

A few social fraternities were established during these years. Meanwhile, several organizations were noted for annual celebrations that ranged from amusing to vulgar. For many years on Washington's Birthday the neophytes of the Sigma senior society paraded about town and ended by kneeling in front of the Kahle statue of George Washington, patron saint of the group. There a spokesman delivered a "litany" that was sometimes clever but sometimes in questionable taste. Of somewhat similar character was an annual mock trial conducted by the professional legal fraternity Phi Delta Phi. Various "ribbon societies" presented shows which were attacked by President Smith in 1917 at a University assembly. For some time the ribbon societies were abolished but later they were inexplicably revived in milder form. For a few years after 1918 there existed "Kappa Beta Phi," a burlesque dedicated to activities as far removed from scholarship as the reversal of the Greek letters implies. Its membership key bore the engraving of a beer mug.

Dancing developed even more than formerly into an outstanding feature of Washington and Lee's social life. In the fall of 1913 the largest assemblage of college girls ever seen in Lexington attended a dance at the University, three hundred "blooming and pretty young lady students" accompanied by three "lady instructors." Washington and Lee became known far and wide for its "Fancy Dress Ball," an annual affair that had evolved from the "Bal Masqué" of 1907, under the direction of Miss Annie R. White. One of these balls prompted the strait-laced Professor Addison Hogue publicly to condemn modern-style dancing as well as indecency of attire. The shocking dances were performed beyond the sight of chaperones. Professor Hogue warned ominously: "We are gliding towards a precipice." Among those supporting such views were Professors Farrar and Latané, trustee Penick, and the *Rockbridge County News*. The Terpsichorean trend was obviously against the old-fashioned and the conservative; yet in the fall of 1919 the student body assembled in Lee Chapel to discuss and unanimously adopt a Cotillion Club resolution condemning "all distasteful and exaggerated forms of dancing such as the 'shimmy' " and banning them from future University events.

A drinking problem existed at Washington and Lee and sometimes damaged the University's reputation. President Denny noted in his final annual report in 1911 that certain students had been adjudged guilty of intemperance and disciplined, and he commented on the general problem of discipline. He observed that nearly all Virginia colleges had had recent troubles, but he thought Washington and Lee's situation relatively good. Postwar conditions in the prohibition era were far from satisfactory, when bootleggers flourished and drunks abounded.

Campus politics drew recurrent criticism, as it has done since. A letter to the *Ring-tum Phi* in April of 1914, signed "A 1912 Alumnus," denounced "politicking" as being least harmonious with the ideals and activities in other aspects of University life. The writer presented a detailed picture of the practices of the day. A candidate selected his campaign manager who with his associates conducted a carefully planned and intensive drive. A rushing committee was formed. Its members bestirred themselves "cutting classes and everything else except possible voters," haunting McCrum's, the Co-op, Newcomb Hall reading room, the dormitories, and the campus in general. Tammany Hall itself could not have been more efficient: "Carriages are often hired in order to convey to the polls those who are so wanting in true college spirit and intelligent interest in the competing candidates." Indeed, "1912" had known "hacks to be sent from two to three miles out into the country in order to convey some rural students to the polls. . . ."

Faculty members sometimes cited extracurricular activities, official or otherwise, as reasons for students' academic failure. Professor Hogue wrote that one lad failed to pass "because preaching, courting, and Greek did not mix well." He added sagely: "A little less courting and a little more Greek would no doubt have carried him over the line." Another youth blamed an attack of measles for his failure, but in Professor Stevens' opinion "much more potent factors were such amusements as glee club, boating, and athletics."

To BE SURE, not all student efforts and interests outside the classroom were frivolous. College men at this tradition-steeped institution began on occasion to write publicly and frankly regarding national and even racial issues. A student editor of the *Southern Collegian* boldly defended Theodore Roosevelt's invitation to Booker T. Washington to dine at the White House in the fall of 1901, and assailed the asinine comments of the Virginia press. But Southernism was still entrenched at Washington and Lee, and this youth was roundly abused both on and off campus. *Ring-tum Phi* editors questioned the propriety of the magazine's expression. One shocked observer in the newspaper predicted that readers of the controversial article would inquire: "Can this come from that dear old College, dear to all Southern hearts as a stronghold of Southern principle?"

While such Virginia papers as the Radford *Advance* condemned "the young upstart" who had defended T.R., Herbert Welsh published the *Collegian*'s remarks in his Philadelphia *City and State*. Zealously attempting to raise funds for Washington and Lee, Welsh cited this example to show Northerners that there was "a more progressive and better spirit in the South than that which many Southern newspapers have given utterance to on the race question."

Student government also had its merits despite the "politicking." Students gradually worked out procedures for control of their affairs in the years before 1914. Faculty interference, occasionally noted as late as the nineties, was gradually withdrawn, leaving students the management of elections and of the honor system. Although the honor system on occasion perhaps was extended to cover more than was capable of enforcement, it had come to embody the code of the "gentleman" (in the sense in which the term was used in General Lee's time), in which lying, stealing, and cheating were beyond the pale. It might be fair to say that the honor system at Washington and Lee, while contributing much to over-all decent student life, has been most successful as applied to quizzes, examinations, and the like.

ONE OF THE NATION's most highly regarded student organizations, Omicron Delta Kappa, was founded at Washington and Lee on December 3, 1914. Publicly known as "the Circle," it is generally described as an "honorary leadership fraternity." It spread to a hundred colleges and universities and by the late sixties boasted some 40,000 members.

The founders stated the society's essential purpose was to provide "a formal means of recognition to men who have distinguished themselves along some line of college activity." Their statement continued: "Membership . . . is conferred for merit alone without consideration of a student's fraternal or other society affiliations." At the outset, members were to be elected each spring "for special attainments in one or more of the following phases of college life: 1. Scholarship 2. Athletics 3. Conspicuous service on the campus 4. University publications 5. Literary society work."

Student founders of "the Circle" were William Moseley Brown, Carl. S. Davidson, Philip P. Gibson, J. Purver Richardson Jr., John Eppes Martin, Edward Parks Davis, William C. Raftery, J. Carl Fisher, Thomas McPheeters Glasgow, Edward A. Donahue, James Edwin Bear, and Rupert Nelson Latture. Faculty members chosen were President Smith, Dean Humphreys, and Dr. D. B. Easter. From its inception election to membership in "the Circle" became a coveted honor among undergraduates, many if not most of whom regarded it as infinitely more desirable than election to Phi Beta Kappa—the "well-rounded" versus the grind or the bookworm.

ANOTHER OF THE COUNTRY's truly distinctive student activities originated at Washington and Lee in these years—the quadrennial mock convention in which the collegians "nominate" a presidential candidate for the party out of power. The first convention was held on May 4, 1908, a few weeks after the appearance in Lexington of William Jennings Bryan, then preening himself for a third attempt to win the White House.

Bryan spoke at the town skating rink. He must have been encouraged by the formation of a Bryan club at Washington and Lee and by a cordial reception at V.M.I., where he was greeted by yells from cadets and students. Superintendent Edward W. Nichols introduced President Denny, who in turn presented Bryan "as a man of clean, strong, courageous life, whom every one admired, and the foremost citizen in private life in the United States today." Times had changed since '96!

The origin of the mock convention seems to have reflected genuine student interest in national affairs rather than merely a desire to stage a spectacular "activity." In preparation for the first convention students published a weekly newspaper, *The Democrat,* devoted to discussion of the party's candidates and politics. Student sentiment was reported to be much divided among several currently prominent figures such as Bryan, Senator John A. Johnson of Minnesota, ex-Senator Gray of Delaware, and Senator Daniel of Virginia. From the viewpoint of attempting to forecast the eventual party nominee the conventions began well, for Bryan was chosen by both the students and the Democratic party.

In 1912 the Democratic nomination loomed as an especially worthwhile prize, for prospects of ending the Republican tenure looked good.

The party in power was riven by the rise of Progressivism and the developing schism between conservative President Taft and his erstwhile friend and mentor, rambunctious Theodore Roosevelt. Speaker "Champ" Clark and Governor Woodrow Wilson emerged as the most prominent of several Democratic hopefuls. Wilson-for-President clubs sprang up at American colleges and one was organized by eighty students at Washington and Lee with the active encouragement of Professor Latané, a personal friend and ardent proponent of the "Scholar in Politics." Speaking at the organization meeting Dr. Latané correctly labeled Wilson as the foremost progressive in the party and glowingly concluded: "This is an age when it is a joy to live, and be a Democrat." Less joyful student Republicans organized a Republican club, carefully avoiding the Taft-Roosevelt imbroglio.

As in 1908 the students again published *The Democrat*. An entertaining if somewhat sacrilegious feature was "T. R.'s Creed," a parody on the Apostles' Creed, authorship of which was attributed to a Southern senator. But despite the interest in the Virginia-born Wilson the young politicos of 1912 were far off the mark in their mock convention, for they nominated Governor Judson Harmon of Ohio for President and alumnus Senator Robert L. Owen of Oklahoma as his running-mate. Governor Harmon acknowledged the honor by writing in longhand of his pleasure in learning that "the students were not all for the Professor candidate."

With Wilson in the White House the 1916 convention turned to the selection of a Republican candidate, and accurately nominated Associate Justice Charles Evans Hughes for President. Some "hometownism" was again evident in the vice-presidential nomination as the students chose Senator Miles Poindexter of Washington, alumnus and native Rockbridger.

No mock convention was held in 1920. However, after the Harding landslide the Washington and Lee Harding-Coolidge-Slemp club gazed into a very clouded crystal ball and issued a prediction that history would refute: "The next administration will meet with great success in our domestic affairs by the application of the principles of economy and humanity to its problems. America will not shirk her duty to the world."

The conventions were revived in 1924, and the student event of that year was most notable in calling the turn of what was to happen at the Democratic National Convention. John W. Davis, a native of West Virginia and Washington and Lee alumnus and trustee, was appropriately and eloquently placed in nomination by a law student from his state, John C. Morrison '25. Davis was then practicing law in New York after a distinguished public career as Congressman, solicitor general, and ambassador to Great Britain. He was chosen after the fight had narrowed to a contest between Davis and former Secretary William G. McAdoo. Davis' University connections no doubt helped him. But he proved to be the authentic Democratic nominee, although the party convention took 103 ballots to select him and did so only after elimination of initially stronger aspirants including McAdoo, Governor Al Smith of New York, and Senators Carter Glass of Virginia and Oscar Underwood of Alabama. The students nominated Senator Joseph T. Robinson of Arkansas for Vice-President but the party did not follow suit. Yet Dr. R. Granville Campbell, '98, beloved political science professor, commented concerning the mock convention: "It was not lacking in a single detail when compared to the real convention." Davis manfully accepted leadership of the divided Democratic party but he fought a hopeless battle in the face of the complacency induced by "Coolidge prosperity."

In general, the conventions have been more accurate in the nomination of Democratic than of Republican candidates. They chose Al Smith in 1928, Franklin D. Roosevelt in 1932, Adlai Stevenson in 1956, John F. Kennedy in 1960, and Barry M. Goldwater in 1964. They did not properly identify any of Roosevelt's challengers although they chose General Dwight D. Eisenhower over Senator Robert Taft in 1952.

The mock convention has become firmly established as a valuable staple of campus life at Washington and Lee. It has not only attracted national attention every four years but has received the sincerest form of flattery, imitation at a number of other institutions.

AN UNUSUALLY COMPREHENSIVE (and not very pleasant) view of student life at Washington and Lee in the years 1910–1911 has been preserved in an autobiographical work by a student of that time, Harvey Fergusson of New Mexico. Although published years afterward, the description of college life is rich in detail and certainly reflects deep feeling.* Fergusson's father had been one of "General Lee's boys." He had walked from Alabama to Washington College with three hundred dollars and a gold watch. General Lee advised him on personal economy. He later became prominent in the politics of New Mexico Territory.

The younger Fergusson had been sent to his father's beloved alma

* Harvey Fergusson, *Home in the West: An Inquiry Into My Origins* (New York, 1945).

mater apparently much against his will—usually if not always an unfortunate situation. He found both town and campus dominated by the
elderly and suffused by their memories. Lexington had changed but
slightly since his father's time, save only that history had become a
glamorous myth and that bitterness had mellowed. Young Harvey, as
he has described himself, was a self-conscious non-conformist, who
recollected with gall what he had experienced at Washington and
Lee.

It pained Fergusson to be served hot bread thrice daily. At the
literary societies he heard the fire-eating oratory of secession times,
and learned that it was a sign of poor breeding to sound the consonant
"r." In these years the ideal of blood aristocracy was carefully nur-
tured at Washington and Lee. The Menckenesque Fergusson wrote
that snobbery always flourished on a college campus, but at Washington and Lee it was backed up and hallowed by tradition. Fraternity
members spoke with condescension to non-fraternity men on campus.
In order to be "rushed" by a fraternity in Fergusson's day, a prospect
had to pass muster on the score of family and be endorsed by an
alumnus. Even though he was but little suited to the role of fraternity
man, Harvey's "grandpappy" had been a Confederate officer, a fact
which caused his election to Phi Kappa Psi.

Fraternity initiation proved to be but the beginning of the upward
social climb, in the college, of an ambitious Mink (slang for student).
He described two grades of ribbon societies, above which was the
Cotillion Club, a goal of all college men. As Fergusson remembered it,
the senior who attained to the presidency of the Cotillion Club commanded a prestige similar to that of a Tibetan lama or the Pope.

With more than a touch of malicious humor, Fergusson has described the formula for social success on the campus of 1910. A
"B.M.O.C." must possess certain talents and diplomacy: to ascend the
social ladder, a youth must have a natural gift for conformity, be a
good fellow ("a good boy," he was sometimes in the twenties), combine in the proper proportion deference and pride, and—this was
sometimes the hard part—have brains enough to pass his work with a
minimum of study.

Sociologists might be interested in this frank appraisal of pre-World
War Washington and Lee and its setting. Fergusson observed that the
Old South's worship of women had been continued as a cult and had
been transformed into an art. With a tinge of satire on General Lee,
who exemplified this attitude, Fergusson remarks that incredulously
(or regretfully, Mr. Fergusson?) no scandal had been uncovered
touching the Southern leader. Chivalry pervaded the campus, but that
code was honored more through lip-service than in practice.

Feminine society of Lexington was divided into three categories, Fergusson recollected. The first group's eminent status derived from family; those in the second rank could be called on or escorted to an entertainment (but never to dances); while to those in the third class a clandestine approach was employed. Young ladies of the elite held court on Sunday nights, where they exchanged badinage with groups of admirers. Lexington abounded in formidable grand dames, most of whom dated from the Confederacy. These dominated social life and vigorously chaperoned the college dances, to which "dates" came from a distance. Even this non-conformist had to admit that the latter furnished on such occasions "an impressive display of beauty." The strictly formal dances, "veritable rituals of gallantry and ladyhood," opened with grand marches and were chaperoned by fierce dowagers. All this to the strains of such current favorites as "Little Gypsy Sweetheart," "Garden of Roses," and "The Blue Danube"!

Nor does Fergusson lightly pass over phases of student life not ordinarily included in solemn histories of colleges. Yet he confessed that these activities were not for him because they were too exotic for his taste. Sex mores have changed gradually but nonetheless greatly since Fergusson's day; no doubt in this area as in others, World War I had its effect.

In the beautiful fall seasons the unhappy New Mexican sometimes went hunting with gun and dog, while in bad weather he read Lafcadio Hearn and *Anna Karenina*. Frequently, however, he plunged into gloom and stagnation, from which condition he sought relief in— alcohol. Some then and now would dissent from his assertion that if alma mater had taught him only one thing, it was how to drink. Lexington had been a dry town for a decade, but numerous bootleggers serviced the thirsty.

Liquor had the effect of drawing this misfit from his shell. One of his brothers "in liquor and fraternity," whom he calls "Blake Randolph," appears to disadvantage in Fergusson's recollection. This person who "had ancestors" was a thorough cad, a spoiled fellow, a confirmed skirt-chaser—but alas! nearly all women liked the roué.

At commencement of 1911, when the disconsolate misanthrope was to receive his diploma declaring him an A.B., he remembered that an English professor, with a slight peculiarity of speech, spoke and that Senator Owen, '77 M.A., of Oklahoma delivered the principal address. Owen made an impression upon the blasé young man as he alerted the graduates for revolutionary changes. "Get ready!" exclaimed the senator. For what? demanded Fergusson, distinctly unprepared, as he left behind the snobbery and conformity of Washington and Lee. Like Henry Adams on an earlier, similar occasion, he knew that he did not know anything when he quit forever the colonnade of General Lee's College.

MANY MATTERS that appeared important to Fergusson and other students faded into insignificance as the nation was drawn into the First World War. Response to the war effort affected the personnel and programs of Washington and Lee more drastically than had any other influence in the institution's collegiate history except the Civil War.

As usual when war is impending, American students at first were uncertain in their attitudes but became more enthusiastic as the issues and the needs became clear. In the two years of American neutrality advocates of pacifism and isolation combated the forces of preparedness and militarism headed by Colonel Theodore Roosevelt and General Leonard Wood. An organization known as the "Collegiate Anti-Militarism League" compiled figures to demonstrate that American collegians did not favor stronger military measures.

At Washington and Lee, in a poll conducted in May of 1915, students participating voted that the military reserve and the national standing army should be enlarged. This result caused the college paper to conclude that "a warlike spirit" prevailed on the campus. A slight majority, however, was recorded against the adoption of universal military training. After the Germans reopened unrestricted submarine warfare in February of 1917 a student writing in the *Ring-tum Phi* called for the organization of a student military company as an expression of Washington and Lee's patriotism. Invoking the spirit of an earlier crisis, the memory of which had not dimmed, he wrote: "The Liberty Hall Volunteers of 1861 set a noble precedent for the Washington and Lee men of 1917."

Of course students were not lacking for advice from those who were older and presumably wiser than they. At Washington and Lee's commencement in 1915 President Charles W. Dabney of the University of Cincinnati commented upon the unfortunate effect of the war upon youth and the restlessness for military action. He advised that the combative urge be channeled into constructive activity. He believed that the college men of the day must somehow save the world of tomorrow—a hope held for every class that ever graduated. A differing viewpoint was indicated by General Edward West Nichols, superintendent of V.M.I., in an address to the students in March of 1916. As was to be expected the soldier advocated preparedness, citing the timeworn maxim: "Put your trust in God, but keep your powder dry."

Somewhat more specific and practical was the counsel given to the National Conference of College and University Presidents in May of 1917 by Secretary of War Newton D. Baker, '94 Law, who urged that all students under twenty-one remain in college and enroll in military training. Practically every able-bodied student at Washington and Lee at that time was undergoing such training.

The trimmings and incidentals of war were everywhere evident in Lexington after America's entry into the conflict. Intercollegiate athletic contests were canceled in the spring of 1917 (but the spring dances went on with those new-fangled antics that disturbed the old fogies). A handsome United States flag, a gift of the faculty, floated over Washington Hall. Lest the young men should fail to grasp American war objectives, they were treated to oratorical discussions of the issues on a "patriotic day," May 14, when the V.M.I. cadets, the Washington and Lee student battalion ("Rookies"), and others marched to town for the celebration. Rector William A. Anderson compared the crisis of 1917 to the critical hours of 1776 and 1861, with the suggestion that 1917 was more serious than either. President Smith, who in September of 1914 had deplored "the show of barbarism by the highly civilized countries," now declared: ". . . it was a war for democracy on the supremacy of which the happiness, liberty, and welfare of the common people rested." The conflict was part of a warfare that had raged for 400 years, he believed. Germany contended for what all Americans had tried to sweep from the earth, the doctrine that might made right, and that civil power should be subordinate to the military.

UPON AMERICA'S ENTRY INTO WAR Washington and Lee sent the institution's greetings and best wishes to the universities of France. Dr. Smith enlightened the French (and this historian): "Our University here was founded by George Washington [sic] and holds among its treasures Peale's portrait of Lafayette. Our whole student body is drilling every day in preparation for efficient service . . . in breaking forever the force of tyranny and oppression and making the world a place of safety and freedom for such great democracies as France and America."

A strain of soberness permeated the commencement exercises of 1917. Flags of the United States and of the Allies mingled with flowers and decorations, and references to the war were sprinkled throughout public utterances.

In October of 1917 several alumni from Camp Lee attended a football rally, where appeals were made to students "to do their bit" in subscribing to Liberty Bonds ($3,800 had been pledged by mid-November), and to contribute to the Y.M.C.A. war fund (by November 6 this had reached $2,509). At a November assembly President Smith urged students to request boardinghouse keepers to observe "wheatless" and "meatless" days each week consonant with the "Hooverizing" of food. The students unanimously adopted a resolution on the subject.

The session of 1917–1918 was characterized by war savings and Red Cross campaigns. The Fancy Dress ball of February 7 had a patriotic theme and all proceeds were destined to the Washington and Lee ambulance unit "over there." Fraternities displayed service flags.

There were many speeches on war issues. Dr. John H. Latané, who had moved to Johns Hopkins University, returned to the campus to receive honorary membership in "the Circle" and spoke on "America's Traditional Policy of Isolation." He opposed that course, assailed a possible "Pax Germanica," and called upon the United States to become a world power. At commencement exercises of 1918, with thin ranks of graduates especially in law, the speaker was Bainbridge Colby, a founder of the recently defunct Progressive Party and afterward Secretary of State. He warmly praised President Wilson, to the accompaniment of applause, and declared: "When he speaks . . . his voice is heard around the world. His will be the final voice in determining the question of liberty and democracy for the world."

The hysteria that was often evident in American attitudes and actions during the war appeared in Lexington at least to a degree. The professor of German at Washington and Lee (a native Virginian and holder of three degrees from the University) experienced some heckling. "A Student" in the spring of 1917 wrote the college newspaper suggesting that the state of mind of Lexingtonians had been unbalanced by the excitement. He referred facetiously to rumors of spies and suspicions of strangers. He doubted that there was much in the area to interest the Germans although Lexington boasted "an arsenal of academic and legal knowledge." There was one consolation: if the Germans came they would be forced to "back in" (a reference to railway ingress), and the citizenry would have time to prepare.

Less amusing was an exchange between a Washington and Lee faculty member and the *Rockbridge County News*, edited by M. W. Paxton. In September of 1917 the paper ran an editorial captioned "Unworthy and Dangerous," condemning hysteria and the suppression of freedom of speech. This courageous analysis elicited from Professor W. LeConte Stevens a sharp rejoinder, indicting all German people from the Kaiser downward as advocates of "the military religion of frightfulness." Dr. Stevens characterized Lord Bryce's famous report, in after years the target of revisionist historians, as a "singularly judicial investigation in Belgium. . . ." The *County News* questioned the alleged fiendishness of the Germans, causing Dr. Stevens to comment: "Nobody but a pro-German any longer pretends to deny the contents of the Bryce report."

President Smith, eight Washington and Lee professors, and seven V.M.I. colonels were among nineteen local citizens who dissented from the *County News* editorial in a signed statement assailing the frightfulness of the "Huns," the Belgian atrocities, and other despicable deeds attributed to the Germans.

The direct effect of the war was felt by Washington and Lee with the opening of the 1914–1915 session, even though America's involvement was more than two years in the future. The hostilities in Europe had depressed the already low price of cotton to five cents a pound, creating a "cotton panic" that cost the University about fifty students in fall enrollment. The waiting list was sufficient to fill the vacancies but during the ensuing session about a tenth of the students withdrew, principally because of the financial condition of the South. Moreover, the conflict persuaded Dr. Smith to postpone until later years an endowment drive.

When the United States declared war in April 1917 Washington and Lee "mobilized" immediately. The executive committee of the board of trustees requested President Smith to apply for installation of a senior Reserve Officers Training Corps unit. The trustees also tendered the campus and buildings in part or in entirety to the national government. The faculty ordered that any senior in good standing who joined the armed forces before commencement would receive his degree.

The student body *en masse* endorsed the ROTC but responded with only moderate applause when Dr. Smith suggested that military training supplant athletics. Within a few days, however, 400 students were drilling each afternoon on Wilson Field, 40 in an ambulance unit and the rest in an unofficial officers reserve corps. Until the War Department could supply instructors, V.M.I. made available Major Murray F. Edwards and Captain W. C. Brown of its faculty and 51 first classmen who served as officers and sergeants. Corporals were chosen by the military committee of the Washington and Lee faculty from the junior and senior classes and the Law School. Dr. Smith and student president E. S. McCord warmly praised V.M.I. for its cooperation, and McCord recalled that V.M.I. had aided in training the college company more than fifty years before. The students drilled first in mufti and gradually acquired khaki shirts while waiting for complete uniforms.

The ambulance unit had been organized in response to a request to school authorities from the government to provide 36 men for an ambulance corps of 1,400 to be sent to France. The local unit left early in June under the charge of Sergeant Forest Fletcher of the athletic department. After training near Allentown, Pennsylvania, it arrived in Europe in January 1918.

A number of other students left school to volunteer and the roll of degree announcements at 1917 commencement was punctuated by the laconic words "at a training camp" or "away with the Washington and Lee ambulance unit."

Faculty members joined in the battle to win men's minds. In 1917–1918 a course in "War Aims" was introduced in the Department of History. Professor Riley, head of the department, offered a six-week course at Camp Lee to "educate" the soldiers in recent European history, so that they might better appreciate the justice of the cause for which they fought.

The fall term of 1917 began with an enrollment of 355, about a hundred fewer than the preceding year. On opening day President Smith discoursed on "Washington and Lee in War Time," and shortly afterward a military training battalion assembled in front of Doremus gymnasium for preliminary inspection by Major Edwards and a staff of student officers.

By February 1918 an official ROTC unit was installed on the campus with Lieutenant Guy E. Manning, '93, as Professor of Military Science and Tactics. The unit was officially inspected in April amid a driving snowstorm. The campus soldiers as yet had no rifles although the weapons were reported to be "on the way."

The University went through the 1917–1918 session, its only full academic year under war conditions, short on personnel but with its basic functions and curriculum relatively intact. Prospects were quite otherwise for 1918–1919. A national "Students Army Training Corps" had been created for men between the ages of 18 and 21. At the beginning of the session it appeared as if the United States government would take over the colleges (as it had the railroads of the nation), to operate them as a means of training officers for the huge army being developed. It was reported that the War Department would dictate the curriculum, but that the faculties of the institutions would teach the prescribed courses. No attempt would be made to continue the usual degree programs because advanced academic classes and the dead languages were unlisted by the War Department. In law schools only military and international law were to be taught. (The Washington and Lee Law School was temporarily suspended in October.) A compulsory course in "War Aims" was to occupy a central role involving students and faculty, leaving little time for anything else. The *County News* remarked that "Learned professors may be expected to be seen teaching for the first time since their youth the junior grades in other departments than their own." All was confusion amidst rapidly changing conditions.

Soon Lexington swarmed with SATC men, housed in improvised barracks at Castle Hill, East Dormitory, Lees Dormitory, and Doremus gymnasium. All were fed in the basement of the gymnasium. Toward the end of September nine young lieutenants reached town to become instructors in the program. The abnormality of academic conditions is indicated in the statement that Professor Easter had been attempting to teach French to 474 SATC men. He was much relieved when an assistant arrived in October. Captain J. C. Harper assumed the military command and 450 uniforms were received.

Adding to the difficulties, the worldwide influenza epidemic of 1918 reached Lexington and the disease raged through the barracks. Lexington's schools, churches, and moving picture house were closed. Eighty cases were reported on October 10, causing the conversion of East Dorm into a hospital. The influenza situation continued to be serious throughout October but gradually abated and passed.

The nightmare of the SATC was short-lived, for the Central Powers cracked in the fall of 1918. The premature news of the armistice caused President Smith to announce at 4 P.M. on November 7 that the war was over. Washington and Lee men, under quarantine, assembled the band to celebrate long after dark. Word of the actual German surrender four days later was received quietly and with understandable skepticism. During the following months the Lexington institutions went about the task of returning to their normal operations and "sloughing off" the SATC.

MEANWHILE, Washington and Lee men were giving a good account of themselves in France. There were 625 men in the University's service star in 1918. Long before America's entry alumni had joined up in the Canadian, French, and British armies. The first known casualty among them was Kiffen Yates Rockwell, who had attended Washington and Lee in 1909–1911 and had won fame as a brilliant aviator. At the end of

September, 1916, Lexington learned that he had been shot to death over the Alsatian front.

In the fall of 1917 news began to appear in campus publications from Washington and Lee men in the American Expeditionary Force. A group of alumni including R. N. Latture, '15, H. W. Kelly, '13, James C. Ambler, '13, and Horner H. Fisher, '16, reported that in November they had consumed a "luscious" dinner at the YMCA and afterward had talked of "the good old days" when "Eddie" Davis had been "the power behind Doc. [J.W.H.] Pollard." In a grimmer vein was a letter to his mother from Brown Lewis, '11, intelligence officer with the 25th Infantry, telling of his experience wandering about "No Man's Land" in the middle of the night. He remarked that "the best part of my trip was I killed a Boche—sniped him at 250 yards." How he could draw a bead at that range in the middle of the night was not explained.

News and letters of other alumni came in throughout and after the hostilities. The *Rockbridge County News* in July 1918 quoted French praise of R. N. Latture, '15, later for more than forty years a faculty member, for "calmness and sang froid . . . during . . . a heavy bombardment." In October 1919 he was notified that he had been awarded the Croix de Guerre for calmness and devotion to duty in 1918 under the most perilous conditions.

Lewis Preston "Pat" Collins, '20, wrote President Smith from France in September 1918 describing the Allied drive of the summer, the hard work of the Washington and Lee ambulance unit, as well as the obstacles, dangers, and casualties—fortunately few. Collins, afterward Lieutenant-Governor of Virginia, had met British Field Marshal French and had shown him pictures of Lexington and the campus. Collins was surprised at the clear knowledge French possessed of General Lee and was pleased (as a Mink if not as an American) when the hero of Ypres remarked: "General Lee is the first and only great general that America has yet produced. . . ."

Lt. John A. Graham, '14, wrote his father from Trier, Germany, in December 1918, a thoughtful and pertinent commentary in the light of subsequent years. He described the entrance into Germany of General Pershing, with whose forces Graham served as an interpreter, adding ironically: "I, who never spoke more than five German words in my life." The people seemed polite and anxious to please, but he commented prophetically: "The thing that makes you indignant is the realization that these people, despite the wooden soles to their shoes and their sawdust bread have never known anything like the destruction and devastation that whole French towns have suffered." Graham favored a somewhat more severe peace than had been given to the unrepentant Germans: "I don't believe in trying to inoculate in our people and in the Germans an undying hatred for each other as some of our Allies I fear would like to do, but still I think they should be made to pay and pay dearly for what they have done."

WHILE WASHINGTON AND LEE furnished no unit comparable to the Liberty Hall Volunteers of '61, the institution was represented by the ambulance unit composed of students, townsmen, and alumni. Letters to homefolk told of the busy work of the unit and of torrid fighting. In the spring of 1918 George Irwin, '20, afterward a longtime faculty member, wrote that William S. Hopkins, '18, had been recommended for a Croix de Guerre (subsequently awarded). Forest Fletcher commented that "Willie Hopkins is as cool and undisturbed under fire as he usually is and Leon ['Jabbo'] Morris is splendid." Sergeant Fletcher told President Smith of gory conditions in mid-April: "We carried five times as many dead and wounded in twenty-four hours as there are students at Washington and Lee. The section has been cited and at least two of the boys (Hopkins and A. S. Johnston '18) will receive French war crosses." None of the unit had been killed, though there had been some narrow escapes. In the same month John A. Kinnear, '20, mentioned that the unit had been in the line of the German offensive, facing hazards of ambulance driving on rainy nights. Word later came to Lexington that Allen Jones, '19, and Henry Baker, '20, also had received the Croix de Guerre.

The Lynchburg *News* waxed eloquent in an editorial, "To Washington and Lee's Renown," on the occasion of the award of the Croix de Guerre to the ambulance unit as a whole. Private Raymond Womeldorf's account at the end of July depicted the unit in the second Battle of the Marne, as did his classmate, R. Bruce Morrison, '17, in a vivid description. About the same time Sergeant Fletcher reported that "Willie Hopkins has just brought in five German prisoners." In August Hopkins modestly told his family that ". . . we have had front seats right along in the big show which started some weeks ago."

Cited three times by the French government, the unit spent some time in Belgium at the close of the war before returning to America.

As always, victory and glory had their price. Somber notes were sounded when lists were compiled of alumni killed in battle or who otherwise died in the service of their country, among them sons of President Smith and Professor Kern. Another sad report was of the death in action of Lt. Clovis Moomaw, a promising young man who had taught briefly in the Law School. By January 13, 1920, thirty-five alumni were listed as having died in service.

AMERICANS and the Washington and Lee community moved into the ensuing decade confident that "the war to end war" had banished forever that frightful pursuit of armed conflict. Seeds of future international tensions, however, were sown, 1919–1939, culminating in the greatest war in history. In that contest Washington and Lee, together with all American institutions of higher learning, was to be deeply and honorably involved.

But meanwhile, the derby-hatted and high-collared youth was transformed by changes following the First World War into the Jazz Age collegian of the twenties, so vividly depicted by F. Scott Fitzgerald, Percy Marks, and John Held, Jr. College rolls swelled in numbers, but seriousness of purpose led only a fraction of the young men to pursue their studies to graduation. Many had come mainly for the enjoyment of college life and these often appeared to dominate the scene.

The School of Law

1] The Lexington Law School, 1849–1866

A NUMBER OF REFERENCES have been made in the preceding chapters to the School of Law, and especially to the involvement of its founder Judge Brockenbrough and Dean Harry St. George Tucker in affairs of Washington College and the University. Because of the school's separate origin and distinctive function, however, a summary of its own history is believed to be in order.

As early as 1804 the Board of Trustees of Washington Academy considered the establishment of a law professorship and even tendered such a position to Paul Carrington, a prominent Virginia lawyer and friend of Thomas Jefferson. Judge Carrington declined the offer and no effort was made to set up a law school at Washington College until after the Civil War.

Early legal education, like that in medicine, was obtained by studying in association with a practitioner of the profession. The first law lectures in an American educational institution were given by Chancellor George Wythe at the College of William and Mary in 1779–1789. Wythe also operated a noted private law school. The University of Virginia opened its doors in 1826 and from that date a school of law there began its valuable career of service. A number of distinguished

[*324*]

private law schools rendered useful training in the early nineteenth century, among them a school conducted at Winchester by Judge Henry St. George Tucker and one operated by Judge Lucas P. Thompson in Staunton from 1840 to 1849.

In the summer of 1849 the Lexington *Valley Star* announced that Judge John W. Brockenbrough planned to open a law school in town and that he had good prospects for a class. This paper, with which the judge had once been associated, warmly praised his qualifications and personality, and wished him success in the project. The Richmond *Enquirer* noted that, as Judge Thompson's school at Staunton was to close, that in Lexington would be the only law school in the state west of the Blue Ridge. Another journal, the Richmond *Republican*, praised the intelligent population of Lexington, as well as the town's beautiful and healthful location. Judge Brockenbrough's urbanity, learning, and experience at the bar and bench qualified him as a teacher.

John White Brockenbrough was born in Hanover County, Virginia, December 23, 1806, into a well-connected Old Dominion family. His father had been a distinguished jurist. Young John attended William and Mary and was one of the first matriculates at the University of Virginia. He subsequently studied law at Judge Tucker's school in Winchester, and became commonwealth's attorney of Hanover County. In this phase of his career he prepared and published a two-volume work of Chief Justice Marshall's decisions in the United States Circuit Court at Richmond.

Shortly before 1837 he moved to Rockbridge County where he met and married Mary Bowyer, daughter of Colonel John Bowyer, a leading citizen. Brockenbrough soon established himself as a successful lawyer and political figure and for a short time edited the local Democratic organ, the *Valley Star*, succeeding John Letcher. Having espoused the principles of the Democratic party "from infancy," Brockenbrough became a party leader of some consequence in Lexington and Rockbridge, where the Whig party generally dominated the scene. Therefore, after Democrat James K. Polk had won the Presidency in 1844, Brockenbrough actively sought the federal judgeship for the western district of Virginia which became vacant in 1845. Despite Letcher's covert opposition he won the appointment in 1846, and the praise of Whig newspapers in Lexington and Staunton.

Judge Brockenbrough's Lexington Law School, as it opened in 1849, was appallingly primitive by present-day standards. It had a one-man faculty and no library. It also had no campus or building although it held classes in Franklin Society Hall, a prestigious and well-omened location. A prospectus for the school announced that the session would run from October 29 to the following March 16. Two classes, junior and senior, would be offered concurrently, so that an ambitious student could enroll in both without additional expense. Such a student could thus earn his law degree in about four and a half months, less than a fifth of the study time in the modern three-year program interspersed with holiday and vacation periods. A few additional lectures on jurisdiction and practice of federal courts, however, were promised at the close of the course. The announcement stated also that law students might attend lectures at Washington College. Many students attended college before beginning the study of law, but as they were not required to do so some young men entered law school with no more academic preparation than those starting in college. The tuition fee was sixty dollars per session.

Textbooks announced for the new school suggest the scope and limitations of the subject matter to be covered. For use in the junior class were Stephen's *Blackstone*, Starkie on evidence, Stephen on pleading, and Volume 1 of Greenleaf on evidence. Adopted for the senior course were Tucker's commentaries, Greenleaf and Starkie on evidence, Stephen on pleading, Gould on pleading, Chitty on pleading, Lube on equity pleading, Mitford on pleading, Lomax's digest of real property, and Lomax on executors and administrators. An official announcement at the close of the first session said of Tucker's commentaries, the principal textbook in the senior class, that "the numerous errors of the text will be corrected by very full quotations from the modern decisions of the Court of Appeals of Virginia."

In the manner of the nineteenth century, Judge Brockenbrough formally opened his Law School in an "Introductory Address to the Law Class of Lexington." Acceding to a request from a committee of the senior class, the speaker consented to publication of his remarks in the press and in pamphlet form. The judge spoke earnestly of his new enterprise, outlined his proposed methods, and enjoined upon the students "systematic and unwearied study." He promised to amplify the textbooks, to note recent decisions, and to consider the civil code which had been adopted a short time earlier by the Virginia legislature. The code contained new features of municipal law. The judge would catechize his students, and promised to set up a moot court during the closing two months of the session.

Their teacher also offered advice to the young men about to embark upon the study of law. He held out tempting rewards to those who should become successful in their profession. He warned that a long probationary period often awaited the young man called to the bar, and illustrated his point by citing the difficult early career of Chapman

Johnson, a distinguished Virginia lawyer. "When you shall come to the bar," he advised, "make it an inflexible rule to be always found during business hours in your offices." The judge then described the moment in a young lawyer's career when he delivered his first important and eloquent speech—to score a triumph. He alluded to an eminent English lawyer of the eighteenth century who established his reputation by a single great speech: from making nothing a year he suddenly found his income at £2800.

There can be little doubt that the community of Lexington strongly supported the new school, and doubtless agreed with the *Valley Star* in wishing it success. As noted above, Lexington in the fifties could boast a number of intellectual institutions. The "Athens of Virginia" welcomed another.

At the close of its first session the Lexington Law School graduated five men, and six completed the course in March of 1851. Of the latter group John Goode, Jr., became a well-known Virginia political leader, member of Congress and solicitor general of the United States; James W. Massie served as professor of mathematics at V.M.I. and as assistant to Judge Brockenbrough in his school during 1860; and William McLaughlin became a local judge and rector of Washington and Lee.

During the fifties enrollment rose as high as thirty-eight. In 1854 an incident in which a law student killed a V.M.I. cadet caused much press comment and only eleven young men matriculated in the 1854–55 session. But in December 1857 the Richmond *Dispatch* reported that the Lexington school, with twenty-eight students, was "the largest private law school in Virginia at present, or with a single exception, at any former time."

The *Dispatch* described Judge Brockenbrough's teaching methods: "The chapters, given to the class the previous day for investigation and study, are made the subjects of individual examination, and, instead of a formal lecture . . . the Judge gives a running commentary on the text as contained in the answers of the students. It is a union of the catechetical and the lecture system, and invests the elaborate duties of instruction with a kind of conversational interest."

Another teaching device employed by Judge Brockenbrough was taking along his law students when his duties as U.S. district judge required him to hold court throughout western Virginia. John W. Davis' father, John J. Davis, recalled with pleasure the valuable experience that this practice afforded him as a student. In March 1859 the judge wrote a kinsman that while cares and troubles beset him his law teaching kept him too busy for melancholia. Those who believe that teaching is a lazy man's vocation would do well to ponder Judge

Brockenbrough's private description of his situation: "This business of lecturing three hours a day to a large class of educated young men, walking to town and back, studying six or eight hours in preparation for the next day's recitation and lecture is no child's play, depend on it."

It is probable that the pattern of his school outlined by the founder in 1849 was adhered to throughout the ante-bellum period. According to official records, 207 students attended the Lexington Law School down to 1861. Many were former students of Washington College but a large number came from distant places, and without benefit of previous college work. From this school went scores of men destined for legislative work, and for the bench and bar. The rolls are studded with notations of service in the Confederate army, and a number were fated to give their lives for the lost cause.

Although a member of the federal judiciary, 1846–1861, Judge Brockenbrough seemed ever responsive to the disturbing political developments of the fifties. He expressed annoyance at a suggestion that he become a candidate for governor of Virginia on the Know-Nothing ticket, stating in plain words his cordial detestation of the "principles" of that party. During 1858 he was strongly urged for the governorship on the Democratic ticket by the Richmond *Enquirer*, a newspaper dominated by Henry A. Wise and hostile to the pretensions of John Letcher. Thus for a moment the two prominent Lexingtonians clashed, but Letcher won the nomination and election.

In the crisis years 1860–1861 Judge Brockenbrough, a warm States' rights Democrat, leaned markedly toward the Southern cause. He, Colonel Massie, and E. F. Paxton carried the States' rights banner in the contest for delegates to the Virginia convention of 1861 which considered the fateful issue of secession. Rockbridge County, overwhelmingly Unionist at the time, defeated the judge and his associates. In January 1861, however, the Virginia General Assembly appointed him a delegate to the ill-starred "Peace Convention" that met in Washington and vainly sought an acceptable compromise to ward off the impending disaster. His law class praised his appointment, "however detrimental to them," and wished him Godspeed. Events tended to strengthen Judge Brockenbrough's hand with his neighbors, compelling a reversal of their opinion after April 15, 1861, which brought unity of the people for secession.

This is not the place for a full examination of Judge Brockenbrough's services during the Confederate era. Suffice it to say that he served in the Provisional Confederate Congress and in October, 1861, was appointed Confederate States judge of Western Virginia, a position he occupied until the overthrow of the Southern government.

2] Tentative Years at Washington College

ONLY A FEW WEEKS after Appomattox the Lexington *Gazette* carried the announcement that Judge Brockenbrough proposed to reopen his Law School, which had been closed during the war. The program would be much the same as before but the session would be extended to nine months and the tuition would be a hundred dollars. The School operated a special summer session in 1865 and attracted twenty-three students to the regular 1865–1866 session.

Meanwhile, as related in Chapter XIII, the trustees of Washington College were confronted with pressing problems including the selection of a president. Judge Brockenbrough had been a trustee since 1852 and in the reorganization of the board in the summer of 1865 he was elected rector. Thus he found himself in the unusual position of heading two separate institutions of higher learning.

We have seen how the board took an inspired action in electing General R. E. Lee to the presidency of Washington College, and how Judge Brockenbrough was authorized to visit the Southern hero in an effort to obtain his acceptance of the post—a mission executed with success.

The coming of General Lee to Washington College infused into the venerable institution new vigor, broadened its field of patronage, and converted its classical curriculum into that of a university. In view of the expanded program it is not surprising that at the close of Judge Brockenbrough's first postwar session in April, 1866, the proposal was broached to unite his Law School with Washington College.

A committee of trustees reported June 28, 1866, on the projected Law School annexation. The report recommended that it should be distinct from the academic department and known as "the School of Law and equity." Judge Brockenbrough was to be the professor, although he was not a member of the academic faculty, and was to control discipline. Law students were not to be entitled to use the library or to occupy the college buildings. Academic students might attend either class in law, upon payment of a $60 fee in addition to the $40 tuition fee for academic studies. No dismissed or expelled academic student could enter the Law School. Upon completion of the entire course, the student would receive the Bachelor of Law degree. Such was the tentative, quasi-independent status of the Law department of Washington College for the first few years of the arrangement, subject to annual renewal.

Judge Brockenbrough reviewed the work of the Law School in his first report submitted to General Lee, June 18, 1867. Of 27 students enrolled, 21 were candidates for the B.L. degree. The latter had stood the ordeal of examination conducted at the Court House by Judge Brockenbrough June 13, 14, and 15, attended on occasion by General Lee and several members of the faculty. Town lawyers also were present, as were many "intelligent strangers, one or two of them Lawyers by profession. . . ." Judge Brockenbrough described the details of the examination:

> A large number of legal problems, was prepared with much care & labor by myself, ranging through almost the whole field of jurisprudence, and three of these were assigned to each candidate, by lot, and written answers were required to be prepared in the immediate presence of myself & the audience, without reference to text books or other authorities. They were all prepared & handed to me on the first day, and were publicly read by the candidates respectively on the following day. They were in a high degree accurate, full & satisfactory. The forenoon of Saturday was devoted to an oral examination on the subjects not drawn from the Lottery & this part of the exercise was especially gratifying & satisfactory. The remaining exercises consisted of the reading of essays on legal subjects, each candidate having prepared one, by my direction, during the April recess of the school.

Judge Brockenbrough highly praised these essays, in style and in research, as well as an earlier series, which General Lee and others had heard read. Student conduct was excellent throughout, according to the professor, and was commented upon by townsmen. The judge wound up his first report by assuring the president that he had heavily taxed student "powers of application and apprehension" during the session. On Monday following the close of the examinations, members of Judge Brockenbrough's class presented him with "a beautiful gold-headed cane," and the town bard and wit, "Lawyer" James D. Davidson, then spoke in humorous vein.

The cautious trustees renewed the connection of the Law School in 1867 and again in 1868, declaring in the latter year that it was not then expedient for the College to establish "a School of Law in regular connection with the institution as one of its departments of instruction." Later it become plain that the Law School should be strengthened by the appointment of another professor. It was clear, also, that the enrollment of the School had not increased; in 1869 only 14 students attended, of whom 12 were recommended for the degree. According to Judge Brockenbrough's report of June 10, 1869, the class had performed well on the written and oral examinations. He admitted, however, misgivings about grading students: "It would be uncandid to deny that there were marked degrees of excellence & proficiency among the candidates, but it would be difficult to apply, with entire correctness, a graduated scale to mark their relative proficiency, in a science so varied & extensive as that of law & Equity." Several members of the Law class of 1869 attained subsequent distinction, the best known of whom included J. Harvey McLeary, who became attorney general of Texas and associate justice of the supreme court of Montana; D. Gardiner Tyler, son of President Tyler; and Charles T. O'Ferrall, later a member of Congress and governor of Virginia.

Radical Reconstruction was in full operation in Virginia, as throughout the South, during the late sixties, and much bitterness was engendered among the former ruling class. Judge Brockenbrough privately scorned radical politics, and resented deeply the activity of the Freedmen's Bureau and its allies in Lexington. His feeling was hardly assuaged by the pressure to pay his federal taxes in 1868. Indeed, because of several factors the last nine years of Judge Brockenbrough's life were anticlimactic.

An able committee of trustees, composed of William McLaughlin, William H. Ruffner, and W. T. Poague, in June of 1869 prepared a thoughtful report on the problem of legal instruction. The report asserted that a single professor could not possibly do all the work of the School, demanded more chairs, a broader curriculum, and better integration of law courses with other studies. The committee quoted with approval Blackstone's remark that the study of law was an important part of a polite education. But there was an even more compelling reason to build up the Washington College Law School. It appeared to the committee that the mission of educated young Southerners was to "guard from pollution and overthrow that Palladium of the political and civil rights of the people, the Constitution of the United States; and the only means of restoring and preserving these rights, under Providence, is to imbue the youthful minds of the South with a profound knowledge of Constitutional law and political science."

Furthermore, the report noted, the entire direction of legal instruction had sharply altered within the past twenty-five years. It had shifted from study in a lawyer's office to attendance at well-equipped law schools. Unless Washington College could furnish the modern type of school, students would go elsewhere. Enrollment at the University of Virginia Law School, in 1866–1869, ranged from 109 to 121, while the figures from Columbian College Law Department (Washington, D. C.) for the same years were 173 to 200. Why could not more pupils be attracted to Lexington? The group recommended the appointment of two professors of law, with salaries and perquisites sufficient to attract the highest-level talent in the nation, and to enable them to devote their exclusive time to the duties of their chairs. The committee did indeed set its sights high; and at once correspondence was opened with the Kentuckian, General John Cabell Breckinridge, former Vice-President of the United States, to tender him one of these professorships. General Breckinridge, who had sons at Washington College and was emerging from a "flight into oblivion," declined the offer.

3] John Randolph Tucker and Judge Brockenbrough

THE HIGH PURPOSE of the trustees to obtain the services of a brilliant lawyer and teacher was fulfilled in 1870 when John Randolph Tucker, an eminent Virginia attorney then practicing in Baltimore, son of Judge Henry St. George Tucker, accepted a professorship. An arrangement in regard to the salaries of the law professors, adopted in 1870, proved to work to the advantage of Mr. Tucker and to the disadvantage of Judge Brockenbrough. By action of the trustees the law professors (and the president) were excepted from the rule forbidding faculty members to accept employment outside their regular duties; whereupon both Judge Brockenbrough and Professor Tucker engaged in the practice of law in Lexington.

For several years the two professors worked in harmony. They submitted a report to President G. W. C. Lee calling attention to the great need of the Law Department—an adequate library. This library, said the professor, should be always accessible to the students, and would make the moot court a valuable adjunct of instruction. "We urge this the more—because there is *absolutely no law library here.* ..." This startling deficiency had embarrassed students. It was the rule in Northern colleges to have law libraries adjacent to lecture rooms.

Despite the addition of Tucker the Law School did not immediately flourish, students numbering only 31 in the spring of 1871 and but 17 in 1872–1873. Judge Brockenbrough's salary proved inadequate. Depending upon fees, it fell far below that paid his colleague. He conceded that he had no legal ground for complaint but it became evident that the judge had signed an unfavorable contract. With a measure of pathos he referred in a letter to trustees Moore and Davidson to "my Law School," which seemed to be slipping from him. With deep feeling he wrote: "That I should under any circumstances be compelled to abandon this favorite scheme of my life, so long as a Kind Providence leaves me in possession of my mental & physical powers, is a possibility too painful to contemplate. . . ."

With the onset of the Panic of 1873 the difficulties of the Law

School mounted. A showdown was inevitable and was not long delayed. Judge Brockenbrough resigned in June of 1872 as rector and trustee of the University. The other board members in June of 1873 were faced with a painful decision, for they were forced to discriminate in the salaries of their two law professors in order to retain the services of Professor Tucker, which they were determined to do. Thus Judge Brockenbrough's resignation was virtually demanded and was forthcoming the next day, June 26.

The wound to the judge was deep and the village reverberated with the echoes of this conflict. About the same period Washington and Lee experienced one of its several recurrences of sectarianism. The battle of the Law School was involved, with Judge Brockenbrough himself believing that, as an Episcopalian, he had been discriminated against. In fact he appealed to the forum of public opinion by spreading his grievances through four columns of small type in the Richmond *Enquirer*.

Before this disagreeable episode is closed one may ponder the issues it raised. The trustees had made a brilliant stroke when they obtained the services of Mr. Tucker, as will be demonstrated in the next section. He was vigorous, able, magnetic—exactly the man needed to infuse energy into the lagging Law School. It was unthinkable to let him go. Sentiment, however, pleaded strongly for Judge Brockenbrough: founder of the School, one who as trustee and professor had rendered the most important services to his institution, but at the same time one beyond his prime and in straitened financial circumstances. The board immediately accepted the latter's unconditional resignation, with the usual words of praise and expression of hope that "kind providence" might sustain him. Unfortunately, "kind providence" did not smile on his efforts to open another private law school in Lexington in the fall of 1873. The times were most unfavorable to such an enterprise. Many of his old students expressed warm sympathy for their "learned Gamaliel"; but by 1875 it was clear that "the distressing poverty of our people" had defeated this last effort. Death came in 1877. The historian may well conclude that Washington and Lee owed much to the kindly and scholarly John White Brockenbrough.

4] Guardians of the Constitution

IT HAS BEEN STATED that in the summer of 1870 the trustees adopted the plan of a more permanent and extended law school than had previously existed. Thereafter the Law Department received designation as one of the "schools," and its professors became members of the regular University faculty. Law students were to matriculate in the same manner as other students at the College, and were to be subject to the same government and control.

The coming of John Randolph Tucker to the Law School faculty proved to be an event in the history of the institution and of the community, despite disappointment of the hopes for an immediate increase in enrollment. Born in Winchester in 1823, Tucker was educated at the University of Virginia where he studied law under his father and was graduated in 1844. From 1845 to 1857 he practiced law in Winchester, and entered Democratic politics as an ardent States' rights champion. He won the office of state attorney general in 1857 and held it until 1865. After the war he became general counsel of the Baltimore and Ohio Railroad, which position he left to come to Washington College.

The Lexington *Virginia Gazette,* hailing Tucker's election to the faculty, described him as one "who has a national reputation for Attic wit, irrepressible humor, thrilling eloquence, high legal attainments, unspotted private character, and wide personal popularity." This was hardly an overstatement as his career in Lexington was to prove. His personality impressed itself profoundly upon the town and region. The anecdotes of his wit and humorous antics became legion, his eloquence in classroom and on platform was unsurpassed, and his sincere piety impressive.

In accordance with the dispensation granted him by the trustees he opened law offices in Lexington and Staunton. Already a practiced hand in the game of politics, the new professor frequently offered his services to the Conservative (Democratic) party of Virginia, appearing on the hustings in the heated campaigns of the Reconstruction period. He was reported by a sympathetic newspaper on one occasion to have "skinned alive" his radical Republican adversary. Throughout his years in Lexington, as congressman or professor, his home "Blandome" was the scene of gay social life. Student publications described parties there with appreciation; and in a time when the student body receded to smaller numbers, the Tucker home brought town and gown together in an atmosphere of friendliness.

We have noted that a reorganization of the School of Law was effected by the trustees in 1873 with Tucker as director of the department. He was voted an assistant professor in the person of young Charles A. Graves, whom he had trained at Washington and Lee and whose career as student and professor in Lexington was to span thirty-three years. This combination of Tucker and Graves functioned only two years, however, as the former won election to Congress in the

Democratic landslide of 1874. He had a distinguished career of twelve years in the House. Although he resigned his professorship in 1875, he retained a nominal connection with the Washington and Lee Law School, through lectures delivered each year to students, addresses to other college groups, and an occasional commencement oration.

At graduation exercises in 1878 Tucker gave an exposition of his ideas of law and society. As reported in the *Southern Collegian* the orator opened with a strong affirmation of the necessity of religious faith. Warming to his subject, Tucker assailed class legislation and advocated a laissez-faire doctrine. He then reviewed the course of the South and Virginia to secession, maintaining that that action had been undertaken not to perpetuate slavery but "to defend the right of each state to say how long slavery should continue in its borders." He enjoined his young hearers to labor in defense of Constitutional liberty; all hope was by no means lost. Noting the agricultural character of the South, he prophesied that the section would perform a conservative function in the future history of the nation.

These doctrines John Randolph Tucker taught in the Law School at Washington and Lee and expounded on the floor of Congress. Student Lucius Desha attested to this in August of 1871 when he wrote to his fellow student Hugh A. Moran: "I can blow for our Law School and for Mr. Tucker especially. He is a fine man and a good teacher, and I venture to say there is no school in the country anywhere that teaches the States' rights doctrine in its purity like he does here." During the seventies, also, the attention of Northern conservatives was attracted to the Law School at Washington and Lee. Many Northern professional men, especially lawyers, distrusted the centralizing tendencies of the radical Republicans, and became disgusted wth the performance of the Grant administration.

One of these was the railroad attorney, Vincent L. Bradford, a resident of Philadelphia. Mr. Bradford, who had been immensely flattered by the award of an honorary LL.D. degree from Washington and Lee (and who subsequently received, at his indirect suggestion, the honorary degree of Litt.D.), heartily endorsed the Constitutional interpretations expounded in the Washington and Lee Law School. This feeling he phrased in a letter to Dr. Alfred Leyburn, Rector, on July 4, 1874: ". . . I am in full sympathy and accord with the essential Truths and Doctrines of Constitutional and Public Law, inculcated by Washington, Jefferson, Madison, Taylor of Caroline, and an Host of Statesmen and Jurists, noble sons of 'the Mother of Commonwealths,' and still recognized and taught by 'the Washington and Lee University' of Virginia."

Bradford, who continued to send an annual contribution to the law library (and who left Washington and Lee a substantial legacy), developed the theme of the mission of the Washington and Lee University Law School. He viewed the School as "a Depository of the soundest principles of Constitutional Law and polite learning. . . ." and conceived of it as a beacon light "in the midst of prevailing political darkness." So long as such an institution "of sound and correct Learning" as Washington and Lee should exist, Bradford would not "despair of regaining a decentralized and restored Federal Republic. . . ." This far-seeing conservative anticipated by many years the shift of conservatives in general from centralization to decentralization as a device best suited to the protection of their property interests. Yet an occasional critic even in Tucker's bailiwick could feel that his Constitutional doctrines were obsolete. Some of these were probably defeatist in outlook during the post-Civil War generation. Whatever his motivation, the bucolic local humorist, "G. Whillikens," wrote his friend "Josiah Simpkins" late in 1886: "Ran Tucker has been lecturin' the boys on the Constitution. Lecturin' on the Constitution these days in like singin' Psalms to a dead hoss." There are those who would feel this comment more applicable to the fourth, fifth, and sixth decades of the twentieth century than to Tucker's day.

Meanwhile the Washington and Lee Law School was carried on in its day-to-day instruction from 1875 to 1889 by Professor Graves. This was a period of decline and discouragement at the University, of faculty resignations and sharp falling-off in enrollment. Years later Professor Graves modestly said that if he deserved credit for his work at Washington and Lee it was for remaining with the institution during those dark days.

Young Professor Graves came to his work well grounded in academic as well as legal subjects. A native of Bedford, Virginia, Charles had come to study in General Lee's College as did two brothers. Charles took the A.B. and M.A. degrees, twice winning the Robinson Prize medal for scholastic excellence, and served as assistant professor of English and modern languages in 1869. He then studied law with Professors Tucker and Brockenbrough, taking the B.L. in 1873. At the beginning of his law study he wrote his father: "I am going to be a lawyer, and a good one if possible. I am sorry I cannot take both courses this year, so as to be able to begin practice next year if I desired."

But when he had finished his course in 1873 he was appointed assistant professor of law. He was named adjunct professor the next year and in 1875 succeeded Tucker as professor of Common and Statute

Law and Equity Jurisprudence. Although this was a formidable assignment for so young a man, who understandably felt his limitations and
lack of reputation, Graves admirably justified the appointment.

In the summer of 1875, however, misgivings lingered about the future of the Law School. Professor William Preston Johnston, a former
member of the academic faculty and lecturer during the seventies in
the Law Department, wrote trustee Francis T. Anderson that the Law
School had always been a heavy drain on the University's funds. The
school could be discontinued, he added, but such a course would entail
a loss of prestige and impair the institution's University status. For the
session 1875–1876 Johnston's plan of having Tucker lecture on Constitutional law, mercantile law, and conflict of laws, with "free" lectures
by distinguished lawyers supplementing the instruction, was adopted.
But from 1876 onward Professor Graves carried the burden alone,
although the catalogues of those years were made impressive by the
listing of special lecturers as staff members.

During the period when Professor Graves directed the Law School
"single-handed and alone," the number of students fluctuated from 14
in 1875–1876, 28 in 1877–1878, 26 in 1878–1879 (drawn from ten states,
11 of the total from Virginia), 19 in 1879–1880, to 15 in 1882 (Graves
urged an increase in enrollment, and suggested advertisement), and
varied but slightly from these figures for the rest of the eighties. Students could still carry both the junior and senior classes and complete
the law course in one year. For example, in the class of 1883, 13
attended both classes, 13 the junior class only, and only 2 the senior
class exclusively.

Better and more commodious quarters were provided in the Washington College building for the Law School. In his report to President
G.W.C. Lee for June, 1885, Professor Graves recapitulated ten years
of stewardship. In a decade a hundred and nine students had been
awarded the B.L. degree; and he also pointed out with satisfaction that
the school had become more than self-supporting. He calculated that
the tuition fees from the Law Department were enough to pay the
professor's salary, the cost of advertising, and incidental expenses.

Although the sources of information concerning life among the law
students in the seventies and eighties are meager, a few items are available. At commencement of 1876 the law supper was a happy occasion.
In attendance were the law graduates with the law and academic faculties. According to the *Southern Collegian*, "There was everything in
abundance that could tempt the appetite, and soon the champaign [sic]
began to flow and the spirits of all were raised." Before the toasts were
drunk, student Bradley of Kentucky, on behalf of the class, presented a

"beautiful arm chair" to Professor Graves. The sage professor then offered advice to the graduates, the essence of which was: "First make lawyers of yourselves, for it was the legal logic of a Tucker which overcame the political intrigues of a Blaine." With the spirited presidential election in the offing, the diners drank to the toast, "The Supremacy of the Democratic Party essential to the preservation of the liberties of the People."

Auxiliaries to the regular course of instruction in law were the Law Society and the Moot Court. At a meeting of the society in March of 1877 student F. M. Cockrell delivered an oration on "The Grand Jury," which was followed by a debate on the subject, "Should parties to an action be allowed to testify in a civil case?" Moot Court had been held for about six weeks in February and March of that year with Judge William McLaughlin presiding.

A writer in the June, 1888, issue of the *Southern Collegian*, presumably a "bic,"* described Professor Graves' teaching: ". . . the text-books which give the principles are not the real authority for the law; that is to be found in the application of these principles by the courts, and collected in their reports. . . . Professor Graves, by patient and systematic work, has looked up . . . the leading cases on all the most important subjects; of these some are assigned as required for the examinations. . . . Others are given as marginal notes, that, to a student who intends to practice in Virginia, are invaluable."

This article also commented on Judge Hugh White Sheffey's lectures to seniors on wills and corporations. Juniors were required to attend the month-long course; but when Judge Sheffey began, the juniors did not have even "a bowing acquaintance with Corporations." The writer suggested that the juniors be introduced to the subject before listening to Judge Sheffey's lectures.

At the close of the eighties it occurred to several trustees that the Law School could be placed on the "best possible basis" by the reappointment of John Randolph Tucker as a full-time professor. One trustee believed that the combination of Graves and Tucker would permit the School to compete effectively for students with the University of Virginia, especially since a noted member of the Virginia faculty, Dr. John B. Minor, seemed near the end of his career. Tucker, who had retired from Congress, was available and would bring to the institution his national prestige.

The appointment was offered and accepted. The press throughout the country applauded the return to Washington and Lee of the

* Victorian slang for law student, derivation uncertain.

"statesman-professor"; joining in the praise were "Marse Henry" Watterson of the Louisville *Courier-Journal,* the Richmond *State,* and the Baltimore *Sun.* The *Sun* quoted Tucker's views of his future work: "I come back . . . to this University after years of separation, and I have come to stay. I propose to devote the residue of my life to teaching young men who assemble here, the truth of our Constitutional system, which my experience in public affairs shows to be essential for the protection of our institutional liberties." It was reported also that Tucker planned to write a book embodying his views on the Constitution, that document which was by no means "an obsolete compact whose restrictions upon greed and insolence are to be considered inoperative."

The *Southern Collegian* expressed enthusiasm for the Tucker appointment. This "true disciple of Jefferson and Calhoun" had put behind him the "fitful fever" of politics. He was returning to the campus, where his purpose would be to imbue "young minds and young hearts with his ideas and his principles of government, that they may . . . carry on the work left by him, and thus keep our government pure, and teach men to know that it is 'an indissoluble Union of indestructible States.' " The *Collegian* confidently predicted a brightened future for the Law School.

The School may be said to have entered a new era of prosperity—a "Golden Age"—during the closing decade of the century. John Randolph Tucker, speaking to a student rally in the spring of 1890, expressed the desire to see more young men enter the University, "from the North and West, as well as from the South, from all over the land as from the Valley of Virginia. . . ." He foresaw with broad vision a much greater institution which would boast more professors, more buildings, more students. A progressive note indeed, sounded at a time when discerning critics were disturbed by stagnation at Washington and Lee.

In June, 1890, Tucker and Graves recommended certain improvements to the trustees. The board approved a summer session, gradual enlargement of the regular course, and higher standards for graduation, pointing to an eventual requirement of attendance at two sessions for the B.L. degree. The trustees also sharply cut the free tuition that had been granted certain favored groups.

Enrollment increased markedly in the Law School during the early nineties. Tucker's appointment was no doubt a factor; and it was a boom season in these parts of Virginia. At Commencement of 1891, while only 3 students received the A.B. degree, 29 gained the B.L. The law professors reported to President Lee in June of 1892 that their department had 63 students, the largest number in history, and that they expected 75 the next session. Every year, they said, the school became better known through its alumni.

A succession of honors that came to Tucker, and the continued attention paid him by the press, also advertised favorably the Washington and Lee Law School. Harvard University conferred upon him the honorary degree of LL.D., which he already held from William and Mary and Yale. The New York *World* compared him to General R. E. Lee in character, and after the return of the Democrats to national power in 1892 he was mentioned for Cleveland's cabinet. In 1893 he was chosen president of the American Bar Association, and in the same year appeared before the United States Supreme Court in a case involving South Carolina railroads. During the nineties he wrote many articles and delivered many orations. Tucker's wide circle of friends became aware of the Law School in which he taught, and a number of gifts of books and money were made to the school by his friends. His friendships transcended sectional and party lines. Tucker's admirers during his career included President Garfield, the eminent legal reformer and codifier David Dudley Field, and Richard Vaux of Philadelphia.

At the suggestion of Professor Graves, the trustees in 1893 conferred the title of dean upon Tucker. For the remaining years of his life he ceaselessly urged upon the board increased instructional staff, larger quarters, and expansion of the library. Despite the impact of the Panic of 1893 and the depression years that followed, the law enrollment held its own at least to Tucker's death in 1897. During these troubled years, too, a number of the school's eminent alumni received their training. Perhaps the two most distinguished graduates in this period (both of whom served for many years as trustees of Washington and Lee) were John W. Davis, A.B., 1892, and B.L., 1895, and Newton D. Baker, Jr. (A.B., Johns Hopkins), B.L., 1894.

Davis' public career as Congressman, solicitor general, ambassador, and presidential candidate has been mentioned in earlier chapters. At his death in 1955 he was hailed by the Richmond *Times-Dispatch* as Washington and Lee's most eminent alumnus. Baker attained distinction as reform mayor of Cleveland, Secretary of War in President Wilson's cabinet, and eloquent champion of the League of Nations. He was considered a distinct possibility for the Democratic nomination for president in 1932, a year in which that nomination was tantamount to election. Both Davis and Baker rose to heights of professional success in the practice of law.

Fortunately each of these distinguished graduates was called upon to place on record his thoughts of society and the law. Baker wrote an article for the *Southern Collegian*'s May, 1896, issue, "Academic Preparation for the Study of Law." He observed that lawyers were becoming "experts in technical business," a tendency which he decried, and called upon the "lawyer of the future, true to his traditions . . . to again become the regulator and upbuilder of the social fabric." He thought he saw favorable omens that this was to be the case, and proceeded to discuss the lawyer as a man of affairs. Young men believed in progress, in some ages painfully slow but sure; at other times revolutions occurred and progress was rapid. The present, he asserted, doubtless with the free-silver agitation in mind, was such a time when old forms of government were being tested as never before. "Communism, anarchy and socialism are no longer the amusements of dreamy social philosophers and romancers, but are coming to be investigated by serious people with a view to diminishing evils, which if not new to society are more oppressive and more apparent under our new conditions. Socialism, indeed, is a great and growing system of thought. . . ." Here the guidance of lawyers would be needed, Baker maintained.

The passing of the narrow classical curriculum he did not deplore. Regarding the college program of the nineties he wrote that it appeared to fit students better for the study of law than did only Latin and the higher mathematics. The newer subjects provided broad cultural values; and also the intrinsic merit of such studies as history, economics, and politics bore directly upon the law itself. A law student, Baker contended, should have been grounded in English institutional and constitutional history, political science, the natural sciences, logic, mathematics, metaphysics, and modern classical languages. In conclusion, he asked, what should the model lawyer be? And his answer was brief and clear: "Simply an honest man with a good mind and all the training of mind and heart that his best efforts can attain from the best opportunities."

John W. Davis' Law Class Oration of 1895 was entitled "The Call of Our Age to the Lawyer." Davis noted the rise and fall of civilizations and declared that "we, as heirs of all who have gone before us, seem to stand at the apex of a mighty pyramid, in a purer atmosphere than those who lived below, and with a broader, clearer view." Like Baker, he examined the defects and dangers of modern society. On one hand he saw the Scylla of discontented masses, restless and explosive, ready perhaps to set up a bitter and unenlightened despotism. On the other was the then even more dangerous Charybdis of American plutocracy. Between these dangers lawyers must steer the nation through adherence to the doctrine of "reverence for the Law." Davis called upon his classmates of 1895 to protect and defend the law, and make the United States an exemplar to the entire world.

In the spring of 1896 Professors Tucker and Graves recommended a number of improvements necessary to maintain the Washington and Lee Law School abreast of others. They felt they were overburdened and urged the appointment of a third teacher. Many areas were ignored or taught inadequately: practice in federal courts, criminal procedure, admiralty law, insurance, agency and partnership. To cover carriers, title to personal property, and contracts in the regular schedule, one of the teachers carried an extra hour each day, in addition to his regular hour-and-a-half lecture. This was more than a man ought to do, they argued. At the University of Virginia no professor had more than four lectures a week, while at Washington and Lee he who did the extra hour was burdened with fourteen hours!

This memorandum advised the trustees that nearly all law schools had from three to six or seven professors, and many also employed assistant professors and lecturers. A school of only two professors, even though they did the work of three or four, was in those times likely to become discredited. The University of Virginia faculty consisted of three full professors and an adjunct professor, while West Virginia University had three full professors. The memorial urged also an increase of tuition fees from $80 to $100 or $125, depending on whether a student elected one or both courses. The faculty admitted that while much could be said on both sides regarding a one-year against a two-year course, the majority of Washington and Lee men attempted the entire course in one year. Tucker expressed himself as ready to seek funds for these improvements, and believed that he could get them.

The board hearkened to this strong representation and appointed young John W. Davis as assistant professor of law for 1896–1897. Davis confessed that he fancied himself the occupant of a law chair at some point in his career, although his first ambition was to achieve success as a practitioner. He modestly doubted his abilities to fill the post, but decided to accept.

Nor was the coming of so able a young teacher postponed a moment too long; for Tucker fell ill late in 1896 and, retaining his zest until the end, died early in 1897. The whole state mourned his passing and the general sentiment seemed to have been expressed by William Henry Ruffner, who wrote his daughter: "We shall ne'er see his like again. Everybody loves him."

As the century closed, more changes affected the faculty of the Law

Department. Harry St. George Tucker was chosen Professor of Law in 1897, "the worthy successor of a worthy sire." Tucker, A.M., 1875, B.L., 1876, about whom so much has been written in these pages, had served in Congress for several terms prior to 1896 (when the silver issue forced his retirement), and as member of the board of trustees of Washington and Lee. In a general way the younger Tucker subscribed warmly to the constitutional views of his father, and also possessed a genial personality which made him a charming companion. As successor to John W. Davis the board chose Dr. William Reynolds Vance, an alumnus who held four degrees including the Ph.D. Professor Vance thus began what was to be a long and distinguished career as law teacher, winding up at Yale University. Professor Graves was elevated to the deanship.

But this combination was not to endure, for in 1899 Dean Graves resigned to accept a position at the University of Virginia. The departure of such a fixture was a blow to the Law School, which the trustees attempted to remedy by the election of Harry St. George Tucker as dean. The broadened law course by 1898–1899 had been so arranged as to discourage completion of the B.L. in one session—"extremely difficult, if not well-nigh impossible." Since, however, the faculty did not forbid it, some able and industrious youths, like Henry Watkins Anderson, B.L., 1899, successfully achieved the double course in one year —and surely Anderson's distinguished career in law and politics justified him. Meanwhile, Professor Tucker had busied himself with the filial tasks of aiding in the collection of a fund with which the John Randolph Tucker Memorial building could be erected, and with editing for publication *The Constitution of the United States by J. Randolph Tucker, LL.D.*, which appeared in 1899.

The cornerstone of Tucker Hall was laid June 13, 1899, with Masonic ceremonies. Funds to finance it had been gathered from among the late J. R. Tucker's friends, alumni, and others. Notable contributors included Mrs. James A. Garfield, John E. Russell of Massachusetts, and James C. Carter of New York. The building was ready by the spring of 1900, a substantial gray stone structure described by the Lexington *Gazette* with understatement as presenting "a striking contrast" to the other college buildings.

In seeking an able teacher to fill the third post at the Law School, the board chose Professor William L. Clark, Jr., a prolific writer of law volumes, whose zealous industry it was hoped would infect the students. But Mr. Clark's tenure at Lexington was short-lived; in an unpleasant incident in the fall of 1899, he was said euphemistically to have "vacated" his chair at President Wilson's "suggestion." Professor John

N. Pomeroy and Mr. Frank T. Glasgow of Lexington took over Clark's work, and the board appointed Martin P. Burks of Bedford, Virginia, A.B., 1870, B.L. (University of Virginia), as professor of law.

5] The Twentieth Century

IN OCTOBER OF 1900 President William L. Wilson died. The board turned to Dean Harry Tucker, who served as acting president until the following June. When the trustees failed in 1901 to elect Tucker president, for which office he had strong backing, he continued as dean of the Law School only until the end of the session 1901–1902. Around the turn of the century the Vincent L. Bradford legacy had become available and in June of 1902 Professor Vance, who had succeeded to the deanship, could report that the law library contained around 6,000 volumes. The Bradford income was used to purchase *Official Reports* of the Supreme Court of the United States and of the Virginia Court of Appeals, *American State Reports*, and *Lawyers' Reports Annotated*, Southeastern, Southwestern, Southern, Northeastern, and Atlantic *Reporters*.

President Denny, however, while noting the increase of Law School attendance in his annual report of 1903 to the trustees, said that the resignation of Dean Vance in June had brought "us face to face with the embarrassing situation that has continually confronted the School in recent years." Stability was provided, however, for many years to come, by the election of Professor Burks, who made an enviable record, to the deanship. In 1904 he was joined in the faculty by Professor Abram P. Staples of Roanoke, Virginia. Also, in 1903, the trustees authorized the use of a limited number of scholarships in the Law School. Despite additional teaching by Professors H. Parker Willis and John H. Latané, the regular staff of Dean Burks, Professor Joseph R. Long, and Professor Staples felt itself overburdened during 1903–1904.

During President Denny's decade in the pesidency the enrollment of the University climbed until it exceeded 600 by 1911–1912, of which the Law School claimed 207. Meanwhile gradual curricular changes had been made, as well as tentative progress toward higher standards. As early as 1902 the catalogue recommended at least one year of academic work before engaging in law study, but this was not a requirement. In 1906 the trustees authorized that the law degree require two years and the form of the degree was changed from B.L. to LL.B. By 1908 the number of credits requisite for college entrance was made a requirement for admission to the Law Department. In his 1912 report Dean Burks suggested that, while the two-year course be continued, an optional three-year program be offered.

Responding to Dean Burks' request for another full-time professor, the trustees in 1912 appointed Mr. Robert Withers, giving the School a four-man faculty. But Professor Staples died in September of 1913; Mr. Withers resigned at the close of the 1913–1914 session; and Dean Burks was granted a two-year leave of absence to accept appointment by Governor Stuart as one of the code revisers of the state. D. Clovis Moomaw, who was fated to meet his death in action in World War I, replaced Professor Staples in 1914. Dean Burks' leave was extended and in 1917 he was appointed to the State Supreme Court of Appeals. William Haywood Moreland, '07, of the Norfolk bar, joined the faculty in 1914 and assumed the courses formerly taught by Dean Burks.

At the close of the 1914–1915 session the trustees considered the fact that leading law schools in North and South had expanded their curricula to three-year programs. The retention of the two-year course at Washington and Lee had subjected its Law School to discussion and criticism. During the previous fall and winter the law faculty had made an exhaustive study of the subject, and in April unanimously adopted resolutions which "in effect put the school on a three-year curriculum." Actually, the three-year course for a time remained optional.

Professor Joseph R. Long was elected Dean in 1917; and after the close of the first World War a staff of five full-time teachers was appointed, courses were expanded, and the curriculum was modernized. Beginning with the 1920 session three full years of residence were required for a degree. At this time the school adopted the "case system," by which "the cases are the basis of instruction and the text book and law review articles are the reference works." By 1926 all courses were taught by the case method. Of much significance was the admission of the Washington and Lee Law School into the Association of American Law Schools in 1920. Another indication of the relative standing of the school came in 1925 when the American Bar Association placed Washington and Lee in "Class A" rating, enjoyed at the time by only thirty-nine law schools. In 1923 two years of college work was made a requirement for admission.

The remaining decades are too close to the present to be described in detail or viewed in the proper perspective. Mr. Moreland became dean in 1923, upon the resignation of Mr. Long, and by the end of the decade the faculty included Professor Clayton E. Williams, LL.B., 1912 (who had joined the faculty in 1919), Professsor Charles P. Light, Jr. (LL.B. Harvard), Professor Raymond T. Johnson (J.D., Chicago), and Professor Charles R. McDowell (LL.B., Yale). This staff continued with the institution through the thirties, unbroken in ranks until the deaths of Dean Moreland in 1944 and Professor Johnson in 1948. In the meantime additions were made to the faculty in the persons of

Professor Theodore A. Smedley (J.D., Northwestern) and Professor Charles V. Laughlin (J.S.D., Chicago).

On December 16, 1934, the old Tucker Hall building was destroyed by fire. Plans were immediately drawn up to replace it with a more modern and beautiful edifice, synchronous with the architectural pattern of the Washington College group. The result was the present model structure. Conforming to the practice of the best American law schools, the *Washington and Lee Law Review* was founded in 1939; and in 1950 a chapter of the Order of the Coif, an honorary scholastic legal society, was installed. Despite the impact of the Second World War, which all but emptied the Law School of teachers and students, a thread of existence was preserved, and at war's end students flocked to Tucker Hall in unprecedented numbers. Professor Williams became Dean (1945–1960), to be succeeded in that office in 1960 by Professor Light and in 1967 by Robert E. Royall Huntley, '50, LL.B., '57 (LL.M., Harvard, who joined the faculty in 1958). With a full complement of staff, the venerable Law School enjoys an excellent reputation and favorable prospects (though facing especial problems) as it progresses through the second half of the twentieth century.

Chapter

XXV

Epilogue

A COMMON FAULT of college and university histories is that, as they approach recent years, they become uncritical and fulsome in praise of their institutions. Yet the agreed-upon terminus of this history, *ca.* 1930, now is a generation ago. It may be, therefore, appropriate to conclude with a brief statement upon the period since, with some suggestions for the future historian of Washington and Lee.

FOLLOWING AN INTERIM, 1928–1930, in which a search was conducted to find a successor to President Smith, and during which the Panic of 1929 struck, only to be followed by the Age of the Great Depression, the trustees in February of 1930 elected Dr. Francis Pendleton Gaines, President of Wake Forest College, to the presidency of Washington and Lee. He assumed his new office in July 1930, and was inaugurated as president on October 25, 1930. The young and debonair leader was destined to guide the venerable institution for nearly a generation until his retirement in 1959, through deepening depression, the Second World War, postwar adjustments, the Korean War, and the decade of the 1950's.

Succinctly stated, Washington and Lee during the 1930's followed the pattern of the preceding era, employing the traditional curriculum taught by an unexpanding faculty. Yet it is fair to say that academic standards were upheld and strengthened, and a much-needed building program produced a rebuilt and modernized Washington Hall complex of administrative and faculty offices and classrooms, renovated dormitories, a new Tucker Hall (brought into architectural harmony with the Washington group), a student union, and a rebuilt, enlarged McCormick Library. On the whole, student morale remained high, though the same could not be said for faculty morale because of depression salaries. Enrollments fluctuated from 931 in President Gaines' first session in 1930–1931, to 874 registered on February 1, 1935, upward to 938 on February 1, 1938, and 944 on February 1, 1940.

President Gaines' annual reports during the decade make rather discouraging reading. Facing a decreased income, necessitating economy and consolidation, the president called for a "living within the University's income" in 1933, while next year a sharp reduction of faculty salaries (none too munificent already) was put into effect.

On the brighter side, Washington and Lee staged, together with the nation, the George Washington Bicentennial celebration in 1932, and also commemorated "the centennial of the Reaper," honoring the invention of Rockbridge County's Cyrus Hall McCormick. A statue of McCormick was unveiled on the campus, and various ceremonies and entertainments rounded out the happy occasion.

In view of modern needs, the University created the office of dean of students, occupied with dedication from 1932 until his retirement in 1962 by Frank J. Gilliam, '17, who also served during these long years as admissions director. Indeed, it can be said that Dean Gilliam came to be almost the personification of Washington and Lee to generations of students and alumni. His program provided for a freshman camp, required freshman residence in the dormitories and dormitory councillors, orientation week for freshmen, and faculty academic advisers for the incoming students.

Long-time (1913–1940) treasurer Paul McNeel Penick ('96, Law) no doubt was cheered by the realization in 1937 of the Robert Parker Doremus bequest, awaited since 1913, in the amount of $1,459,571.35 (which had been designated in President Denny's time). In that same year Washington and Lee received $256,115.63 from the funds of Virginia-born John Barton Payne of Chicago, and in 1940 a gift of $100,000 was put to use in reconstructing the old Carnegie Library as a modernized McCormick Library.

Despite continued decline in earnings from endowment in that period, President Gaines' annual report for 1940 could say that academic work had been strengthened and that a larger number of students than formerly were continuing to graduation. In this document, Dr. Gaines furnished a convenient summary of his first decade, which showed a doubled endowment, a tripled endowment for scholarships, increased applications and enrollments, and a stronger teaching staff. Though he did not say so, President Gaines enthralled students and public alike with his eloquent oratory, redolent of the Old South, and contributed heavily in the field of public relations. His figure striding across the campus from his nearby residence, gaily beheading dandelions with one of his numerous canes, became a well-known and beloved part of Washington and Lee life.

BUT THE WASHINGTON AND LEE of the interwar epoch came to an abrupt end with the advent of the guns of September, 1939. Echoes of war once again affected the quiet and seemingly remote campus, and the fall of France in the spring of 1940 produced a shock. Japanese bombs at Pearl Harbor terminated ordinary campus pursuits, and when somber commencement was held in June, 1942, students and faculty alike had entered the armed services or war work. Three years later President Gaines could announce that one-third of the alumni and one-half the staff were so engaged.

Sensitive to disruption, Washington and Lee adjusted to wartime conditions, through the adoption of summer sessions and acceleration. For a time the United States government sent a group of student-soldiers, known as the ASTP, to the campus (closed in April 1944), and meanwhile other facilities were employed by the Army School for Special Services (1943–1945), which brought to Lexington familiar faces of the entertainment and athletic worlds. The grim session 1943–1944 witnessed the smallest enrollment of civilian students in eighty years.

As fortunes of war changed, however, the uncertainty of the period gave way by 1945–1946 to preparations for the postwar University, causing enrollments to swing by 1947–1948 in the widest arc from lowest to highest enrollments in modern history, the latter bringing new problems. It should never be forgotten that Washington and Lee men numbering a hundred and thirty-six made the final sacrifice in this greatest war of history.

IN VIEW OF THE FACT that Dean Robert H. Tucker—who had joined the faculty in 1915, and had become dean of the University in 1933 after a brilliant career as teacher of economics—had retired in 1946, a new dean was sought. Dr. James G. Leyburn, Professor of Sociology at Yale and a descendant of Lexington's Scotch-Irish pioneers, was elected dean of the University, assuming his duties in 1947. Dean Leyburn championed new ideas of curricular reform at Washington and Lee, amidst considerable student enthusiasm. The Leyburn "Plan", though not fully realized, emphasized the integration of knowledge, and broadened the curriculum especially in the field of Fine Arts (music, painting, and drama), philosophy, and the humanities. Several new faculty members were appointed to teach in these areas. Dean Leyburn, an extraordinarily gifted teacher, returned to full-time teaching in 1956.

The Bicentennial celebration of Robert Alexander's "Academy in Augusta," which covered two years, during which honorary degrees were awarded to eminent persons and addresses delivered, was accompanied by a fund-raising drive. Both in connection with this campaign and otherwise, President Gaines demonstrated his ability to interest patrons of learning in Washington and Lee, notably Mrs. Alfred I. duPont (who also was an honorary degree recipient and elected to membership in the Board of Trustees) of Wilmington, Delaware and Jacksonville, Florida, and Mrs. Arthur Kelly Evans of Atlanta, Georgia and Hot Springs, Virginia, who made very generous gifts to the institution.

ANOTHER EPISODE, beyond the ken of this historian, but which has significance in the history of Washington and Lee, was the decision in July 1954 to replace "subsidized" football, with a non-subsidized program, and which "gave the game back to the boys." While the years before had seen many excellent young men receive their education through athletic subsidies, some persons were brought to the campus who fitted into no program at Washington and Lee. This situation was recognized by the trustees, who courageously terminated the subsidized football program. Loud and vigorous criticism rang through the land from alumni and sports writers, and the students themselves appeared to be unhappy about this decision. But eventually the new program came into its own under the direction of Professor Twombly, Athletic Director, and Coach Lee McLaughlin of the football team, with widespread approval of faculty, alumni, and an endorsement from *Sports Illustrated*.

No SOONER had this disturbing problem been disposed of than Washington and Lee, with all other Southern and American institutions of higher learning, was faced with the question of integration and admission to college of qualified Negro applicants. The matter became especially pressing after the Supreme Court Decision of 1954. While Washington and Lee, together with some other Southern colleges and universities, had scarcely considered the issue before the 1950's, especially since it considered itself to be "a private" institution, this problem has become a highly sensitive and importunate one. Recently a beginning has been made at Washington and Lee; even this has been painful for some schooled in the older values of the South and nation. The University community, however, is in general agreement that Washington and Lee should seek and welcome qualified students without reference to race or religion. This policy is being vigorously implemented by the administration and faculty.

THE NEEDS of Washington and Lee of the sixties are great, and have been pointed out increasingly in recent years by faculty self-study and by student critics. One may hope that the leadership requisite to meet the challenges of our own troubled times will be forthcoming. Enough has been written to demonstrate that, as Harry St. George Tucker once observed long ago, Washington and Lee's fortunes are inextricably interwoven with the destiny of America. It may be appropriate finally to refer to the Washington and Lee motto, "Non In Cautus Futuri," and as a benediction to quote the two concluding stanzas from poet Margaret Junkin Preston's *Centennial Poem for Washington and Lee University, Lexington, Virginia, 1775–1885:*

> Oh! ye who tread these classic halls,
> Baptized once more in patriot blood,
> Think what exalted memories flood
> These doubly consecrated walls!
> The hoary lore of Oxford's towers,
> Made sacred by her Alfred's name,
> Can never boast a prouder fame
> Than shrine these aisles of ours!
>
> Ye will not walk ignoble ways:
> Ye dare not seek unworthy aims:
> Ye cannot do a deed that shames
> These heroes of our holiest days!

Your oath a Roman oath must be,
Sworn with a faith that will not yield
Sworn on the doubly sacred shield
OF WASHINGTON AND LEE!

Index

FIRST REPRO HP
8–V-2884–Random House–General Lees Col.　　4　3　2　1　　7-JSD
April 4, 1969

ABOUT THE AUTHOR

OLLINGER CRENSHAW, a native of Georgia, was graduated from Washington and Lee University in 1925. Shortly thereafter he became a student instructor in history there, subsequently serving as instructor, assistant professor, associate professor, professor of history and, since 1962, head of the history department. He took his doctorate in history at Johns Hopkins. He has taught summers at the College of William and Mary, the University of Wisconsin, West Virginia University, Johns Hopkins, and the University of Virginia. During the academic year 1956–1957 he occupied the Ernest J. King Chair of Maritime History at the United States Naval War College, Newport, Rhode Island.

Over the years Mr. Crenshaw's scholarly interests have centered in the general history of the United States, the Old South and the Civil War, and the history of American foreign affairs. He has contributed articles and reviews to the *American Historical Review*, the *Journal of Southern History*, and the *Mississippi Valley Historical Review* (now the *Journal of American History*). His book *The Slave States in the Presidential Election of 1860* (1945) enjoyed a generally favorable reception from scholars. At present he is engaged in a study of ante-bellum South Carolina, secession, and the opening of the Civil War.

In 1939 he was married to the former Marjorie Burford of Texarkana, Texas, and they have a son, Albert. As a hobby Mr. Crenshaw coached the Washington and Lee intercollegiate tennis teams during the 1930's.